Power Lines

POLITICS AND SOCIETY IN TWENTIETH-CENTURY AMERICA

Series Editors

William Chafe, Gary Gerstle, Linda Gordon, and Julian Zelizer

Power Lines

PHOENIX AND THE MAKING OF
THE MODERN SOUTHWEST

Andrew Needham

PRINCETON UNIVERSITY PRESS

Princeton and Oxford

Contents

Acknowledgments

SCHOLARSHIP IS COLLABORATIVE. MANY PEOPLE MADE THIS BOOK POS-sible. Without their kindness, support, and encouragement, it would not exist.

As a young scholar, I benefited from terrific graduate mentors. At San Francisco State, Bob Cherny and Barbara Loomis helped me transform my interest in history into the practice of research and writing, in the process introducing me to the environment as a site of historical inquiry. In classrooms, offices, and hallways at the University of Michigan, Carroll Smith-Rosenberg, Richard Tucker, Maris Vinovskis, Sue Juster, David Scobey, John Carson, Michael Witgen, Fernando Coronil, Gina Monantz-Sanchez, Geoff Eley, and Matthew Countryman encouraged me to pursue historical writing that was complex and multisided. An amazing cohort of fellow graduate students including Andy Ivaska, Barbara Berglund, Dave Salmanson, Jose Amador, Andrew Highsmith, Nathan Connolly, Allen Dieterich-Ward Anna Lawrence, Shaun Lopez, Mario Ruiz, Tom Romero, Tom Guglielmo, and Larry Hashima all taught me that excitement and fun could be part of an academic career. I am indebted to Scott Campbell, Terry Macdonald, Phil Deloria, and Matt Lassiter who served on my committee. Finally, María Montoya has been a part of this book from its origin as a seminar paper through to its publication. She displayed incredible generosity: reading countless drafts, pushing me to develop its arguments, asking "why do I care about this?," and providing other forms of timely encouragement.

I have been incredibly lucky to have María both as an advisor at Michigan and as a colleague and friend at New York University, where she has continued to encourage and support me. In NYU's history department, Tom Bender has been a terrific and patient mentor, a model of how to balance scholarly and professional work with a deep commitment to public life. Linda Gordon has believed in and supported me and this book since the first time we met. Michele Mitchell, whom I have known as a teaching assistant, professor, and colleague, has been a source of friendship, advice, and chile. Rachel St. John has been a fabulous influence as a friend, co-teacher, and scholar since arriving at NYU. Other colleagues at NYU including Andrew Satori, Guy Ortolano, Marilyn Young,

Martha Hodes, Niki Eustace, Hasia Diner, Fiona Griffiths, Karl Appuhn, Karen Kupperman, Barbara Weinstein, Kim Phillips-Fine, Jennifer Morgan, Danny Walkowitz, and David Ludden have all given me tremendous encouragement. Graduate students at NYU, including Tracy Neumann, Matt Shutzer, Lana Povitz, and Jeannette Estruth, read the manuscript and provided vital feedback.

This book has received support from multiple institutions. Michigan provided generous funding throughout my graduate career. NYU's Goddard Fellowship for junior faculty allowed leave from teaching to complete revisions of the manuscript. The Newberry Library awarded me the Lewis Lloyd Fellowship in American history and fellow scholars at the Newberry, including Danny Greene, Scott Stevens, Leon Fink, Brodie Fischer, Liesl Olson, and Susan Sleeper-Smith, helped me through a difficult revision that became the book's first chapter. Finally, the Clements Center at Southern Methodist University provided an amazing location in which I could begin transforming dissertation into book. At the Clements Center, Ruth Ann Elmore and Andrea Boardman welcomed me to Dallas and provided assistance on a daily basis, including vital image scanning. Tom Sugrue and Bill Cronon generously agreed to serve as outside readers for a manuscript workshop so important that the tapes of the proceedings eventually disintegrated. Clements fellows, Debbie Kang, Monica Perales, Chris Wilson, and Cynthia Radding, proved terrific colleagues, as did the wider Clements Center community, including Sherry Smith, Bob Richter, Ben Johnson, Michelle Nickerson, Andy Graybill, Ed Countryman, and Jim Hopkins. I was deeply fortunate to be at the Clements Center before the passing of David Weber, who provided a model of how to combine grace, intellect, and generosity, with scholarly commitment to the places and people of the Southwest.

This book would not have been possible without the work of librarians and archivists at the National Archives in Washington, D.C., College Park, and Denver; at the University of Arizona, Northern Arizona University, Arizona State University, and Dineh College libraries; at the Arizona Historical Society in both Tempe and Tucson; at the Interlibrary Loan Offices at NYU and Michigan; at the Native American Rights Fund in Boulder and the Navajo Nation Museum. At the Arizona Historical Foundation, now the Arizona Historical Society, Linda Whittaker, Susan Irwin, and Rebekah Tabah have gone above and beyond to find documents, photographs, and other materials, sometimes based on only the merest hint. I am grateful for all their work. My research trips to Denver and Tucson were made more enjoyable by the hospitality of Tom Romero and Laurie Blumberg-Romero, and Kit and Saundra Taylor.

I have presented portions of this book at the Western History Association, Organization of American Historians, the American Society of

Environmental Historians, and the Urban History Association as well as at the Huntington Library, the D'Arcy McNickle Center at the Newberry Library, the School for American Research, and Princeton, Northwestern, Arizona State, and Yale universities. A vast number of scholars have provided useful input, including Darren Dochuk, Cathleen Cahill, Kevin Kruse, Elizabeth Tandy Shermer, Julian Zelizer, Jeani O'Brien, Dana Powell, Dalain Long, Don Fixico, Juliana Barr, Ned Blackhawk, Margaret Pugh O'Mara, Stephen Amerman, Leah Glaser, Brian Frehner, and all members of WHiNERs. At Princeton University Press, Clara Platter encouraged me to write this book for a broad scholarly audience. Gary Gerstle as well as two anonymous reviewers gave me detailed and helpful advice on revisions. Eric Crahan, Jill Harris, and Eric Henney have helped shepherd it to completion, and Marsha Kunin helped me complete the final revisions.

My family has been a part of this project since I first saw Four Corners Power Plant through a car window, long before I became historian. Throughout my family's long experience with this book, my parents, Todd and Ellen Needham, and my brother, Shawn, have maintained their faith that my initial question "What is *that* doing *here*?" was worth asking. They also believed that I could answer that question, even when I doubted my own ability to do so. I owe deep thanks as well to Bruce, Sharon, and Kristin Darga, who have endured laptops, papers, and books scattered throughout various family gatherings. They all deserve a power salute.

The long years of writing this book have been filled with joy because of Jack and Raymond Needham and Kim Darga. Jack and Raymond have made me laugh, filled me with wonder and incredible pride, and spurred me to complete this book through the past six years. It is dedicated, in part, to them. Kim Darga has lived with this book as long as she has lived with me. The debts I owe her are unrepayable. She has accompanied me to libraries, dams, canyons, and power plants, listened to spoken versions of this book for more than a decade, read every word in countless forms, and granted me wisdom, patience, and love. The dedication is only a small measure of my love and appreciation.

Power Lines

Beyond the Crabgrass Frontier

THE THREE-BEDROOM RANCHES AT GLENVIEW AND TENTH STREET HAD been carved out of a grapefruit orchard during the Korean War. Construction crews put them together, their developer remembered, "just like on an assembly line." The subdivision had been considered among the best on the market at that time. Potential buyers flocked to see the model home at the 1952 Phoenix home show, examining the GE ranges and Westinghouse refrigerators that came with the $7,400 purchase price. They stood before the Frigidaire air conditioners, a $1,500 option, feeling the cool of the refrigerated air on their skin. Buyers purchased all ninety homes even before the subdivision was complete.[1]

By the mid-1960s, most Phoenicians would have considered these old houses. In the intervening decade, the city's population grew more than 400 percent. New subdivisions sprung up seemingly overnight, placing new houses atop the cotton and cantaloupe fields that had once dominated the valley. While the appliances in the homes on Glenview and Tenth had aged and the lack of central air turned off many potential buyers, the homes retained their value. Builders continued to describe the area as a "prestige neighborhood."[2] It was close to parks, golf courses, and other outdoor activities. The houses had wonderful views of Camelback Mountain to the east and Squaw Peak to the north.[3] They lay only a short drive from the new aerospace and electronics plants clustered around Deer Valley Airport, and the houses filled with the families of engineers and junior executives working for Sperry Rand, Motorola, and other companies that had recently arrived in the Valley of the Sun.

A generation of scholarship has given us a vast number of stories about suburban houses similar to those at Glenview and Tenth Street. The burgeoning subdivisions of northern Phoenix demonstrate the powerful actions of the federal government to subsidize and underwrite postwar growth. They stand as evidence of the diligent efforts of the local "growth machine" to capture federal subsidy and locate it in place. Their nearly uniform racial character—among the 200,000 people living in northern Phoenix's subdivisions in 1960, only 83 were African American and fewer than 4,500 had "Spanish surnames"—shows the federal government's "possessive investment in whiteness."[4] The commercial strips and shopping malls developed nearby symbolize postwar consumer culture in its affluence and its banality. The high-tech manufacturing plants of northern Phoenix represent the effects of the Cold War's "military Keynesianism." The setting of those plants amid subdivisions displays a vision of an "industrial garden" that would unite "smoke-free industries" with nearby residences. The subdivisions of north Phoenix were home to people whose identities as homeowner, taxpayer, and school parent reshaped postwar politics. They were the physical manifestation of both the dream of homeownership and the nightmare of sprawl: "Dream Homes by the Dozen," and "The BLOB That Ate Arizona." And nowhere do these stories about the forces of change that lay at the heart of postwar growth seem clearer than on the outer fringes of suburban space.[5]

The names scholars have used to describe these boundaries point to similarities in the stories they tell. Newly built homes sit on the "Metropolitan Frontier" or the "Crabgrass Frontier," or they are part of "Edge Cities," places where people experienced "Life on the New Frontier."[6] The low-density metropolises carved from the formerly agricultural and desert landscapes of the American West were "urban oases," in the words of one of their early historians, urban spaces radically different and separate from the barren lands that surrounded them.[7] These narratives of "sprawl," moving progressively outward from the metropolitan center, would likely seem familiar to the historian most centrally associated with the frontier. Frederick Jackson Turner, of course, famously described the western frontier as the key force of American history, a line of the "perennial rebirth" of American values and ideals. The arrival of the frontier represented the beginning of development, and therefore of history. It was the initial process in the creation of modern America. Opposite "civilization" was "savagery," a space without history or connection to the ongoing stories of civilization and progress, a space providing undeveloped ground to be transformed.[8] The stark line separating subdivision from farm or desert has functioned much the same way in metropolitan and suburban history. The arrival of the bulldozer represents the beginning of urban time. The crabgrass frontier represents the outer boundary of the wave and lies at the hither edge of "undeveloped" land—the meeting point not between savagery and civilization, but between the modern metropolis and the "undeveloped" periphery beyond.[9]

If we angle our line of sight slightly above the roofs at Glenview and Tenth, however, a new geography becomes visible. Carried atop wooden poles thirty feet high, a grid of electrical power lines paralleled the street grid below. From transformers attached to each pole, small distribution lines carrying 240 volts of electricity ran into the homes. It was such power lines that had inspired the geographer Henri Lefebvre in the early 1970s to imagine the modern home as "permeated in every direction by streams of energy which run in and out of it by every imaginable route."[10]

The power lines that entered the homes on Glenview and Tenth did not, however, run along every imaginable route. They followed a definite path. The 7.2 kilovolt lines carrying electricity to the houses led to a small substation six blocks away at Eighth Street and Ocotillo where the substation's maze of transformers and circuit breakers reduced the voltage of electricity entering the station at 34 kilovolts for distribution to local homes. The 34-kilovolt power line feeding the substation headed east. It cut north of Camelback Mountain, and then turned and ran almost due north. Passing the last subdivision, it proceeded through cotton fields in northern Scottsdale before terminating, like the numerous strings of 34-kilovolt lines that ran to other parts of Phoenix, at a larger substation named "Pinnacle Peak." There, local transmission lines received electricity carried by twin strings of 365-kilovolt extra-high voltage (EHV) lines, whose path led north.[11] Leaving the Salt River's alluvial basin, the lines cut northeast through the Tonto National Forest, following 120-foot-wide rights-of-way cut through dense stands of juniper, oak, and ponderosa pine.[12] As they headed north, the EHV lines climbed the 3,000 vertical feet of the Mogollon Rim and, after cresting the rim, arrived in a landscape far different from the suburban subdivisions and irrigated fields of Phoenix or the surprisingly green forests of central Arizona.

Most Americans in the mid-1960s knew the landscape of the Colorado Plateau, even though they didn't know it by that name. They had seen it in the spires of Monument Valley that formed the setting of *Stagecoach* and *My Darling Clementine*. They had witnessed it in their homes as the Marlboro Man ambled across their television screens. The EHV lines traveled, however, to a part of the Plateau rarely seen on film or television. A few miles north of Interstate 40, they passed over an unmarked border, entering the Navajo Nation.[13] They passed east of Window Rock, that nation's capital, and the small community of Burnham, where the power lines towered over Navajo hogans. Thirty miles past Burnham, they entered a small basin that local shepherds had once called "No Fat Valley" because its sparse vegetation made it a difficult location to sustain their flocks of sheep and goats.[14] Since the late 1950s, the valley had been transformed. Much of its land had disappeared under the waters of Morgan Lake, a 1,600-acre cooling reservoir. Just east of the lake, 200-foot-tall draglines operated by mixed crews of Navajo and Anglo workers removed topsoil and sandstone before blasters used dynamite to shatter the coal seams the dragline had revealed. Along a newly built road, trucks larger than the houses on Glendale and Tenth carried the coal a short distance away from Navajo Mine to a dense collection of pipes, conveyors, and boilers known as Four Corners Power Plant.[15]

Within Four Corners, unearthed coal was set afire and released fly ash, nitrogen, and sulfur dioxide, heavy metals, and carbon dioxide, all of which traveled up the power plant's stacks and into the sky. Mercury and fly ash fell to earth relatively quickly, making their way into the arid soils and limited water of the Colorado Plateau, as well as the bodies of the people and animals that lived upon it. Nitrogen and sulfur dioxide stayed in the air longer, until they mixed with moisture and fell to the earth as rain significantly more acidic than normal. The plant's carbon dioxide remained aloft, mixing with similar emissions from the power plants and automobiles that burned fossil fuels in the region, nation, and world.

Utility officials labeled these emissions "byproducts": the unvalued, if inevitable, results of unleashing coal's energy. The product they valued was electricity. As burning coal heated boilers, water within turned to steam. Channeled upward, the steam struck turbine blades, spinning them at a controlled rate of sixty times per second. On the opposite end of the turbine, giant magnets rotated within coils of copper wire at the same speed. The opposed charges of the spinning magnets grabbed electrons in the copper wire, causing them to flow from atom to atom. These flowing electrons—electricity—left the plant via a step-up substation that fed twin strings of EHV power lines. Coursing through circuits at the speed of light, electricity zipped out of No Fat Valley, crossed the Colorado Plateau, traveled down the Mogollon Rim, and arrived into the homes at Glenview and Tenth.

In Phoenix, Four Corners' electricity powered a social order that the historian David Nye has called "high energy society."[16] Evidence of this society appeared in Phoenix's newspapers, where retailers, homebuilders, and public utilities boasted of the labor electrical appliances could save and the leisure they could produce. Advertisements urged husbands to buy their wives an "electric valentine," a vacuum, washer/dryer, or electric skillet that "will help her get more fun out of life by making her homemaking easier—and remind her of your thoughtfulness every day of the year." Wives were urged to take steps to ensure that their husbands would remember them. "HINT TO THE LADIES: If your husband hasn't seen this page, maybe you should prop it up in front of his coffee cup this morning."[17] High-energy society also defined the lifestyles reporters discovered when they traveled to Phoenix to investigate the "Big Boom in the Desert" and "The New Millionaires of Phoenix." As banker Herbert Leggett explained to a writer from the *Saturday Evening Post*, "I awaken in my air-conditioned home in the morning. I take a dip in my swimming pool. I dress and get into my air-conditioned automobile and drive to the air-conditioned garage in the basement of this building. I work in an air-conditioned office, eat in an air-conditioned restaurant and perhaps go to an air-conditioned theater."[18] No evidence of the electricity that powered Leggett's air-conditioned lifestyle existed in the pages of the *Saturday Evening Post*. Indeed, mention of electricity in literature explaining and promoting Phoenix's growth is rare. Little exists beyond pledges by Phoenix's utilities "to provide adequate supplies of ENERGY—economically—to meet the future requirements of Arizona's dynamic progress."[19]

Electricity had not always gone unnoticed. Earlier in the twentieth century, Americans had gaped in wonder at its power. Standing before the electrical dynamo in the Great Hall of the Exposition Universelle in fin-de-siècle Paris, Henry Adams felt "his historical neck broken by the sudden irruption of forces totally new."[20] Adams likened the changes he foresaw in the dynamo as second only to the birth of Christ in their historical impact. Other Americans saw electricity as evidence of new human control over the natural world. Gazing at New York's illuminated skyline from the Brooklyn Bridge in 1910, Ezra Pound declared, "Here is our poetry, we have pulled down the stars to our will." Americans flocked to see illuminated midways at World's Fairs and to witness spotlights trained on natural wonders like Niagara Falls.[21] In the 1920s and 1930s, politicians and planners including Gifford Pinchot, Lewis Mumford, George Norris, and Rexford Tugwell had envisioned the proliferation of electrical networks throughout rural America leading to social modernization, economic equality, and an amelioration of the inequities of both rural and urban life.[22] And the beginning of electrical transmission from Boulder Dam to Los Angeles in 1936 drew one million Angelinos into the streets, the largest civic celebration since the armistice to cheer and dance in suddenly well-lit streets. By the 1960s, however, wonder had disappeared. Electricity and power lines had become second nature in Phoenix, an assumed and expected aspect of modern life. Appearing in Phoenix's homes, businesses, and factories at the flick of a switch, electricity seemed to exist in neither time nor space. It simply was.

This book aims to make those power lines historically visible. In so doing, it broadens narratives of postwar growth, both in scale and subject. By tracing the development of the power lines that ran between Phoenix and the Navajo Reservation through time and across space, *Power Lines* constructs a broad new map of postwar urban, environmental, and political change. Exploring the relationships between natural resources and metropolitan expansion; supplies of energy and demand for electricity; urban boosters, federal officials, and Navajo political leaders; and prosperity and underdevelopment in an emerging region, the book reveals the intimate and unequal connections power lines forged between electrical consumers in Phoenix and the people and landscape of the Navajo Nation. By introducing the expropriation of resources from distant, yet materially vital hinterlands into accounts of postwar metropolitan growth, *Power Lines* expands historical understanding of postwar inequality to include peoples living far from metropolitan centers. By connecting the ecological transformation of the Colorado Plateau to the ever rising demand for inexpensive electricity in metropolitan Phoenix, it demonstrates that suburbanization triggered environmental changes that reached far beyond America's growing subdivisions. By following power lines from the Colorado Plateau to Los Angeles, Albuquerque, and elsewhere in the Southwest, it suggests that metropolitan growth was spatially far broader than currently understood. Indeed, it argues that accounts of metropolitan growth must reach beyond isolated city-suburb pairings to investigate regional formations created as the collective material demands of growing cities and suburbs created new bonds with human societies and natural landscapes located far beyond metropolitan borders. This book is the story of one such region: the modern Southwest.

By telling this story at the regional, rather than the metropolitan, level, *Power Lines* challenges the borders of recent political history. Over the past decade, a compelling synthesis of postwar American history has focused attention on metropolitan space as the central battleground of American politics. This synthesis has highlighted two central dynamics of postwar politics. First, federal growth politics created new forms of spatial inequality. Extending and expanding New Deal programs after World War II, the federal government took unprecedented steps to subsidize middle-class consumption in ways that were both racially exclusionary and deeply invested in the promotion of capital accumulation in undeveloped metropolitan space. In so doing, these programs led to the development of the new residential and industrial spaces of the postwar suburbs. At the same time, the exclusionary nature of suburban development served to fix poor and minority populations in place in the inner city. Growing metropolitan areas acquired stark inequalities as suburbs formed a "White Noose" around increasingly poor, nonwhite inner cities, strangling them as suburbanites demanded lower taxes, limits on public spending, and other forms of local protection.[23] Second, local growth machines pursued economic development, at least in part, by undermining the hopes federal planners had invested in growth. Economists working for the federal government saw their growth politics as a rising tide that would lift all boats.[24] As an emerging national security state underwrote capital mobility on an unprecedented level, however, local growth machines—coalitions of politicians, businessmen, and property owners—competed with other cities to attract capital by attacking the New Deal state's support for unionization, regulation, and social subsidy. This competition created clear winners. Relatively undeveloped cities of the South and West, lacking the burdens of established regulatory and social welfare states at the state and local level, offered tax and labor incentives to newly mobile industrial capital and quality-of-life amenities to newly mobile people. The result was the Sunbelt. Cities in the South and West grew at nearly twice the rate of their Midwestern and Northeastern counterparts, reshaping the American economy, national politics, and eventually making its built environment of subdivisions, commercial strips, shopping malls, and industrial and office parks the vernacular landscape of the majority of the American people and its deregulatory, anti-union, low tax policies the successor to the New Deal state.[25]

The pages that follow owe much to this synthesis. The method contained within reflects its emphasis on foregrounding economic and political structures within the broader story of how people attempted to transform their local circumstances. *Power Lines* also reflects the belief that space is a historical text in which can be read the outcome of political struggles as well as a structure that constrains historical agency. This story contains many familiar actors: federal policy makers promoting metropolitan growth, and local businessmen, politicians, and homeowners struggling to turn federal policies toward their own divergent benefits. And it shares the conclusion of the metropolitan synthesis that these struggles have caused profound and enduring geographical inequalities.

Power Lines, however, also argues that the metropolitan synthesis has drawn far too narrow a map of metropolitan space and of the politics of growth. In some cases, containing narratives of historical change within cities and suburbs has left important stories half told. Set almost entirely in metropolitan America, the story of the emergence of a "consumer's republic" exists in narrative and spatial isolation from the new production that enabled it. Similarly, the story of metropolitan boosters' work to draw capital to their cities has lain unconnected to their efforts to capture the energies that stirred that capital to life in its new forms of suburban houses and factories. Stories of metropolitan inequality, as well, have largely sidelined the "devil's bargains" that faced distant communities as new demands pulled their resources—whether fossil fuels, landfill space, or landscapes desirable for tourism—into the metropolitan orbit even as ideas of the underdevelopment and primitivism of the countryside naturalized these inequalities.[26] As the pages that follow show, metropolitan growth structured a series of choices for hinterland residents between continued poverty, outmigration, and damaging ecological transformations.

Metropolitan history's narrow map has also elided the broad assumption shared by federal planners and local boosters that metropolitan growth represented the engine of national economic expansion. "Metropolitan preferences" in federal policy making reflected broad beliefs that urban demand for resources and labor could be agents of hinterland modernization and development. At the same time, those policies channeled resources from periphery to center, creating new unequal regional connections and positioning peripheral nature as fuel for extending metropolitan growth. In focusing on the struggles for power within the metropolis, then, the synthesis has failed to consider the political and ecological disruptions that metropolitan growth initiated far beyond metropolitan borders.

Assumptions about the metropolitan nature of growth in the postwar Southwest have rendered Indian people marginal to the postwar history of a region with the nation's largest Indian population. In a generous reading, this marginalization reflected political developments in Indian history that seemingly ran counter to dominant stories of American political development. As a federal welfare state born in the New Deal gradually expanded the people included in its provisions during the postwar era, Indians faced termination, a policy characterized by the cessation of federal services and the extension of state authority over Indian lands. As the long civil rights movement shifted to an emphasis on demanding rights and equality, Indian activists pursued the separate legal statuses of sovereignty and self-determination. At worst, the absence of Indians from many narratives of postwar history has reflected an implicit belief that Indians occupied a marginal and relatively unimportant place in modern American history, even in regions that contained significant populations of Indian peoples, a belief abetted by the increasing historical focus on metropolitan America as the locus of historical agency.[27] By introducing Indian peoples into the broader story of Phoenix's growth, *Power Lines* attempts to alter these narratives. The termination era's emphasis on replacing federal with state authority over reservation lands represented part of the political process whereby metropolitan officials attempted to claim and incorporate the resources of distant territories to supply metropolitan demand, a process of "unlock[ing] the natural resources known to exist on the reservations," as Barry Goldwater stated in 1950.[28] Similarly, Navajo demands for sovereignty, self-determination, and decolonization reflected the particular circumstances that faced people experiencing dramatic changes to their land. *Power Lines* demonstrates how Navajo leaders sought to take advantage of energy development, initially by employing similar policies as Phoenix's boosters in an attempt to attract industry and later by seeking the nationalization of energy reserves on reservation lands. It also suggests that the legal structures of the American polity as well as cultural ideas about Indian primitivism combined to defeat these efforts. Most importantly, it demonstrates the centrality of energy supplies on Navajo land to the growth of the Southwest, and the social and environmental inequalities that resulted. Metropolitan development and Indian underdevelopment, it shows, went hand in hand in postwar America.

Finally, remapping metropolitan history at the regional level brings nature into the story of postwar metropolitan development in new ways. Recent scholarship has looked to suburban growth to explain the rise of environmentalism. Witnessing the transformation of open spaces and the air and groundwater pollution that accompanied metropolitan growth, suburbanites, as scholars have shown, demanded new controls on growth, worked to preserve "open land," and turned to nature in increasing numbers as an escape from life that seemed excessively materialistic.[29] Indeed, Phoenix's history reflects both the suburban desire for environmental amenity and the belief that suburban sprawl destroyed nature. Beginning in the 1930s, Phoenix's boosters posed their city as an alternative urban experience that allowed both modern life and easy escape to nature. By the 1970s, however, environmentalists described Phoenix as the poster child of uncontrolled growth, "The BLOB That Ate Arizona," in Edward Abbey's account.[30]

Nature was constitutive of metropolitan experience in a more material way. In using electricity produced both by the combustion of fossil fuels that had stored prehistoric energy in place and by the transformation of water's kinetic energy flowing through canyons that energy had created, Phoenicians created connections to nature. The power lines that reached into their houses brought energies from the Colorado Plateau's present and past into the daily life of Phoenicians at every moment of the day. They represented an artifact of a vast ecotechnological system, a phrase coined by the historian of technology Thomas Hughes to describe the "intersecting and overlapping natural and human-built environments" created as technological change created hybrid systems that blended nature and culture, ecology and economy. While ecotechnological systems, as both William Cronon and Richard White have detailed, harness nature to distinct human purposes, they remain embedded within the flows and constraints of the natural environments on which they rely.[31] Indeed, while the electricity that powered Phoenix seemed, to its consumers, to materialize from the wall sockets of suburban homes, it remained deeply connected to the places where, over time, geological forces had located bituminous coal or had directed flowing water. While those places might be peripheral for consumers, they remained central to the system as a whole.

The relative imbalance of power between the residents of Phoenix and the Navajo Reservation, places on opposite points of the Southwest's ecotechnological system, reflects the metropolitan preferences of postwar policy making that from the 1940s to the 1970s encouraged energy resource development as a core feature of metropolitan and economic growth. As *Power Lines* demonstrates, the interest in making inexpensive energy available to metropolitan residents overrode, by the early 1960s,

long-lasting beliefs among liberals that electricity generated from resources on federally controlled land should be publicly controlled. Advocates of public power had long seen public power as providing a yard-
stick that would discipline the private sector while bringing electricity to
underserved consumers in rural America.[32] By the 1960s, however, the
possibility of interconnecting with private utilities and creating a vast
power pool that could guarantee reliable service across space overrode
those concerns. Federal officials found willing partners in officials from
private utilities and boosters across the Southwest, who welcomed the
potential for new energy supplies on federally controlled lands to meet
burgeoning metropolitan demand and expand both metropolitan populations and corporate profits. Phoenix's spectacular postwar growth, then,
was not only the artifact of successful boosters or savvy politics; it also
occurred because of vast supplies of energy located on the Navajo Reservation and the success of metropolitan actors in claiming this energy for
their own benefit. These changes transformed the geography of electrical
production in the region. In the 1950s, consumers had relied on natural
gas burned in their immediate vicinity, as well as large hydroelectric dams
on the Colorado River. By the early 1970s, they relied overwhelmingly
on coal that was both mined and transformed into electricity on Indian
land. By that time, Navajo Mine fed 4,200 tons of coal per day to Four
Corners Power Plant. Black Mesa and Kayenta Mines sent an additional
15,000 tons to two other power plants.[33] These were small signs of an
industry-wide shift toward coal in energy production during the 1960s,
a shift that both shaped the environmental history of the Southwest and
created today's environmental future.

Power Lines places its narrative of metropolitan growth within a broader
regional context, then, in order to expand the spaces and peoples included
in chronicles of postwar growth. It demonstrates that the decentralization
of power that metropolitan historians have charted—the construction of
the suburban "white noose"—was accompanied by powerful centralizing
tendencies that drew distant landscapes into metropolitan orbits.[34] The
search for the natural resources required for metropolitan growth, and
for spaces to discard the waste produced by metropolitan consumption,
led federal, state, and local actors to create new infrastructures. These
power lines, aqueducts, and landfills reorganized economies, ecologies,
and societies in distant landscapes. Once constructed, they shaped possibilities and limited opportunities for change.[35] These infrastructures invested metropolitan actors in the transformation of distant landscapes
while drawing distant people into new relationships with metropolitan
centers. The result was not only metropolitan sprawl but also the reorganization of politics, society, and nature in new, far-flung regions. Coming
to terms with these distant changes requires new stories that illustrate the

connections forged between cities, suburbs, and distant hinterlands in the processes of metropolitan growth.

Power Lines tells this story of regional formation in four parts. Part I—"Fragments"—tells the prehistory of the modern Southwest. It begins with the natural history of energy in the Southwest, detailing how energy, as coal, became located in particular places and, as water, reshaped others, creating the landscapes of the Colorado Plateau and the Salt River Valley where Navajos and Phoenicians, respectively, developed ways of life tied to the conditions natural energy had created. While these places developed atop landscapes shaped by the work of the same natural system, few connections existed between them. This part extends to the 1930s, when federal efforts to develop the Colorado River's energy at Boulder Dam dramatically altered that natural system by controlling the energy of flowing water that had, for millennia, shaped the Southwestern landscape.

Part II—"Demand"—details the population and manufacturing growth that dramatically increased electrical use in the postwar years. It foregrounds the efforts of Phoenix's powerful growth machine to rebrand their city as a place with modern amenities and high quality of life, to gain control of local institutions, and to reshape politics to make Phoenix and Arizona a low-tax, low-regulation, anti-union magnet for business. These efforts helped bring billions of dollars' worth of manufacturing capital and new housing development to metropolitan Phoenix as well as hundreds of thousands of new residents to the desert Southwest. These actions transformed Phoenix, as symbolized by the deliberate change of the colloquial name for Phoenix's surroundings from "Salt River Valley" to "Valley of the Sun." Underlying this change was a transformation in land use, as subdivided agricultural fields and open desert became a landscape of homes and light industries that consumed 2,000 percent more electricity in 1970 than it did in 1945.

Part III—"Supply"—explores how coal from the Navajo Reservation became the energy source that met first Phoenix's, and then other Southwestern cities' demand for electric power between the early 1950s and the late 1960s. In part, the story told in this part is one of technological change. As extra-high-voltage power lines became capable of transmitting electricity hundreds of miles with minimal energy loss, the construction of power plants far from metropolitan areas became economically viable. More important in this story, however, are political decisions about the nation's public lands and the people who lived on them. Political actors in the Interior Department, metropolitan Phoenix, and Navajo Tribal Government came to believe that energy development could resolve both potential electrical shortages in metropolitan areas and poverty on the Navajo Reservation. These actors had very different ideas, however, of energy development's political dynamics. Navajo tribal leaders envisioned energy development leading to tribal industrialization, which they envisioned as a means of protecting their people in an era in which Indian policy threatened the eventual end of federal services. Interior officials, including members of Phoenix's growth machine serving in the first Republican administration in twenty years, valued regional, rather than reservation, development. Their policies, offering generous lease terms to private developers, functioned to make hinterland energy available to metropolitan consumers at low costs. Energy development proceeded rapidly. In 1961, power plants generated 175 megawatts of electricity using coal from one mine on the Navajo Reservation. Ten years later, including those power plants under construction, power plants on or near the Reservation generated 8,690 megawatts of electricity, drawing coal from three large strip mines on Navajo and Hopi land. This new generating capacity, more than five times the amount of electricity of that at Hoover Dam, changed the politics of energy in the Southwest. From the 1930s to the 1950s, federal agencies, namely the Bureau of Reclamation, had directed the development of the region's electrical networks. In the mid-1960s, however, private utilities in the region formed a new a consortium to develop power plants using Navajo coal, which now set the course of development. By the late 1960s, the Bureau of Reclamation purchased and sold electricity into the massive pool of power that the consortium controlled, a public-private system, largely controlled by private companies with long-term leases on power plants, that directed the terms by which energy was produced, transmitted, and consumed in the region.

Part IV—"Protest"—explores how this new system of coal-fired power plants shaped political efforts to critique Southwestern growth in the 1960s and 1970s. Chapter 6 tells the story of the broad-scale environmentalist attack on Phoenix as the apotheosis of America's misguided ideas about growth that was sparked by a Bureau of Reclamation proposal to build new dams near the Grand Canyon. Intended to provide electricity for an aqueduct carrying Colorado River water to Phoenix and Tucson, the dams symbolized to environmentalists the insatiable destructive capacity of metropolitan demand. Even as environmentalists attacked the excesses of Southwestern growth, however, they helped forge a compromise in which coal-fired power plants, rather than hydroelectric dams, powered the new aqueduct. The resulting accord divided hinterland space in the Southwest into sacred spaces of pristine nature, set aside for the enjoyment of tourists, and productive spaces where energy development benefited metropolitan consumers.

The proliferation of power plants also led to new critiques by young Navajo activists and tribal officials in the late 1960s and 1970s. For many Navajos, the plants served as a symbol of, in the words of tribal chairman Peter MacDonald, "the colonial relationship between the Navajo Nation and the cities of the Southwest." By the late 1960s, Navajos increasingly criticized energy development and called for greater tribal control over tribal lands, a movement they termed "nationalism." Navajo nationalism took markedly different paths among tribal leaders and young activists, however. MacDonald and other tribal officials in the 1970s looked to the OPEC (Organization of Petroleum Exporting Countries) nations currently reorganizing the world's petroleum supplies as providing an example of how control of energy development could create new political power for "the emerging Navajo Nation." At the same time, young Navajos challenged the authority of both energy companies and the Navajo officials to claim lands occupied by long-standing Navajo communities. They successfully used grassroots organizing tactics and new federal environmental laws to stave off new development. Navajo tribal officials and grassroots leaders were less successful, however, in transforming the conditions or the existing infrastructure of energy development, which continued to supply power to metropolitan consumers. This history, then, provides powerful evidence for the structural constraints created by capital-intensive infrastructure once it was set in place.[36]

With its focus on the regional development of electrical power networks in the Southwest, *Power Lines* largely avoids two topics that readers might expect to find. First, it contains little discussion of the uranium mining and processing that occurred on the Navajo Reservation from the late 1940s into the 1970s. The eastern portion of the Navajo Reservation existed as the westernmost portion of a geological belt containing the majority of uranium reserves of the continental United States. Uranium mining did replicate many of the social and spatial dynamics explored herein. Indeed, the public health effects of uranium mining are far more proven than those related to coal mining and coal-fired power production. Both Navajo uranium miners and Navajos who resided near uranium mills have suffered from increased rates of lung and thyroid cancers, pneumoconiosis, and tuberculosis, and have received "compassionate payments" from the federal government in recognition of their contribution to the postwar national security state. No such compensation has been forthcoming for the increased rates of asthma and other respiratory diseases observed in Navajos living near areas undergoing energy development.[37] Such epidemiological patterns demonstrate that, as Brett Walker argues, "people really do physiologically experience nations' policies and priorities" in the form of industrial diseases that represent "physical inscriptions of the nation's policies on the body."[38] At the same time, uranium mining and processing had significantly different spatial and temporal dynamics than electrical energy development. Until 1971, the Atomic Energy Commission was the sole purchaser of American uranium. Uranium development thus forged links between the postwar national security state, private companies, and Navajo workers. These connections existed on the federal level, with few of the ties between metropolitan consumption and hinterland production that form the heart of *Power Lines'* analysis.[39]

Second, *Power Lines* deliberately avoids use of the term "Sunbelt." In part, this choice reflects the language used by the people whose history is recorded herein. Few people in Phoenix before the mid-1970s used "Sunbelt" to describe the places they lived.[40] This rhetorical absence was a national phenomenon. "Sunbelt" became widespread as a regional description only after Kevin Phillips used the term in his 1969 *Emerging Republican Majority* to describe the fast-growing cities of the South and West that he saw as the Republican Party's future political base, and gained greater currency in the 1970s with the increasing use of "Rustbelt" or "Frostbelt" to describe the industrial cities of the Midwest and Northeast hit hard by deindustrialization.[41] As elected officials from these diverse metropolitan locations came together in shared appeals for fairer distribution of federal dollars, in the case of the Rustbelt, or in defense of growth and opposition to new federal regulation, as in the case of the Sunbelt, the "Sunbelt" and "Rustbelt" began to exist as organized worlds of meaning, in short, as places, in a way that they had not in the immediate postwar period.[42] Before those changes in the 1970s, however, the Sunbelt did not exist. What did were a series of regions that grew as they competed with one another for the capital set loose in the postwar political economy even as they benefited from federal-policy preferences for metropolitan development.

Power Lines instead uses terms that people living in both Phoenix and the Navajo Reservation used to describe the region and their visions of its future: "modern" and "Southwest." As early as 1941, the Phoenix Chamber of Commerce explained that "Phoenix's strategic location, the largest city between Dallas and Los Angeles, makes it the logical wholesaling and retail outlet for the Southwest."[43] By the mid-1950s, these representations had become more colorful. Phoenix, the title of one promotional pamphlet boasted, was *The Economic Capital of the Great Southwest Sun Country!* while ads boasted that Phoenix was "*the* important distributing center for quite a chunk of the Southwest."[44] These claims to centrality served as claims to authority. Drawing on long-held booster theories of development, Phoenix's growth machine suggested the resources of the countryside should flow, naturally, to the dynamic center.[45] Reference to the "Southwest" in Navajo political discourse was less frequent, but still prominent. Navajo political leaders deployed "Southwest" when appealing for the extension of metropolitan prosperity to reservation lands. At the dedication of Four Corners Power Plant, Paul Jones announced that energy and industrial development would make "the Navajo Tribe a force in the Southwest . . . coupled with the further development of Phoenix, Tucson, and other cities."[46] As those dreams became increasingly unfulfilled by the early 1970s, Peter MacDonald, Jones's successor as tribal chairman, criticized "the colonial relationship between the Navajo Nation and the cities of the Southwest" and promised renewed steps to "fully develop the Navajo Nation as an important economic, social, and political force in the Southwest."[47] Navajo critics of energy development, as well, used "Southwest," but to attack the continuing environmental and social inequalities that regional membership imposed on their homeland. "People across the Southwest," one student wrote to the *Navajo Times*, "destroyed our land so they can use electric can openers and tooth brushes." Another writer denounced Arizona governor Jack Williams for delivering the "same speech he has given to the great white middleclass children of Phoenix, even though they are sustained by water stolen from the Navajos."[48] The Southwest, then, was not merely a regional description but a form of organizing space politically, a means toward claiming resources and contesting their proper distribution. "The Southwest" was the result of political and economic changes that took and made place.[49]

Similarly, *Power Lines* uses "modern" to reflect the terms by which people in the Southwest represented the trajectory of the changes that surrounded them. Visions of an explicitly modern Southwest emerged as Phoenicians sought to distinguish their city from an earlier regional association with primitivism and underdevelopment. Locals portrayed "the metropolitan city of Phoenix" in the 1930s as "a jewel of modernity set in the green carpets of year-round crops," dramatically different from "the more ancient cities of the Southwest."[50] Phoenix also stood in stark contrast to the Navajo Reservation, where Indians, one Arizona magazine explained in the 1950s, "dance in the ancient way, sing the old chants, retell tales of olden days, cling to habits and customs hoary as the hills." "Navajoland," the same article explained, represented a place to escape "the swish and zoom of the times."[51] For Navajo leaders, Phoenix served as guidepost and counterpoint as well. Phoenix's residential comforts and industrial expansion represented a goal for Navajo leaders in the late 1950s, as they imaged "many industries" on the reservation and "two light bulbs in every hogan" leading to "a modern way of living."[52] By the early 1970s, Navajo visions of modernity had fractured. Peter MacDonald and other Navajo leaders envisioned tribal controls over energy supplies as enabling the creation of a powerful "emerging Navajo Nation," part of an "Indian OPEC" that would assert tribal rights over resources to shape politics and space throughout the region. At the same time, Phoenix increasingly represented the perils of modernity that many Navajos hoped to avoid. Letters in the *Navajo Times* portrayed preservation of the "fresh, clean air" and "beautiful landscape" of northern Arizona as a priority of Navajos' economic future, while "the highways and new houses of Phoenix," which threatened to "spoil our beautiful home" represented "the kind of modern development we wish to avoid." "We do not want and will not live the life of an ulcerated white, middle-class Christian suburbanite," Michael Benson wrote to the *Navajo Times*. Instead, Benson called for a "Navajo road" that allowed Navajos to drive pickup trucks and live in "warm, modern homes with electricity" without abandoning "a heritage, unique and secure, in this time of chaotic and rapid change."[53]

The modern Southwest emerged not only as Phoenicians and Navajos used common language to describe space, but also as a region linked in the material and spatial connections that carried energy from the Navajo Reservation into the homes of Phoenix.[54] My focus on these regional connections, their role in the emergence of the cultural and material region I call the modern Southwest, represents a second reason I avoid "Sunbelt." Too often, historical studies focused on the Sunbelt have taken region for granted conceptually, assuming that the metropolitan complexes that grew explosively after World War II possessed not only a shared moment of historical emergence but a shared regional identity. Promising recent work, such as Elizabeth Shermer's work on Phoenix's postwar growth machine and Joe Crespino's explorations of Strom Thurmond's attempts to appeal to voters in the West, has demonstrated how historical actors worked across space to forge regional connection. Too often, however, case studies located solely within single metropolitan spaces have attempted to suggest a regional identity, particularly in the emergence of postwar conservatism, based in a suburban anti-statism common across the nation.[55]

In using "modern Southwest" to describe the space that emerged in regional linkages created after World War II, *Power Lines* argues for an understanding of regional formation produced both in the material ties that connected spaces and in the shared understandings of space that those connections abetted.[56] It focuses on electrical power networks because the infrastructure that connected energy supplies with consumer demand represented a powerful source of such connections. Power companies and federal officials mapped energy resources on a regional level, they planned power lines to connect regional "load centers," and, by the late 1960s, collaborated closely to distribute electricity throughout the region.

Power Lines also focuses on electrical power networks to reveal the unequal and frequently unperceived systems of commodity production, distribution, and consumption that underlie and abet daily life in metropolitan America.[57] Commodities from the countryside have long fed and clothed urban consumers while playing a fundamental role in creating the structures of modern capitalism.[58] The power lines that ran between Phoenix and the Navajo Reservation intensified the structural inequalities that had long existed between city and countryside. Electrical networks require the simultaneous and constant balancing of supply and demand. Electricity does not so much flow, as we are accustomed to thinking about the motion of commodities in a market system, as flash, annihilating the space between consumption and production in both the immediacy and the constancy of its usage. For such a system to function, surety of energy supply became vital. The temporal lag between production and market entry involved in other forms of peripheral commodity production—the attempt by the farmer, or the mining conglomerate for that matter, to bring commodities to market when prices were high—threatened to destabilize metropolitan energy networks. To avoid such conditions, the terms of energy production granted extensive control—in the form of long-term contracts, fixed prices, and limited opportunity for renegotiation—to mining companies and electrical utilities. These terms were not merely the function of economics, they were political decisions reflecting the determination that metropolitan economies stood as the vital agent of postwar growth and the belief that Indian people possessed limited capacity to participate in contemporary economic life. Energy development granted Navajos money, but left them little meaningful power over the production occurring on their land once infrastructure was in place. That final point is vital. Navajos did retain political and economic power before contracts were signed and capital took material form as drag lines, generator turbines, and transmission lines. Navajos could and did attempt to shape the terms of energy production to meet their needs as they understood them at particular points in time. Once capital was fixed in place, however, the possibility for systemic change faced significant limits.

The practices of electrical consumption made it difficult for consumers to appreciate their inequalities. While Navajos quickly came to recognize the inequalities created by Phoenix's "air conditioned lifestyle," the practices of electrical consumption made them less evident to consumers. In an electrified home or factory, the connections to the distant landscape of electrical production are constant and readily available at the flick of a switch. Electricity's constant presence, other than in exceptional moments of blackout, in short, obscures appreciation of the spatial breadth of the connections in which consumers are engaged. Electricity comes with no label saying, "Made in China." As public and private utilities combined various sources of energy—flowing water, burning coal, and natural gas—into a massive pool from which they drew their electricity, these connections became more obscured, even as energy development on Navajo land intensified. Metropolitan residents, thus, created and intensified the modern Southwest's deeply unequal regional connections in the practices of daily life, even if they never spoke of the Southwest.

By the late 1960s, the act of turning on a light switch or air conditioner in Phoenix, Albuquerque, or Los Angeles led metropolitan consumers to participate in material networks that linked them intimately to the Navajo Reservation. Such connections remained largely unacknowledged in the daily lives of metropolitan consumers. They were far more visible on the Navajo Reservation. Ash and tailing piles, power-plant stack emissions, and the stark sentinels of transmission towers became signs of regional subordination. Peter MacDonald suggested as much to an audience of Western officials in 1975, "Our own people have the pleasure of watching giant transmission lines march across the land," he told the Western Governors Association, "at the same time as they are denied the opportunity to have electric service to their own homes which sit beneath the transmission lines."[59] MacDonald spoke to the central dynamic of the modern Southwest as it developed from the 1930s to the 1970s. The uneven distribution of energy had produced a region in which economic prosperity and high quality of life in metropolitan centers required the dual exploitation of people and nature on the Colorado Plateau, creating significant, frequently unrecognized, costs for distant environments and marginalized peoples.

This is a story rooted in particularities of time and space in the Southwest, but it has connections to the history of the United States, and to the world at large. The high-energy society of postwar America turned to natural resources on the periphery not only in the Southwest. In the late 1960s, just as coal from the Navajo Reservation came to supply increasing numbers of consumers in the Southwest, the Crow Tribe in eastern Montana signed lease agreements to mine coal across their reservation lands for use by utilities in Illinois, Minnesota, and Wisconsin. In the early 1970s, coal companies began blasting the tops off mountains in West Virginia, Kentucky, and Pennsylvania to reveal the coal beneath, filling nearby hollows with leftover debris, and shipping coal to power plants serving the vast metropolitan area stretching from Richmond to Philadelphia. As high-energy society became the goal of development worldwide, the strip mines run by Shenhua Group and ChinaCoal in Shanxi Province and Inner Mongolia replaced the mines at Black Mesa as the largest strip mines in the world in the 1990s, providing energy for Beijing, Shanghai, and other burgeoning urban centers. And in recent years, natural gas companies have begun injecting high-pressured water into geological formations deep below the earth's surface in upstate New York, central Pennsylvania, and eastern Ohio, fracturing subsurface geologies below some of the areas most hard hit by postwar economic restructuring.

In each case, these natural energies, long stored in place, became the fuel of modernity. Many of the people who lived above them experienced new opportunity in the form of wage work or royalty payments. They also faced environmental exploitation as the lands they knew changed dramatically. Transformed into electricity, energy from these lands traveled through power lines into the lives of people living far distant, people who ignored electricity even when they relied upon it. That ignorance appears no longer an option as the emissions created in the transformation of fossil fuels to electricity are likely to shape the human future itself. That potential future makes it important to notice power lines anew. It is the hope of this book to participate in that process, and make power lines and the unequal connections they have created more visible, both in the Southwest and in the world at large.

Ansel Adams, "Power Lines from Boulder Dam Cross the Mojave Desert." NARA 79-AAB-2. 1940.

PART I

Fragments

CHAPTER 1

A Region of Fragments

AT 7:36 P.M. ON OCTOBER 9, 1936, ELIZABETH SCATTERGOOD, THE daughter of the chief engineer of the Los Angeles Bureau of Power and Light, lowered "the most powerful fingertip in the world." At that instant, telegraph wires carried a signal from Scattergood's finger to the power-house at the base of Boulder Dam. Hearing the telegraph's staccato alert, an engineer in the powerhouse threw a switch, opening circuits that sent electricity coursing through the power lines that surmounted the canyon walls downstream from the dam. An instant after Scattergood lifted her finger, sixteen arc lights on the top floor of City Hall burst to light, ex-tending "long fingers of brilliance into the darkness," in the words of an *LA Times* reporter. "The dim-lit city, starting up like a sleeper," Thomas Treanor wrote, "was in an instant clothed with such a flaming radiance as man has never made before." More than one million Angelinos flooded the streets in the city's largest civic celebration since the Armistice. Ad-dressing the throng, Mayor Frank Shaw promised benefits not only for his city, but for a far broader region. The dam's power would trigger, Shaw announced, "a higher order of social and industrial development that will bring us happy results in the Southwest."[1]

Boulder Dam had been an object of national fascination since its con-struction began five years earlier. Seven hundred fifty thousand annual visitors flocked to see the dam's creation, thrilling at the high-scalers swinging from ropes hundreds of feet long and marveling at the massive buckets of concrete lowered to the dam's rising crest, activity that formed a welcome contrast to the photos of bread lines and migrant labor camps that filled the nation's newspapers in the Depression's depths.[2] Franklin Roosevelt's secretary of the interior, Harold Ickes, certainly realized the dam's potent symbolism. He was in office for less than a month before removing "Hoover" from the dam and replacing it with "Boulder."[3]

Roosevelt realized its symbolic power too. In September 1935, as he began his reelection campaign, Roosevelt traveled to Black Canyon. With ten thousand spectators "fringing the parapet like pygmies," as the *Times* reported, Roosevelt explained the dam as a manifestation of the trans-formations the New Deal had set in motion.[4] "The largest generators and turbines yet installed in this country, machinery that can continu-ously supply nearly two million horsepower of electric energy," Roosevelt

FIGURE 1.1. Los Angeles's celebration of Boulder Dam's electricity represented the largest civic celebration in almost twenty years. Copyright © Corbis. 1936.

explained, would soon "power factory motors, street and household lights and irrigation pumps." In so doing, the dam's energy would transform the region and the nation at large. No longer would the Southwest be known primarily as a land of "unpeopled, forbidding desert." Its residents would no longer "dread the coming of a flood" or fear "a shortage of water" caused by the "turbulent," "unpredictable" river. Instead, the dam would create industrial modernity, benefiting "the millions of people who now dwell in this basin, and the millions of others who will come to dwell here in future generations." In closing the frontier stage of development in the Southwest, the dam promised to benefit the nation at large. "The mighty waters of the Colorado were running unused to the sea," Roosevelt proclaimed. "Today, we translate them into a great national possession."[5]

The crowd gathered on the dam's crest roared, but people elsewhere in the Southwest were less enthusiastic. Many Arizonans feared that the benefits Roosevelt outlined would be distributed far more unequally than he suggested. Since a 1922 interstate compact dividing the river's waters had placed Arizona and California together in the Colorado River's lower basin, California's demand for water seemed an existential threat. A year before the dedication of Boulder Dam, Arizona governor Benjamin Mouer had declared martial law on the Arizona shore of the Colorado, deploying forty infantrymen and twenty machine gunners to Parker, Arizona, and dispatching the "Arizona Navy"—five state guardsmen aboard the ferryboat *Julia B*—to prevent federal workers from completing preliminary work on Parker Dam, which, downstream from Boulder, would divert the now controlled waters of the Colorado to Southern California. To Mouer, the planned aqueduct was little better than theft of Arizona's rightful resources. "We may get licked in this affair," Mouer proclaimed, "but we will go down fighting." The *Los Angeles Times* dispatched a "war correspondent," who archly reported on the mobilization of "troops into this theater of war to protect the State of Arizona from invasion by all or part of the State of California." A member of the Arizona Navy took his anger out on California literally, firing a shotgun into the Colorado's western shore. The incident ended in farce. The *Julia B* became entangled in cables cast across the river, and its sailors suffered the indignity of being rescued by a boat owned by the City of Los Angeles. The conflict moved to the Supreme Court, which enjoined further work on the dam before Congress settled the matter by passing the 1935 Rivers and Harbors Bill expressly authorizing Parker Dam. While it did not prevent the dam's completion, the voyage of the Arizona Navy signaled the fears among many Arizonans that the development of the Colorado's energy did not foretell shared regional and national growth. Rather, they saw competition in which Arizona's needs were subordinated to those of California.[6]

The state capital in Phoenix was not the only place in Arizona where officials had reasons to fear Boulder Dam. In 1933, Commissioner of Indian Affairs John Collier spoke before the Navajo Tribal Council in Fort Defiance, Arizona. "Down there on the Colorado River," Collier told the council, "is the biggest, most expensive dam in the world . . . which will furnish all southern California with water and power. The Boulder Dam will be filled up with your fine agricultural soil in no great number of years if we do not stop erosion."[7] Collier warned the council that the dam's construction might lead other federal officials to identify erosion from the Navajo Reservation as a threat to regional development and national investment. Either Navajos could stop erosion voluntarily, Collier warned, or someone would do it for them. Attempts to control erosion, however, entailed new regulation of grazing land, new limits on herd sizes, and, more generally, the destabilization of the subsistence economy that had allowed Navajos to mount perhaps the most successful response to American conquest of any American Indian tribe.

The beams of light that lit Los Angeles, the Arizona Navy traveling up the Colorado River, and the warnings to the Navajo Tribal Council all reflected the Southwest's fragmentation. Across Arizona and Southern California, human history had created something akin to "island communities," to use Robert Wiebe's description of late nineteenth-century America's spatial form.[8] Phoenix and the Navajo Reservation lay deeply connected to markets both national and global. They had little relation to each other, however. The construction of Boulder Dam, and the politics surrounding it, signaled a change. It suggested that efforts to turn the energy of the river to human purposes had begun to tie the fates of those places together. Boulder Dam had begun the creation of a new region.

ENERGY'S PAST

"As an unregulated river," Franklin Roosevelt told the crowd at Boulder Dam, "the Colorado added little of value to the region this dam serves."[9] Flowing unimpeded to the Gulf of California, the Colorado's history seemed to Roosevelt one of great waste, a story of productive resources left unclaimed. Natural energy has a productive history, however, that exists independent of human history. It wrote that past on the landscape that surrounded Boulder Dam. Indeed, the results of energy's productive past enabled the productive future that Roosevelt's dedication envisioned in the form of the walls that held Boulder Dam's abutments and contained the upstream waters of Lake Mead.

The canyons of the Colorado were only one element of energy's history. One hundred million years before crowds joined Roosevelt atop Boulder Dam, the location where they stood had been starkly different. Rather than a high plateau bisected by the deep canyons of the Colorado, the land was flat and swampy. It lay a mile lower than it would in the twentieth century, almost at sea level. Waters trickled slowly across the land, not west, toward the Pacific, but east toward a vast shallow sea that stretched across what is today the intermountain West.[10] Plants grew thickly along the fluctuating shores of the Cretaceous Seaway. Ferns, palms, and cypress raised their leaves to the sun, gathering solar energy. Using photosynthesis, they converted that ephemeral energy into carbohydrates, which took form as stalks, branches, and leaves.[11] When eaten by the triceratops or other dinosaurs that roamed the swamps, carbohydrates fueled biological life. Most carbohydrates, however, went unconsumed. Upon death, those plants sank into the swamp. They formed a thick mat of vegetation that decomposed slowly as bacteria harvested carbohydrates. Decomposing plants formed an oozy muck on the swamp floor where oxygen and bacteria grew scarce. Decomposition slowed. Sediment from inflowing rivers pressed from above, squeezing sap and other liquids from the ancient plants. Pressure also broke loose weakly bonded oxygen and hydrogen atoms from the carbohydrates, leaving mostly carbon behind. As they bonded in hexagonal rings, those molecules formed a dense substance known as peat.[12]

Peat represented a concentration of the energy prehistoric plants had stored. It will smolder steadily if lit. For decades, even centuries, burning peat beds will slowly release the energy of their bonded carbon until little but ash remains.[13] Most of the peat in the prehistoric Southwest did not ignite, however. Instead, it slowly changed, assuming an even more energy-rich form. Additional pressure from overlying rocks and underlying geologic forces compressed peat, rendering it more and more carbon-rich as pressure broke all but the strongest chemical bonds. Peat first became a jellied substance the consistency of soft cheese, called gyttja, then it solidified. Slowly over aeons, prehistoric plants became bituminous coal.

Coal beds clustered in seams across present-day Arizona, New Mexico, Colorado, and Utah, mapping the Cretaceous Seaway's ancient shorelines.[14] Those coal beds stored ancient energy in place beneath the surface of the Colorado Plateau until humans discovered it, and more importantly, until they found it valuable and accessible. Those beds remained buried not only through the long history of geologic time, but through most of the shorter history of the industrial age. Lying far from industrial and urban centers, the Southwest's coal remained buried while coal fired Manchester mills to produce cloth for a world market; while coal heated tenements to warm immigrants in New York, Philadelphia and Chicago; and while coal drove railroads across the American West. It remained buried until technology, demand, and politics made it accessible. Eventually, humans would claim ownership of the ancient energy that underlay the Colorado Plateau while debating whom these vast stores of natural wealth should enrich. No humans, however, had a hand in that wealth's creation. It was the work of the sun, the earth, prehistoric life, and time itself.[15]

Unlike coal, water's energy history does not sit in place. Instead, over aeons, it has created place. The Southwestern landscape that exists today, not only iconic sites like the Grand Canyon, but the vast valley of the Salt River and the thin soils of the Colorado Plateau, represent its creation.

The process by which water made new places in the Southwest began with the dramatic geologic changes that helped transform peat beds into coal seams. Seventy million years ago, the tectonic changes that caused the Rocky Mountains to rise from sea level dramatically transformed the lands to their west as well. Entire tectonic blocks rose steadily upward, like corks in water, forming the Coconino, Kaibab, and Colorado Plateaus.[16] Over the course of forty million years, the Colorado Plateau, what today forms most of southern Utah, northern Arizona, and western New Mexico, rose more than a mile. Its location in the new geography of North America, sandwiched between the Pacific Ocean and the Rocky Mountains, meant that its landscape received the brunt of water's energy as it exited the mountains in the spring melt seeking the ocean. Water rushing out of the mountains eventually established a common path, and a powerful river formed; explorer John Wesley Powell wrote in 1869, "a million cascade brooks unite to form a thousand torrent creeks; a thousand torrent creeks unite to form half a hundred rivers beset with cataracts; half a hundred roaring rivers unite to form the Colorado, which rolls, a mad, turbid stream, into the Gulf of California."[17]

Powell witnessed a relatively young landscape, geologically speaking, when he journeyed down the Colorado in a flat bottomed boat in 1869. Geologists currently believe that, until eight million years ago, the water flowing out of the Rockies collided with the plateau lands to the west and turned south, flowing into a massive inland lake they have named Lake Bidahochi. At the same time, an ambitious stream to the west had been cutting its way through the Kaibab Plateau for millions of years. As the headwaters of that stream reached farther and farther east through a process called headwall erosion, they gathered more water, carving the channel wider and deeper. One momentous day, the stream broke through the plateau's last redoubt and met the main stream of the prehistoric Colorado River. In a flood of unbelievable magnitude and duration, the Colorado changed course, choosing the stream's steep gradient over the relatively level course toward the lake. Lake Bidahochi gradually drained, forming the bed of the Little Colorado River. At the same time, the Colorado's water tore into the Plateau, digging deeper and deeper, and forming, over the past eight million years, the Grand Canyon.[18]

Similar canyons formed across the Plateau as the Colorado's tributaries—the San Juan, the Virgin, and the Salt Rivers—cut their way through its land. Water's energy dug canyons deep, isolating water and leaving the Colorado Plateau's surface dry and arid.[19] The steep slopes and thin soils on the Plateau created a landscape prone to erosion. And the river's rapid current served as a conduit, carrying massive amounts of silt, soil, and sediment downstream from the Colorado Plateau. River gauges placed near Yuma, Arizona, in the early twentieth century, before dams impeded the river's flow, estimated that the river carried 500,000 tons of reddish soil every day.[20] Silt ran so thick in the Colorado that swimmers who ventured into its waters emerged with a strange second skin, a coat of silt that Barry Goldwater found in 1940, "dries as tight as a weiner skin and is about as comfortable."[21]

Erosion left the Plateau's soil thin. Most of its landscape varied between desert and grasslands. In locations where slickrock sandstone dominated the landscape, the Plateau's scant rainfall rushed away at the moment it struck the earth. In locations where soil and slope allowed water to linger, grama, western wheat, and galleta grasses grew, thick during wet years, but disappearing during long droughts that expanded deserts.[22] The Plateau contained other microenvironments: alpine forests with aspens, ponderosa pines, and Gambel oaks, and pockets of alluvial soil near mesa bottoms where cottonwood trees grew amid rushes, goldenrod, and thistle.[23] By the fourth century CE, Puebloan migrants, later known as *Anasazi*, located settlements near such washes. For a thousand years, they built increasingly more elaborate and protected dwellings, beneath cliffs and in isolated canyons, before an extended drought drove most, other than Hopis that remained in villages on Black Mesa, elsewhere. Shortly thereafter, Athabaskan migrants arrived into a land that their stories told had been prepared for them by powerful beings. Residents of Tewas Pueblo called them "*navahu'u*," meaning "farm fields in the valley," a reflection of the alluvial agriculture they adopted. They called themselves *Diné*, meaning "the people." In the subsequent six hundred years, they would work to make the stingy environment of the Colorado Plateau their home.[24]

The soil that washed away from the Colorado Plateau formed new landscapes downstream. Swift river currents in canyons rushed soil downstream before the great conduit rivers of the Southwest exited their canyons and slowed. At flood times, they deposited their cargo in valleys whose soils eventually reached almost unfathomable depths. Boosters in the Imperial Valley, close by the Colorado in Southern California boasted of "a 500,000 acre bowl filled with a conglomeration of soils . . . not the usual six to ten inches deep, but a full mile or more."[25] In central Arizona, the Salt River deposited alluvium 10,000 feet deep.[26]

These valleys came with severe limits attached to their rich soils and nearly year-round growing season. Annual rainfall amounted to less than eight inches, far below the level needed to support agriculture, and temperatures regularly soared to over 100°F. Despite these difficulties, however, settlers called the Hohokam arrived in the Salt River Valley around 450 CE and discovered that its loose soils could support extensive agriculture if the river's waters could be manipulated. Redirecting those waters into what became an extensive canal system that laced the valley floor, the Hohokam cultivated as many as 250,000 acres by 1300, supporting a population that may have reached 200,000 people. If the Hohokam's fluorescence demonstrated the potential of the valley's soils, their disappearance from the archaeological record demonstrated the limits of the valley's environment. Archaeologists believe climate changes in the early fifteenth century produced first devastating floods, which destroyed irrigation works, and then an extended drought that created new social conflict. By 1450, the Hohokam had abandoned the Salt River Valley.[27]

The first Anglo-Americans to settle in the Salt River Valley saw destiny in ruined Hohokam canals. Watching teams of oxen excavate the sand-filled canals in 1867, an English émigré named Darrel Duppa proclaimed that "a new city shall spring, Phoenix-like, upon the ruins of a former civilization."[28] Duppa's proclamation coined the name of the new settlement. It also stood as testament to the possibilities the energy of flowing water had set in place throughout the Southwest. In alluvial valleys and washes, grasslands and canyons, water's energy had created ecological niches that humans could manipulate to store and collect energy. At the same time, the ruined canals of the Hohokam and the empty dwellings of the Anasazi stood as stark warnings about the limits of the landscape falling water had created.

EMPIRE

Most Americans in the early twentieth century did not view the Southwest as rich with energy. Apart from its Southern California periphery, they saw the region as backward, primitive, and unproductive. That image had value. By 1921, 750,000 Americans flocked annually to the Grand Canyon to gaze from the rim at Zoroaster and Shiva Temples, to descend on mules down Bright Angel Trail, or to watch Hopi artisans work with silver and clay and dance daily at 5:00 p.m. Farther east, bohemians gathered at Mabel Dodge's home near Taos to experience a rugged landscape and to live among local Pueblo people, writing, painting, and photographing experiences that felt somehow more authentic than those available in Greenwich Village. The growing trade in "Indian-made" goods by Hopi, Pueblo, and Navajo artisans made the authenticity of primitivism available to eager consumers in the East. Altogether, such institutions created an image of the Southwest as, in Leah Dilworth's words, "the place of the unique, the handmade, the rural, and the authentic," a place starkly opposed to the modern metropolis.[29]

In Los Angeles, on the Southwest's western periphery, that image was more complex. To be sure, Charles Lummis's Southwestern Museum, perched above the Arroyo Seco between downtown and Pasadena, contained large collections of Hopi kachina, Pueblo pottery, and Navajo rugs, to go with religious icons carried by Father Kino and the Bear Flag carried by John Fremont.[30] For Lummis, however, the close proximity of "the Great Southwest" formed part of the charm of Los Angeles. An easy day's train journey could carry Angelinos to "the land of poco tiempo," where "the opiate sun soothes to rest, the adobe is made to lean against, the hush of the day-long noon would not be broken."[31] Indeed, the opportunity for both productive work and ready leisure made Southern California, for Lummis and other Los Angeles boosters, then and now, a type of paradise.[32]

Other Angelinos viewed the areas to their east with a more materialist eye. Instead of escape, they saw resources that could fuel their city's industrial growth. In a 1923 editorial, the *Los Angeles Times* called on the city's businessmen to reach "further into the back country to get coal and iron and wool and cotton to feed the industries which will grow." As early as 1914, the Los Angeles Chamber of Commerce affixed "Nature's Workshop, the city where nature helps industry most" to its letterhead, suggesting not only that the city's benign climate and sunshine improved workers' morale and productivity, but that the water, power, and other resources necessary for manufacturing flowed naturally from the surrounding hinterlands toward the city. Indeed, this view of resources flowing, as if by nature's intent, from metropolitan periphery to center, shaped the way Angelinos talked about their city's presumed ownership of those resources.[33] "There it is, take it," formed the entirety of William Mulholland's dedication of the Los Angeles Aqueduct, which carried most of the Owens River from the eastern Sierra Nevadas to the San Fernando Valley.[34]

Boulder Dam, in the minds of Los Angeles's municipal officials, formed a natural extension of these imperial tendencies. Shortly after federal officials began developing plans for the dam in 1920, Ezra Scattergood, chief engineer of the Los Angeles Department of Power and Light and the father of the woman who would eventually trigger the flow of electricity from Boulder Dam, suggested that electrical power sales could be used to pay for the dam's construction. In 1924 he elaborated while testifying before Congress that, "the City of Los Angeles would be perfectly willing to become wholly responsible for all carrying charges and operating expenses of the Boulder Canyon dam . . . to receive the right of development of the power possible at that point." Mulholland, chief engineer for both the city's Bureau of Water Works and Supply, and the Metropolitan Water District of Southern California, was equally enthusiastic. Testifying before the House Irrigation subcommittee in 1924, Mulholland contended that the dam could solve his city's "appalling drought." In return, the city's consumers could provide security. "The coming of the city of Los Angeles into this proposition, I think, adds amazingly, immensely, to the sureness of return to the United States government," he testified, estimating that Los Angeles's electrical demand could grow 25 percent annually. "We promise to be a very large customer."[35]

Such early assurances came as relief to officials from the Bureau of Reclamation. Established by the National Reclamation Act (NRA) of 1902, the U.S. Reclamation Service represented the junction of two visions: those of late nineteenth-century "irrigation evangelists" who sought to revitalize the family farm by uniting "landless men" in the East with the "manless land" of the West, and those of early twentieth-century engineers who sought to transform turbulent Western rivers into controlled systems that could provide irrigation water and electric power. The authors of the NRA saw those dreams as mutually constitutive. The sales of "reclaimed" farmland and irrigation water could be used to pay for the construction of new dams and irrigation works, creating a nearly endless cycle that would cause deserts across the West to bloom.[36] By the 1920s, however, these dreams had come apart. While engineers had proven mostly adept at building dams to control Western rivers, irrigated farming proved a tougher task than most evangelists had believed. Despite the optimistic claims of Frederick Newell, the first Reclamation commissioner, "the dead and profitless deserts" needed more than just "the magic touch of water to make arable lands that will afford farms and homes." They also required expertise, taxing labor, and economic stability. All proved in short supply. The expertise of the Bureau of Reclamation (the agency's name was changed from the Reclamation Service in 1907) was stretched thin by political demands that located projects in every western state, and the fluctuations of the commodity cycle drove many prospective farmers away. By 1925, one-sixth of all Reclamation farmland lay fallow and 60 percent of Reclamation loans were delinquent.[37]

With Eastern Congressmen criticizing annual appropriations to a supposedly self-supporting agency, Arthur Powell Davis, Newell's successor in the early 1920s, was relieved when Scattergood and Mulholland indicated Los Angeles's consumers would, in effect, fund a dam on the Colorado, which he viewed as essential as a first stage in a broader development plan. In 1922 Davis proposed a dam "built as high as appears practicable" in the vicinity of Boulder Canyon. The dam would allow downstream flood control, would enable construction of a new irrigation canal for the Imperial Valley, and would be paid for entirely through "revenues from leasing the power privileges" of the dam itself. Understanding clearly who would lease these privileges, Davis directed surveyors searching for a dam site to explore no farther upstream than 350 miles from Los Angeles's City Hall.[38]

Businessmen in Los Angeles were initially less enthusiastic than Los Angeles's civic officials. Harry Chandler, publisher of the *Los Angeles Times* and the wealthiest, most powerful figure in Southern California politics, feared the project would devalue the vast amounts of land he owned south of the U.S.-Mexico border.[39] Other opposition related to power. Southern California Edison, the region's largest private utility, feared that Boulder Dam's inexpensive public power would drive more and more cities to municipalize their electrical service, as Los Angeles had in 1917. In the early 1920s, Chandler and Southern California Edison pursued a furious campaign to defeat the dam, joined by private utilities across the nation. Altogether the utilities spent $1 million a year in the 1920s to lobby Congressmen against the dam, to fund newspaper editorials promoting free enterprise in electrical distribution, and to support scholars who attacked public power. The *Times* led the charge, denouncing the dam's power scheme as a "socialistic attack . . . on our free enterprise system."[40]

Two events altered this opposition. Increasing anti-American sentiment in Mexico in the years after the Mexican Revolution led Chandler to fear nationalization of his property, and he steadily reduced his Mexican landholdings. Second, Reclamation officials proved willing to include private utilities in its plans. While public power advocates hoped the dam would serve as "an arrow aimed directly at the heart of the Power Trust," Interior Secretary Raymond Wilbur, prioritizing repayment of the federal investment in the dam, eventually granted Southern California Edison rights to purchase 9 percent of the dam's power, enough to supply almost 800,000 homes, as well as additional rights to purchase electricity unused by other utilities.[41] Reclamation also divided management of the dam's power plant between Edison and Scattergood's Los Angeles Department of Power and Light (LADPL). Finally, because the Boulder Dam Act required utilities to build their own power lines to connect their systems with Boulder Dam, Edison began carrying much of the power for small municipal utilities outside of Los Angeles, charging "wheeling fees" for the service. Indeed, Donald Pisani has suggested that "Southern California Edison was, perhaps, the greatest beneficiary of 'public power' at Boulder Dam."[42] Even before those benefits were determined, however, the general contours of Boulder Dam's development became clear to Harry Chandler. The dam's power would be put in service of his city's growth. In late 1927, the *Times* suddenly called for "quick action by Congress" to pass a measure it had opposed since 1922. Henceforth, the newspaper, according to Michael Hiltzik, "would be the most vociferous booster of the Boulder Canyon Project in all the West."[43]

Chandler's change of heart also owed to the distribution of the dam's power. While the Interior Department reserved 18 percent of the dam's power for use in both Arizona and Nevada, the terms of the legislation, particularly the requirement that utilities build their own power lines, made it unlikely that utilities in those states would claim their shares. Indeed, in 1930, when utilities returned contracts to purchase $327 million of electricity over the course of fifty years, the dynamics of the dam's power distribution became clear. Ranging from the largest contract (the Metropolitan Water District of Southern California) to the smallest (the City of Burbank), all of the dam's power would flow to metropolitan Los Angeles.

Angelino's used a word to describe the new geography that linked their city with the Colorado River. Like Americans in New York and Chicago before them, they described the infrastructure connecting their growing city with the resources of its hinterland as empire.[44] "Imprisoning a mighty river," Chester Hanson wrote in the *Times*, Boulder Dam "opens the gates of a new empire."[45] Empire suggested that the power lines that reached from Boulder Dam to their city were an inevitable, an almost natural consequence of their city's growing power. They also suggested that those power lines would have broadly distributed benefits, bringing light to the dark places of the region. A cartoon in the *Times* the day of the dam's dedication conveyed a similar sentiment. As Lady Liberty, wearing a sash emblazoned with "The Great Southwest" raised a flag for "Hoover Dam," a light shone behind the dam in the east. "The Gateway of Empire," the cartoon declared, seeming to suggest a new dawn for the Southwest in which Los Angeles's influence would spread ever farther.[46]

Boulder Dam did represent the dawn of a new phase of state power, both in the West and in the nation, in which the state's distributive powers would be targeted in increasingly powerful ways toward the landscape of metropolitan America. The distribution of the dam's power stood as one of the first manifestations of an emerging metropolitan preference in policy making, that saw metropolitan growth as the surest means toward regional and national prosperity. Such preferences would soon manifest themselves in the form of suburban homes and federal highways, and eventually in other power lines built throughout the Southwest. Eventually, metropolitan growth and the public good would become almost synonymous in the eyes of Southwestern liberals and conservatives alike. At the moment of Boulder Dam's creation, however, those preferences, and the new alliance between federal officials and the Los Angeles growth machine they reflected, appeared troubling, even dangerous, to people elsewhere in the region.

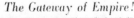

The Gateway of Empire!

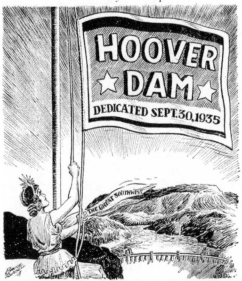

FIGURE 1.2. Los Angeles's civic officials articulated the flow of Boulder Dam's electricity toward their city as a natural manifestation of urban empire. "The Gateway of Empire," by Bruce Russell. Copyright © 1935. *Los Angeles Times*. Reprinted with permission.

STATES' RIGHTS

The distribution of Boulder Dam's power did not initially trouble most Arizonans. Water was different. In stopping the wild Colorado, Boulder Dam transformed its water into potential property. Ownership of the river's water, however, was a vexing question. Unlike land, upon which the idea of property is grounded, water does not remain in place. Instead, it crosses the borders between property, between states, and between nations that humans have placed upon the land. From the planning of Boulder Dam onward, people in the West debated how the controlled waters of the Colorado should be divided. The river and its major tributaries flowed within the borders of five states—Wyoming, Utah, Colorado, New Mexico, and Arizona—and the river's main stream created state borders between Arizona, Nevada, and California on the lower river. How much could each state claim? Before those states had formed, the lands had been national territory. Had the federal government granted water to the states when they became sovereign? These questions remained particularly vexed in the arid West, where controlled water, which was scarce, represented in many ways more valuable property than land itself, which was abundant. Reclamation held out the potential for water to make the desert bloom and create irrigated Edens. It also raised the possibility of dystopic social collapse, of another Hohokam, if water could not be procured. "Water," one Arizonan asserted in 1940, "means future."[47]

For Arizona's officials, the plan for Boulder Dam, which diverted Colorado River water to Southern California, represented not only resources flowing away from their state, but the foreclosing of their own imperial dreams. "The Colorado River is our great resource," Arizona governor George Hunt declared in 1924, "and unless we conserve it and get the maximum benefit from it, we can depend on becoming a sort of vermiform appendix to Los Angeles, instead of becoming one of the great empire states of our nation."[48] Two years earlier, Hunt's words could likely have been spoken by any of the governors who occupied statehouses in the Colorado River basin as cooperation between officials from Southern California and the Bureau of Reclamation threatened visions of prosperity up and down the river.

By 1924, however, Hunt stood alone. In 1922, officials from the seven Colorado River basin states had met in Santa Fe and negotiated an interstate compact dividing the river's waters. After determining that the river had an annual flow of 15,000,000 acre-feet (overestimating the actual number by some 2,000,000 acre-feet), delegates had split the river at Lee's Ferry, the site where the river crossed the Arizona-Utah border.[49] The upper basin states of Colorado, Wyoming, New Mexico, and Utah would receive 7,500,000 acre-feet, and the lower basin states of Arizona, California, and Nevada would receive the same. This solution proved doubly disappointing to most Arizonans. At the meeting, Arizona's delegate, W. S. Norviel, had pressed Arizona's rights to 44 percent of the river's water, arguing it contained 44 percent of the lands that drained toward the river. California, by this calculation, would receive 3 percent. Not only did the meeting fail to accept Norviel's suggestion for dividing the river, it failed to adjudicate whether the water Boulder Dam would transfer into property belonged to the states, as Arizonans believed, or the federal government, as the commission's chairman, Herbert Hoover, insisted. Worse, this question remained open even as the compact placed Arizona in the lower basin with California. Rather than seeing its rights to 6.6 million acre-feet acknowledged, as Norviel's proposal had hoped, Arizona would have to share the lower basin's waters with California.[50]

Arizona officials responded both obstinately and opportunistically. George Hunt, who had been Arizona's first governor after statehood in 1912, revived his political career by defending Arizona's "superior and natural rights" while opposing the "selfish private interests" of California. If Jesus walked on water, his constituents joked, George Hunt ran on the Colorado.[51] Following his example, the Arizona legislature adamantly refused to even consider ratifying the compact, forcing an amendment to the Boulder Canyon Bill allowing the compact to go into effect with the endorsements of six out of the seven basin states. Senators Carl Hayden and Henry Ashcroft mounted a semisuccessful eighteen-hour filibuster, running out the clock on one Senate session in 1928, only for the dam's advocates to place it first on the Senate's docket for the following session, leading other senators to invoke cloture. Even after passage of the bill, the Arizona legislature refused to ratify the compact until 1944. "Signing the compact," one state legislator stated in 1940, "would be like signing [our] own death warrant."[52]

These state demands for protection of water rights reflected local history. Until 1900, floods and drought had alternately plagued the Salt River Valley, making Darrel Duppa's description of the city as a Phoenix reborn only partly accurate. Valley farmland expanded and receded according to the river's flow, which ranged between 300,000 and 52 cubic feet per second during the 1890s alone, preventing development of what one booster termed "rich bottom-lands . . . not equaled by any portion of the great West."[53]

In 1902, the fledgling Reclamation Service chose Phoenix as the location of its first signature project, after local grower Dwight Heard intervened with his personal friend Theodore Roosevelt. Located seventy miles upstream from Phoenix, Roosevelt Dam would control the waters of the Salt River and apportion them to the valley's waiting farmers. The choice of Phoenix did not come without administrative difficulty. The National Reclamation Act had envisioned the development of unclaimed lands in the public domain. Most of the Salt River Valley, however, had long since passed into private hands, either through the Desert Lands Act of 1877, which allowed families to claim up to 640 acres or through the actions of the private irrigation companies that sought to purchase land and sell it at great profit after building irrigation works. Envisioning this difficulty, two Phoenicians who were also members of the National Reclamation Association successfully advocated for an amendment to the act, allowing private landholders to jointly collateralize their lands to guarantee repayment of construction costs. Shortly after passage of the act, owners of 240,000 acres of valley land did just that, forming the Salt River Valley Water Users' Association, and indenturing their land to fund the dam's costs and purchase private irrigation works in the valley.[54]

The location of the Bureau of Reclamation's first major project in the Salt River Valley did not result in a powerful federal presence in the valley. The Salt River Project (SRP), as the Water Users' Association became known, governed the distribution of water and collected delivery charges, forming a local authority that distributed water to farms surrounding the small cities of Mesa, Tempe, Glendale, Peoria, and Phoenix. In 1917, SRP assumed responsibility for all future costs and revenues from the project.[55] In short, the Bureau of Reclamation, the epitome, in Donald Worster's words, of "state power, state expertise, state technology, and state bureaucracy" in the twentieth-century West, virtually abdicated authority over its first major project shortly after its completion.[56] Rather than a centralization of federal authority, SRP suggested the continuity of the nineteenth-century state practices of dispersing resources into private hands.

SRP's development produced particular views of natural resources in Phoenix. Regardless of whether they were owned by the state or, like 75 percent of the land within Arizona, federal property, natural resources, many Phoenicians believed, were essentially local property. The proper role of government entailed action to pass resources to their local owners. Such beliefs had a long life. On Roosevelt Dam's fifty-year anniversary, Barry Goldwater wrote a column in the *Los Angeles Times* praising the SRP as "the proper kind of partnership between a free people and their government." SRP's development involved, Goldwater wrote, "local interests solving their own problems in co-operation with the federal government."[57]

While Roosevelt Dam regulated the Salt River, it did little to stabilize the booms and busts of commodity agriculture. After cotton prices rose with the beginning of World War I, growers transformed their valley into what they soon referred to as the "Nile Valley of Arizona," planting more than 190,000 acres of long-staple Egyptian cotton, up from only 7,400 acres four years earlier.[58] In 1921, the cotton economy collapsed as cotton prices fell from $1.35 to $0.35 per pound. Tens of thousands of acres entered receivership. SRP cut off water service to 75 percent of its members for nonpayment, and local merchants saw million-dollar losses. Phoenix's relief rolls swelled and its jail cells filled with Mexican farm workers arrested for vagrancy after bankrupt farmers refused to pay their wages. The Mexican consulate intervened, leading the Arizona Cotton Growers, the trade organization of Arizona's cotton industry, to fund a voluntary repatriation program.[59]

In the longer term, the cotton bust led to greater crop diversification as SRP funded a program allowing farmers to borrow capital to finance the costs of transitioning away from cotton. Crop diversification increased Phoenix's importance as an industrial and administrative center. Phoenix banks held the loans that allowed crop diversification. A new geography of canning plants, packing houses, and feedlots emerged in the land between the Southern Pacific and the Salt River south of Phoenix, and new office buildings housed the headquarters of the cooperative marketing associations that sponsored Buy a Turkey Day, the Arizona King Cotton

Festival, the Cantaloupe Queen competition, and other more mundane forms of agricultural marketing.[60] Such efforts were broadly successful. In 1937, as the nation recovered from the Depression, 2,800 carloads of Salt River Valley Sweet-Eating Cantaloupes, 13,000 carloads of lettuce, and innumerable railcars filled with 2.1 million grapefruits, 113,512 bales of Egyptian long-staple cotton, and 5 million pounds of honey rolled out of the valley.[61]

Recovery from the cotton bust also led to the electrification of Phoenix's farm fields. Growers desperate for cash aggressively irrigated their fields, raising the entire valley's water table. Standing water covered one-third of the valley's farmland, threatening to turn soils alkaline. Hydraulic pumps could clear the water relatively easily, however, Phoenix's farms, like 95 percent of agricultural land nationwide, lacked electrical service. While hydroelectric generators had been installed at Roosevelt Dam in 1907 and Phoenix's private utility had received power from the dam since 1913, almost none of the farms were electrified because of rural power-line construction costs that averaged $1,000 per mile.[62] Fearing the potential loss of farmland, SRP's board decided to fund construction of power lines. In 1923, SRP floated a $6 million bond to build a system of rural power lines and two additional dams on the river—Horse Mesa and Mormon Flat Dams—insured by a contract with the Central Arizona Light and Power Company (CALAPCO), Phoenix's private electric company. Five years later, SRP offered a second $4.1 million bond allowing SRP to complete its system and fund construction of a fourth dam on the Salt River, Stewart Mountain Dam. By 1930, the Salt River descended through four dams in a series of stairsteps before reaching the valley, each one generating power for both country and city alike; 90 percent of the project's farms had electrical service, representing, SRP bragged, "the largest block of electrified farmland in the world."[63]

In 1928, SRP and CALAPCO formalized the division of the valley's electrical spaces. That year, they signed an operating agreement establishing the territory where each would provide electrical service. CALAPCO agreed to serve no more than 15 percent of the customers on SRP's land. Otherwise, it would serve urban residents living in Phoenix, Tempe, Glendale, and Peoria. While this territory may sound capacious given the sprawl of contemporary Phoenix, the city's 1928 borders encompassed only 9.6 square miles, containing a population of roughly thirty thousand people.[64]

Electrical service area determined more than just the address to which electrical customers sent their utility bill. It also determined the experience of electricity itself. Receiving funding from American Power and Light, a holding company that purchased controlling shares of the utility's stock in 1924, CALAPCO built a distribution system that integrated power from Roosevelt Dam with Phoenix Power Plant, a natural gas–burning generating plant completed in 1930. These sources of electricity complemented each other. "During times of plentiful water supply a large portion of the power comes from [Roosevelt Dam]," a local business-man explained in 1938, "and during times of shortage or large power de-mands the steam plant acts as insurance for a steady supply of electrical power for the homes and industries of the valley." CALAPCO's system, in brief, provided ample reserve supplies as insurance against shortage.[65]

SRP's system differed. With widely distributed consumers, SRP con-nected long chains of customers to a single source of electricity. Small windstorms routinely knocked out power to large sections of the valley. If too many farmers used their pumps simultaneously, voltage could drop, causing brownouts that damaged motors. In order to utilize the limited kinetic energy supplied by the Salt River, most SRP generators were de-signed to rotate slowly, providing electricity at 25-hertz, rather than at the industry standard 60-hertz. Lights flickered noticeably, and standard appliances would not function. As south Phoenix resident Ruth Staley remembered, "When we moved out here [in the early 1930s], it was only 25-cycle, you know. . . . And oh, it was such a nuisance. . . . We had to replace all our motors."[66]

Despite Ruth Staley's flickering lights, SRP joined CALAPCO as tan-gible symbols of Phoenix's modernity. In 1938, Al Morairty, president of the Phoenix Chamber of Commerce, described a potential tour of "the metropolitan city of Phoenix, a jewel of modernity set in the green carpets of year-round crops," designed for a visitor who had followed enticements from one of the valley's new resorts to "winter among the palms and roses" in "a land where winter never comes." Downtown, such visitors would find "colored Neon and fluorescent tube lighting of the most modern kind." On the way to their resort hotel, in addition to the cotton and vegetable fields, citrus orchards and livestock corrals, visitors would also see "many suburban and farm homes cheerily lighted from electric supply lines which traverse every road and lateral in the valley" within the "first completely electrified rural district in America." All of these elements distinguished Phoenix from "the more ancient cities of the Southwest."[67] In other booster materials, such messages were more pointed. Phoenix's City Directory of 1920 boasted "a modern town of forty thousand people, and the best kind of people, too. A very small percentage of Mexicans, negroes or foreigners."[68] Such materials paid little attention to the agricultural laborers in the fields that surrounded the city. Instead, whether they focused on electrification or racial purity, they sought to distinguish Phoenix as a modern redoubt within a region broadly considered backward and underdeveloped.

The Depression did threaten that modernity, at least as it was supplied by SRP. Drought early in the 1930s led to crop failures, low water supplies, and a severe limitation on generating capacity, even with the project's four dams completed. Forced to purchase electricity from CALAPCO and unable to meet debt payments, SRP stood on the brink of financial collapse, until the state legislature, in a complicated maneuver, split SRP into two overlapping entities that were legally municipal subdivisions of Arizona's state government. After 1936, SRP consisted of a power district in charge of electrical supply, and an agricultural improvement district. This maneuver enabled the utility to remain solvent, to refinance its debt with tax-free bonds, and to use electrical sales to underwrite water costs.[69]

Despite these struggles, SRP resisted any attempts to use electricity from Boulder Dam to resolve its power shortages. In 1937, a group of self-described "public-minded citizens" formed the Boulder Dam Power Transmission Association of Arizona, aiming to create a state authority charged with claiming Arizona's share of Boulder Dam's power. The association promised broad benefits for SRP and the state at large. The dam's power would bring "the re-establishment of the Water Users [SRP] as the dominating factor in the power business in Central Arizona, a position which it once held." It would also allow greater industrialization in the valley. Indeed, the association promised development akin to what Franklin Roosevelt had promised in his dedication of Boulder Dam. Manufacturing would flock once the dam's inexpensive power became available. "Air-conditioning for the long, hot period" would become more affordable. More Arizonans could afford to use electrical appliances. In short, the dam's power would truly modernize Arizona. As the first line of the association's newsletter proclaimed, "ELECTRIC ENERGY IS AS NECESSARY AS WATER AND AIR FOR THE EXISTENCE OF MODERN ECONOMIC LIFE."[70]

Despite such appeals, SRP joined CALAPCO in fighting the proposal. In part, this rejection reflected the general absence in Phoenix, before the 1950s, of the battles between public and private power that characterized much of the nation's electrical politics. It also reflected the belief that Boulder Dam could undercut SRP's own rates. An analyst examining the decision after World War II wrote that "As a *power* producer and distributor, [SRP] is commonly understood to function, to all realistic intents and purposes, essentially as private companies function."[71] In a larger sense, however, SRP's opposition to Boulder Dam power demonstrated how ingrained opposition to Boulder Dam, and to the federal government's management of the Colorado River more generally, had become in Arizona's political culture. That political culture envisioned Phoenix as the center of a Southwestern empire. It sought to create local development by drawing nearby resources to the state's center in Phoenix. Standing athwart that vision, channeling resources to Southern California, federal authority remained suspect, even if it brought short-term benefit. The outcome was ironic. Managers of the Bureau of Reclamation's first major project actively worked against the distribution of power from Boulder Dam within the borders of their state because they feared excessive federal control thwarted their imperial dreams.

STOCK REDUCTION

On the Navajo Reservation in northern Arizona and western New Mexico, federal authority assumed a more direct, and bloody, form. Between 1934 and 1938, federal agents ventured across the Colorado Plateau, counting Navajos' sheep, goats, horses, and cattle, and judged those numbers against the range's "carrying capacity." At times, they attempted to purchase animals. At other times, they resorted to slaughter. Billy Bryant recounted his memories forty years later. "Our goats" he remembered, "were put in a large corral where they were all shot down. Then the government men piled the corpses in a big heap, poured oil or gasoline over them and set fire to them. . . . Not only the goats, but the sheep, too, were slaughtered right before the owners. Those men took our meat off our tables and left us hungry and heartbroken."[72]

The deaths were a result of stock reduction, a Bureau of Indian Affairs program that attempted to "stabilize" the Colorado Plateau's rangelands by limiting Navajo herd sizes and confining animals to specific grazing districts. Stock reduction represented the BIA's response to the severe erosion increasingly evident on reservation lands in the early twentieth century. It represented only one of several federal efforts led by BIA commissioner John Collier to rationalize the Navajo Reservation's natural resources and political organization with a goal toward enabling economic self-sufficiency. These efforts crashed on the rocks of stock reduction, however, as Collier failed to understand Navajo subsistence, the place of sheep in Navajo culture, and Navajos' understanding of the broader environmental crisis facing the reservation. Navajos, for their part, rejected those of Collier's policies they could and created new tribal governing institutions dedicated, in part, to resisting federal authority.[73]

The journey of sheep north into New Mexico in the sixteenth century, accompanied by Spanish settlers, remade Navajo society. Until sheep arrived, Navajos had farmed alluvial washes west of the Pueblo settlements in the Rio Grande Valley, in a place they called "Dinétah." As they encountered sheep in raids on Pueblo and Spanish villages and returned with them to Dinétah, Navajos discovered sheep opened a new energy supply.[74] As was the case with horses for plains tribes, sheep converted energy stored in grass into a new, mobile form that could supply Navajos with sustenance in the form of milk and meat as well as wool for clothing and blankets. Navajo shepherds gradually pushed west from Dinétah onto the Colorado Plateau in search of new supplies of grass's energy, and, by the early nineteenth century, organized their lives in migratory cycles in territory reaching from central New Mexico to the Grand Canyon. Pastoralism made Navajos energy rich, allowing them to use the Colorado Plateau's grasses to transform, as Marsha Weisiger writes, "a stingy environment into a land of plenty."[75]

Sheep provided not only sustenance. Navajos formed relationships with their animals that were affective, spiritual, even familial. One origin story told that Changing Woman had formed Navajos, sheep, and horses, simultaneously by combining corn pollen and dew. "From now on," she told the sheep and horses, "people will live by means of you."[76] In turn, she charged Navajos to sing the songs that kept their animals healthy and maintained hózhó, the balance or harmony that surrounds all life, animates the universe, and maintains the health of all living things, including the land itself. Such songs and stories taught Navajos of the deep connection that tied them to their animals, according to Navajo scholar Percy Deal, who has explained, "The sheep is our mother. They will care for you."[77] Navajos reciprocated care with migration. By leading sheep to ungrazed grasslands, they supplied them with energy, fulfilling obligations of reciprocal care.[78]

Sheep also allowed Navajos to mount the most successful response to conquest of any group of Indians in the nineteenth century. Between 1863 and 1866, the U.S. military launched a campaign of total war against Navajos, destroying animals, food stores, and peach orchards, and offering a brutal choice between exile or continued violence. The army forcibly marched surrendered Navajos three hundred miles east, in what became known as "the Long Walk," to a pestilent camp called the Bosque Redondo.[79] In 1868 Navajo leaders negotiated a treaty; 7,400 Navajos returned to a reservation along the Arizona–New Mexico border, on "10,000 square miles of the most worthless land that ever laid out of doors," in the words of one Bureau of Indian Affairs (BIA) agent.[80] Obligations to sheep soon outweighed reservation boundaries as Navajo shepherds led their herds into ungrazed grasslands beyond the reservation. Expansion enabled population growth. With sheep growing fat on lush grasses, herds exploded in size. By the 1910s, one million sheep, goats, and horses grazed reservation lands. Large herds enabled Navajos to enjoy a protein-rich diet of milk and meat, contributing to a fivefold increase in Navajo population by 1930. At the same time, the large size of the herds limited need for federal subsidies. Indeed, federal officials ratified this accretion, expanding the reservation through executive and congressional actions until, by 1907, the reservation covered most of the southern Colorado Plateau.[81]

Pastoralism allowed Navajos to mitigate many of the traumas that Indians faced at the turn of the century. Most Navajos had little reason to interact with Indian agents, and agents found it difficult to keep track of Navajos, even after the reservation was divided into six separate agencies. Indeed, the difficulty of travel made any estimate of herd sizes at best, in Weisiger's words, "a guesstimate." The need for children to work as shepherds meant that fewer Navajos attended assimilationist boarding schools than other Indian groups. And relatively low interest in the Colorado Plateau's lands meant that only the far eastern edges of the reservation were allotted under the terms of the Dawes Severalty Act of 1887, which divided tribal landholdings into individual allotments ranging between 40 and 160 acres and led, nationwide, to the passage of 90 million acres of tribal lands out of Indian possession.[82]

None of this history should be taken to imply that Navajos lived in pristine isolation from the surrounding world. Federally licensed traders became an increasing presence on the reservation at the turn of the twentieth century. A small number of Navajos became full-fledged commercial stock raisers. The largest stock owners, Chee Dodge and his wife, Nánibaa', owned five thousand head of sheep, controlled 131,000 acres of reservation land, and possessed the largest private bank account in nearby Gallup. Other Navajos engaged markets in more limited ways. Female weavers sold rugs to traders eager to meet the demand of collectors of "primitive crafts."[83] Some men sought wage work on railroads and nearby ranches. Sheep allowed most Navajos, however, to feed and clothe themselves without becoming dependent on the market. Pastoralism, in short, enabled subsistence. Subsistence has long held an association as the opposite of capitalist modernity: a meager, hand to mouth existence that the market's surpluses would relieve. From another perspective, however, subsistence offers an alternative to market capitalism, an ability to stand firm in the ability to self-provision while engaging the market on controlled terms.[84]

Subsistence relied ultimately, however, on a combination of energy and isolation. Since returning to the Colorado Plateau, Navajo territory expanded to meet the energy needs of the growing herds, enabled by relative economic and political isolation. In the 1910s, however, Anglo and Hispano stock raisers began to drive large herds onto the Colorado Plateau and to fight further reservation expansion. In 1911, political pressure led federal officials to rescind two earlier additions to the reservation. Commercial stock raisers also constrained Navajo mobility by fencing water holes, springs, and grazing areas on and off the reservation. Seasonal migrations had previously enabled grasses to reproduce themselves and mitigate the Colorado Plateau's tendency toward erosion. With forage increasingly scarce, goats and sheep began to graze the same land repeatedly. As early as 1904, E. O. Wooten, a botanist at New Mexico A&M University, reported that the Checkerboard region of western New Mexico, where competition for grazing land was particularly fierce, "is nearly denuded of grass."[85]

Climatic fluctuations exacerbated the damage. A severe drought between 1899 and 1904 desiccated the Colorado Plateau. A series of subsequent wet years pounded the Plateau with violent thunderstorms. On denuded lands lacking rooted grass, torrential rain cut arroyos deep into the Plateau's surface, carrying increasing amounts of soil away from the Plateau. As water ran into deep arroyos, the water table itself fell. Alluvial washes no longer received sufficient water for agriculture. Cocklebur, bugseed, and other unpalatable plants began to replace native grasses, and the Plateau's lands produced less and less consumable energy. One petition to the BIA, signed by almost three hundred Navajo men and women, complained that "many of us find it difficult to graze our sheep and cattle properly, and must keep them constantly on the move."[86]

Many Navajos supplemented subsistence through different means. Some sought off-reservation wage work on ranches or railroads. Others, near Fort Wingate, on the eastern portion of the reservation, began excavating seams of coal visible on mesa walls, selling it to BIA agencies or in nearby Gallup. BIA inspectors found that coal could be obtained "very cheaply and with very little trouble." By the mid-1930s, thirty-four mines on the reservation produced 3,300 tons of coal annually. It also provided ready cash of $6 a wagonload. Coal served as an almost seasonal crop that could be exchanged for cash or credit, as wool was at the trading posts. Indeed, one BIA official described these mines as "subsistence mines," explaining that "when it's time to plant or tend other agricultural matters, most coal production comes to a halt." For many Navajos, as Colleen O'Neill argues, mining coal was like herding sheep. Both required specific ritual actions. As miner Burton Yazzie explained, "you have to make an offering to her when you disturb . . . mother earth." Coal mining and sheep herding also rested on similar equations. They both relied on abundant energy and relative economic isolation. Coal mining remained a subsistence activity because demand remained low. BIA agencies needed only so much coal. Farmington and Gallup were small towns of a few thousand people. The costs of transporting the coal elsewhere literally outweighed its value.[87]

Struggles to maintain subsistence, then, faced Navajos at the moment John Collier became Commissioner of Indian Affairs in 1933. Collier had long been a critic of federal policies that allotted land, restricted native religion, and stressed assimilation, describing the BIA as "the nexus of a conspiracy of robbery under quasi-legal forms."[88] Collier believed Navajos, in their relative isolation, possessed a purer, more authentic way of life than that imposed on Indians by American industrial society. "Their tribal, family, and rich inner life remains unaltered," Collier wrote in 1924, "an island of aboriginal culture in the monotonous sea of machine civilization."[89] While Collier ended bans on native religion and advocated a return to tribalism as BIA commissioner, he was also an ardent modernizer, arguing that Indian self-government and "doing business in the modern, organized way" represented the means to counter the disorganization created in Indian societies by assimilationist policies. His Indian Reorganization Act sought to extend the New Deal's emphasis on the organization of economic activity to Indian people by empowering tribal governments to manage resources and expand reservation economies. "You can't govern yourselves," Collier told a crowd of tribal leaders from the northern plains in 1934, "you can't do business, you can't protect yourself, unless you organize."[90]

Collier's plans for Navajos involved the reorganization of tribal government and the rational management of reservation resources. Until 1922 the Navajo Tribe had no formal government.[91] That year, Secretary of the Interior Albert Fall created a six member Navajo Business Council for the express purpose of ratifying oil leases, as required by existing federal law. The Council was small, including one representative and one alternate from each of the six agencies of the reservation. While the council made the vital decision to hold revenues in common rather than issuing per capita payments, it remained largely powerless. "None of its early actions affected the lives of the Navajo people," one anthropologist wrote, "and many said they had never heard of it."[92] Collier envisioned a dual centralization: the six BIA agencies would be consolidated into one central agency, and Navajo tribal government would be expanded to form a more representative assembly. Both would be located at a newly created government center in Window Rock, a sparsely populated area notable for a prominent sandstone arch. From there, federal and tribal officials could coordinate reservation economic activities.

These activities included new regulations of coal mining. A 1934 U.S. Geological Survey (USGS) report commissioned by Collier concluded that the reservation had too many mines that operated with "almost no responsibility for safety or good mining practice" and that this represented "a great disadvantage and hazard to the tribal wealth" because miners paid no royalties to the tribe. The report called for mining by individual Navajo groups to end, the implementation of a mineral development plan "approved by a mining engineer . . . with long experience in the management of coal mines," and the royalty payments from Navajo miners.[93] Collier, in short, sought to replace the dispersed and atomistic strategies of subsistence with an economy directed and managed by centralized authority. Collier formalized these ideas in the Indian Mineral Leasing Act of 1938 (IMLA), which both brought uniformity to a confusing welter of laws governing the leasing of minerals on Indian lands and granted broad authority to the secretary of the interior to accept or reject leases on behalf of Indian tribes, a manifestation of the federal trust responsibility that granted the federal government exclusive authority over Indian peoples. While royalties and bonus payments from any leases would go into tribal treasuries, the IMLA generally reflected Collier's belief that most tribes were incapable of operating in the complicated world of energy development. The law required that all leases be put out for competitive bid, gave the secretary of interior veto power over any lease terms, and forbade tribes engaging in mineral development on their own. As James Allison argues, these provisions served to sideline tribal governments, until the late 1960s, from an active role in shaping the terms of energy development on their reservations.[94]

Erosion, however, represented the greatest threat to Navajo security in Collier's view. The soil rushing away from the Colorado Plateau constituted, in the BIA commissioner's mind, an economic crisis that would speed a confrontation between previously isolated Navajos and a rapidly modernizing world beyond the reservation's borders. "The crisis consists in the fact that the soil of the Navajo reservation is hurriedly being washed away into the Colorado River," he wrote in *Survey Graphic* in 1934. "The collision consists in the fact that the entire complex and momentum of Navajo life must be radically and swiftly changed to a new direction and in part must be totally reversed."[95] Collier worried this combination would limit Navajo economic possibilities for the foreseeable future. Collier also feared that erosion, in combination with the Boulder Dam, posed a political threat to potential Navajo autonomy and self-government. As early as 1929, the USGS had written of the "major silt problem" facing Boulder Dam. With the dam stopping the river's flow, silt would accumulate behind the dam, rather than being carried downstream. Indeed, the amount of silt passing Yuma dropped from 500,000 to 80,000 tons daily after the dam's completion. The USGS worried this silt would quickly choke the reservoir, reducing its electrical generating capacity and endangering the dam's financing plan. The USGS's report also pointed a finger. The "Navajo Reservation," it contended, "is practically 'Public Enemy No. 1' in causing the Colorado Silt problem." Collier worried that, unaddressed, silt's threat to the dam would lead federal and local officials to demand new regulation of the reservation landscape that would hamstring Navajo development. Eliminating a significant proportion of grazing animals, in Collier's mind, would improve the range, solve the silt problem, and allow economic modernization to proceed in a noncrisis atmosphere.[96]

Collier moved swiftly after becoming Commissioner. In October 1933, he proposed a reduction of 400,000 animals, promising new wage work to supplement losses. The six-member tribal council endorsed the plan after Collier told them stock reduction would occur with or without their permission. Finding the initial program ineffective after large stockowners culled only their oldest animals, Collier announced a reduction of 150,000 goats, which scientists for the Soil Conservation Service judged particularly destructive to the range. After finding that these first two policies had decimated small herds while leaving the largest herds intact, Collier introduced a new system in 1937 aimed at distributing stock more equally. The SCS divided the reservation into nineteen grazing districts and calculated the maximum number of animals each district could accommodate. BIA officials then divided that carrying capacity by the number of stock owners in each district and issued grazing permits to everyone, enabling each holder the same number of "sheep units." For Collier and government scientists, the policy paired conservation's emphasis on the efficient use of resources with the New Deal's emphasis on economic equality.[97]

Navajos, however, found the entire program disastrous. Large stockowners held social obligations to provide for their less fortunate clan members and allowed stock-poor Navajos to herd shares of their animals. For less fortunate Navajos, reducing large herds eliminated the last subsistence resource of the impoverished. Promised jobs replacing pastoral income failed to materialize. As Capiton Benally explained, "After I reduced my sheep I asked for a job . . . but the U.S. officials told us there were no jobs. . . . [T]he jobs they had talked about had been just fakes." Furthermore, some BIA officials carried out reduction with marked cruelty. On occasion, agents shot animals and burned their carcasses in front of astonished families that had formed lifelong relationships with those animals. Collier's continued demands for greater reduction and new regulations rankled. "He had taken a large part of our sheep, goats, and horses," Eli Gorman stated, "and he acted just like this was nothing."[98]

Most importantly, as Marsha Weisiger has detailed, Collier failed to understand how many Navajos understood both their sheep and the world around them. Some Navajos understood erosion merely as a function of drought and believed that erosion would cease when the rains returned. Many others saw it as a result of an absence of hózhó, a world out of harmony because specific ritual actions had not been practiced. In this view, stock reduction exacerbated the crisis, because it violated the mutual obligations that Navajos owed to their animals. In much of the reservation, Navajos reacted with anger, tearing down fences that divided grazing districts. Others threatened violence against BIA employees. Some BIA officials responded with arguments that Navajos were beyond rationality, that their belief system contained no sense of cause and effect. It well did, but those understandings differed dramatically.[99]

Collier misjudged, as well, by introducing the Indian Reorganization Act (IRA) to Navajos in March 1934, in the midst of goat reduction, probably the most painful moment of the stock reduction era for many Navajos. Collier presented a plan for an expanded and reorganized tribal government that could not be destroyed by the BIA or Interior Department, with access to a $10 million revolving loan fund, educational changes that would "equip an Indian to hold any position in the Indian Service," religious freedom, and a tribal court system. Collier erred by explaining the program in excruciating detail, including pages of his address dedicated to allotment, a policy that barely affected Navajos. Details became more confusing when translated into Navajo for the 90 percent of the people in attendance who did not speak English. One attendee compared the presentation to a game where a "person hides the ball and others guess where it is."[100]

Collier's proposals for Navajo economic and political modernization sparked opposition from a seemingly unlikely source. The small number of returned boarding-school students had been, since the 1920s, the loudest voice encouraging the tribe to move away from stock raising and embrace new economic strategies, including jobs in energy development. In part, these politics had to do with their particular position in Navajo society. Absent from the reservation during years when Navajos began acquiring their herds, boarding-school students tended to be stock-poor. Fluent in English, they attained an outsized voice in the tribal politics most Navajos ignored. Their power also, however, had to do with their experience off the reservation. The leading figure of the Returned Student's Association, Jacob Morgan, had attended boarding schools in New Mexico and Colorado and had graduated from Hampton Institute in Virginia. He had converted to the Christian Reformed Church and engaged in missionary work. He also advocated grazing fees on large stockholders to reduce the number of sheep on the reservation six years before Collier became BIA Commissioner. Morgan and other members of the Returned Students Association, however, feared that the IRA would lead to the isolation of the reservation economy from the surrounding region and that Collier's stress on religious freedom would block missionary efforts. Morgan, in particular, became a full-throated opponent of Collier's plan, denouncing him for seeking to "segregate the Indian, keep him an

Indian . . . [and] cut him off from the greatest education for citizenship, namely personal contact with American life."[101]

Significant numbers of Navajos supported the IRA as a means to self-government. Morgan's Returned Students Association forged an alliance, however, with pastoralists from the western portions of the reservation, where stock reduction was particularly fierce, and who saw the vote against the IRA as a rejection of stock reduction. In a close vote, the referendum failed, 8,197 to 7,679. Morgan boasted that "the Indian commissioner has met more than a match in the young progressive Navajos who want the benefits of civilization for themselves and their children." "This self-government idea," he continued, "would result in the loss of those challenged rights of equal citizenship with their white brothers."[102]

John Collier's and Jacob Morgan's vision of the Navajo future were compatible in many respects. Both envisioned a shift away from pastoralism to a more "modern" economic future. Both advocated new controls on Navajo herds to mitigate both the effects of domesticated animals on Navajo land and their importance to the local economy. Both envisioned Navajo tribal government as a source of power. Soon after the rejection of the IRA, Morgan would help expand the tribal council until it contained representatives from 101 reservation subdivisions called chapters. In 1937, Morgan ran for, and won, the tribal chairmanship, which he held in uneasy truce with Collier. Indeed, the tribal council would grow in importance over the following thirty years in its new home in Window Rock.[103]

Both, however, failed to conceptualize their visions of the Navajo future in much depth. Collier suggested that the availability of a paltry amount of credit—$10 million—and a new cadre of educated Navajos would lead to industrialization. Morgan argued that new contact between Navajos and local businessmen would lead businesses to flourish on the reservation. Those ill-defined plans, however, illustrated their differences. They divided on a question that would bedevil Navajo development efforts for the following decades: Should Navajo leaders aim for autonomy, seeking to develop the reservation as a source of economic power, or should they attempt to connect to the broader economy of the Southwest, aiming to grow in concert and connection with the economic growth of the region? Tribal leaders would have to face this question, because the subsistence economy, by the late 1930s, had cracked. By the 1940s, even the four thousand families lucky enough to hold grazing permits had, on average, fewer than fifty sheep that struggled to survive on a range containing sparse vegetation. Such families had to be frugal to avoid literally consuming their flocks. Another 2,500 families had no livestock at all. While many Navajos worked to restore their flocks after the tribal council ended stock reduction in 1943, others despaired. "Many of the people have lost their ambition and pride," Councilman Tseche Notah lamented. "Every day I hear people say, 'What's the use? What's the use of trying to do anything?'" As Richard White argued, the ultimate, painful irony of stock reduction was that Collier had sought, above all, a form of economic organization that would allow Navajos to remain self-sufficient, but instead his policies produced Navajo dependency.[104]

The lines between stock reduction and Boulder Dam are not as direct as the power lines between the dam and Los Angeles. John Collier worried about erosion from Navajo land before heading the BIA. He pursued his plans not with a concern for protecting the federal investment in Boulder Dam but fearing what that investment might mean for Navajos who were perceived to be endangering it.[105] In those fears, though, were signs that the dam had changed the place of the reservation within the Southwest. Soil from the reservation lands had washed into the Colorado River for years, long before there was a reservation. In the wake of the dam, however, erosion had new meaning. It was now linked to federal investments and to electricity that flowed away from the river's canyons and toward waiting consumers in Los Angeles.

Since the publication of Kenneth Jackson's *Crabgrass Frontier* nearly thirty years ago, scholars have come to understand the New Deal's metropolitan policies as sources of profound inequality. As we will see in the following chapters, New Deal housing policies rooted racial and class inequalities in space by offering generous terms to white middle-class homebuyers and denying those same terms to African Americans and most Latinos. Even before Roosevelt's "brains trust" wrote the National Housing Act of 1934, however, metropolitan preferences embedded in the actions of federal agencies had already begun the uneven development of the Southwest. The choice to route energy and water toward metropolitan consumers furthered the development of Los Angeles at the expense of the Salt River Valley and Navajo Reservation. Such preferences also began to create a new region.

In 1920 the Southwest was a region of fragments. The Salt River Valley and Navajo Reservation existed in relative isolation from Los Angeles. Boulder Dam began to draw these places into new relationships with one another. Navajos experienced these relationships primarily as dispossession, as the historical moment when the erosion that was the by-product of their relationship with animals gained a new political meaning. The metropolitan logic that led those power lines toward Los Angeles created feelings of dispossession in Phoenix as well, though not nearly with the same consequences as in northern Arizona. It also led to new visions of the future in Phoenix, visions whereby energy from the Colorado Plateau, energy that Phoenicians viewed as theirs by right, could create a new kind of valley that would perhaps follow the path blazed by Los Angeles.

Power lines did not only change relations between places. They changed politics, as the effort to claim energy, and the lands upon which it was contained, became one of the central political struggles of the following years. Finally, the power lines changed nature itself. For millions of years, natural systems had stored energy beneath the earth's surface and channeled it across the landscape of the Colorado Plateau. Beginning with Boulder Dam, this energy began to flow through to new systems, systems built not by natural forces of geology and topography, but according to the dictates of human economic and political demands. Those dictates created systems that distributed energy in profoundly uneven ways. It was in this mutual reshaping of political power and natural energy that the modern Southwest took shape.

PART II

Demand

CHAPTER 2

The Valley of the Sun

BETWEEN 1940 AND 1960, PHOENIX CHANGED FROM AN IRRIGATED OASIS to a Southwestern metropolis. Hundreds of thousands of Americans moved to Phoenix, including almost 200,000 between 1955 and 1960 alone. The majority came from the East and Midwest, from the industrial cities and small towns of a region not yet known as the Rustbelt.[1] In twenty years, the city's population grew from 65,000 to 440,000. And the lands north of the Grand Canal changed from the agricultural heartland of the Salt River Valley into a landscape of residential subdivisions containing 62,000 homes—58,000 more than in 1940. The names the city's boosters used to talk about Phoenix symbolized that transition. In the early twentieth century, visitors learned that Phoenix was located at the center of the Salt River Valley. By the postwar years, they found themselves in the Valley of the Sun.

Early in this era of mass migration, Raymond Carlson, editor of *Arizona Highways*, tried to explain its underlying dynamics. "Lots of folks, apparently, . . . have decided that living in the sun is a lot more fun than living in places where the climate and other living conditions are less conducive to a full and happy life."[2] Carlson's magazine displayed the various aspects of this "full and happy life" in vivid color photographs and often purple prose. In Phoenix, new residents would find a modern city with all the comforts of contemporary life. Phoenix home buyers shopped in a market providing "more house per dollar . . . than in any other section of the country."[3] Within the city, residents could enjoy golf, tennis, even horseback riding in the many parks. If Phoenix's leisured life became overbearing, undeveloped landscapes nearby allowed people to "sit quietly under a mesquite tree and watch the clouds cavort, or hum a tune or ponder the sweet and bitter mysteries of life or puzzle out the ways of mountains and mice and of meek and mighty men."[4] If residents had particularly "jangled nerves," the spectacular landscape of the Colorado Plateau, "where our scattered Indian tribes live complacently, completely undisturbed by the frenzied civilization about them," was only a short drive away.[5] The Valley of the Sun, in short, was a place that presented its residents with a lifestyle that balanced suburban living, stripped of the long commutes, cold winters, and other problems that plagued Eastern cities, with easy escape to the Grand Canyon, "Navajoland," or numerous other natural spaces.

"The Valley of the Sun" was not only an idealized place. It was also a political project, the result of two of the most powerful forces in the postwar American political economy. The first was the ongoing legacy of New Deal policies that sought to fuel the national economy through debt-driven personal consumption. Part of the general postwar economic philosophy historians have labeled "growth liberalism," policies such as the National Housing Act, the Banking Act of 1935, and the G.I. Bill, offered federal loan guarantes to a select population of white Americans choosing suburban living. Manifesting the same metropolitan preferences that underlay the distribution of Boulder Dam's power, the authors of these policies viewed residents of the metropolitan periphery as the vital agents of postwar growth and offered credit at terms advantageous for both borrowers and lenders. The resulting "landscape of mass consumption," to use Lizabeth Cohen's term, was plainly evident in Phoenix, both in the huge numbers of homes built after World War II and in the increasing numbers of electrical appliances that filled them.

Local efforts to attract these consumers, and the potential capital they embodied, was the second force that created the Valley of the Sun. Migrants to Phoenix in the 1940 and 1950s were not fleeing the Rustbelt. Rather, they were enticed to Phoenix by a series of appeals related to the quality of life and cost of living available there. State officials and local businessmen alike presented Phoenix as different from other cities as a means to attract capital. As we will see in the following chapter, much of this capital took the form of high-tech manufacturers and other elements of the Cold War military-industrial complex, which Phoenix's officials wooed with a range of political guarantees and economic enticements. In the economy of postwar America, however, white, middle-class Americans to whom the federal government guaranteed credit were also a form of capital. By attracting such people to their city, Phoenix's bankers, retailers, home builders, electric utility officials and other businessmen profited dually, first as their businesses became the conduits through which the federally guaranteed credit of growth liberalism flowed into the local economy and then as consumers gradually paid off their locally incurred debts. Their concentration in space represented a pool of capital that, by their presence, created more capital.

Place mattered as well in this political economy. Representations of Phoenix as a locus of clear skies, warm weather, open space, cheap homes, and individual opportunity attracted new residents seeking "quality of life." There were also material and political consequences, created by expectations about "quality of life" that disciplined local officials to maintain the opportunities for lifestyles that were particularly desirable, included among them residential segregation and the environmental amenities of clear skies, open space, and recreation that Phoenix's boosters emphasized. The result, by the 1960s, would be the very particular form of spatial inequality that is this book's focus. By then, the center of Phoenix's landscape of mass consumption would exist in residential neighborhoods that were almost entirely white, isolated from the neighborhoods of black and Mexican American Phoenicians, and powered by distant power plants on Indian land. In the 1930s and 1940s, this spatial arrangement had not yet come to be. Instead, Phoenix remained a small city, reliant on commodity agriculture and marginalized within the new regional space created by Boulder Dam. The efforts that recast the Salt River Valley as the Valley of the Sun were local political efforts by a class of businessmen attempting to change these economic conditions and regional dynamics. To understand them, we need to start not at the metropolitan periphery, but downtown.[6]

DOWNTOWN

When Phoenix's businessmen were asked about the growth of their city in the 1970s, they told two stories. Technology usually came first. "Airplanes and air conditioners," Phoenix lawyer Frank Snell told an interviewer in the 1970s. "If you hadn't had either we'd never grown."[7] Passenger air service had reduced travel time to Phoenix from the East Coast and Midwest, Snell explained, from a journey of days to one of hours. And Phoenix's emergence as "the Air Conditioned Capital of the World," Snell declared, allowed Phoenix to become a "year-round city."[8]

Following these stories about technology, however, Phoenix's businessmen spoke of personal initiative. Talking to the oral historians of the Phoenix History Project, they portrayed their compatriots as historical agents who had taken a small agricultural town and, using little more than will and ingenuity, transformed it into the nation's ninth largest city. "I'll never forget it," Snell said of Walter Bimson, president of Valley National Bank, "when banks practically said, 'No more mortgages on homes,' Walter takes a full-page ad. . . . 'Our bank is prepared to loan money on homes.' . . . 'We have money available for first mortgages.'"[9] Bimson had arrived in Phoenix in 1933, leaving a position at Harris Trust of Chicago to assume control of a bank whose deposits had fallen from $17.7 million to $6.1 million in the preceding three years. Seemingly in free fall, Valley Bank appeared likely to become Arizona's twenty-seventh bank to fail during the 1930s.[10] Bimson's loan policies reversed the slide. Lending money far and wide to individuals and businesses, Valley Bank rapidly recovered, becoming "Arizona's central bank" by the late 1940s, with 70 percent of the state's deposits. Bimson became hailed as a miracle worker: "the Bank Knight in Arizona" and "Arizona's Indispensable Man."[11] The last title was apt. As Snell remembered, "Walter was pretty much the leader of the group."[12]

Frank Snell, for his part, became "the original dark glasses man," in the words of Walter Bimson's brother, Carl, legendary for his ability to organize Phoenix's businessmen behind myriad institutional and political goals.[13] Like Bimson, Snell was a new arrival to Phoenix. A native of Kansas City, Snell moved to Phoenix in 1927 after a brief time practicing law in the copper-mining town of Miami, Arizona. With his partner Frank Wilmer, Snell established a law firm that became the city's largest by 1940. After conducting interviews with a vast number of prominent postwar Phoenicians, Wesley Johnson concluded that Snell held Phoenix's levers of power. Acting behind the scenes, Snell could, as Johnson wrote, "sit down for lunch at the Arizona Club with a few friends and develop either public or private policy for Phoenix, as the occasion demanded."[14] Snell himself boasted to Johnson about one small element of that power, his ability to organize "15 or 20 important men" to "bring Central Arizona Light and Power back to Phoenix" and end Wall Street's control over Phoenix's local utility.[15]

While Bimson and Snell were new to Phoenix in the 1930s, other members of their circle came from families that were as long established as possible in a city incorporated for fewer than sixty years. Edward O'Malley headed a building-materials and real-estate empire built by his father. Orme Lewis had grown up swimming in the irrigation canals that ran through the city before joining his father's legal practice, which he built to be the city's second largest by 1950. Lewis attended elementary school with two other scions of Phoenix's elite. Barry and Robert Goldwater's grandfather Michael had immigrated to Arizona in 1860, establishing a dry goods store in Gila City, before moving his operations to Phoenix in 1872. Their father, Baron, had built Goldwater's into the state's largest department store by the time the two brothers came of age and assumed ownership in 1929.[16]

These second- and third-generation Phoenicians forged a dense social network with the newly arrived professionals in the compact business environment of downtown Phoenix. Today, Phoenix stands as the archetype of "Sunbelt sprawl," with office parks and corporate campuses spreading sixty miles across the valley from Gilbert to Glendale. Until the 1960s, however, its business life occurred within a downtown core of little more than twelve square blocks. Valley Bank's headquarters at Central Avenue and Monroe Street stood one block north of the Dwight Heard Building, where the offices of Snell and Wilmer and the *Arizona Republic* were located. Goldwater's department store lay one block east, on North First Street;

FIGURE 2.1. By 1951, Central Avenue formed the heart of a compact downtown where most of the valley's business was transacted. Courtesy of the Arizona Historical Society. 1951.

the offices of Lewis and Roca and the headquarters of O'Malley Lumber lay one and two blocks west on West Adams Street. At noon, Bimson, Snell, Lewis, O'Malley, Goldwater, and other businessmen could walk to the south edge of downtown to eat lunch in the Arizona Club atop the Luhrs Building. After work, they could meet for drinks at the Kiva Club inside the Hotel Westward Ho, just north of downtown. This spatial proximity created their identity not only as businessmen, but as downtown businessmen, united spatially by their centrality within the city.

As downtown businessmen, they distinguished themselves from an earlier generation of elites. Bimson, Snell, the Goldwater brothers, and most others in their circle had only indirect ties to the valley's agricultural economy. Unlike Philip Tovrea, a cattleman who led the Phoenix Chamber of Commerce in the early 1930s, or Dwight Heard, who owned more than 7,000 acres of cotton and alfalfa fields and whose name graced the headquarters building for the Arizona Cotton Growers Association, the businessmen who rose to prominence in the 1930s and 1940s were professionals who ran banks, law firms, and retail outlets.[17] Their businesses may have catered to ranchers and growers, they may have had them as clients, but they had a separate identity. Bimson even lived downtown, in a 4,000-square-foot house atop the Phoenix Security Building.[18] And though the Salt River Valley's growers continued to produce tremendous wealth from control of land, labor, and water, they became the subject of subtle mockery among the newer generation of businessmen. Asked what surprised him upon taking a position as general manager of the Phoenix Chamber of Commerce in 1947, Lewis Haas chuckled and answered, "Beards." "There were some funny things about that old Chamber," Haas told an interviewer, "I could hardly believe my eyes when I saw what was being sent out! Pictures showing Phoenicians with beards."[19] Haas's words indicated more than the different masculine sartorial choices that defined the worlds of industrial agriculture and downtown business. They also illustrated downtown businessmen's broader ideological understanding of themselves as a modernizing force within what they regarded as a relatively backward city.

It was this understanding that led them to the "Valley of the Sun." Interested in rejuvenating local tourism, the Phoenix Chamber of Commerce commissioned a survey in 1935 on perceptions of the "Salt River Valley" among potential visitors. The results spurred calls for a new name, after most respondents suggested the "Salt River Valley" called to mind an alkaline wasteland. The survey only reinforced downtown businessmen's unease with Phoenix's emphasis on commodity production. "Too much reliance on commodities that fluctuated on the world market," Walter Bimson later told an audience of Western businessmen, had "harmed the state's development."[20] The Depression, which crippled Arizona's "Four C's," shaped these beliefs. Between 1929 and 1932, copper prices dropped from 18.1 cents to 5.6 cents per pound, and most of the state's copper mines severely curtailed operations. Agriculture and cattle ranching suffered as well, with annual revenues over the same years falling from $41.8 million to $13.8 million and from $25.5 million to $14.7 million, respectively. The collapse of the state's extractive economy reverberated through Phoenix, causing the widespread bank failures that left Valley Bank teetering on the brink when Bimson arrived, and swelling the city's relief roles as unemployed miners and farmworkers flocked to the city in search of work. Finding little work at any rate, more than fifty thousand people fled the state's economic woes, reducing Arizona's overall population by 12 percent.[21]

Shortly after the Phoenix Chamber publicized the results of their survey, the Phoenix-Arizona Club—a group that brought together tourism boosters with the chambers of commerce in the valley—called a meeting to determine a new place name. A group of cotton growers suggested "Roosevelt Valley," referring to the dam that had spurred the valley's growth. Objections were raised. Some attendees complained that the name would suggest an endorsement of the current president, whose policies, in their thinking, had resulted in the theft of Arizona's water. Others expressed concern that the name did little to extol the valley's merits. Whatever the case, when Jack Stewart, owner of the Camelback Inn, a resort in Scottsdale, suggested "the Valley of the Sun," Frank Snell recalled that it received nearly universal acclaim. By 1937 "Phoenix, in the Valley of the Sun" appeared atop the Phoenix Chamber of Commerce's letterhead, where it would remain for most of the postwar years. "The Valley of the Sun" received not only a featured place on stationery, however, the campaign also received financial support from Bimson's Valley Bank. As Snell remembered, "Jack Stewart had a great idea of tourism not for his hotel but for the whole community and Walter got in and really supported him and with money."[22]

"The Valley of the Sun" represented more than a name change. It reflected a new vision of Phoenix as a place whose reputation for leisure would draw residents. Initially, Phoenix's businessmen targeted wealthy Americans who retained disposable income for travel and recreation in the midst of the Depression. The Phoenix-Arizona Club's 1938 publication *Life in the Valley of the Sun* featured photos of well-manicured resorts and the luxurious homes of winter residents such as Philip Wrigley and Henry Luce. As Snell recalled, "They were seeking people who could afford to come here and were not looking for jobs." The hope was, Snell explained, that resort visits by wealthy Americans would lead such visitors to establish "winter residence, then build businesses here."[23]

Following World War II, the Phoenix Chamber of Commerce spread the appeal of the Valley of the Sun more broadly. Beginning in 1949, the Chamber initiated both a national advertising campaign, underwritten by financing from the city's general fund, proclaiming that "It's Fun in the Valley of the Sun." It also began a long-running program in which the Chamber invited writers from "trade journals, national magazines, syndicated writers, and leading newspaper editors" to visit Phoenix on five- to six-day junkets, usually between December and April.[24] In 1960 the Chamber sent such invitations to *Life, Newsweek, U.S. News & World Report*, the *Saturday Evening Post, Time, Ladies' Home Journal, Better Homes and Gardens, Good Housekeeping, Saturday Review*, and seventy-nine additional newspapers.[25] The results could be seen in articles titled, "Fun in Sun City," "It's Fun to Live in Phoenix," "Big Boom in the Desert," and "What It's Like to Live in Arizona."[26] Articles in national magazines followed similar narrative patterns. Almost all commented on the bountiful recreational possibilities of the "Sunniest City in the U.S.A.," according to *Holiday* magazine. *Good Housekeeping* wrote that Phoenix was "perfect for whatever outdoor activity a family wants." Magazines targeted at men almost universally emphasized the possibility of "Golf! Year-Round!" as *Esquire* excitedly announced. A separate *Holiday* article detailed the natural recreation located in close proximity to downtown: "City dwellers can escape to desert and mountain picnic areas of untouched natural beauty, 10 minutes from Phoenix. Rugged South Mountain Park is the nation's largest city park, and Papago one of the most picturesque."[27]

Climate did not only shape recreational possibilities in these profiles. It also shaped domestic life. Phoenix boosters coined a phrase, "outdoor living," to describe the ways in which Arizona's climate allowed a different everyday experience from that of the East Coast. "Back there [in Boston] a house was important because we had to stay inside so much. We resent it here when we have to stay inside," one transplant explained in *Better Homes and Gardens*. "We spend our money for more pleasurable things. We have a swimming pool, and our recreation is simpler, more oriented to the outdoors, and less expensive. We don't have to buy snow suits or pay those heating bills."[28] Other articles pointed to designs that made outdoor areas a virtual extension of the home. *Life* portrayed a family eating dinner on a terrace "built around a spiky yucca tree with a view extending past [a] 600-year-old giant cactus to Camelback Mountain," while *Architectural Record* examined the ways in which a home nearby had "three separate outdoor living areas," one for dining, a second for "enjoyment of the cool summer breezes," as well as a children's play area.[29] Finally, articles in women's magazines suggested that "outdoor living" was particularly beneficial to their audiences. Regular articles in *Redbook* and *Good Housekeeping* touted the fashions being worn in Arizona during the winter: "trim little jackets . . . designed for the outdoor life in patio and at poolside," "a short cotton cocktail outfit laden with gold rickrack," "backs are out—in the open, beautifully bared by shadow brown maillot that merely loops the shoulder."[30] Not only did the climate allow women to wear lighter, more flattering clothes throughout the years, "outdoor living" was presumed to encourage women to stay active and thin. One article in *Vogue* went so far as to say, "I never saw a fat person, except tourists, while I was there."[31]

The similar themes contained in the articles suggested the success of the Chamber's junkets in conveying the central message of the Valley of the Sun campaign. In the pages of national magazines, Phoenix came across as a place with a remarkable possibility not only for outdoor living, but self-invention through individual lifestyle choices. As the subject of "What It's Like to Live in Phoenix" told the readers of *Better Homes and Gardens*, "Back in the East, everything is defined for you. Here the whole place is growing, expanding, and there's no limit. . . . If I do something, it's my triumph. If I fail, it's my failure. I'm a lot more of an *individual* in Arizona."[32]

No magazine exported the message of Phoenix's businessmen more consistently, however, than *Arizona Highways*. Founded in 1921, the magazine spent its first two decades instructing readers on the finer points of Arizona's development, including "must see" sites including the vast open-pit copper mines near Bisbee and the newly paved highway linking Prescott and Phoenix. The latter site reflected the magazine's dual emphasis on Arizona's development and the promotion of paved roads, best seen in its early motto, "Civilization Follows the Improved Highway." In 1937, however, *Arizona Highways*' focus began to change. That year, the state hired Raymond Carlson, a recent graduate of Stanford, to be the magazine's first non-engineer editor. Carlson quickly changed the magazine from a staid black-and-white journal whose articles featured passages such as "From the dim dawn of history on the great Babylonian plains . . . each age has embalmed its ideals, ambitions, its very spirit, in its bridges," to a lush photo journal in the style of *Life*, filled with two-page color spreads of cactus flowers, canyon sunsets, and Navajo and Hopi dancers, and featuring a new motto, "House Organ of Heaven." The magazine's circulation also increased dramatically, from fewer than 8,000 in the early 1930s to 250,000 in 1951, with more than 150,000 of those subscribers being "vicarious Arizonans" who lived out of state.[33]

Carlson quickly fell in with Phoenix's downtown businessmen, likely due to the downtown location of the magazine's office. Carlson lunched daily at the Arizona Club and bonded with Goldwater in particular over their interests in photography and recounting Arizona's history. And by the middle of World War II, the promotional rhetoric of the Valley of the Sun had assumed a central place in the magazine. "You may think of January as a cold, dismal, gloomy month," a 1943 article titled "The Sun Is Our Fortune," explained, "but Phoenix will enjoy two hundred and thirty-nine hours of the sun's friendly presence." Another article told servicemen overseas, "You enjoy the pictures of fun in the Sun Country with this invitation in mind, 'This can be you when the war is won.'" Such rhetoric filled the magazine in the following decades in articles such as "Phoenix: City in the Sun," "You'll Like Living in Phoenix," "Phoenix, City on Wings" and "Dream Homes by the Dozens."[34] Carlson's interactions with Phoenix's businessmen extended to other areas as well. Goldwater, who had traveled since his childhood throughout northern Arizona, flew Carlson in his Cessna to various natural settings that could be featured in the magazine. Carlson reciprocated by publishing Goldwater's photography of northern Arizona and its Indian people. Moreover, he adopted Goldwater's sense that, in Peter Iverson's words, "The 'real' Arizona could not be found among the tall buildings lining Central Avenue in Phoenix" as the central visual message of the magazine. Between 1946 and 1955, photographs of the natural landscapes of northern Arizona and its Indian people and their material culture made up 85 percent of the magazine's covers. As Iverson writes, "Again and again, the magazine and thus its readers returned to the Arizona north of old Route 66 and the Santa Fe Railroad and from the Grand Canyon eastward to the New Mexico line."[35]

Arizona Highways represented those landscapes as providing perspective on the modern world. "There's room enough to get off by yourself," Carlson wrote of the canyons of the Little Colorado River. "And you and your little affairs become very little indeed when placed in such spacious and majestic surroundings." In portraying the yawning, empty canyons of the Little Colorado as, in the article's title, a "Happy Land," Carlson flipped the nineteenth-century notion of the sublime on its head. Rather than an awe-inspiring confrontation with nature's immense scale and elemental power, a hiking excursion on the Little Colorado would quiet dissonance caused by modern life. Rather than revelation, the goal was rehabilitation. Arizona's nature provided inner peace that could remain with individuals and fortify them upon their return to the duties of modern life. As Joyce Muench suggested in "Pilgrimage into Spring," "When the work at your desk . . . grows dull, you have only to listen to the call of Arizona's awakening. Close your eyes and see the breezes tousling the heads of flowers on the Desert. . . . Then open them again and start off on your work."[36]

Arizona's native peoples served a similar purpose of reminding modern Americans of a simpler life. A 1953 article about the Navajo, "Colorful People," explained that "Many of them have never seen a train or a plane, have never basked in the glow of Neon lights, have never been carried away by the high emotions inspired by the stridence of a juke box. . . . They manage to entertain themselves without movies, radio, or television." Without the constant distractions that characterized modernity, the article suggested, Navajos were free from anxieties that could even drive many people to illness. "They manage to be happy in their own little worlds, they find the ways of their fathers sufficient for full and complete lives, they accept their lot with a philosophical calm. They live a life of slower tempo, less hectic than ours, much freer from nervous tensions and ulcers."[37] Again and again, the magazine returned to such portraits of Navajos, and other Indians, living not only spatially, but temporally distant from the ills that plagued modern Americans. Navajo children cared for their sheep and respected their elders, adults worked hard and provided for their families, and Navajo life continued "completely undisturbed by frenzied civilization about them."[38]

Such portraits, of course, bore no resemblance to the actual experience of Navajos, who, at the time Carlson wrote, were struggling through the dire aftereffects of stock reduction. Indeed, one year before Carlson wrote that Navajos were "completely undisturbed by frenzied civilization," the Red Cross had airlifted 95,000 pounds of food, medicine, firewood, and forage to Navajos, an operation likened by one reporter to "a domestic Berlin airlift."[39] While photos of Navajo sheep herders filled the pages of *Arizona Highways*, Navajos relied on pastoralism less and less, drawing only 10 percent of their income from stock raising by the mid-1950s.[40]

Accurate representation of Navajos' lives, of course, was not Carlson's intent. Instead, "the Navajo" represented difference, in two senses. "The Navajo's" presence in the magazine served to highlight Phoenix's modernity, which, as we will see in the following chapter, its businessmen sought to buttress by creating artistic institutions, funding the architecture of Frank Lloyd Wright, and most importantly, attracting high-tech industry. The presence of native culture on Phoenix's periphery showed the city as the state's modern center. At the same time, representations of Indians served to distinguish the Valley of the Sun from other locations where people might consider relocating. The presence of Indians could be added to the valley's other attractions to create a sense of endless possibilities for personal invention lacking in other areas. This sense of possibility shaped portraits of Phoenix in other magazines as well. As a former New York executive told *US News*, "I used to commute from Oyster Bay . . . everyday—an hour and a half each way. Now I live on the desert just beyond town. . . . I can go home at lunchtime and take a dip in my pool. After work or on weekends, I play tennis and golf. Sometimes I go prospecting for uranium in the Superstition Mountains with an Indian friend of mine. I just enjoy life about 10 times as much."[41] By encouraging such representations, *Arizona Highways* helped turn Phoenix's parochialism on its head. No longer was it a source of grievance, a reason why the Colorado River's water and energy flowed toward Los Angeles. Instead, it was an attraction, allowing a life perfectly balanced between the modern and its escape.

The efforts to reshape Phoenix's image were widely successful. It is rare today to find a reference to the Salt River Valley even in Phoenix itself. The Valley of the Sun, by contrast, became ubiquitous, its name gracing commercial enterprises and community institutions alike. The name change and the efforts to create a sense of Phoenix's uniqueness, however, would be rather unimportant had they not occurred in concert with the federal policies remaking metropolitan America at the same time. In Phoenix, the transition from the Salt River Valley to the Valley of the Sun was not only a rhetorical change. It was also manifested in the transformation of property itself.

SUBDIVISION

Perhaps no institution in Phoenix benefited more from federal intervention in the economy than Valley National Bank. Policies initiated early in the New Deal that regulated private banks, provided capital, and underwrote a vast array of lending practices fueled the bank's rise to the largest in the intermountain states. These policies facilitated, in the words of David Freund, "a monetary and credit revolution" that "made it easier—in many cases risk free—for the private sector to lend and borrow."[42] Most prominently, the Federal Housing Authority (FHA), created by the National Housing Act of 1934, guaranteed mortgage loans for 80 percent of the value of approved residential property and for 20 percent on smaller home-improvement loans. Such extensive federal guarantees encouraged banks to loan money, since, as Kenneth Jackson wrote, "there was very little risk to the banker if a loan turned sour."[43] In guaranteeing mortgage loans, the FHA worked indirectly, subsidizing private banks, in order to, in terms used by FHA officials, "unleash" and "unloosen" "sleeping capital."[44]

Valley Bank was well positioned to take advantage of the FHA's guarantees. Carl Bimson helped write legislation creating the FHA and testified before Congress in its support. After joining his brother at Valley Bank, Carl Bimson "made a crusade" of spreading word of the new policies, "organizing crews to ring doorbells and talk up loans" for home improvement or large appliance purchases guaranteed by the FHA. According to Bimson, in the program's first year, Valley Bank established 59 percent of such loans made in Arizona while the state's eight other banks made a mere 7 percent.[45] Even during the Depression years of the late 1930s, the bank made 198,000 federally guaranteed loans. Many of these were smaller Title I loans for home improvements and appliances. Those loans cascaded through the depressed local economy, employing contractors and bolstering sales at Goldwater's and other retail outlets selling large appliances.[46] As returning veterans flocked to Phoenix after World War II, many familiar with the city after training in one of Phoenix's four military bases, the bank's business in more substantial home-mortgage loans exploded. The annual dollar amount of FHA mortgages offered by Valley Bank rose from $11,335,407 in 1947 to $203,552,084 in 1970, representing between 16 percent and 25 percent of the bank's lending portfolio throughout that period. VA loans under the GI Bill represented another 8 percent to 14 percent. Federal mortgage underwriting, Carl Bimson later explained, provided a baseline of secure loans that allowed the bank to loan money to new commercial, real estate, and manufacturing enterprises.[47]

Such loans encouraged small contractors to enter into the mass production of homes. Take the case of John F. Long, the largest home builder in postwar Phoenix, and the nation's second largest builder in the late 1950s after Levitt & Sons. After his discharge from the military in 1946, Long returned to his boyhood home in Phoenix and began building a home for his wife and child using a GI Bill loan through Valley Bank. "Took six months to build it," he recalled, "and then we had an opportunity to sell it, before we had it finished." Selling the house for $8,450, Long made a profit of $4,500. Long repeated the process with multiple homes. As he told an interviewer in 2000, he "sold about twelve houses before we built our own," each time taking out small loans to cover construction costs and repaying the loans upon sale of the house.[48] By the early 1950s, Long had become a developer, purchasing agricultural land, dividing it into smaller plots ranging from thirty to ninety houses, and building homes upon it, such as the plot of homes at Glenview and Tenth that open this book. By 1954, however, he had a grander vision, a planned community of thousands of homes built using mass-production techniques on the western edges of Phoenix, interspersed with "parks and swimming pools and recreation buildings and so forth" designed so that "the whole spectrum of living could be in one . . . area."[49]

The success of Long's master plan, the creation of a community he called Maryvale, depended not only on his ability to apply the mass-production techniques pioneered by William Levitt on the former potato fields of Long Island, but also on Valley Bank's willingness to finance the project. Long's purchase of two hundred acres of agricultural land at roughly $2,500 an acre and his construction costs of $6,000 per three-bedroom, two-bath house required a loan of approximately $9 million for Maryvale's first phase of 1,380 houses.[50] Long remembered this as a gamble for Valley Bank. The land "was considered a long ways out," and "Walter Bimson made the comment . . . my financial statement didn't warrant the kind of loan that I was asking for." Bimson, Long recalled, "felt I definitely had something on the ball. So they made the loan."[51]

If Bimson was gambling, however, he was doing so on short odds. The postwar years witnessed a mass migration to Phoenix of largely middle-class workers who made eager home buyers. As we will see in greater detail in the following chapter, Walter and Carl Bimson helped extend this migration by participating in promotional campaigns that attempted to draw new manufacturers to Phoenix. These campaigns touted the low housing costs potential employees would enjoy. Phoenix, one pamphlet distributed to prospective manufacturers stated, has "More house per dollar . . . than in any other section of the country."[52] Even as Maryvale's homes went on the market, Carl Bimson was president of the Chamber of Commerce while it oversaw the advertising programs aimed at attracting new residents. Valley National Bank thus helped produce demand for new housing at the same time it profited from residential expansion. That, as one historian writes, "no one seems to have questioned this as a potential conflict of interest" signals the central place of residential growth within Phoenix's political culture.[53] Business and community development were linked inextricably. Indeed, with the complete sale of Maryvale's first phase occurring, in Long's words, "almost overnight," both Long and Valley Bank prospered. Long cleared an estimated $1.5 million in profit, roughly $360,000 of which went to Valley Bank as interest when Long repaid his commercial loan.[54]

The 1960 census showed the results of such metropolitan expansion. Between 1955 and 1960, the population of Maryvale's three census tracts grew from 1,547 to 22,547. Photos of the "Greatest Home Show on Earth," held in 1955 to announce the opening of Maryvale show a lone cul-de-sac containing seven houses, giving way, at the surrounding fence, to bare fields with tractor marks still visible. Indeed, the 1960 census map for Phoenix captures a frozen moment in the process whereby agricultural property became residential real estate. Census tract 66, which formed the southern portion of Maryvale, showed the area surrounding the Grand Canal dense with new streets named "Cherry," "Hollyhock," and "Mulberry." The southern portion of tract 66 remained unmarked on the census map, awaiting its imminent remapping by suburban streets and cul-de-sacs whose names gestured broadly at an agrarian past.[55]

The homes clustered along these streets and cul-de-sacs became known, in Phoenix and throughout the nation, as "subdivisions." Across the suburban landscape, the spatial divisions established by home builders rapidly became vernacular descriptions of place, articulated by the people who came to call that landscape home. Place-specific names such as "Northeast Village," "Sherwood Vista," and "Winona Park" made the new landscape of homes built using similar materials and production techniques legible and memorable places.[56] Calling these "subdivisions" has become second nature in the suburban landscape. It is easy to forget that before subdivisions were places, "subdivision" was a process, a process in which the value of property was transformed by the new residential marketplace underwritten by federal guarantees. In the process of subdivision, the ability of banks and home builders to finance the construction of new housing drove land prices up exponentially. Home builder Ralph Staggs remembered that agricultural land valued at $250 per acre before World War II cost $1,000 per acre by 1950 and $6,200 per acre by 1962. At times, the demands to proceed with residential construction overrode even the value of crops almost ready for harvest. When John Long began Maryvale's second phase of development in 1955, he

FIGURE 2.2. Leveled agricultural land could rapidly be transformed into subdivisions, such as Cox Meadows in northern Phoenix. Note the electrical transmission lines and poles in the background that accompanied suburban home construction. Courtesy of the Arizona Historical Society. 1953.

was so eager to begin construction that he paid the cantaloupe farmer whose land he purchased for his crop as well. "We disked it and all of that," Long recalled, grinding the cantaloupes into the soil, "and here we were having our grand opening."[57]

The agricultural past did not disappear on these landscapes. Many home builders gave their subdivisions names such as "Melrose Groves," "Orangedale," and "Country Estates." Others appealed to buyers through direct connections with the land's former productive use. Universal Homes urged buyers to "pick yourself a sweet home," in its "Pomelo Estates" subdivision, where homeowners could enjoy "country-style living" in homes "surrounded by your own fruit bearing trees."[58] Other home builders advertised their houses as "located on choice citrus lots."[59] In making such appeals, however, the way in which land itself was valued changed. No longer valued for the wealth its soils could produce, it was valued according to the idea of place—"country-style living"—its agricultural past enabled its sellers to market. In short, residential development revalued land whose "productiveness" earlier boosters had touted as "not equaled by any portion of the great West" according to the dream of the suburban home in the garden.[60]

Occasionally, home builders went beyond this familiar "home in the garden" vision and made the process of subdivision overt. One 1955 ad for Paradise Park announced that "We will accept clear lots northeast or northwest of Paradise Valley Acreage as Down Payment!"[61] The description of agricultural land as "clear lots" itself demonstrated the transition taking place. Land that, through the application of capital, labor, and water, had been "reclaimed" from the desert into productive farmland became, in the new world of metropolitan Phoenix, "clear lots," awaiting residential development.

The subdivision of farmland was not, however, a simple story of the transition of metropolitan Phoenix from agricultural to suburban. Rather, suburban home construction facilitated the extension of agriculture into undeveloped desert lands farther from Phoenix. John Long explained that he rarely purchased agricultural land outright. Instead, he bought undeveloped desert or fallow acreage elsewhere in the valley and exchanged it, two acres for one, for the existing farmland he sought to develop. The land for Maryvale's shopping center, for instance, was purchased from a farmer whom, Long explained, "owned twenty acres at that site and we bought forty acres out by 75th Avenue and Indian School Road, traded him his twenty for forty, and then, later . . . I bought 80 acres further out yet, and traded it for his forty for the 80." Long's policies not only expanded the footprint of agriculture around Phoenix. In putting desert lands to the plow, in investing capital in place in the form of graded, tilled, and irrigated lands, he helped to prepare the landscape for future subdivision, with irrigated fields providing the ideal setting for the mass construction of housing.[62]

As a large-scale builder, Long subcontracted mortgage services to a California firm, the Stalford Mortgage Company, which opened an office in Maryvale and paid Long's company a small fee for each mortgage it made. When Valley Bank provided development loans to smaller builders, however, it profited doubly from the conversion of agricultural property into residential property. Ralph Staggs began building houses in Phoenix in 1949, buying fourteen lots at Twenty-Ninth Street and Oak, using a loan from Valley Bank. "I built the houses myself in the daytime," he recalled, "and sold them at night." After four months, he sold the houses and repaid his commercial loan. Like Long, his business grew steadily. Eventually Staggs developed fifty-eight different subdivisions financed by Phoenix's three main banks: Valley National, First National, and the Bank of Douglas. Because Staggs focused on building smaller subdivisions scattered throughout metropolitan Phoenix, rather than a large planned development such as Maryvale, he did not subcontract mortgages like John Long did. Rather, home buyers initiated mortgages through Phoenix's private banks. Even with the low mortgage rates of the 1950s, mortgages on suburban houses proved lucrative. In 1957, a $12,000 mortgage on a 1,700-square-foot Staggs-Bilt Home, located in a "prestige neighborhood" called Northeast Village near Camelback Mountain would return, over the course of one of the thirty-year mortgages the FHA made standard, $12,500 in interest payments. Given that Staggs built "2,500 houses in that area," Phoenix's banks generated roughly $150 million in interest payments from FHA mortgages in Northeast Village alone.[63]

The potential profits from the production of residential space also created new connections between Valley Bank and the nation's financial centers. A mortgage is an agreement lodged both in space and time; it invests capital in space with the promise of repayment across time. Even if the FHA mortgages that Valley Bank originated were assured against loss by the full faith and credit of the United States, Valley Bank provided the capital that flowed from home purchaser to home builder, capital the purchaser promised to repay, with interest, across the extended life of the mortgage. Left on its own, however, Valley Bank's capital reserves would have been quickly depleted by the rapid development of Phoenix's residential real-estate market, leaving the bank unable to offer new mortgages. Phoenix's banks simply did not possess sufficient capital to fund the spatial transformation of their metropolis. The solution lay in the creation of a secondary mortgage market. If Valley Bank and other lenders could sell the mortgages they established to other financial institutions, they could exchange the temporal payment obligations of home buyers for liquid capital that could be newly located in space via the establishment of new mortgages. As was the case with the primary mortgage market, the New Deal state played the central role in the creation of these secondary markets. Chartered under Title III of the National Housing Act of 1938, the Federal National Mortgage Association, or Fannie Mae, purchased mortgages from initial lenders, thus freeing up capital by creating a secondary mortgage market in FHA loans.[64] The establishment of Fannie Mae had dual results. First, it encouraged banks to offer FHA mortgages. As legal scholar Charles Haar later argued, Fannie Mae's "willingness to buy FHA mortgages encouraged lenders to make them," thus underwriting the steady development of lands on the suburban periphery.[65] Second, the notes and bonds Fannie Mae created offered insurance companies, mutual savings banks, investment banks, and other large financial institutions investment vehicles to participate in the federally subsidized mortgage market.

It was not only federal policy that encouraged institutional investors to purchase mortgages from Valley Bank. The bank's executives aggressively recruited investors, using their city's amenities as a lure. "They can buy any of the mortgages they want," Carl Bimson explained, "but they can't find a vacation spot like Phoenix." Bimson recalled the bank's pitch: "Why don't you and the wife come to Arizona for a week or two weeks vacation—while you're out here, we'll show you some of the best loans you ever saw in your life. . . . [W]e'll sell you these loans at a discount—if you don't buy them, you've had a legitimate business expense. . . . [I]f you do buy them you can also charge off your expense and you've got yourself a nice portfolio of good mortgage loans."[66] Walter Besson, another Valley Bank executive, remembered Walter Bimson's persuasion of these visiting executives as akin to sexual seduction: "Walter stroked the eastern bankers—I'm talking about the investment bankers—well and long and hard." When Bimson's seduction was successful, the bank directed capital back into the local mortgage market. If a banker said, "I'll buy a million dollars of the loans," Carl Bimson detailed, "we came back and ran full page ads in the paper saying we have a million dollars of mortgages to lend."[67]

Rather than mere direct relationships between lender and home buyer, then, mortgages on the homes built on Phoenix's formerly agricultural lands were elements in a massive cycle of capital, in which federal monies and investment dollars flowed from the nation's political and financial centers through local institutions and became fixed in space and time in the form of Maryvale, Pomelo Terrace, Northeast Village, and the hundreds of additional subdivisions built on Phoenix's urban periphery. As the largest initiator of mortgages in Phoenix, Valley Bank had "Changed the face of Arizona," Walter Bimson told the bank's stockholders in 1956.[68] The audience celebrated that message. Indeed, they had invested in it. As Walter Besson explained, "From an investment standpoint, our stock made a pretty good impression . . . because of the phenomenal growth that Walter and the Valley Bank were doing."[69] If Valley Bank remade the state's face, however, growth liberalism provided the structure and the incentive in which that makeover took place. Insuring a large percentage of the bank's loans against failure, the FHA encouraged Valley Bank to make aggressive bets on metropolitan growth while cushioning it from the effects of potential failure. Fannie Mae provided capital to underwrite Phoenix's growth. The ability to profit from the new markets in metropolitan space also enriched Valley Bank, which, by 1945, was the largest financial institution in the Intermountain West. The effect of the New Deal's housing policies on Valley Bank ranged beyond financial success however. In establishing the bank as the key local conduit through which capital flowed, those policies helped establish Bimson and his downtown associates as the central figures in Phoenix's postwar growth machine.

GROW-AND-BUILD

It was not only in regard to housing that New Deal policies bolstered the position of Phoenix's downtown businessmen. The New Deal's reforms of the electric utility industry also allowed them to gain control of the state's largest electric utility. In the New Deal, reformers launched a series of attacks on the "Power Trust," holding companies owned by Wall Street bankers that controlled 80 percent of the nation's electrical supplies, and whom reformers blamed for evasion of state regulation, the corruption of state and federal legislators, and overcharges that limited the spread of electrical modernization.[70] The Public Utility Holding Company Act of 1935 (PUHCA), electrical reformers' great legislative triumph, mandated the dissolution of any holding company that served "no demonstrably useful and necessary purpose." Following its enactment, only utilities operating within a single state or contiguous area could be jointly managed. The act also forbade agents of Wall Street firms from occupying seats on utilities' boards of directors. Both the geographical and administrative dictates of the law, then, conceived the connection between private companies and local communities as the means of stemming the industry's abusive practices.[71]

CALAPCO's history reflected the patterns of abuse that reformers decried. Controlling shares in CALAPCO had been purchased by American Power and Light (AP&L), an electrical holding company itself owned by a second entity, the Electric Bond and Share Company (Ebasco), the largest utility holding company in the nation. CALAPCO paid management fees to AP&L and engineering fees to Ebasco. AP&L also paid management fees to Ebasco, layering another set of charges within the bills paid by CALAPCO's customers and raising the price of electricity for residential consumers an estimated 40 percent.[72]

The small population of local businessmen capable of directing a utility in a state like Arizona, however, produced a different form of centralization, even as the PUHCA attempted to decentralize control of electrical utilities. When the Securities and Exchange Commission ordered AP&L's dissolution in 1945, an investment bank managing the divestment of its utilities sought out Frank Snell, asking him to assemble a local board of directors. In return, the "15 or 20 important men" that Snell tapped to serve on CALAPCO's board received a stock discount of .50 per share. An examination of the board of directors for CALAPCO and its successor, Arizona Public Service (APS), between 1945 and 1966 demonstrates the dominant position held by Phoenix's downtown businessmen. Sixteen out of twenty-six members of the board, during that time, resided in Phoenix. More striking still is the dominance of Phoenix businessmen on the utilities' executive committee. All but one of the eleven members who served on the committee between 1945 and 1966 lived in Phoenix. In addition to Frank Snell, who served as chairman of the board for both CALAPCO and APS, and the utilities' corporate officers, President Walter Lucking and CEO William Reilly, Phoenix's downtown businessmen—including W. R. Wayland and C. W. Bond, both of Valley Bank, Edward O'Malley, and J. B. Ryan, head of the largest drugstore chain in Phoenix—occupied most of the positions. While five ranchers or growers from throughout the state sat on the board of directors, only one, John Jacobs, a carrot grower who was, as we will see in the following chapter, closely aligned with Phoenix's downtown businessmen, served on the executive committee.[73]

The PUHCA also led to consolidation of private electrical service within Arizona. Shortly after its sale, CALAPCO expanded its customer base by purchasing Northern Arizona Light and Power Company, which served Flagstaff, Winslow, and other small communities in northern Arizona. Snell and four other members of CALAPCO's board also joined the board of directors for Arizona Edison, a small utility that served areas north and west of Tucson in 1946. In 1951 Arizona Edison faced financial and management difficulties. The already interconnected boards agreed to merge the companies, choosing the name "Arizona Public Service" to signal the new utility's statewide reach.[74]

While Valley Bank's growth materialized in the form of new homes in northern Phoenix, APS's growth took shape as the infrastructure that supplied electricity to those new houses. At its formation in 1952, APS owned 803 miles of power lines. By 1970, that number had grown to 3,255 miles. The growth in the utility's power-line mileage represented the hundreds and hundreds of miles of new power lines required by the subdivision of the lands of northern Phoenix.[75] It also, however, represented infrastructure that tied together the scattered systems of the three utilities that composed APS. To examine APS's service maps throughout the 1950s is to see the ongoing connection between Arizona's hinterlands and Phoenix. Indeed, the utility's power lines came to replace the networks that had brought cotton, cattle, and lumber to Phoenix on their way to the national market as the clearest manifestation of Phoenix's place as Arizona's central city. New lines reached north to Tuba City and Page, west to Yuma and Parker, south to Casa Grande, Bisbee, and Douglas, and east to Miami, Holbrook, and Show Low. As APS extended lines across the state, they drew the state's outlying areas into new relations with not only the utility but with the interests of Phoenix's downtown businessmen.[76] On a more basic level, the breakup of holding companies tied APS's success to the growth of Phoenix's economy. No longer a cog in AP&L's vast national conglomerate, Arizona's utility now existed on its own, its future tied indelibly to the growth of Phoenix and the state at large.

APS's growth also manifested itself in the form of power plants. In the late 1940s, CALAPCO faced a dire shortage of electricity. When Phoenix's businessmen gained control of the utility, CALAPCO owned one generating plant, the natural gas-fired Phoenix Power Plant, whose 42.5 megawatt capacity stood far below the area's electrical needs. To cover its margins, CALAPCO purchased power from SRP's dams on the Salt River and the Bureau of Reclamation's Parker Dam on the Colorado River. Once the target of the Arizona Navy, Parker Dam supplied much of Phoenix's electrical demand during World War II. In 1945, the first year for which statistics are available, CALAPCO purchased 86 percent of the total energy it distributed from the Bureau of Reclamation and other outside sources, reflecting both the wartime emergency and Reclamation's suspension of rules giving public utilities first claim on electricity generated at its dams.[77] In the war's aftermath, however, this arrangement seemed unsustainable due to political, economic, and environmental factors. Shortly after the war ended, the Bureau of Reclamation reinstated preference policies, raising the price of electricity to private companies substantially. At the same time, an extended drought reduced the total generating capacity of the dams on the Colorado River. Across the region, utilities attempted to restrain electrical use in the late 1940s, restricting agricultural pumping to late-night hours when demand was low, instituting daylight savings time to decrease electricity use in the early evening, and even cutting power to some large industrial users in Southern California. Still, Phoenix experienced three blackouts between 1946 and 1948 along with numerous brownouts when voltage was reduced due to unsustainable demand.[78] The Federal Power Commission's (FPC) *National Power Survey* of 1947 warned that the Southwest was "dangerously underpowered in light of the expected future population." The report continued, "New supply must be developed to avert a crisis situation in southern California and in Arizona."[79]

This energy crisis, as we will see in chapter 4, sparked Reclamation's interest in building a "500,000 kilovolt system" that would link its dams with new coal-fired power plants located on the Colorado Plateau. It led CALAPCO and APS, however, in different directions. First, it led to new construction within metropolitan Phoenix. In 1945 the utility expanded Phoenix Power Plant, eventually raising its capacity to 145 megawatts. As the electricity from that expansion came on line, APS began construction of Saguaro Power Plant between Phoenix and Tucson to serve Arizona Edison's former territory and to provide backup power to the Phoenix metropolitan area. Completed in 1955, the plant possessed two units each capable of generating 100 megawatts of electricity. In 1953 the company began building the 220 megawatt Ocotillo Power Plant in Tempe. When Ocotillo was completed in 1956, the utility's generating capacity stood at 635 megawatts, all fired by natural gas drawn from the Permian Basin of West Texas, an energy source that caused few noticeable emissions and resulted in few complaints about power plants located within metropolitan Phoenix's small industrial districts or just beyond its metropolitan borders. By the mid-1950s, APS had succeeded in reducing the percentage of electricity purchased from outside sources to 19 percent of its total use. In 1956, APS actually broke even, selling 19 percent of the electricity it generated to other utilities with which it had established interconnections as its power lines stretched ever broader in the 1950s.[80]

Second, APS pursued interconnections with other utilities. By building lines connecting its system with Utah Power and Light, the Public Service Company of New Mexico, and Southern California Edison, APS could mitigate the seasonal nature of electrical demand while maintaining the economies of scale possible when power plants were run to their maximum capacity. Interconnection with Utah Power and Light was particularly beneficial. In the winter, when APS had more supply than demand, it could sell electricity northward when electrical demand in Utah was high. In the summer, the utility could purchase power, avoiding the need to utilize older, less efficient plants. In this manner, both utilities realized increased sales levels and offset the fixed costs of their plants in wages, bonded debt, and tax payments.[81]

APS also concluded a brief period of conflict with SRP over provision of service to the subdivisions developed in the public utility's service areas by negotiating an agreement that solidified the borders between the two utilities and calling for "close coordination and integration of the generation and transmission facilities of both firms." The two utilities negotiated the interconnection of their transmission systems, the pooling of reserve capacities, and the course of future power plant construction. While each utility would rely on its own generating capacity for the bulk of its power, they each agreed to utilize the others' plants for reserve capacity. Much like the agreement between Utah Power and Light, this agreement allowed greater economies of scale as each company could run its most efficient power plants to maximum capacity more frequently. Furthermore, the agreement to plan future construction allowed the two utilities to stagger their schedule for installing new plants so that plants would be used to their maximum capacity. Where each utility had planned to install new units in 1957, the new plan called for SRP to add almost 400 megawatts in 1957 and 1958 while APS installed a similar amount in its own system in 1960 and 1961.[82]

The steady expansion of APS's generating capacity testified to the utility's ability to finally embrace the growth-based development strategies that utilities in more populous regions had relied on since the 1910s. Since the age of Edison and Westinghouse, utilities serving large and growing customer bases had built generating capacity in advance of demand, relying on population growth and promotional activities to sell increased amounts of power. Holding companies generally avoided such strategies for small, isolated utilities under their corporate umbrellas in the 1920s and 1930s. Fearing that small customer bases could not grow quickly enough to consume new supplies and that the vast distances between urban "load centers" would not allow effective interutility sales of electricity, AP&L, CALAPCO's holding company, planned no new construction after completion of Phoenix Power Plant in 1930s.[83] CALAPCO possessed enough generating power to meet existing demand, but little excess. Once independent of holding company oversight, however, APS began to build its generating capacity, significantly embracing a "grow-and-build" strategy. This strategy had three components. The first was technological. APS banked that improvements in generation technology would allow electricity to be produced more efficiently in greater quantities, thus lowering the unit cost of electricity through greater economies of scale.[84] Because power plants took three to five years to come online, however, power plant construction had to occur in advance of demand. Indeed, the strategy's name represented a misnomer. Rather than grow-and-build, suggesting that construction occurred in response to demand, it might have more accurately been called "build-and-grow," reflecting the predictions of growth upon which the strategy relied.

The second component was financial. Because power plants required capital to be invested years in advance of revenue, grow-and-build required deep engagement with the nation's financial markets. In order to garner the additional capital needed to expand its generating capacity, APS offered 2.1 million additional shares of common stock, 955,000 shares of preferred stock, and $115 million in bonded debt, between 1952 and 1965, raising a total of $263.6 million. The company offered consistent rationales to the *Wall Street Journal*: "Expects to put $20 million into new plants and equipment in 1952 and 1953," "To reduce short term loans incurred for construction," "$33 million for construction in the next 2 years [1956–57]," "To repay construction loans and finance expansion," "Expects to spend $39.1 million on construction." APS's preferred stock offerings in particular targeted the same Wall Street investors that electricity reformers had demonized. The company sold its first preferred stock offering in 1954 exclusively to "twelve institutional investors," and New York Life Insurance Company bought fully one-third of APS's August 1961 issue of 240,000 preferred shares. Phoenix's downtown businessmen profited handsomely from the financial and material expansion of the utility. When AL&P was broken up on November 8, 1945, these same men purchased CALAPCO stock at $12.625 per share with their $.50 discount. After slow growth for five years, the stock rapidly gained value, tripling in price from 1952 to 1960, splitting two-for-one in early 1961, and returning to 1960 price levels by May 1961. At that point, stock originally purchased for $12.625 was worth $64.61.[85] More important than the personal wealth that the dissolution of AP&L brought to Phoenix's downtown businessmen, however, was the new position it gave them in the local and national political economy. Like Valley Bank, Arizona Public Service served as the local conduit through which capital from the nation's financial centers flowed before becoming fixed in space in the form of power lines and electrical generating plants. That the utility occupied this position was an ironic outcome of New Deal policies that saw local control as a bulwark against Wall Street influence.

Increased consumer demand represented the final component of grow-and-build. To match increasing supply and to serve bonded debt, CALAPCO and APS needed electrical consumption to exceed population growth. This problem was not unique to Phoenix. Articles with title such as "Sell or Die!" and "Sell—and Sell and Sell," filled utility-industry journals throughout the 1950s. Utility executives in the postwar years, however, believed they possessed broad control over domestic consumption of electricity. Speaking at the Edison Electric Institute, Philip Sporn, president of American Gas and Electric, told the audience: "The most important elements that determine our loads are not those that happen, but those that we project—that we invent—in the broad sense of the term 'invention.' You have control over such loads: you invent them, and then you can make plans for the best manner of meeting them."[86] Such invention was manifest in the real estate section of the *Arizona Republic* throughout the 1950s. Next to ads declaring "Oh-h-h! How Wonderful!" it was to live in a three-bedroom Whitmore Villa home "completely air conditioned by refrigeration," lay APS advertisements explaining the inexpensive work that Reddy Kilowatt, the cartoon mascot of the electric utility industry, could do: "No other family servant will do so much for so little! For only a nickel, Reddy will do five loads of laundry, vacuum the house for a month, do the dishes for two days or provide five full evenings of radio entertainment."[87]

New Deal housing policies laid the groundwork, or more accurately, installed the wiring, that allowed APS to pursue such campaigns. Until the 1930s, the ownership of large appliances such as refrigerators or washing machines remained almost exclusively the province of American households in the top 20 percent of income. Appliance prices remained high and most houses were wired for only limited amounts of electricity, enough to provide illumination but not the heavy circuits necessary to support such large appliances. Fewer than 25 percent of American homes owned more than one small appliance such as irons or vacuums. The FHA democratized electrical use. While Title I of the National Housing Act guaranteed loans for home modernization and appliance purchases, much as the NHA guaranteed home mortgages, the most important change was the institutionalization of a uniform set of expectations about home electrification. The FHA underwriting manual adopted codes requiring multiple electrical outlets distributed throughout the house to allow use of portable appliances and sufficient illumination. Furthermore, it mandated that, for mortgages to receive FHA guarantees, homes should have separate circuits for light and large appliances, ensuring that home wiring would be able to handle increased electrical loads. The FHA, as Ronald Tobey writes, "effectively created the national mass market for electrical modernization of the home."[88]

Judging by the pages of the *Arizona Republic*, the ability of domestic electrical circuitry to handle increased electrical loads remained a concern of electrical utilities into the 1950s. As late as 1959, the paper's home maintenance section contained articles reminding readers that "the first practical step in home modernization is the electric wiring," while APS ran ads throughout the decade emphasizing that Phoenicians should ensure their homes were "adequately wired . . . for modern, electrical living."[89] Such warnings, however, were far outweighed by calls urging consumers to "Live Better, Electrically." "A Freezer Pays for Itself," declared one ad; "An Electric Dryer Beats the Sun," another. Housing advertisements attempted to attract buyers through the range of appliances they offered: RCA Color Televisions, Easy Automatic Washers, and Westinghouse Frost-Free Refrigerators, Electric Ranges, and Laundromats.[90]

Such ads displayed the combination of appeals to domesticity, technological advancement, female leisure, and male purchasing power that were characteristic of postwar consumer culture.[91] "Electricity is a Family Affair," explained a series of APS ads. One portrayed a mother watching television with her son, a "dream of a few years ago but a reality today." Another showed "Dad" relaxing at home with Reddy Kilowatt, happy in the "real buy" he received from his "family servant." "He knows electric service from Reddy is his biggest household bargain."[92] The Appliance Merchandisers Association's paired advertisements for electric dryers showed an unfortunate woman straining to carry her washing machine to the clothesline—"more than 2,000 pounds of lifting a year"—while her companion relaxed on the sofa as electricity allowed her to "skim through the washing, drying and ironing and enjoy more leisure time."[93] Ads encouraged husbands to purchase their wives "an electric valentine": a household appliance that "will help her get more fun out of life by making her homemaking easier—and remind her of your thoughtfulness every day of the year." An advertisement for the Forrest Cox subdivision made a similar appeal, suggesting men show their wives that "she's your favorite valentine . . . by placing her in a home . . . designed specially to make homemaking easier." To assure that men would pick up on the message (and perhaps to suggest that women were not simply inanimate objects that could be "placed" in whichever house their husbands chose), the ad concluded with a "HINT TO THE LADIES: If your husband hasn't seen this page, maybe you should prop it up in front of his coffee cup this morning."[94]

APS did more than appeal directly to consumers. Representatives of the utility also appeared regularly at meetings of the Homebuilders Association of Central Arizona, with ideas for and incentives to integrate greater use of electricity into home designs. In February 1955 Bill Downey, the residential sales coordinator of APS, spoke to the group about "residential lighting," followed by a screening of General Electric's film, "See Your Houses in a New Light." Downey visited again later that year to explain ways in which home builders could extend electric service beyond the home, onto the patios and barbecue areas that were essential parts of home builders' appeals to "outdoor living." Downey suggested installation of an "electric barbecue and rotisserie" and the placement of exterior outlets that would allow homeowners to use "lights, radios, even televisions" on their patios. At least one home builder embraced this message as a 1957 Hoffman Homes ad that detailed the "loads of electrical outlets" on the patio that allowed "western living at its best." Two years later, another APS representative appeared to explain that to receive the Edison Electric Institute's "Living Better Electrically Gold Medallion," homebuilders needed to install an electric space heater, water heater, heavy wiring, and four built-in appliances. There were rewards beyond medallions for homes designed to consume large amounts of electricity. In 1955, APS rewarded the home builder who promoted "the utmost in modern electric living" at the annual Phoenix home show with a two-week, all-expenses-paid trip to Hawaii.[95] And in 1958, John Long toured Maryvale with GE spokesman Ronald Reagan after the community was named a winner of "GE Award Homes."

APS was not the only utility in Phoenix to run such campaigns. Indeed, it was the Salt River Project, not APS, that had urged husbands to purchase their wives an "electrical valentine." Such ads illustrated the transition the public utility experienced during the postwar years. While subdivision had remapped property lines north of the Grand Canal, the lines that separated the service areas of SRP and APS, of public and private power, largely remained in place following the utilities' 1955 agreement. As rows of houses replaced rows of cotton, SRP gained residential customers at annual rates that regularly exceeded 15 percent. The total gain was dramatic. In 1949, SRP had 17,391 residential customers. By 1970 that number had grown to 163,955. During the same period, its residential electricity consumption increased from approximately

FIGURE 2.3. John F. Long shows GE spokesman Ronald Reagan features of Maryvale's GE Award Home. Courtesy of John F. Long Foundation, Inc. 1958.

36,000 kilowatt hours annually to 1.9 million. The absolute number of irrigators using SRP's power actually fell, and their electrical consumption remained essentially static, increasing only from 350,000 to 460,000 kilowatt hours annually between 1945 and 1970. Unsurprisingly, SRP's business in residential energy sales increased apace, rising from 13 percent of SRP's revenue in 1949 to 43 percent in 1970. To meet this growing residential demand, SRP pursued its own version of grow-and-build, replacing its antiquated 25-hertz distribution system with a standard 60-hertz system and building two new natural-gas-generating plants during the 1950s. SRP's business shifted, in large part, from agricultural to suburban, and the utility began to function, in the words of one analyst in the 1950s, "essentially as private companies function."[96]

Both utilities experienced great success in their efforts to increase consumer demand. In 1945, CALAPCO's average domestic consumer used 1,453 kilowatt-hours annually, which cost an average of $46.76. By 1960, APS's annual residential consumption had reached 3,958 kilowatt-hours with annual payments of $107.18. SRP's customers used even more electricity, increasing from annual per capita consumption 3,254 kilowatt-hours and payments of $46.76 in 1947, to 5,519 kilowatt-hours and $130.98 in 1960. Two reasons accounted for the higher usage of SRP's customers. First, they tended to live in newer homes built on the former agricultural lands of the Salt River Project. Second, whereas APS sold both electricity and natural gas, SRP was only an electric utility and thus urged developers to build all-electric homes, which used substantially more power.[97] Statistics accounting for average domestic use capture, however, only part of the story of increasing electrical consumption in the Valley of the Sun. Combined with the dramatic increase in population, the years between 1945 and 1960 saw CALAPCO's and APS's domestic consumption increase tenfold, while SRP's increased by more than a factor of twelve.

These dramatic increases in residential electrical consumption before 1960 occurred prior to the democratization of air conditioning. Until the early 1960s, electrically powered air conditioning remained a luxury. When Valley Bank vice president Herbert Leggett boasted to a reporter for the *Saturday Evening Post* in 1961 that "I awake in my air-conditioned home in the morning. . . . I dress and get into my air-conditioned automobile and drive to the air-conditioned garage in the basement of this building. I work in an air-conditioned office, eat in an air-conditioned restaurant and perhaps go to an air-conditioned theater," he conveyed an experience reserved largely for Phoenix's elite.[98] Home builders equipped most mass-constructed houses with "swamp coolers," devices that cooled homes by blowing air through water-soaked asbestos pads, raising the relative humidity inside homes. In February 1955 the least expensive home listed for sale in the *Arizona Republic* featuring refrigerated air conditioning was priced at $11,750, 150 percent as expensive as the base unit in Maryvale. By February 1963, however, the price for refrigerated homes had dropped to $9,400. After 1965, swamp coolers had virtually disappeared from new homes.[99] The resulting electrical consumption caused the average domestic use of both utilities to again double in the 1960s. Altogether, between 1947, when statistics for both utilities are available, and 1970, domestic consumption of electricity increased from 110,000 to 2.4 million kilowatt-hours annually. By that time, the utilities combined drew revenues of more than $70 million from residential service, an increase of 2,400 percent since 1945. It is little wonder that a 1955 article in a stockbrokers' journal rated APS the nation's safest electrical stock.[100]

This electrical use reflected the rise of the society Lizabeth Cohen has called the "Consumer's Republic," in which use of domestic appliances became increasingly linked to status and even citizenship. It also reflected the promises businessmen made to potential residents when they explained the meaning of the Valley of the Sun. They promised a place that would possess both recreational and domestic quality of life. Residents of the Valley of the Sun could enjoy golf and swimming outside the home. Within it, they would be guaranteed all the amenities of modern consumer life, electrical modernization and electric valentines alike. This bargain proved beneficial for many people who learned to enjoy the possibilities of life in northern Phoenix, with all the recreational and domestic rewards it afforded. At the same time, the residence of these people proved beneficial to the businessmen who controlled Phoenix's electric utility, for whom new residents were, as much as houses and power lines, a form of capital fixed in space whose mortgage checks, purchases of appliances on installment plans, and payments to electrical companies represented the return on capital invested by both Phoenix's businessmen and the nation's investors who underwrote their faith in the Valley of the Sun's growth.

"APARTHEID IS COMPLETE"

In 1930, Phoenix was a spatially small, relatively dense city, with 48,118 people living within its limits and that contained a little more than ten square miles, a density of 7.4 people per acre. The city's population was located primarily between Van Buren Street and the Salt River. The city's northern border lay at McDowell Boulevard, only three miles north of the river. By 1960, the city had grown dramatically, in both population and size. As agricultural land north of the Grand Canal became residential property, Phoenix's municipal government pursued an aggressive annexation policy, an attempt by city officials to maintain control over the fiscal benefits of metropolitan growth. Fearing the incorporation of suburbs that would garner the tax dollars created by the subdivision of property and cause the city's core to decay, Phoenix's municipal government aggressively promoted the benefits of annexation among the new developments. As Phoenix mayor Timothy Barrow later explained, "we annexed the suburbs." By 1960, the city covered 290 square miles, with its northern border lying more than twelve miles north of the Salt River. Annexation dramatically lowered the city's density. Even as Phoenix's population grew by over 900 percent in thirty years, reaching a population of 439,170 by 1960, its territory grew more than 2,800 percent, with density dropping to 2.3 people per acre.[101]

As in cities nationwide, New Deal housing policies made it virtually impossible for nonwhites to participate in the new, federally underwritten markets in residential property. Believing that integration represented a risk to stable property values, FHA officials had, at the agency's inception, instituted policies that prevented the agency from insuring mortgages in

neighborhoods with any significant nonwhite populations while reject-
ing nonwhite applicants for homes in newly built subdivisions.[102] These
policies shaped the practices of the real estate industry in general. Real
estate agents pledged to maintain the racial character of neighborhoods
as a condition of licensing. "That the entry of Non-Caucasian[s] into districts where distinctly Caucasian residents live tends to depress real estate
values," wrote realtor Stanley McMichael in *Real Estate Subdivisions*, an
industry textbook, "is agreed to by practically all real estate subdividers
and students of city life and growth."[103] Such agreements held firm in
Phoenix. As local civil rights activist Lincoln Ragsdale testified at a hearing of the U.S. Commission on Civil Rights held in Phoenix in 1962, out
of 31,000 homes built by three builders in northeastern Phoenix, homes
all "built, directly or indirectly, through FHA commitments," not a single
home, "not one," Ragsdale testified, "has been sold to a Negro."[104]

As subdivisions sprawled northward, racial inequality in Phoenix assumed a new spatial scale. As was the case for minorities in cities across
the West, the racial segregation and squalid living conditions facing Phoenix's relatively small minority population had been the rule since before
World War II. Schools were segregated by law until 1953. Local theaters restricted African Americans, Mexican Americans, and Indians to
their balconies, while public pools and parks on the Salt River informally
forbade all nonwhites from swimming.[105] The city's black population
lived in two small enclaves, one on the east side and the other on the
north bank of the Salt River, while others lived south of the river, beyond
the city's limits.[106] Similarly, Phoenix's Mexican Americans, composing
roughly 10 percent of the population, lived close to the river, in houses
with limited plumbing and minimal, if any, electricity. Indeed, a 1946 report by Maricopa County officials reported "Steinbeck-esque Joad families living in dilapidated housing, row after row of open backyard toilets,
which smelled to high heaven, and dust blanketed, littered streets and
even dirtier alleys." Even larger numbers of Mexican migrant laborers
lived in the 150 to 160 agricultural labor camps that lay beyond the city
limits with accommodations that included abandoned stables, and flies
everywhere "on the garbage, the excreta, the soiled mattresses . . . and
on the children's dirt-encrusted faces," in one social worker's account.[107]

As the city's population and territory boomed after World War II, its
minority populations continued to be contained in those small areas.
The 1960 census showed that 90 percent of Phoenix's African American
population lived in just 9 of the city's 108 census tracts. These tracts,
all located south of Van Buren Street within the city's 1930 limits, also
contained one-third of the city's residents with "Spanish surnames." John
Camargo, who grew up just south of downtown Phoenix in the 1950s
recalled, "There were just Hispanics and blacks. I don't remember any

whites." The tracts contained the oldest housing stock in the city. Whereas 55 percent of the housing in Phoenix had been built between 1950 and 1960, only 24 percent of the houses in South Phoenix were new. While these predominantly nonwhite areas of Phoenix contained less than 10 percent of the city's total housing units, they were the location of 27 percent of Phoenix's deteriorating units, houses which had one or more defect requiring repair for the house to remain habitable, and 46 percent of its dilapidated dwellings, houses which did not, according to the census worker, provide safe and adequate shelter.[108] In 1966 a British magazine reported that "Phoenix . . . finds itself saddled with square mile after square mile of some of the most run-down, dilapidated housing in urban America. . . . [W]hole blocks are served by one or two water taps." In a city where the "housing dollar" went further than in any other part of the country, fewer than half the dwellings in the census tracts that housed the majority of the city's black and Mexican American population were owner occupied. As poor wiring and limited electrical outlets formed one of the key standards by which census workers measured deteriorating or dilapidated dwellings, a minority of homes housing the city's nonwhite population could use more than two large appliances. Nonwhite populations were, in large part, excluded from electrical modernity both by selective credit policies that favored whites and by housing stock that foreclosed the possibility of "living better, electrically." In only one of those tracts, at any rate, did the median income exceed the lowest median income north of Van Buren. Visiting South Phoenix in the wake of Barry Goldwater's failed presidential bid, a reporter for the *New Republic* found a "squalid slum" that "looks like a cross between a Mississippi Black Belt Negro ghetto and a Mexican border town. . . . Streets are unpaved, sewers unconnected, and public utilities inadequate; many houses have outdoor toilets, and many houses are no better than outhouses."[109]

The new landscapes north of Van Buren developed between 1950 and 1960 formed a stark counterpoint to southern Phoenix. During the 1950s, over 67,000 homes had been built on that territory, 85 percent of Phoenix's new housing construction. Only 4 percent of the homes were deteriorating and 1 percent dilapidated. Most strikingly, this landscape was almost exclusively white. Out of the 305,178 people who lived in this newly residential area, 235 were listed as "Negros," representing .07 percent of the population. The majority of the African Americans in North Phoenix lived in the census tracts with the highest median incomes, suggesting that most worked as live-in domestics. The census counted 9,252 people with "Spanish surnames"—3 percent of the population—north of Van Buren, suggesting that Mexican Americans possessed significantly more residential mobility in metropolitan Phoenix than African Americans. A closer examination, however, shows the "Spanish surname" population most heavily clustered into two types of census tracts. First, they located in tracts immediately north of Van Buren, suggesting that while Mexican Americans may have had more mobility than African Americans, their mobility was limited to houses recently vacated by whites moving farther north. Second, they located in tracts that, on the census's tract map, show significant undeveloped space, suggesting populations of farm laborers on agricultural land annexed in advance of residential development. Still, a small population of people with "Spanish surnames" did manage to reside and presumably buy the some of the new homes built in north Phoenix. The two census tracts covering Maryvale's moderately priced homes, census tracts where all but 4 of the 3,886 homes were built between 1950 and 1960, showed 397 people with "Spanish surnames" and 3 "Negros," out of 16,421 total residents.[110]

It was not only the FHA that maintained the color line between North and South Phoenix. "If you were black or Hispanic," John Camargo remembered, "you couldn't go north of Van Buren. . . . You would drive through there and just would be risking a fight with white kids that were in that area, and even . . . older whites that, you know, didn't like Blacks or Hispanics."[111] White violence also met African Americans who sought to integrate northern Phoenix. In the late 1940s, African Americans who purchased homes even south of Van Buren were met with petitions from white neighbors and found garbage dumped on their lawn and graffiti defacing their homes. Lincoln and Eleanor Ragsdale, who managed to purchase a home in the exclusive Encanto neighborhood of northern Phoenix by having a sympathetic friend serve as a buyer and transfer title, faced threats from neighbors, defacement of their property, and harassment from Phoenix's police force. Reflecting on the police's actions, Ragsdale stated, "I looked suspicious. And all you had to do to look suspicious is to be driving a Cadillac and be black."[112] Reverend Bernard Black remembered that Willie Mays lived on his street in South Phoenix into the late 1960s because the San Francisco Giant, in Phoenix for spring training, could not find a willing renter anywhere north of Van Buren. John Camargo, as well, emphasized that Phoenix's police played a major role in enforcing the city's racial borders. Venture north of Van Buren and the police would, he explained, "stop you and talk to you and ask you what you were doin' there. . . . We never reacted, you know, it was almost a fact of life."[113]

Appearing before the U.S. Commission on Civil Rights in 1962, Phoenix mayor Sam Mardian portrayed his city as a center of enlightened race relations within a nation increasingly divided by race. He pointed to the Phoenix school board's desegregation of local schools one year prior to *Brown* (though he neglected to mention the state supreme court ruling that forced the school board's hand). He explained that Phoenix's hospitals had been opened to all people "without enactment of laws" and related that restaurants served patrons "without regard to race or color." Mardian told the commission that "the voluntary nature of desegregation" in Phoenix, which he regarded as "much healthier than forced integration," resulted from the particular nature of the city's growth. "There are many newcomers from all over the country, and I think," Mardian testified, "they are all anxious to be friendly and to treat other people in a friendly manner so that they might reciprocate and treat *them* in a friendly manner." The intersection of unfamiliar people had created, in Mardian's telling, a type of exceptionalism, in which individualism had won out over group prejudice.[114]

Mexican Americans and African Americans testifying before the commission as well as the 1960 census told a different story. Northern Phoenix, with its 99 percent white population defended by both state policy and popular violence, and southern Phoenix, where John Camargo did not "remember any whites," replicated the patterns of growing metropolitan areas in the nation at large, where, as Thomas Sugrue writes, "whiteness and blackness assumed a spatial form."[115] The spatialization of race in Phoenix also created a new form of invisibility even more profound than in Detroit or Philadelphia. As we will see in the following chapter, changes in the city's charter that placed municipal elections on a citywide basis produced political invisibility in the sprawling metropolis, as candidates had little reason to appeal to the relatively small and powerless populations living south of Van Buren. Indeed, the city's annexation policy excluded predominantly minority areas south of the Salt River until close to the 1960 census, when its annexation promised to push the city over a population of 400,000.[116]

Invisibility manifested itself in public space as well. As new commercial strips and enclosed malls like Park Central developed in northern Phoenix, the city's middle-class whites no longer shared the downtown shopping district with blacks and Latinos. As Rev. Brooks told the Civil Rights Commission "the white community leadership for the most part is unaware of the problems, because the opportunities for exchange, intellectual, social, or economic, just do not exist."[117] As Andrew Kopkind, the reporter for the *New Republic*, explained the city in 1964, "Apartheid is complete. The two cities look at each other across a golf course."[118]

Such patterns were repeated across the nation. As the federal government underwrote postwar metropolitan growth, the patterns of race and residence in Phoenix resembled those in Charlotte and Atlanta, and Detroit for that matter, with a prosperous white noose surrounding neighborhoods of racialized poverty. These stark patterns of residential inequality were not, primarily, a consequence of overt discrimination, though as John Carmago's interview indicates, violence lingered not far below the surface. Indeed, Barry Goldwater bragged of his NAACP membership and his actions to integrate his department store just as Sam Mardian pointed to the voluntary nature of desegregation of movie theaters, department stores, and restaurants. While other Phoenicians testifying before the U.S. Commission on Civil Rights stated that they rarely saw Blacks or Mexican Americans dining in those restaurants, they too admitted that discrimination was not the main problem facing Phoenix. Rather, it was the uneven distribution of resources between northern Phoenix, where both public and private capital flowed into new subdivisions, and the nonwhite areas of the city, which remained underserved, underdeveloped, and ignored by both federal and local officials who focused their efforts on exclusionary metropolitan development. These dynamics were a consequence of the ways in which federal policy imbued with value not only space, but individuals. Capitalizing, in a sense, individual whiteness, growth liberalism helped determine where public money would flow to attract new people, and where private money would flow to serve them.

Walter Bimson delivered an address at the Western Area Development Conference in 1954 titled "The Businessman as Area Developer." The speech evoked Alexis de Tocqueville in a paean to the central role local businessmen had played in community formation. De Toqueville, Bimson explained, had grasped the timeless benefits of private efforts at local improvement. While a businessman might be "working for his own advantage" when he sought the development of his community, "he is not entirely selfish in this," Bimson explained. "He knows that his keenest competitor will also prosper and that many people and businesses unknown will be better off because of his efforts." Bimson warned his audience that this voluntarism was endangered by increasing federal involvement in local development. Warning of excessive federal oversight contained in the Housing Act of 1954, Bimson asked, "Where and when has any country, any area ever been developed except by businessmen for business purposes?" The federal government should leave development, he declared, "to those of us who know our areas best."[119]

Was Bimson being willfully blind in ignoring the federal government's role in underwriting his bank? Was Barry Goldwater, when he had asked suburban audiences gathered to hear his Senate campaign stump speech, "Do you believe in expanding federal government?"[120] Such patterns of attack on federal authority by those who benefited from them most remain one of the central paradoxes of modern political history. The following chapter will suggest one possible answer to this conundrum by arguing that efforts to draw manufacturing industry led Phoenix's businessmen into an open attack on the New Deal regulatory and social-welfare state even as these men resided in the warm embrace of programs that subsidized new housing and easy consumer credit and that privileged local control of utilities.

Those policies, however, created changes that tore at the image that Phoenix's businessmen created and the spaces where they once operated. Postwar policies created an intensive impetus toward residential growth. Searching for the Valley of the Sun's combination of recreational escape and domestic modernity, Phoenicians, new and old alike, moved farther and farther from the city's center. Soon, they moved to areas outside of Phoenix itself, in Scottsdale, Gilbert, or the unincorporated land north of Phoenix. As the center of Phoenix's gravity moved north, commercial businesses, somewhat reluctantly, followed. In 1955 Ralph Burgbacher, a California developer, purchased the 46-acre Central Avenue Dairy, three miles north of downtown, and began building Park Central Mall. Downtown merchants were initially skeptical. Goldwater's "had a hell of a time seeing the handwriting," Burgbacher remembered, "downtown . . . three miles away." The owners of Korrick's Department Store, too, "felt that we were crazy, you know—go out there in the sticks—and downtown. So they spent about 2 million remodeling that old deal and it never worked, see?"[121] After business at the mall boomed, the merchants closed their downtown stores. Soon, office buildings began to rise nearby, in what became considered "uptown." Many downtown businesses left, drawn by cheaper rents, or built their own offices, subsidized by federal tax policies that allowed generous write-offs for new construction.[122]

Even as downtown declined, residential construction spread out ever farther over the valley's lands. In the late 1960s, corporate homebuilders, mainly from California, moved in. In John Long's eyes, they lacked the social responsibility that had seen him outfit Maryvale with a swimming pool, playgrounds, and a local school. "Most builders now go in and they buy forty acres or eighty acres and then they move away; someone else plunks down beside them." Long worried that this process would be the end of the Valley of the Sun. "If no plans are made for the open space, and if we lose that, we'll lose a lifestyle that most—that's what people came here for."[123] Long was optimistic that this lifestyle could be preserved. The environmental writer Edward Abbey was, unsurprisingly, skeptical. Writing in the *New York Times Magazine* about the city that he found "swollen worse than a poisoned pup" in 1975, Abbey told of a visit to Fountain Hills, a development on Phoenix's outskirts where a fountain shot water two hundred feet into the air. There, Abbey encountered a group of women "glad to be out of Phoenix itself, or Los Angeles, or Minneapolis, wherever they'd come from." They believed, Abbey wrote, they had escaped "the crime, the noise, the crowding, the denser smog of the city. It would have been cruel to remind these cheerful and friendly people," Abbey thought, "that Fountain Hills is destined to become, if growth trends continue, a part of The Thing creeping toward them. . . . There is no escape."[124]

While people embodied as capital might move farther away and establish another mortgage to avoid what Abbey described as "the Blob," the houses remained. In periods of economic decline, such houses would lie vacant, as John Long experienced when the recession of 1968–69 led the FHA and VA to foreclose on more than one thousand homes in Maryvale causing "a real drag on the community. . . . Kids would knock out windows and weeds grow up and so forth."[125] The infrastructure that had been created in the process of subdivision—roads and sewers and power lines—remained, though. While the federal policies that created a local economy dependent on ever increasing levels of residential growth might turn the house into a commodity to be exchanged, the material infrastructure that surrounded and supplied that house did not adjust. It remained fixed in place to supply the seemingly ever increasing level of demand within which the house was embedded.

CHAPTER 3

Turquoise and Turboprops

WHEN THE EXECUTIVES FROM SPERRY RAND STEPPED OFF THEIR PLANE AT Sky Harbor Airport in September 1955, Thunderbirds were there to meet them. The officials of the Phoenix Chamber of Commerce's special event committee—the Big Chief (President), Little Chief (Vice President), Mis Chief (social director), Sachem (Secretary), and Medicine Man (Treasurer)—had planned the visit for weeks. Wearing their trademark high-necked blue velvet jackets, silver and turquoise belts, and silver thunderbird medallions, the Thunderbirds whisked the executives on a quick tour. Driving north, they pointed out Camelback Mountain's stark red-rock slope studded with saguaros. On the mountain's northwestern slopes, the Thunderbirds showed off the fine homes of Paradise Valley and the golf course at Phoenix Country Club. Passing beyond the subdivisions of northern Phoenix, they stopped just south of Deer Valley Airport and stepped out of the car to tell Sperry's executives the good news. Over the previous seventy-two hours, Phoenix's Industrial Development Commission had raised $650,000, financing the purchase of the land where they stood. It would become Sperry Rand's property, the Thunderbirds promised, if the company moved its aviation electronics operations to Phoenix.[1]

Returning to Phoenix Country Club, members of the Chamber of Commerce met with Sperry's executives to explain the site's advantages. One member informed them that "there was a lot of land available to them for their testing and elbow room out there on the Grand Canyon Highway." Ralph Staggs spoke of the wide range of modern subdivisions that lay within easy commuting distance of the factory. John Jacobs, chairman of the board of APS and the property's owner, told them the water rights he held on the company's prospective land, currently a carrot farm of John Jacobs' Farms, would provide ample water for industrial purposes.[2] Other Chamber members told them of the Valley of the Sun's business-friendly politics, its sunny skies and low humidity, its open space, right-to-work laws, and attractiveness to potential employees. All these qualities made Phoenix, the Chamber members explained, the ideal place for Sperry's operations. After the meeting, the executives were taken to the Camelback Inn, where they could play golf, ride horses, or merely sit by the pool. Returning to the airport, the Thunderbirds informed the executives of one final matter: A bill repealing a tax on products manufactured for sale to the federal government had advanced to a final vote in the state legislature.[3]

This tax cut evidently tipped Sperry's decision in Phoenix's favor. In December, the day after passage of the tax bill, a Sperry Rand spokesman in New York announced the company would move their aviation electronics division to Phoenix. By 1966, the corporation's new branch, Sperry Phoenix Company, occupied an 800,000-square-foot plant in northern Phoenix, employed four thousand workers, and purchased materials from more than ninety subcontractors within Arizona. Asked in 1962 whether the Sperry Rand made the right decision, Percy Halpert, manager of Sperry Phoenix, replied: "We have ample opportunity almost daily to compare Phoenix's advantages with those of many other areas. In weighing these with the other complex considerations important to the growth of an aeronautical and electronics enterprise, we believe we could not have made a wiser choice."[4]

The successful appeals to companies like Sperry Rand remade Phoenix's economy. By 1955, manufacturing passed agriculture as the city's largest economic sector. By 1960, manufacturing employed thirty thousand people and generated income of $435 million in Phoenix, compared to fewer than one thousand employees and income of $5 million twenty years earlier. It also remade the landscape. In Phoenix's industrial boom, the "clean" factories of companies like Motorola, Lockheed, and Honeywell located operations outside of Phoenix's traditional industrial areas south of downtown, on the metropolitan fringe and among subdivisions, creating a landscape that Robert Self has labeled the "industrial garden," a booster dreamscape in which "neighborhoods and factories, workers and managers, homes and highways were to coexist in a delicate balance."[5] The demand of "clean" industries for ever increasing amounts of electricity grew at double-digit rates annually from 1950 to 1965. This demand represented not only the manifestations of a new industrial landscape, it also reflected the increasing political power of Phoenix's boosters and others like them across the West within the postwar American political economy. By the early 1960s, that combination of industrial demand and political power would send power lines reaching toward the coal reserves of the Navajo Reservation.

WARTIME

Phoenix's industrial age began late. World War II may have made Detroit the "arsenal of democracy," but the war transformed Phoenix in even more profound ways. At the war's beginning, Detroit had been industrial for a half century. Ford's assembly lines had long been icons of modernity that had reshaped work culture across the globe. None of these industrial techniques had reached Phoenix, however. In 1940, Phoenix's manufacturing sector, if it could even be called that, consisted of a number of agricultural processing plants clustered between the Southern Pacific Railroad tracks running along Madison Street and the north bank of the Salt River, south of the downtown offices of Phoenix's businessmen.

The workscape of South Phoenix was remarkably foul. Meat-packers, lard- and tallow-rendering plants, metal shops, brick and ice factories, and canning facilities shared a landscape with the majority of Phoenix's nonwhite population. Smoke from sugar beet factories hung in the air, and waste from packing plants fouled the water. Polluted water and industrial waste baked in the desert heat, mixing with "the odors of a fertilizer plant, an iron foundry, a thousand open privies and the city sewage disposal plant," according to one contemporary account. Phoenicians of the "better classes" sought to keep industry south of the tracks. Indeed, Phoenix's limited zoning ordinance, adopted in 1930, was used primarily to prevent both industry and nonwhite people from moving north of the railroad tracks in order to protect property values.[6]

World War II brought new industry, and new people, to Phoenix. Fifteen thousand people flocked there to work in plants built by Goodyear Aircraft, AiResearch, and Reynolds/ALCOA. During the war, both "cotton pickers galore out of Tennessee, Mississippi, Arkansas and Kentucky," and "skilled workers, people that could work machine tools . . . not cowboys," according to varying accounts, moved to Phoenix to build flight decks for naval aircraft, cabin pressurization equipment for B-29 bombers, nose cones and guidance systems for B-17s, and other components for the nation's growing air forces.[7] In "clean," "garden-type" plants set amid cotton fields, they worked with precision equipment on the orderly environment of the assembly line.[8]

The war also exposed Americans to Phoenix in a way that surpassed the wildest dreams of the founders of the "Valley of the Sun" campaign. Hundreds of thousands of servicemen cycled through training camps scattered around the valley. "Where you can grow cotton," an Army Air Corps officer determined, "you can grow aviators."[9] On bases that replaced cotton fields, the officer's evaluation proved true. Falcon Field near Mesa graduated five hundred new pilots with basic flying credentials every three months. Luke Field, located fifteen miles west of the city, served as the Corps' largest advanced combat school, graduating over seventeen thousand fighter pilots who buzzed the valley in AT-9s and P-38s.[10] Farther west, troops at Fort Huachuca trained in desert warfare, preparing to face Rommel's panzers in North Africa.[11]

Arizona Highways assured its readers that these "soldier guests" would be wonderful ambassadors, spreading word of the valley's charms around the globe. Their experiences in Phoenix would be sure to "confound some of the wise acres who long have joked about that 'Arizona desert,'" Stephen Shadegg, later Barry Goldwater's campaign manager, wrote in 1943. "A lot," Shadegg reported, "are planning to come back," suggesting that wartime would soon trigger a population boom.[12] According to the ledgers of Phoenix's electrical utilities, Shadegg's prediction proved accurate. In the years between 1945 and 1950, both SRP and CALAPCO added new residential customers at annual rates ranging from 8 percent to 18 percent. If these numbers can be understood as largely composed of new migrants, Phoenix and the areas surrounding added between five thousand and ten thousand new households annually in the immediate postwar period.[13]

Wartime brought other surprises. The factories, which manufactured componentry to be shipped off to the center of the aviation industry in Los Angeles, taught Phoenix's businessmen that becoming "a vermiform appendix of Los Angeles," as Governor George Hunt had earlier lamented, was not entirely bad. Wartime manufacturing brought $137 million to the local economy, much of which made its way into the ledgers of merchants, restaurateurs, and theater owners, who kept their businesses open late into the night to meet the needs of workers on the swing shift.[14] It created other, even more lucrative opportunities, such as the $10 million line of credit that Walter Garrett, AiResearch's president, established with Valley Bank.[15] Even the war's low point in Phoenix had a happy ending for Phoenix's businessmen. In 1942, MPs killed three black servicemen in the "Thanksgiving Night Riot." In the wake of the disturbance, all local commanding officers declared the city off limits, citing dangerous conditions, most notably rampant venereal disease in the city's red-light district. Led by Frank Snell, Phoenix's businessmen rallied to demand Mayor Newell Stewart "restore the good name of the city of Phoenix." Stewart complied, dismissing the chief of police, city manager, city magistrate, and even the city clerk. "It was kind of like a coup," Snell remembered, "and we called it the Cardroom Putsch."[16]

If wartime was a time of power and prosperity for Phoenix's businessmen, its immediate aftermath was a time of worry and disappointment. Most businessmen had envisioned the arrival of manufacturing as initiating a vital new stage in Phoenix's development. After Goodyear Aircraft announced its plans to build a factory in 1940, Sylvain Ganz, president of the Phoenix Chamber of Commerce announced: "[I]t seems that the ice has been broken and that from now on Phoenix will become increasingly important, and properly so, as an industrial center." Even earlier, Philip Tovrea, owner of a large slaughterhouse and cattle yard, professed that once it arrived, "manufacturing industry will increase of its own accord."[17] Later in the war, the Chamber of Commerce became less confident as demobilization loomed and created a Postwar Development Committee in an attempt to maintain wartime industries in Phoenix. The committee could do little, however, to prevent demobilization. In 1945, AiResearch relocated its operations to Los Angeles when the federal government canceled $36 million worth of contracts. Goodyear Aircraft ceased operations in 1946, its plant becoming a storage site for decommissioned naval aircraft.[18] Some war workers abandoned Phoenix, following companies to Los Angeles. Others remained, working odd jobs. Former defense workers, Carl Bimson recalled, "were driving trucks or they're doing this or doing that" while Patrick Downey remembered "a PhD., an electronics engineer, that was here working as a gas station attendant." To those who lived in the city through the war, it must have seemed that Phoenix deindustrialized almost as suddenly as it industrialized.[19]

Phoenix's businessmen worried about their city's future, as its population grew at annual rates of 10 percent or higher while wartime manufacturers relocated elsewhere. Such worries were understandable. The combination of simultaneous population growth and industrial decline appeared unusual. Even with the New Deal state guaranteeing mortgages and encouraging the expansion of consumer credit, Phoenix's businessmen worried that a city dependent on winter tourism, real estate development, and service-sector employment could not continue growing. From the perspective of seventy years later, Phoenix appears to have been one of the first urban areas whose growth was fueled substantially by the New Deal's selective credit policies. It looked different from the offices of Valley Bank in 1946. Indeed, the idea that manufacturing represented stability while other economic sectors were more ephemeral influenced Phoenicians' memories of the city's growth. As one of Bimson's deputies later remarked, "an economy based on tourism and real estate, well, that isn't a very solid base."[20]

Reconversion, of course, was a national economic dilemma, a result of the drastic reduction in wartime spending that had fueled the economy for more than a half decade. Politicians across the political spectrum offered national solutions. On the Left, consumer advocates and their supporters in the Democratic Party sought to maintain wartime price and rent controls to cushion the economic slowdown they felt sure would follow the war in an effort to maintain the relative economic equality of wartime. On the Right, the National Association of Manufacturers and the U.S. Chamber of Commerce pushed for an immediate end to price controls, arguing that private enterprise, freed from government controls, would increase production and raise the American standard of living. In the Full Employment Act of 1945, liberals sought to oblige the

federal government to engage in Keynesian job creation if private enterprise failed to provide sufficient employment. After conservatives blocked
the bill, they settled for the compromise Employment Act of 1946, which
merely recommended that Keynesian spending be considered if economic
slowdowns ensued. Labor unions launched a wave of strikes attempting to protect their own standards of living, through demands of higher
wages, and to expand them to unorganized workers, through the continued expansion of industrial unions. Conservatives responded with the
Taft-Hartley Act, a mandate for the open shop and strict limits on union
tactics.[21]

As these national debates proceeded, Phoenix's businessmen turned
to a local solution. In the late 1940s, they engaged more directly in municipal politics, reorganized local government through calls for "reform,"
and reoriented public policy toward the attraction of new manufacturing
and business. They were far from the only businessmen to do so. In Dallas, such businessmen organized the "Citizens Charter Association"; in
Albuquerque, the "Citizens Committee." In southern cities, they joined
the "Southern Leadership Project." In Phoenix, they called themselves
"Charter Government." Scholars have referred to these as "community
power structures," "civic-commercial elites," and "growth machines."[22]
They shared essential beliefs and ways of looking at the world, however:
the tight control of local government by a small coterie of businessmen
oriented around local Chambers of Commerce, the creation of a "business friendly" image for their city, the contestation of elections at the
scale of the city rather than the ward, and the use of levers of power
available in both the public and private sectors to attract manufacturing
industry, particularly defense manufacturing, as a means of spurring economic growth and metropolitan expansion.[23]

CHARTER GOVERNMENT

Phoenix's version of this phenomenon began to take shape within the
Phoenix Chamber of Commerce immediately following the war. Until
the 1930s, the chamber had focused on effectively marketing the Salt
River Valley's agricultural bounty, sponsoring events such as "Buy a Turkey Day" and the "Arizona King Cotton Festival."[24] In the late 1930s,
downtown businessmen gained increasing authority within the Chamber
and began to reorient it away from the promotion of the Salt River Valley's agricultural commodities and toward the Valley of the Sun's goals
of attracting tourism, convention business, and wealthy businessmen to
Phoenix. As a part of this process, Robert Goldwater, seeing a need for
a special events organization within the Chamber, formed the Thunder-

birds in 1937. A small group of initially five, and soon fifty-five members, the Thunderbirds became the shock troops of the downtown business-men's efforts to transform Phoenix. In addition to hosting the Phoenix Open Golf Tournament, they met and shuttled important visitors around the valley, highlighting its attractions.[25]

Wartime gave Chamber members experience in the practices of indus-trial recruitment. The organization played the leading role in securing the site for Luke Field, negotiating purchase options on 1,440 acres for a base site, and raising $40,000 to purchase it through the city.[26] The organization also served as a key liaison between local businessmen and defense manufacturers. And it served as the organizing vehicle for the "Cardroom Putsch." Still, at the end of the war, the Chamber remained relatively small, and bylaws in its charter prevented it from important aspects of industrial recruitment, particularly the ability to own and hold property.[27] Its promotional materials, as well, were outdated by war's end, containing little information about wartime industrialization, and featuring, to Lewis Haas's amusement, Phoenicians with beards.

Frank Snell, Walter Bimson, and others began to address these prob-lems at war's end. Some efforts occurred independently. Bimson's Valley National Bank created a Business Development and Research Depart-ment, which acted as a clearing house, distributing a "vast variety of data on Arizona" to other financial institutions in the hope of attracting busi-ness.[28] Most activity, however, occurred within the Chamber. In 1945, Snell and Bimson worked to amend the Chamber's charter, reiterating their commitment to "promote and foster the civic, economic, and social welfare of its members and the City of Phoenix, the Salt River Valley, and the State of Arizona," but also enabling the Chamber "to acquire, hold, and dispose of property and to do any and all things necessary and suitable to those ends."[29] Then, between 1946 and 1948, the Chamber underwent a dramatic expansion. Reaching out to a broad range of busi-nessmen, its ranks grew steadily. Between 1946 and 1948, its membership increased from 800 to almost 2,800, and its annual income grew from $38,000 to $140,000. The Chamber offered Lewis Haas a position as its chief executive, hiring him away from its San Francisco equivalent.[30] It also increased its number of committees from four to fourteen, including the newly formed fifty-person Industrial Development Committee (IDC), which led a wide-ranging effort to research and recruit potential indus-tries. The IDC, as Elizabeth Shermer has detailed, "compiled information for new firms, improved advertising and publicity, engaged in industrial outreach, coordinated with other Arizona business organizations and raised funds for recruitment campaigns."[31]

If the Chamber was the organizational vehicle for the effort to rein-dustrialize Phoenix, the IDC was its policy shop. Researching industries around the country, its members sought to answer three questions. First, what types of industry would "fit" in the Valley of the Sun? This concern over matching industry with image reflected a real concern that new residents of Phoenix, drawn by "quality of life" appeals, might object to the very question of industrial development itself. As one Chamber member recalled the skepticism later: "'Why have more factories?' one new arrival asked me. 'They'd just clutter up the pretty Arizona landscape and smoke up the pretty Arizona sky, maybe even drive the tourists away.'"[32] Phoenix's wartime experience, however, provided an easy answer. Aviation plants located amid cotton fields had impressed Chamber members as "clean" and "smoke-free," potential realizations of the long-held American dream of uniting the machine and the garden. The IDC found that another, closely allied industry had the same potential. Committee member and recruitment specialist Patrick Downey explained, "We felt that the electronics industry, being of a garden-type variety, would probably be more beneficial to the city than anything else."[33]

Second, what desirable natural qualities did Phoenix possess? Wartime experience again provided answers. AiResearch's representatives had chosen Phoenix because the region's low humidity prevented corrosion in the delicate, high-altitude switches the company manufactured. The valley's 320 days of sunshine provided an ideal environment for testing aviation equipment, much as it did for training fighter pilots. The land surrounding the city provided a variety of possibilities for plant sites. As most potential sites lay on irrigated farmland, the property was already graded and came with water rights attached. Finally, the location within a day's travel distance from the center of the aviation industry in Los Angeles and the atomic laboratories at Los Alamos allowed plants to serve two potential end users. The IDC soon trumpeted these natural advantages alongside the beneficial effect of the sunny skies and open space on workers' constitutions. Employers, one chamber advertisement from 1948 suggested, would get "King-Sized Man Hours." Since the nineteenth century, of course, boosters had promoted Phoenix's "natural advantages," the idea, as numerous scholars have explained, that nature had blessed certain locations with amenities that destined them for greatness. The "natural advantages" promoted by the IDC suggests how this notion evolved in the mid-twentieth century. First, the diversification of manufacturing led boosters to articulate their local environment as advantageous toward particular manufacturing sectors, rather than industry in general. While this could, at times, involve the type of material advantage nineteenth-century boosters had emphasized, particularly in the form of available land, it also involved environmental qualities such as low humidity and open skies that favored particular types of manufacturing. Second, boosters paired natural appeals to particular companies to quality-of-life appeals to workers, seeking to portray their locations as places that could enjoy workplace stability in a time of increased worker mobility. [34]

Finally, what public policies would draw aviation and electronics companies? Answering this question incorporated most of the committee's work. In their early research as well as in the work of an emerging number of locational specialists that advised companies about potential plant sites around the nation, the IDC found that three local public policies concerned the "light industries" they targeted: labor, taxes, and government stability and efficiency. The IDC saw the latter as the most important. As Paul Fannin, the first chairman of the IDC and a future governor and senator, stressed, "industry must have the assurance it will receive a fair deal from the locality in which it locates." But this would require businessmen to take a more active role in politics. [35]

The IDC gained a vital ally in this effort when Eugene Pulliam, the owner and publisher of the *Indianapolis Star*, purchased both the *Arizona Republic* and the *Phoenix Gazette* in 1946. Pulliam, a longtime winter resident of Phoenix, had been, in his early life, an avowed Progressive and supporter of Theodore Roosevelt's Bull Moose campaign. A tour through Depression-era Europe forever altered his perspective. Witnessing the rise of fascism and seeing the effects of Stalinism, he believed, like many conservatives during the 1930s, that free market capitalism represented the core bulwark of American freedom. The New Deal, in this view, departed on a dangerous road toward collectivism. Pulliam filled his papers, both in Indiana and Phoenix, with these views, both in his own editorials and in regular columns by syndicated writers like Westbrook Pegler and Victor Riesel. Indeed, his papers' tendencies tended so far to the right that the Arizona Democratic Party's 1952 convention passed a resolution condemning "the dangerous dictatorship of the press by one man who neither knows nor understands Arizona's problems, and who persists in printing only one side of the news." As the resolution suggested, Pulliam's media monopoly gave his politics outsized influence. With his purchase of both the *Republic* and the *Gazette*, he consolidated newspapers that had provided significantly different political perspectives. Particularly in a city gaining tens of thousands of new residents annually in the late 1940s, Pulliam's control of local media gave him, and his Chamber allies, tremendous power to shape local opinion and politics. [36]

The successful enactment of an amendment banning the closed shop in the state constitution represented the first manifestation of these combined efforts. In March 1946, Herbert Williams, a building contractor recently returned to Phoenix after military service, was refused a construction contract because he employed nonunion building tradesmen. Joining with veterans who found themselves unemployed because of union seniority rules, Williams formed the Veterans Right-to-Work Committee. The Committee launched a petition drive to place a right-to-work amendment on the November ballot. Pulliam and Phoenix businessmen quickly lent their support. Barry Goldwater, who had been writing editorials for the *Phoenix Gazette* decrying the New Deal's pro-labor slant since the late 1930s, agreed to head the committee's retailers' wing. The Right-to-Work movement represented the alignment of unemployed workers and downtown businessmen in a rapidly growing city dominated, at that moment, by real estate and housing development. As Williams's political activity demonstrated, contractors and unemployed workers mobilized in opposition to building trades unions they believed were limiting their employment opportunities. At the same time, downtown businessmen feared the postwar development boom might create powerful building trades unions that could prove to be a powerful countervailing political force.[37]

Press coverage of the initiative was imbalanced, to say the least. Editorials in the *Republic* and *Gazette* likened "domineering, self-serving labor bosses" to both Hitler and Communists while claiming that "good unions . . . have nothing to fear." While leaders of the pro-union "Committee Against the Right to Starve" attempted to challenge such imputations, they were largely closed out of Phoenix's papers. Opponents of the amendment were left to distribute pamphlets that reached a fraction of the readership of the *Gazette* or *Republic*. Union leader M. A. DeFrance bitterly explained later that "we raised a considerable amount of money" and "went on the radio" but, closed out of the newspapers, "we just couldn't win." Indeed, the amendment passed by a margin of 61,875 to 49,557, with the deciding margin of votes coming from Phoenix's Maricopa County. The anti-union amendment, embedded in the state constitution, proved resistant to challenge. Looking back from the 1970s, labor organizer Darwin Aycock, proclaimed that, "Phoenix was to labor-management relations what Mississippi was to the civil rights movement."[38]

It was in Charter Government's 1949 campaign for city council, however, that the combined force of Pulliam's media monopoly and the Chamber's organizational efforts had their longest-running impact. In July 1949 a large group of downtown businessmen gathered in the Phoenix Title and Trust Company to organize a political organization to contest the upcoming municipal election.[39] Calling themselves the "Charter Government Committee," the group represented the culmination of three years of efforts to reform the city's charter, driven by a determination that Phoenix's municipal government was unstable, inefficient, and ill managed. Organized in the 1920s with a commission-style system, Phoenix's municipal government failed to achieve the efficiency such government structures supposedly offered. Ward-based elections were frequent, oc-curring annually, creating unstable councils with inexperienced members. Individual city commissioners held administrative power over munici-pal departments, creating an enmeshed patronage system. Collectively, the commissioners held the power to fire the city manager with a simple majority, which made the position "simply the choicest plum in the pa-tronage game," in the words of one historian. Factionalism on the com-mission led to the frequent replacement of the city manager, with the city employing twenty-three different managers between 1920 and 1940 even as a requirement that the manager live in Phoenix before appoint-ment produced an unqualified pool of candidates. [40] Largely avoided by downtown businessmen, municipal government became a site of power for the city's municipal and building trades unions and small proprietors who profited from their business.[41]

In 1947 newly elected mayor Ray Busey appointed a commission of forty people to consider changes to Phoenix's governing charter. The charter reform panel was "carefully selected," as Busey later explained, "to represent practically every facet of our social structure. . . . Capital, labor, education, national, and racial backgrounds, as well as industrial men were there."[42] The Chamber, however, played the dominant role. Charles Bernstein, a lawyer and the Chamber president, served as chair-man, and Frank Snell and Walter Bimson played prominent roles. After considering several possibilities including partisan elections or a strong mayoral system, the charter reform commission proposed a charter in-creasing the city manager's authority but dropping the residency require-ment; changing the name of the city commission to "city council," in-creasing its membership from five to seven and stripping councilmen of authority over city hiring; and holding biannual at-large elections for the council. While a majority of the city commission, as well as the city's supposed boss, "Dock" Scheumack, and the existing city manager, James Deppe, opposed the measure, voters approved it in a November 1948 election after Pulliam's newspapers promoted it as essential for "clean government" and as "an escape from boss rule."[43]

The new charter failed to stabilize municipal government. The tran-sition to it allowed the existing council to appoint the two additional council members. The three anti-charter councilmen appointed two like-minded supporters, and they voted to reappoint City Manager Deppe, whom the Pulliam press held out as a symbol of corruption. After an audit revealed an unexpected municipal deficit, and allegations arose that pros-titution and gambling were rampant in South Phoenix, the Charter Gov-ernment Committee formed, pledging to run a slate of candidates who understood "the intent of the city charter revisions" in the fall elections. The one hundred attendees decided on criteria for their slate. Candidates, a member of the first selection committee remembered, would be people with business experience, "active participation in community service," whom did not seek politics as their "principal means of employment."⁴⁴

Given the final criteria, it appears ironic, in retrospect, that Barry Goldwater occupied one of these slots. And indeed, the election represented the beginning of Goldwater's formal political career. Three years after the election of 1949, Goldwater would win election to the Senate, where he would serve for all but four of the following thirty-six years, the exception those following his unsuccessful campaign for president in 1964. In 1949, however, Goldwater represented an ideal candidate for the group. He was well known in Phoenix, both for his eponymous department store's advertisements and for his film narrating a 1940 journey through the Grand Canyon. With melodramatic narration and music, the film presented Goldwater as a brave, dashing figure, "a bronze god who had just beaten the river," in one viewer's memory. Goldwater himself later credited the film as his entrée into politics. In exhibitions across the state, the film "gave me access to so damn many Arizonans that it was just a natural step for me to go into politics."⁴⁵ Goldwater had also become a public opponent of the New Deal, endearing him to Pulliam. Since the late 1930s, he had written editorials urging businessmen to take a more active role in politics. In 1937 he wrote of the "Scared-e-cat" businessman who opposed the New Deal but failed to challenge FDR in public. "There isn't a businessman in this country today," Goldwater wrote, "that does not fear the future status of our rising tax figure, yet he confines his suggestions for correcting the situation to his intimates who will agree with him."⁴⁶ Becoming the leading spokesmen for the other six Charter Government candidates, Goldwater promised to bring a businessmen's efficiency to government.

Twenty-three candidates filed for election to the six council seats (the mayor occupied the seventh), but Charter Government and the Citizens Achievement Group (CAG), composed of the anti-charter councilmen, represented the main parties contesting the election. The CAG claimed responsibility for civic improvements such as an airport expansion and improved parks, and received the endorsement of the Phoenix Central Labor Council. Government efficiency, professionalism, and high taxes, however, represented the primary issues covered in Pulliam's papers. "Economy in governmental operations should be the first point of attack," Pulliam argued in a signed editorial on October 10. The following day he framed municipal government as primarily an economic enterprise, one that he felt was being mismanaged. "The vital need is for having the best possible general manager and board of directors at the head of this great people's corporation. For that is just what Phoenix is—a corporation owned by the people, doing a nine-million-dollar annual business." The *Republic* suggested that the city's deficits represented an issue of inexperience. Though Deppe had served as city manager for longer than any figure since 1920, Pulliam portrayed him as "unskilled" at the essential economic business of the city, writing "it must be obvious what waste and losses can occur when a nine-million-dollar business is headed by an unqualified person," and arguing "deficits are evidence of an unskilled hand at the helm." The Charter Government candidates, by contrast, were "successful in business," interested "in the people and in promoting civic welfare," and "not in politics for the sake of graft or personal gain." Calculating total taxes received by the city, Pulliam argued that Deppe's ultimate failure could be seen in the 313 percent increase in property tax receipts over the course of a decade. While neglecting to detail the ways in which population gain had influenced that number, the *Republic*'s editorial page portrayed Charter Government as "an aggressive group . . . fighting the taxpayers' battle in this municipal campaign."[47]

Criticism of another type of taxes was folded in amid the paper's coverage of the election. On October 22, beside an article suggesting that the CAG was attempting to suppress turnout as a path to victory, an article quoted Paul Fannin denouncing Arizona's "horse and buggy days taxes" on manufacturing. Fannin explained that the state's high business taxes led one company to locate its 1,400 employee aluminum factory in California, despite the fact that the company relied on bauxite mined within Arizona. Chamber president John McAtee pitched in, decrying "our medieval system of tax extortion," before detailing that extortion at length: "We have high inventory taxes. We have high machinery and equipment taxes. We have a manufacturers' sales tax. We have an income tax. We have city, county, and state taxes. We have business license fees and taxes . . . and many other taxes too numerous to mention."[48]

The attempt to reduce business taxes was not only a state matter. Initiatives eliminating a city inventory tax on manufacturers and lowering machinery and equipment taxes on manufacturing were on the municipal ballot below the vote for city council candidates. Despite the paper's denunciation of Deppe for driving the city's property taxes to new heights, the paper readily endorsed the tax cuts that shifted $30,000 of the municipal tax load from manufacturing to "the shoulders of property owners." The paper posed the change as a matter of public responsibility, a "small risk to take in the interest of a greater Phoenix," leading to "more employment opportunities and higher values for . . . property by virtue of growth." Located side by side with demands for cleaner government, the Pulliam press's call for policies "that will put Phoenix in a more favorable competitive position with other cities in acquiring new industries" served to conflate demands for "business-like government" with development policies intended to draw new industries. Public-mindedness came to mean both clean government and economic expansion.[49]

The Pulliam press removed all stops the week before the election. Daily, a cartoon figure at the bottom of the front page labeled "the public," threw an apple at "Dock" Scheumack, reminding voters of the importance of their vote. "Today's apple. Put the charter amendment into effect—Get a trained city manager for Phoenix." "Today's apple. Elect a ticket you won't be ashamed of—quit apologizing for your city government." "Today's apple. It's your city, you know—Are you going to let bosses run it?" "Today's apple. Is your tax bill too high? Give a trained city manager a chance instead of a boss."[50]

Charter Government's campaign met with resounding success. Voters swept all of its candidates into office by wide margins. "CHARTER TICKET SWEEPS CITY" a banner headline in the *Republic* screamed. The following day, the Charter Government Committee very publicly disbanded in an announcement on the paper's front page.[51] The new city council proceeded to hire a new city manager, Ray Wilson, from Kansas City and demanded Deppe's resignation. When Deppe refused, arguing that "My resignation would only give substance to the illusion of mismanagement, bossism, graft, corruption, inefficiency, and incompetence that has been successfully created by politically ambitious individuals and a ruthless, unprincipled, power-seeking press," Goldwater cut his statement short, and the council unanimously fired him.[52]

Voices beyond Phoenix recognized Charter Government's victory as a dramatic turning point. "Phoenix Makes a New Start," declared *National Municipal Review* shortly after the election. Despite its pledge to disband, the Charter Government Committee did not disappear. Rather, it reformed two years later to nominate a new slate of candidates, and continued to disband and reappear at election time until 1975. During that time, only one candidate won election to the city council without Charter Government's endorsement. Charter Government's defeat of boss rule became part of the narrative of local politics, a just-so story that explained why Phoenix's businessmen dominated local politics without, supposedly, interfering in its workings. As Mayor Jack Williams explained in his 1959 farewell address, "Charter Government is not in existence now, although two Chairmen were selected when it disbanded, so that, Phoenix-like, it can be reborn at election time."[53]

Metropolitan preferences in federal policy making aided and abetted Charter Government's political dominance. As home builders subdivided the landscape of former farm fields north of the Grand Canal, Phoenix gained more than 200,000 new residents between 1955 and 1960, a population increase that, in its own right, doubled Phoenix's 1950 population, driving the center of electoral gravity in Phoenix ever northward.

In the 1949 election, Charter Government candidates had campaigned in nonwhite parts of the city, appealing for votes at Carver High School and in the predominantly Mexican American Marcos de Niza Homes. As almost entirely white northern Phoenix gained more and more votes, candidates visited neighborhoods in South Phoenix less and less frequently. The structure of local elections, at-large elections held in noncongressional years, discouraged participation as well. Municipal officials made voting itself difficult through onerous registration procedures and aggressive enforcement of literacy tests. In addition to a state law that required registration four months before primaries and six weeks before general elections, Phoenix required annual registration for municipal elections with the only site of registration being the city clerk's office downtown. In her study of reform governments in the Southwest, Amy Bridges found voter participation rates in poor, predominantly nonwhite Phoenix precincts falling below 10 percent in municipal elections, as opposed to 25 percent in more affluent areas to the north.[54] Charter Government, Bridges wrote, created a voting public that resembled a wealthy suburb "in social settings that were considerably more diverse. This was accomplished by writing the rules to win, by organizing to mobilize prospective supporters and bring them to the polls, and by failing to annex communities less likely to support incumbent regimes."[55]

The result could be seen in the unpaved streets and unconnected sewers that *New Republic* reporter Andrew Kopkind found in 1964. The funding that could pave those roads or complete those sewers went toward luring new residents and industry. In the years after 1949, municipal officials and the Chamber of Commerce coordinated their activities ever more intimately. Municipal dollars flowed into the Chamber's junkets that brought reporters from business magazines and industry journals to the Valley of the Sun. With local politics securely in Charter Government's grasp, Paul Fannin, Frank Snell, or Walter Bimson could pursue manufacturing with generous offers, secure in the knowledge that handshake promises would be honored by the City Council. A 1963 report prepared by the El Paso Chamber lamented that in Phoenix, "industrial scouts are met at the plane, entertained, offered free land, tax deals, and an electorate willing to approve millions in business-backed bond issues" while "El Paso does nothing." "Unless we start hustling after new industry," the report continued, "we're going to wind up in serious trouble."[56]

The "trouble" the El Paso Chamber identified reflected the new politics of metropolitan growth that Phoenix's businessmen helped create. In these politics, the public-private coalitions that governed Sunbelt cities competed against one another and their Northeastern and Midwestern counterparts to attract capital. Growth liberalism's metropolitan preferences for subdivision enabled the creation of these politics of metropolitan

competition by off-loading many of the risks of growth to the federal
government, while its emphasis for local control empowered Phoenix's
businessmen, who drove the search for new manufacturers. Competitive growth politics operated on a different logic, however, than that of
growth liberalism. Where the advocates of growth liberalism's selective
credit programs envisioned their policies as creating broadly distributed
wealth, at least among white Americans, the metropolitan competition
for industry was a zero-sum game. In the years following the election of
Charter Government, competitive growth politics would tear at the New
Deal's social compact.

COMPETITIVE GROWTH POLITICS

"A lot of it was punt and pray," Patrick Downey recalled. Beginning in
the late 1940s, Downey was out on the road, part of a three-man IDC
team with Adrian Babcock of CALAPCO and APS, and Floyd Raines,
assistant director of the Chamber. Traveling to different prospective companies, they presented the benefits of what they began to call Phoenix's
"business climate" through "extensive charts, maps, dwelling on the tax
situation, dwelling on the weather, on the lack of rainfall. . . . That coupled with labor, the union situation." Downey described the process as an
endless series of meetings, working through corporate chains of authority
until the three finally presented to an executive with power over locational decisions. Downey described the process as staid. Bob Saback, an
executive at Valley Bank, had different memories: "All I can say, we did
everything we could to attract funds into Arizona. . . . We had a . . . team
of guys that were all goers—man, they could drink all night and into the
day and just hit the road and go and blow 24 hours a day, seven days a
week." Going so far as to suggest that some activities skirted the borders
of legality, Saback told his interviewer, "Ok—all right—that's how the
west was won."[57]

Even before Charter Government's victory, the IDC team experienced
their first success. In 1949, after what Downey almost certainly overesti-
mated as five years of appeals, Motorola announced it was relocating a
research and development laboratory to Phoenix.[58] It was not until the
mid-1950s, however, that high-tech manufacturing became dominant. In
1951, AiResearch reestablished its factory manufacturing high-altitude
switches close to Sky Harbor Airport. In 1955, Motorola built a second plant to manufacture semiconductors. By 1962, the company would
add two more plants, in its Solid State Systems and Military Electronics
divisions. In 1955, Sperry Rand established a subsidiary, Sperry Phoenix, to manufacture missile guidance systems. That year, manufacturing

surpassed agriculture as the Phoenix metropolitan area's leading source of income. The following year, General Electric moved its entire computing division to a plant between Phoenix and Tempe. In the early 1960s, Unidynamics, Western Electric, the Nuclear Corporation of America, and Cannon Electric all built the sprawling, low-slung factories typical of postwar manufacturing architecture.[59]

Their companies' executives offered testimonials in new promotional literature intended to draw additional companies. David Thomas, president of the Nuclear Corporation of America, testified that his experience had been the same: Phoenix "is an area free of the strife and problems normally associated with larger industrial areas." J. E. Hickman, plant manager at Kaiser Aerospace, stated "A modern industry awareness demonstrated by city and state government contributes much toward maintaining a healthy business climate." H. W. Welch, general manager of Motorola's telecommunications division, echoed Hickman's words, "The cooperative attitude of state and municipal employees . . . provide[s] an excellent business climate for Motorola's divisions in Phoenix."[60] Another Motorola executive, testifying to the ease of drawing good employees to Phoenix, claimed that they received twenty-five applications at their branch plant in Phoenix for every one they received at their Chicago and Riverside branches.[61]

Downey, Babcock, and Raines made their pitches to high-tech companies that were increasingly flush with federal money. Just five months after Charter Government swept Phoenix's City Council, the National Security Council issued NSC-68, warning its classified audience that "the cold war is in fact a real war in which the survival of the free world is at stake" and calling for "the rapid building up of the political, economic, and military strength of the free world."[62] Two months later, the Korean War began. Defense spending escalated rapidly, growing from $79 billion in 1949 to $225 billion in 1953. During the Korean War, most military dollars went to established industrial centers for manufacture of combat equipment. Following the war's end, however, Eisenhower's "New Look," with its emphasis on air power and nuclear weaponry, shifted the bulk of military spending to the air force. While intended, in part, for cost effectiveness, the New Look saw only a marginal reduction in defense spending. Military spending fell briefly to $197 billion in 1956 before returning to Korean War levels by 1958. More important, by shifting the most contracting from the army to the air force, the New Look changed the nature of defense spending. The army's focus on reliable heavy combat equipment led it to maintain design and development responsibilities in-house. Seeking technological innovation, however, the air force left research and design responsibility to the firms with which it contracted. These policies created at least ideological distance between federal spending and defense manufacturing, as did the continued paeans of companies such as General Electric to the values of private enterprise. As Ann Markusen has contended, high-tech industries' "impeccable free-enterprise viewpoint removed most of the stigma from the surge in public spending that the arms revolution entailed."[63]

Contracting policies during the New Look era also encouraged locational mobility among defense contractors. Defense procurement contracts allowed companies to charge the federal government for the costs of recruiting and resettling skilled laborers interregionally. Furthermore, such contracts permitted these companies to include those expenses in their cost base. Since contracts functioned on a cost-plus basis, in which companies could take a certain percentage of profit above and beyond their expenses, these policies actually encouraged the movement of skilled labor from region to region. "One might even argue," Markusen suggests, "that the government has been running a massive for-profit population resettlement program in the postwar period."[64] Cost-plus contracts encouraged companies to seek out locations where state and local governments imposed low levels of corporate obligation for policies such as unemployment insurance, workman's compensation, and welfare spending. Beginning in 1951, the Office of Defense Mobilization also ordered that military facilities and defense industries be dispersed away from existing industrial centers to protect against atomic attack. Announcing the policy, it explained that "the dispersion (or deployment in space) of *new* plant development for war-supporting industries can make American production less vulnerable to attack." As a result, plants located in "isolated" areas began receiving preference in contracting.[65]

Dispersal policy granted Phoenix an additional "natural advantage." Soon, the IDC's promotional brochures began detailing the impediments that Phoenix's location, which required "maximum enemy penetration," posed to atomic attack. "Phoenix is surrounded by open desert country which offers no screening for low-flying aircraft," the Chamber of Commerce explained in *Industry Finds Its Place in the Sun*. "The submarine-launched surface-to-surface missile threat is of significance. However, being 400 miles from the coast, Phoenix takes full advantage of the degradation of accuracy with increasing range of . . . guidance systems." Moreover, the brochure suggested, the low density of Phoenix's subdivisions and their culture of outdoor living created a landscape in which manufacturing would be able to recover rapidly, even should Soviet bombers and missiles manage to strike the Valley of the Sun: "Because of the informal, leisurely, outdoor type of living, the population is also well dispersed," the Chamber suggested. "All this will minimize the impact on the production capability of Phoenix in the event of an enemy attack."[66]

While the Chamber's claims that Phoenix possessed natural advantage against atomic attack were unique, cities across the South and West and states across the nation duplicated its appeals to manufacturers based on quality of life, labor peace, and low taxation. In *Fortune* and *Businessweek*, advertisements for Phoenix claiming "This isn't just a vacation spot, Frank!" shared pages with ads informing readers that "This summer, a city larger than Detroit will move to Colorado," that San Diego was "where climate, labor and management form a profitable team," and that "Labor and management agree on Los Angeles." Ads called on companies to "Plant the future in Georgia" and notice that "Industry is turning to Iowa, where comfortable living means happy workers."[67] The advertisements signaled the new politics born at the junction of private manufacturing capital whose mobility was underwritten and encouraged by the Defense Department and local attempts to attract that capital and fix it in space in the form of buildings and jobs.

The presence of new manufacturing reverberated in the local economy. Like the federally underwritten middle-class homeowners of the previous chapter, able to generate interest income for local banks, sales to local retailers, and charges to local utilities, new manufacturing plants represented capital fixed in space that by their presence generated more capital. Indeed, a 1964 Chamber study found that each manufacturing job in Phoenix supported four other jobs in construction, utilities, and other service industries. A company like Motorola, with 8,500 employees, stood to create 34,000 additional jobs. By contrast, tourism, the study estimated, supported only one additional job.[68]

The value of such jobs, as the above advertisements indicate, made them objects of determined metropolitan competition. Almost all aspects of public life in Phoenix came to revolve, at least partially, around growth politics. The creation of the Phoenix Museum of Art provides just one example. In 1959 Frank Snell, Walter Bimson, Orme Lewis, and Mayor Sam Mardian devised a "Case for the Phoenix Art Museum." This project interested Lewis and Bimson, at least, for nonpolitical reasons. Both Lewis and Bimson were avid collectors of high art, owning impressive collections of both European neoclassical and American modern art, including works by Jasper Johns and Robert Rauschenberg, that they eventually loaned to the museum. In their "Case," which appeared in the *Arizona Republic* beside a supportive editorial, however, they argued the museum represented a vital step in the continuation of Phoenix's growth. "Are we content to continue to make rapid strides in population and industrial growth? But to permit our cultural development to lag embarrassingly behind?" Mayor Mardian was later more blunt in his reasons for supporting the museum: "A community needs cultural activities to attract the type of people that Phoenix wants. Electronics people. They'll support these institutions."[69] In short, those boosters involved in founding the Phoenix Art Museum believed modernism would help create industrial modernity. Counteracting beliefs that "cosmopolitan New Yorkers" saw Phoenix as "a wild and woolly West" remained an important project of Phoenix's businessmen, leading to the creation of cultural institutions such as the Phoenix Symphony and the Phoenix Shakespeare Festival. It also led Walter Bimson to provide financial support for Frank Lloyd Wright, who maintained his winter studio, Taliesen West, in Scottsdale. "Walter would buy," one of Bimson's deputies recalled, "a set of plans a couple of times a year just because Frank Lloyd Wright . . . needed money."[70] Wright's buildings, including several Valley National Bank branches, served as vivid examples of a new type of desert modernism emerging in Phoenix, a symbol, as the Chamber's advertising committee put it, "of the modern amenities that we have."[71]

Sperry Rand's employees apparently had such concerns. The Long Island–based company had not originally considered Phoenix when searching for a site for its new aviation electronics plant. Instead, an industrial relocation firm, one of many that sprang up in the early 1950s to advise firms after Defense Department policies made mobility financially advantageous, suggested Phoenix.[72] Advertising, Frank Snell recalled, played little part in gaining the attention of Sperry's executives.[73] Company leaders faced internal resistance against a move to Phoenix, as, according to one account, executives and skilled workers alike feared moving "to an isolated desert city."[74]

The process of competitive growth politics, however, worked dramatically to Phoenix's advantage. Snell remembered that Phoenix's right-to-work law turned the tide. "The Sperry people in particular . . . told me that their . . . productivity was so far ahead of what they could do it to Long Island . . . because of non-union."[75] So too, however, did the close connections between the Phoenix Chamber and local government, allowing rapid public policy decisions to meet terms that Sperry's executives established. At the end of their initial communications with the IDC, Sperry's executives had presented a list of demands, including a secure plant site, property tax abatements, and improvements to Deer Valley Airport, through which the company expected to conduct most of its operations. Within seventy-two hours, Phoenix's boosters responded, raising $650,000 from public and private sources and meeting all of Sperry's terms. Public policy changes in the state legislature, increasingly influenced by the growing power of a resurgent Arizona Republican Party with its base in Maricopa County, also pulled Sperry to Phoenix. As the company deliberated, the legislature passed a law eliminating state sales taxes on goods manufactured for sale to the federal government.[76]

As Sperry's case suggests, in order to attract companies whose relocation became an object of local political interest across the nation, advertising and the direct personal appeals made by Downey, Babcock, and Raines at corporate headquarters or the Thunderbirds at the Phoenix Country Club were not enough. Rather, public policies luring manufacturing industry with promises of control over workers, low taxes, land grants, and other enticements, ultimately shaped most corporate decision-making. As Elizabeth Shermer has recently argued, such policies eventually reshaped American politics. As metropolitan areas in the South and West adopted governing structures similar to Phoenix's, they gained a competitive advantage over Northeastern and Midwestern polities that had incorporated organized labor and industrial regulation into their political structures during the Progressive Era and New Deal.[77]

The unequal results of these policies could be seen in the dilapidated houses and scant social services of South Phoenix. Even as Mayor Sam Mardian campaigned for a municipal bond for the Phoenix Art Museum and helped arrange enticements for companies like Sperry Rand, he rejected a HUD matching grant to rehabilitate slum housing. "Spending money on housing isn't our business," said Mardian, arguing that improving private housing remained purely the place of the private sector.[78] Mardian, himself a subdivision developer, represented perfectly Charter Government's embrace of the metropolitan preferences of the growth liberal state even as they rejected its social welfare provisions. Federal actions that underwrote metropolitan growth—mortgage guarantees, military dispersal policies, or, as we will see in the following chapter, policies to make energy supplies on federal land available to metropolitan utilities—represented acceptable uses of state power. Local governments benefiting from those policies, however, had no compunction to pursue the social welfare provisions that growth liberals believed mitigated the unequal nature of capitalist development. Instead, as they came to understand industrial growth as in the public interest, they clawed away at those provisions to achieve advantage within the broader competition for metropolitan growth.

"INDUSTRY, ENERGY, PROGRESS"

Metropolitan growth politics also determined the practices of the region's electrical utilities. CALAPCO and APS possessed deep ties with the leadership of Charter Government. Frank Snell served as the chairman of the utility's executive committee, and Walter Bimson served as an important financial advisor. APS's president, Walter Lucking, and its CEO, William Reilly, both served terms as Chamber president. CALAPCO and then

APS employed Adrian Babcock, one of the three IDC representatives who traveled the nation promoting Phoenix. The utility's annual reports read much the same as the IDC's promotional material. Arizona was, APS's first annual report in 1953 declared, a "Frontier with a future." Manufacturing was, it announced, "becoming increasingly aware that there is plenty of room in Arizona for industries that want to grow and prosper with the West."[79] Later in the decade, the utility produced its own promotional material, including "Industry Views of Phoenix and the Valley of the Sun," which contained testimonials from executives about the low cost of electricity and the opportunities for growth they had discovered in metropolitan Phoenix. So that the point was not lost, the first page of the pamphlet featured a bold headline, "Industry, Energy, and Progress," and promised: "No matter what form it may take, Public Service pledges to provide adequate supplies of ENERGY—economically—to meet the future requirements of Arizona's dynamic progress."[80]

New industries represented valuable new consumers for APS. Residential users tended to use electricity in peaks. In early mornings, residential consumption rose as people awoke, turned on percolators, radios, and electric skillets. It moderated in midday before spiking again at night when people turned on lights and televisions and other appliances. Such peaks could cause residential use to vary 60 percent or more over the course of a day. If utility service consisted solely of residential customers, utilities would either have to build capacity far in excess of normal demand to account for such peak usage periods or purchase large amounts of so-called "peaking power," which was priced higher than standard "base power," from other utilities. Manufacturing industry, by contrast, used electricity at a relatively constant rate. With production occurring around the clock, frequently in windowless plants that required constant artificial lighting and air conditioning, manufacturers demanded a steady stream of electricity. Supplying manufacturers allowed utilities to avoid the dramatic drops in electrical demand. The resulting flatter demand curve allowed utilities to run generating plants to near maximum capacity, thus achieving greater economies of scale. The more reliable demand of industrial consumers therefore made them valuable elements of utilities' grow-and-build strategy. By steadily increasing their number of industrial customers, a utility could be sure that its advance investment in power plants would not be wasted, with an idle plant dragging down the company's bottom line.[81]

APS's pricing policies for industrial consumers reflected the value of such industries. APS, like most utilities, offered manufacturers significantly lower prices on electricity than other users. The Federal Power Commission's statistical survey of utilities makes it difficult to determine the details of industrial usage and pricing until 1961, when the FPC separated commercial and industrial uses into separate categories. Analysis of annual revenue and electrical use between 1961 and 1965 show residential electrical users paying an average of 2.65 mills ($.0265) per kilowatt hour and commercial users paying 2.2 mills, while industrial rates averaged 1.10 mills. In 1961, the first year such statistics are available, industrial users consumed 41 percent of the electricity APS sold but contributed only 27 percent of its revenues. Residential users, by contrast, consumed 17 percent of APS's electricity but contributed payments of 28 percent. In short, industry as a sector contributed the least amount of revenue to APS, even though it used the most electricity.[82]

Even within an industry where such pricing policies were standard, APS's price differential represented a regional extreme. A comparison with five other private utilities nearby shows APS having the lowest industrial electricity prices in the region by at least 10 percent. A heavy industrial user of electricity in 1961 would have paid Tucson Gas and Electric $429 for 20,000 kilowatt-hours (kwh) of electricity while the same user location in APS's service area would have paid only $351 for the same amount. The only utilities with lower industrial prices were public utilities: SRP and the Los Angeles Department of Power and Water. At the same time, APS had the region's highest residential and commercial prices. A heavy commercial customer, a supermarket for example, would have paid TG&E $131 for 6,000 kwh in 1961 and APS $169; for a heavy residential user, say Herbert Leggett with his air-conditioned lifestyle, the difference would have been $103 for 500 kwh from TG&E versus $111 for the same amount from APS. Reflecting the deep investment APS had made in the attraction of manufacturing industry to Phoenix, the utility used its residential customers to subsidize the cost of electricity to industrial users to a greater extent than any other investor-owned utility in the Southwest.[83]

SRP had many of the same characteristics as APS. Its executives, too, were active in the Chamber of Commerce. Like Walter Lucking, APS's president, R. J. McMullin served a term as a Chamber officer in the 1950s, and as secretary in 1955 and 1956. SRP showed a similar margin between residential, commercial, and industrial prices. SRP's prices, however, ran slightly below those of APS in all categories. Where APS charged an average of 1.1 mills per kwh for industrial customers, for example, SRP charged 0.9. This difference reflected many factors: the lower amount of bonded debt held by SRP, its status as a Bureau of Reclamation preference customer, which allowed it first claim on inexpensive power from Parker and Davis Dams, and its tax-free status.[84]

That price difference represented something else, a marginal difference that could represent, for industries using hundreds of millions of kwh annual, a significant cost savings. It represented, in short, the possibility for intrametropolitan competition for manufacturing within a metropolitan political culture obsessed with its own marginal advantages. The industrial price differences between the two utilities remained relatively unimportant during the 1950s, as new industries flocked into the service areas of both utilities. During the brief recession of 1960 and 1961, however, it sparked substantial conflict between the utilities for the first time. While the rate of increase in electrical consumption by SRP's industrial customers slowed to between 3 percent and 4 percent in both years, APS's industrial consumption actually fell by 2 percent annually. While it is difficult to prove conclusively, the divergence in the two utilities' industrial consumption in the early 1960s suggests that virtually all the agricultural land in APS's service area had been redeveloped by that time and that new factories had moved onto the farm fields of SRP's territory. In the following years, commercial and residential consumption formed a greater and greater share of APS's business. Indeed, by the late 1960s, commercial businesses consumed 34 percent of APS's electricity while industry had declined from a 41 percent to a 28 percent share in less than a decade. SRP, by comparison, saw steady increases in industrial consumption, rising from 24 percent to 34 percent of its share over the same period. In short, APS saw its efforts to draw industry to Phoenix go largely unrewarded, as industry located on the peripheral lands in SRP's service area, while APS increasingly served commercial and residential customers. This economic slowdown began to create fissures in the utilities' previously collegial relationship as APS questioned SRP's tax exemptions in particular and the wisdom of public power in general.[85]

SRP's distribution of electricity to its consumers highlights the nature of change that the efforts to attract manufacturing brought to postwar Phoenix. In 1947, irrigators formed SRP's largest electrical consumers. Irrigated farms used electrical pumps to draw water from deep wells and to pump water from canals to the high point on their property. Commercial, industrial, and residential customers combined consumed almost 20 percent less electricity than did irrigators. Through the late 1940s and early 1950s, that gap actually increased as farmers brought additional wells into production. In 1954, the year before manufacturing succeeded agriculture to become the state's leading industry, irrigators consumed a whopping 57 percent of the utility's electricity. From that point on, however, this percentage fell steadily. In four years, it fell by half. Two years later, in 1960, industrial use surpassed irrigation as SRP's leading electrical consumer. By the end of the 1960s, the percentage of SRP's electricity used for agriculture had fallen to 7.5 percent. Those numbers told the story of the valley's transformation. A small city "set in the green carpets of year-round crops" had grown to encompass the entire valley. By then, metropolitan growth politics had transformed the agricultural Salt River Valley into the high-tech Valley of the Sun.[86]

INDUSTRIAL GARDEN

By the late 1950s, the results of this transformation stood throughout metropolitan Phoenix in the form of low-slung factories. On Grand Canyon Highway in northern Phoenix, Sperry Phoenix manufactured flight-control systems for NASA and the air force in its 220,000-square-foot plant. AiResearch's 675,000-square-foot factory just north of Sky Harbor Airport manufactured jet engines and missile-control systems. West of Phoenix in Litchfield Park, Goodyear Aerospace built airborne electronic systems and missile components in its 1-million-square-foot facility. And Motorola's plants dotted the valley: a 300,000-square-foot military electronics plant in Scottsdale, a 90,000-square-foot research laboratory near Arizona State University in Tempe, and a 1.1-million-square-foot semiconductor plant, a building larger than twenty football fields, northeast of downtown. Other companies that formed key elements of what Dwight Eisenhower had labeled "the military-industrial complex" in his farewell address—Raytheon, Honeywell, General Electric—lay scattered about the valley.[87]

Some of these facilities, like AiResearch's factory near Sky Harbor, were in semi-industrial districts. Most, however, lay amid subdivisions. Single-story, white, surrounded by parking lots and green lawns, the buildings appeared nothing like the images of industry that most Americans knew. On their perimeters, dedicated substations converted electricity from the transmission voltage of 34 kilovolts to the lower voltages needed to power lighting, manufacturing equipment, and the massive air-conditioning units that sat atop factory roofs. Air conditioning was one of the major talking points of Phoenix's recruiters. Frank Snell recalled that he would reassure visitors that "you could air condition a . . . whole factory without any problem. Western Electric came here with acres, almost, of a plant and air conditioned the whole thing, so that the whole thing . . . felt just the same inside in winter, spring, summer and fall."[88]

The Federal Power Commission's annual statistical survey of public and private utilities does not provide definitive ways to determine the amount of electricity consumed by the new industries that moved to Phoenix in the 1950s and 1960s. Until 1960, the FPC combined commercial and industrial businesses into a single category. The combined numbers can, however, provide a basis for conjecture. During the 1950s, the amount of electricity consumed by APS's commercial and industrial customers never grew at a rate of less than 6 percent. Its growth rate saw marked spikes of 21 percent in 1952, corresponding with Motorola's expansion, and 27 percent in 1958, corresponding with the opening of Sperry Phoenix's plant. SRP's growth rate told a different version of seemingly the same story. Its growth rates remained low during the early 1950s, indeed, as low as 0.1 percent in 1954 as most manufacturing growth remained contained within APS's territory. In 1955, however, those rates exploded. That year, SRP's commercial and industrial consumption jumped 74 percent as Motorola opened its military electronics plant in Scottsdale. The gross total of commercial and industrial electricity consumption also hints at the transformation of the valley. Between 1949, when Charter Government took over, and 1970, that number increased over 1,100 percent.[89]

Such numbers make it easy to see the 1950s and 1960s as an era in which growing demand and stable management created security for Phoenix's utilities. Look more closely, however, and turmoil and instability begin to emerge. In the years before CALAPCO began its grow-and-build strategy in the late 1940s, the utility had purchased upward of 80 percent of its electricity in some years from other sources, mainly the Bureau of Reclamation's power plants at Parker and Davis Dams. Expanding Phoenix Power Plant dropped its purchases to 20 percent of its energy in 1951 but it suddenly jumped back to 50 percent the following year. The construction of Ocotillo and Saguaro lowered it again to 19 percent in 1956, but then it varied dramatically in the following years: 33 percent in 1957, 18 percent in 1958, 43 percent in 1959.[90] As much as utility executives liked to believe they could predict and control demand, events remained beyond their control. In 1957, a short circuit at a switching station south of Phoenix prevented electricity at Ocotillo Power Plant from reaching the city for two weeks, forcing the company to purchase half of its electricity from Utah Power and Light, which accounted for a quarter of the company's electrical purchases that year.[91] In 1959 a fire at Saguaro blacked out much of Phoenix and knocked the power plant out of commission for a month, forcing APS to actually import power across Bureau of Reclamation power lines from Southern California. Despite the promises grow-and-build made of secure management of electricity across time and space, the daily practice of supplying power was anything but secure.[92]

Fuel supply, energy itself, represented the largest source of instability facing APS in the 1950s. To supply Saguaro, Ocotillo, and Phoenix Power Plant with natural gas, both APS and SRP had separately agreed to long-term contracts with El Paso Natural Gas, which built two new pipelines to replace an aging line traveling from El Paso's fields in West Texas across southern New Mexico. For El Paso Natural Gas, the grow-and-build strategy employed by both utilities in central Arizona represented only a fraction of its own growth in the decade after the war. El Paso had signed contracts with several major utilities in Southern California in the late 1940s, as those utilities pursued expansion policies similar to those of APS. Buoyed by the boom in Southern California, El Paso had become the second largest natural gas company in the nation, selling almost 650 million cubic feet of gas per day by 1954.[93]

As customers of El Paso Natural Gas, APS and SRP occupied a peripheral place in a system of energy supply and regulation over which they held no control. In 1953 the rate of gas flowing from El Paso's fields in West Texas began to slow. El Paso expanded its exploration for gas beginning a search in newly opened fields in northwestern New Mexico, but its supplies remained unstable. The Federal Power Commission warned El Paso in 1954 that it needed to find more reliable supplies. Despite such warnings, federal regulation of interstate gas transmission was ineffective at balancing supply and demand, with the Federal Power Commission relying on an unsustainable policy that encouraged dramatic increases in sales during periods of growth and tended to lead companies like El Paso to become overcommitted. In early 1955 both APS and SRP began planning new power plants as industrial demand spiked. El Paso, however, informed the utilities that it could not guarantee enough natural gas to supply any additional plants.[94] Even as Charter Government and the Phoenix Chamber were winning the competition for growth, its utilities were losing a competition for natural gas to the massive market in Los Angeles. The story of Boulder Dam was, in a sense, repeating itself.

SRP had a solution at hand. While El Paso Natural Gas posed limits on the energy flowing into central Arizona, Congress was considering legislation authorizing a new project on the upper Colorado River. Intended to finally secure the upper basin's rights to half the river's water, the Colorado River Storage Project (CRSP) proposed several new dams on the upper river, including the largest at Glen Canyon on the Arizona-Utah border, an even more isolated location than the by-then named Hoover Dam. Glen Canyon, like Hoover, was to be a "cash-register dam," built not to supply irrigation or drinking water but to fund CRSP's broader developments in the river's upper basin. And Phoenix represented the closest metropolitan area to the dam other than Las Vegas. While the power was technically reserved for use in the river's upper basin, the Bureau of Reclamation ruled that SRP could claim 100 megawatts of firm, or guaranteed, power by agreeing to fund construction of a steam-fired generating plant of equal capacity in the upper basin. SRP could purchase, Reclamation officials predicted, as much additional power at the peaking rate charged to preference customers as it required.[95]

APS had no such immediate solution. In theory, a lack of the energy needed to pursue grow-and-build did not immediately imperil APS. In the short term, the utility could have drawn upon the electricity available through interconnections with Utah Power and Light and SRP. In practice, such an approach would have been disastrous. Without the ability to build new plants to meet growing demand, APS would have faced rapidly increasing payments to the other utilities for electricity purchases without its own sales to offset the purchases. Neighboring utilities would likely have limited future interconnections with APS, since its generating capacity provided little ability to balance their own peak loads. The lack of energy would have also alarmed financial analysts accustomed to evaluating utilities according to the terms of grow-and-build. APS would have faced difficulty gaining access to capital, leading to lower stock prices, higher interest-rate charges on bonds, and limited interest from investors.[96]

In June 1955 APS commissioned a study from the Stanford Research Institute (SRI), an independent arm of the university that conducted nonpartisan social-scientific analysis on a contract basis. The utility asked for an evaluation of potential energy supplies in the Southwest, including dam sites claimed by the state of Arizona in the 1950s, that could form reliable supplies and that APS could rely on for at least twenty-five years. The report, returned to APS two months later, offered several conclusions. First, it suggested that the supply of natural gas available to APS would remain limited for the foreseeable future. While new discoveries had been made in New Mexico, SRI concluded, "the overwhelming demand of the Southern California Market is likely to constrain the possibilities for exclusive use of this source." Second, it concluded that electric generator design had achieved near maximal efficiency improvements. For a half-century, generators had been producing more and more electricity from less and less fuel. SRI, correctly, determined that efficiency improvements had slowed since 1950. Scale increases—large jumps in the size of individual generating units—rather than more efficient generators would henceforth be the primary means to achieve economies of scale that would lower the price of electricity.[97]

Finally, SRI suggested APS utilize a new fuel. Recent surveys commissioned by the Bureau of Indian Affairs had shown large deposits of coal on the Navajo and Hopi Reservations. While this coal had been utilized locally, the report explained that "transportation difficulties in the rugged territory in which these deposits are located, . . . the generalized movement away from coal to water power and natural gas in the western states," as well as "the stigma coal has in modern society as a dirty fuel," had heretofore limited its appeal. Improvements in long-distance electrical transmission, SRI suggested, promised to surmount these difficulties. Indeed, its researchers referenced a Bureau of Reclamation report linking western population centers with intermountain coal supplies via a "500,000-volt system" that would deliver what the Bureau of Reclamation had called "coal by wire." Such a system, adapted by APS, would enable access to an almost infinite amount of energy. Long-term price trends also favored coal. The FPC, which regulated interstate pipelines, was allowing the price of gas to rise slightly above the rate of inflation. In contrast, SRI reported coal costs were falling as railroads switched to diesel locomotives and many manufacturing industries switched to electricity for power. These cost changes would soon bring coal to a par with natural gas as a fuel for generating electricity. By 1961, SRI predicted, it would take $0.223 of natural gas and $0.265 of coal to produce one million BTUs, the standard measurement for heating the boilers of electrical generators. By 1965, SRI estimated that electricity would be cheaper to produce at coal-fired mine-mouth power plants than at natural-gas-powered plants. Finally, coal had one further advantage. Unlike natural gas, it was not subject to regulation by the Federal Power Commission, allowing utilities much greater control over cost increases. By signing long-term leases with mining companies, electric utilities could guarantee a fixed-cost fuel supply.[98]

APS received the study enthusiastically. Explaining the plan to a *Los Angeles Times* reporter writing a series of articles about the future of the electrical power industry in the Southwest, APS chairman Walter Lucking stated that "The plan has feasibility—we have determined that—and lots of possibilities." Lucking was so enthusiastic, in fact, that an eager headline editor for the *Los Angeles Times* printed that a coal-fired power plant was already planned for the Four Corners region.[99] It was not, but there was reason for Lucking's enthusiasm. Since American Power and Light's dissolution, CALAPCO, and then Arizona Public Service, had always faced an essential dilemma in their strategy of grow-and-build. The broader strategies of growth that brought hundreds of thousands of new residents and millions of dollars of manufacturing capital to Phoenix had created nearly boundless possibilities for steadily increasing electrical demand in the energy-intensive landscape of subdivisions, factories, and shopping malls. APS, however, had never secured the boundless supplies of electricity needed to meet that demand. The coal supplies of northern Arizona, though, were ample enough, according to the Bureau of Reclamation account that SRI cited, to "last one thousand years." And, aside from some small local uses, the coal was virtually untapped. If APS could develop that coal, it could secure its future profitability. All that was required was agreement with the federal authorities that held the coal reserves in trust for the Navajo people who lived on the land atop the coal supplies.

"We did not want dirty industries: we were very particular about that," Frank Snell told his interviewer for the Phoenix History Project. Indeed, the Chamber of Commerce filled its promotional materials with code words describing the types of industry it sought to attract to Phoenix:

"light," "clean," "suitable," and "smoke-free." One publication explained, "The emphasis with industry in metropolitan Phoenix is on cleanliness. Here no ugly smokestacks insult the Arizona sky, no growl of monotonous machines harshly stamp their audible imprint."[100] Preventing pollution within Phoenix was not an empty slogan. In 1961, municipal officials rezoned an area of West Phoenix to block a planned oil refinery while Lew Haas worked to steer industries that "might not 'fit' Phoenix," in the words of one Chamber member, elsewhere in Arizona.[101]

Phoenix's boosters used "clean," however, to refer to the aesthetics of industry. The actual production process of the high-tech industries that flocked to Phoenix was anything but environmentally friendly. Plants for Motorola, Honeywell, AiReseach, and other companies may not have spewed smoke into the air, but they used highly toxic chemicals—trichloroethane, chlorinated solvents, and methoxyethanol among others—which produced serious adverse health effects, including liver and kidney failure, damage to circulatory and reproductive systems, and numerous cancers. In 1982, Motorola revealed that trichloroethane from its Fifty-Second Street semiconductor plant had been leaking from an underground holding tank for an undetermined period of time. Investigators from the EPA discovered a plume of volatile organic compounds that extended in the soil and groundwater several miles to the plant's west. Following the EPA's investigations, the "clean" factory in the garden was ruled a Superfund site.[102]

Chemical plumes, however, were not the only way in which the factory's aesthetics belied its ecological effects. Completed in 1962, the factory received most of its electricity from a different source than El Paso Natural Gas's wells in the Permian Basin. Instead, its power lines received electricity that originated far to the north, from coal on the Navajo Reservation, where it was set afire in Four Corners Power Plant and transmitted—"coal by wire" some called it—to the industrial and residential consumers of Phoenix. The political process of removing that coal from the ground and lighting it afire in Four Corners Power Plant involved a different kind of growth politics, which is to say, boosters working not only in Phoenix, but also in Washington, D.C. It also meant new involvement with the politics and economics of the Indian reservations upon which energy was located. It also required a different type of recruitment—the courting, not of executives from Long Island, but of Indian officials from Window Rock. And this recruitment would be carried out with a different rhetoric. Rather than the language of competitive advantage, Phoenix's businessmen would speak of shared regionality, mutual modernization, and the broad benefits of "land freedom."

PART III

Supply

CHAPTER 4

Modernizing the Navajo

ON JULY 26, 1957, PAUL JONES AND ED LITTLEFIELD SAT ACROSS A CON-
ference table in the Navajo Council House, shuffling contracts back and
forth. As James Stewart, superintendent of the BIA's Navajo Agency
looked on, Jones, chairman of the Navajo Tribe, signed above the lines
marked "Lessor" while Littlefield, executive vice president and general
manager of Utah International Construction Company, signed as "Lessee."
The signed contracts gave Utah International permission to explore for
coal on 24,320 acres of the eastern portion of the Navajo Reservation, beginning in an area known locally as "Ram Springs." On the map appended
to the contracts, however, Ram Springs gained a new name, "Area #1 of the
Navajo Mine." The contracts laid out other terms of the agreement. Utah
Construction, one of the "Six Companies" that had built Boulder Dam,
would pay the tribe fifteen cents a ton for coal used on the reservation
and twenty cents for coal used beyond its borders. The company pledged
"to employ Navajo Indians when available in all positions for which they
are qualified in the judgment of the lessee" and "to work Indians, giving
priority to members of the Navajo Tribe, into skilled, technical, and other
higher jobs." The tribe and corporation also agreed "to cooperate with
each other to the fullest extent for the purpose of erecting a powerplant
on or adjacent to" the leased area, with the mutual understanding that
Utah International would make electricity available "at wholesale bus bar
rates to the Tribe" for use within the Reservation. Jones praised the new
partnership in the *Navajo Times*. "Working together with the companies
developing these resources, we will move into a future of self-determination
and self-sufficiency. These resources will provide the funds, employment
and energy that will make the Navajo Tribe a force in the Southwest."[1]

In the late 1940s and early 1950s, officials within the Interior Department's varying administrative agencies viewed the Colorado Plateau from
different perspectives. Looking for new energy supplies that could meet
the burgeoning demand of the metropolitan Southwest, Bureau of Reclamation officials saw a region rich with possibility. Water in the Colorado
River flowed within deep canyons, providing an ideal setting for new
hydroelectric dams. Beneath the Plateau's surface, massive coal reserves
held a nearly boundless supply of untapped energy. In reports that the
Stanford Research Institute would soon summarize for Arizona Public

Service, Reclamation officials posed coal on the Colorado Plateau as the future source of electrical power for the American West. By contrast, officials for the Bureau of Indian Affairs saw the same land as exhausted and unproductive. Witnessing nearly destitute Navajo Indians struggling to survive in the wake of stock reduction, they developed plans to move Navajos away from the Colorado Plateau.

In the mid-1950s, however, these divergent visions had aligned. As a Republican administration took office for the first time in twenty years, Phoenix businessmen gained access to the levers of power that federal authority held over public lands. They brought with them distinct ideas about the ways in which private development of public lands could meet both metropolitan demands for energy and resolve Indian underdevelopment. Even before Barry Goldwater arrived in Washington, he suggested that "unlocking" energy resources could prove the solution to Indian poverty. "In mineral wealth alone," Goldwater had written Howard Pyle, Arizona's newly elected Republican governor, in 1950, "there is enough . . . within the reservation boundaries to make our so-called Indian problems simple enough."[2] Indian leaders, as well, played a role in this re-envisioning of the Colorado Plateau. Eager to allow Navajos to stay on the reservation, tribal chairman Paul Jones and others viewed energy development as a potential means to create an autonomous future of wealth and power very different than his tribe's impoverished present. This vision of autonomy echoed the visions of John Collier and Jacob Morgan for the Navajo future. It would involve industry and manufacturing and a strong tribal government. It would also involve electrical modernization: "two lights in every hogan," one tribal official promised. Or, as Paul Jones told the Navajo Tribal Council in 1957, "it means a modern way of living."[3]

This alignment of energy development and Indian policy took material form by the early 1960s in a new infrastructure of coal mines and power plants on the Navajo Reservation, and of power lines that stretched across the Southwest. That infrastructure changed the landscape of the Navajo Reservation, not only in the deep gash of Navajo Mine, but in oil and natural gas wells and in power lines spoking outward from Four Corners Power Plant, a 175-megawatt power plant located on the Navajo Reservation in northwestern New Mexico. The political terms in which this infrastructure took place, terms set largely by the belief held by businessmen from Phoenix and elsewhere that the state should facilitate capital location, shaped this infrastructure's meaning and future. These politics meant that private companies, rather than the federal authorities, mined coal and set it alight. They meant that federal policy focused increasingly on unlocking resources on Navajo land rather than ensuring that employment accompanied development. And they meant that the

FIGURE 4.1. Navajo Mine with Four Corners Power Plant in the background. Utah Construction Company/Utah International Collection. Image courtesy of Special Collections Department, Stewart Library, Weber State University, Ogden, Utah. 1962.

power lines leading from Four Corners became the main supply for the electricity demanded in Phoenix, rather than primarily being a source of Navajo economic modernization. Finally, that infrastructure fixed these politics in space—in legal spaces as signed contracts and in material form on Southwest's landscape—as coal mines, power plants, and power lines began to mark the Colorado Plateau.

A 500,000-VOLT SYSTEM

The map on page 11 of the Bureau of Reclamation's 1952 *Study of Future Transmission for the West* showed the Colorado Plateau buried in coal. The black mass reached from northern Arizona into Wyoming and east into Colorado. To its south lay "6,600," the amount of quadrillion ("million billion" the caption helpfully noted) British Thermal Units of energy contained therein. To its west, a stack of coins, standing approximately on the location of Richfield, Utah, was labeled "20¢," the coal's cost at the mine per million BTUs. The map showed the Colorado Plateau containing both the most extensive coal deposits in the West, and the least expensive to mine. This, for the Bureau of Reclamation, was the West's energy future.[4]

The map symbolized the new role the Bureau of Reclamation assumed during the war as the chief planner of the West's electrical systems. During the war, electricity generated at Boulder and Parker Dams had proven vital to the war effort, providing the power that drove assembly lines in Southern California's burgeoning aviation industry. Indeed, defense manufacturing used so much power that Boulder Dam's generating capacity was fully consumed by 1942, twenty years earlier than Reclamation planners in the early 1930s had estimated.[5] The Bureau of Reclamation did more than just generate electricity. Its Transmission Division directed the construction of new power lines connecting Boulder and Parker Dam, as well as connecting Parker Dam to Phoenix, Los Angeles, and other "load centers." By the end of the war, officials in the Transmission Division claimed authority to manage the future development of the Western power grid.

Electrical service in the Southwest gave these planners reasons for concern. Across the region, signs of imminent power shortage grew alarming. Utilities from the Colorado's lower basin filed requests for power from Davis Dam that tripled the dam's generating capacity. "It is clear," a Reclamation planning report in 1947 stated, "that the industrial, agricultural, and domestic economy of these States will be severely impaired and retarded if additional sources of energy are not quickly developed."[6] Fearing such shortages, Reclamation officials recommended aggressive expansion. They called for construction of six new high dams, three on the main stream of the Colorado above Hoover Dam (renamed in 1947), that would produce an additional 3.7 million kilowatts of electricity. The program had little to do with Reclamation's original charge to provide irrigation water. Indeed, the plan earmarked power from only one of the new dams for an irrigation project. Bridge Canyon Dam, just downstream from the Grand Canyon, would, in Reclamation's plans, pump water through the Central Arizona Project, fulfilling long-held dreams of Arizona officials. Otherwise, the dams would generate power for the metropolitan Southwest. "The new plants are needed now," the report stated. "Electrical energy provided by their construction should be absorbed by the load demands of the region's urban areas as soon as it is available."[7]

Bureau officials soon realized that hydropower could not meet the region's increasing demand for electricity. *A Study of Future Transmission for the West* estimated that the West's population would increase from forty-eight million to seventy-one million people by 1975 while electrical demand would grow more than fourfold. The Southwest would grow even faster, the report predicted, doubling in population and increasing electrical demand eight times over. While Reclamation's dam-building program envisioned increases in hydroelectric production from 55 billion kwh to 215 billion kwh by 1975, that supply would still only meet

38 percent of the West's demand. Hydropower's share of the region's energy supply would actually fall by 17 percent despite the expansion. Other energy sources faced limits as well. Utilities had expanded their use of natural gas in electrical generation, but Reclamation officials predicted that "soon our reserve supply will vanish" and that "supplies of natural gas cannot be expected to keep up with the growing demand." The report assumed the amount of natural gas consumed in electrical generation would essentially remain static at 35 billion kwh, and thereby fall as percentage of the West's power supply from 33.5 percent to only 6 percent. Natural-gas-fired plants "will be little used but will be maintained to provide generating capacity for peaking service," the report predicted. "Such use alone can justify the high cost fuel." Atomic power as well would remain too expensive to serve as "a prime source of energy in the foreseeable future."[8]

That left coal. The West, the report argued, had barely touched its coal reserves. Despite containing almost three trillion tons of coal, reserves that "will last upwards of a thousand years" that fuel produced only 10 percent of the region's electricity. Coal had long been seen as a last resort for electrical utilities, a dirty fuel that was difficult to transport, required dedicated trains, and faced high shipping costs. Those conditions, however, no longer held. Improvements in transmission technology allowed larger amounts of energy to be shipped longer distances. In 1947, electrical engineers had perfected 345-kilovolt transmission lines, surpassing previous limits of 138 kilovolts. Transmission lines carry power in proportion to the square of their voltage. If voltage is doubled, four times as much power flows. And while capacity increased exponentially, cost rose only geometrically. Thus, a 138-kv line that could carry 150,000 kilowatts cost $60,000 a mile to build, while a 345-kv line cost $100,000 a mile but could carry 900,000 kilowatts.[9] Such improvements solved the West's long-running problem "of moving energy from relatively remote sources to her principle energy markets." Indeed, it was less expensive, the report calculated, to transmit electricity from southern Utah to Los Angeles with 345-kilovolt transmission lines than it was to transport coal by train. Coal, in short, was both viable and available in large supply. By 1975, the report predicted, coal would supply 55 percent of the West's electrical energy.[10]

Reclamation envisioned new coal-fired power plants functioning more like its hydroelectric dams than traditional fuel-fired plants. Traditional plants, such as APS's Saguaro or Ocotillo plants, were generally located in metropolitan areas, with fuel transported to them via pipeline. The new coal-fired plants would be located near coal supplies. They would be, in the electrical industry's term, "mine-mouth" plants, and from them, transmission lines perhaps as large as 500-kilovolts could carry electricity

METHODS OF TRANSPORTING ENERGY

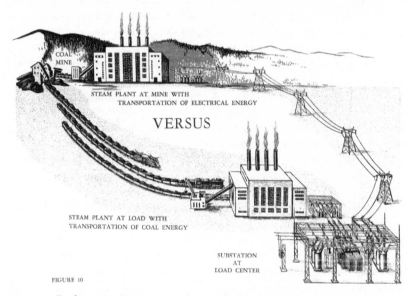

FIGURE 10

FIGURE 4.2. By the 1950s, improvements in extra-high-voltage transmission technology made it increasingly possible to ship "coal by wire," rather than by train. Source: Bureau of Reclamation, *A Study of Future Transmission in the West.* 1953.

across the West to waiting consumers. Indeed, the report's map of "a 500,000-volt power system," showed a power plant hovering over the Four Corners with bulk transmission lines reaching out to Phoenix, Los Angeles, San Francisco, and Seattle. Power lines connected that plant to others along the Montana–North Dakota border and into northern Missouri.[11]

The report also proposed greater coordination of diverse sources of electricity and transmission. New coal-burning plants would be connected to the Bureau of Reclamation's dams across the West. Such a system had benefits beyond the avoidance of metropolitan pollution. Coordination between metropolitan areas would allow locations with deficient supplies of electricity to be supplemented from other regions. It would also diversify loads and smooth demand curves by supplying metropolitan areas with varied weather and by serving customers living in different time zones. It would also allow a minimization of reserve capacity. This "coordinated, cooperative effort," Commissioner Michael Straus wrote in the report's forward, would realize "the ultimate proper utilization of our natural western resources for the benefit of the people."[12]

Straus's vision of "coordinated, cooperative effort" did not require his agency to step beyond its normal realm of hydroelectric generation to build the coal-fired power plants, a decision likely sparked by a 1947 controversy over the Tennessee Valley Authority's move into coal-fired generation. Instead, it anticipated private utilities would pool capital to build and manage such plants. Reclamation officials did, however, argue their agency was best suited to build and manage the system's 500,000-volt power lines. Since the completion of Parker Dam, the agency's Division of Transmission had begun building power lines and transmitting electricity to utilities, charging power recipients carrying fees. Many of its customers, particularly small utilities without the means to pay for large transmission lines, welcomed the new system. If Reclamation built power lines from the proposed power plants, it could link those systems, connecting scattered utilities with dams, into a cohesive network covering the West. In such a system, the report suggested, coal plants, which were difficult to turn on and off, could supply a constant base load while hydropower provided peaking power, stopping generation when necessary merely by stopping the flow of water through turbines. The new system would reorganize the structure of the power industry in the West. Rather than relying on discrete infrastructures of supply and demand, with interconnections only for emergency and surplus, *A Study of Future Transmission in the West* proposed a massive centralization of power generation.

The report also proposed a reorganization of the geography of electrical generation. Local utilities would maintain a few generating facilities. They would only use those they owned in times of extreme demand. Relying on centralized power plants and dams throughout the West linked by a new network of power lines, metropolitan areas would become almost entirely spaces of electrical consumption. Production would instead move to the Intermountain West. While the report listed no specific sites for power plants, map after map showed arrows leading away from the Colorado Plateau to "load centers" on its periphery. The report contained no information, either, about the landscape in which coal lay or the people who lived there. Energy wealth alone constituted the Colorado Plateau in the Bureau of Reclamation's vision.

THE NAVAJO

The BIA saw the Colorado Plateau differently. *The Navajo*, a 1949 report authored for Interior Secretary Julius Krug by BIA officials, portrayed Navajo Reservation as a place of overpopulation and ecological decline. Desperation was the tone of its epigraph, a quote from anthropologists Clyde Kluckhohn and Dorothea Leighton: "Their rapid increase in

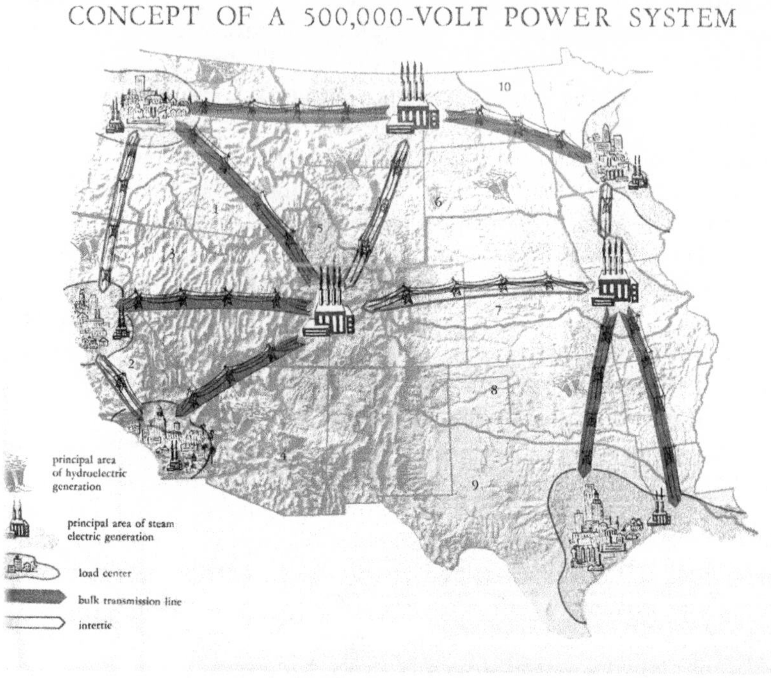

CONCEPT OF A 500,000-VOLT POWER SYSTEM

principal area
of hydroelectric
generation

principal area of steam
electric generation

load center

bulk transmission line

intertie

FIGURE 4.3. The Bureau of Reclamation's study of transmission foresaw the location of power plants within the interior West which would be utilized by metropolitan consumers. Source: Bureau of Reclamation, *A Study of Future Transmission in the West.* 1953.

numbers continues, and the adjacent areas can no longer absorb the overflow. Moreover, the resources of their own ancient lands have been shockingly depleted by erosion. How are The People to make a living?"[13] Side-by-side photos on page 17 of *The Navajo* offered one possible answer. The first showed arroyos cut deeply into the Plateau landscape and an abandoned Navajo hogan. Its caption read, "Erosion limits the range's uses." The second showed neat rows of crops and a Navajo man driving a tractor. This photo, however, did not show the Navajo Reservation. Instead, the report explained that it displayed irrigated farms 200 miles to the west, on a new settlement. The report did not mention that the settlement was the site of the Poston War Relocation Center, a former Japanese internment camp, now repurposed for use by "Indians of tribes in the Colorado River watershed who do not have sufficient land for their own support."[14] The message was clear. Conditions on the reservation were so desperate that abandonment of the reservation, even for some of the most forbidding areas of the West, was the best option.

Following World War II, BIA officials confronted extreme poverty on the Navajo Reservation. Per capita income in 1947 was $82, 7 percent of the American average. Daily diets averaged 1,000 calories, compared to the 1,500 allotted displaced persons in occupied Germany. In the winter of 1947 alone, the War Assets Administration (WAA) distributed 60,000 pounds of rice and more than 200,000 cans of spinach, tomato juice, peaches, and beets, and Congress authorized $2 million in direct aid.[15] Sitting before the House Subcommittee on Indian Affairs in March 1948 to explain the crisis, James Stewart, superintendent of the Navajo Agency, described the attitude of Navajos toward their reservation. "They are very much attached to their country," he explained. "It is a unique area, a picturesque and beautiful area, and they are very much attached to it. They're starving, but they'll stay there unless something forces them to leave." Arizona congressman John Murdock leaned forward and responded. "If men could live on scenery alone they would be rich indeed, but that country does not make it possible for them to live on scenery alone."[16]

The Navajo represented the Department of Interior's, and the BIA's, response to Congress's order to prepare a plan for "Navajo rehabilitation" as a condition of its $2 million appropriation. The emergency had captured national attention. During wartime, the all-Navajo "Code Talker" battalion had become famous for its use of the Navajo language as an unbreakable code. Other Navajos, more than half of the work-age population, had been employed on railroads and in mines, ordinance depots, and wartime manufacturing throughout the Southwest.[17] The deprivation of the reservation, which *Collier's* magazine termed "The Plight of the Navajo," seemed to represent a failed promise to veterans and other Navajos who had sacrificed for their country during wartime. It also symbolized, according to some reports, a sign of the nation's mistaken priorities. "Why do we give millions in Europe," an Indian activist asked in a *Washington Post* story, "while on an arid western desert in our own country 55,000 of our own people . . . are slowly starving to death, because we have not kept faith with them?"[18] *The Navajo* was seemingly designed to answer such critiques. Requesting $90 million for roads, schools, and communication equipment, the program planned an extensive development of reservation infrastructure akin to a domestic Marshall Plan, which was under congressional review at the same time.

The report's authors did not present that infrastructure as a means to rebuild a ruined economy. Rather, infrastructure represented a means of allowing Navajos' eventual escape from their reservation. Testifying to Congress in support of the program, Assistant Secretary for Public Lands William Warne, who oversaw the program's development, testified that, "We must find ways and means of getting them out into the main swim of the economy and civilization down there in the Southwest."[19] Interior Secretary Krug echoed Warne's comments, "Our desire is to bring all of them to the status of American citizens, let them go their own way in our American economy."[20]

Implicit in these comments was a repudiation of John Collier's Indian New Deal. The Indian Reorganization Act had promised to mitigate the disorganization of a half-century of land allotment, coercive boarding schools, and religious repression by creating reservations as protected sites for the rejuvenation of Indian political and cultural life. Collier, in a sense, sought to give spatial, political, and economic form to John Marshall's dictum that Indian tribes were "domestic dependent nations." To be sure, these policies retained a coercive, paternalistic edge. By maintaining the secretary of interior's responsibility for Indian peoples, the Indian New Deal allowed the secretary veto power over any projects or proposals on tribal lands. As both stock reduction and the Indian Mineral Leasing Act had shown, Collier broadly considered Indian people incapable of acting as economic agents in their own right. Still, his policies supported tribal autonomy and self-government in a manner diametrically opposed to the Dawes Act era of allotment and tribal dissolution.

After Collier resigned in 1945, his supporters insisted those policies should be maintained. D'Arcy McNickle, then the BIA's assistant commissioner and an enrolled member of the Salish tribe, called on President Truman to ensure rehabilitation would protect tribal self-rule.[21] Another former assistant in the BIA warned that Navajos required continued protection from the "atomic fission of white materialism," lest they become "Lowgrade Okies."[22] Members of the Association of American Indian Affairs—in the 1940s primarily anthropologists who studied contemporary Indian life—besieged officials in the Interior Department with letters recommending tribally managed development of reservation lands while insisting that Navajos be involved in planning "Navajo Rehabilitation." Anthropologist Ruth Kirk wrote to Secretary Krug in 1947 that "Any plan presented to Congress should have complete Navajo approval— nothing would be more disastrous to Navajo morale and hope than to foist on them any plan on which they have not been consulted, to which they do not agree, and which would be disappointing to them."[23] And Collier himself wrote frequently for western newspapers, warning that critics of his policies were "less concerned with the welfare of the Indians than they are with reopening the door to the despoiling of the Indians of their land."[24]

A growing number of critics, however, challenged Collier's view of tribal autonomy and particularly of the reservation as protected homeland. As Paul Rosier has shown, these critics described reservations not as homelands but as prisons or concentration camps that isolated Indians

from American society and, in the Navajo case, caused Indian destitu-
tion.[25] The Hoover Commission on Government Efficiency sounded a
common refrain when it suggested the IRA's effort to foster Indian self-
determination was a misguided attempt to prop up archaic institutions.[26]
In its 1947 report, the commission argued that "The basis for historic
Indian culture has been swept away. Traditional tribal organization was
smashed a generation ago. . . . Assimilation must be the predominant goal
of public policy." Others, like the journalist Oswald Villiard, accused Collier of retarding Indian progress to satisfy his own romantic yearnings.
The IRA, he argued, represented a misguided attempt to keep Indians
in cultural stasis, as "human museum pieces" and "vestiges of a life that
was picturesque." These descriptions appealed particularly to critics of
Collier's treatment of the Navajos. Writing in *Look* magazine, Will Rogers, Jr., son of the famous humorist, denounced the BIA for policies that
created "starvation without representation" and imprisoned "60,000
Navajo American citizens in a cultural zoo." He, instead, called for policies that would "bring these citizens into the main stream of the nation's
economy."[27] Similarly, Navajo tribal attorney Norman Littell called on
Congress "to throw a bridge across from an isolated society heretofore
maintained deliberately as a matter of erroneous policy, as a museum
piece, to the broader life of American citizens in the world beyond their
reservation."[28]

In the immediate postwar years, beliefs that federal policy should aim
for the assimilation and incorporation of Indian peoples held increasing political sway in Congress and the Interior Department. Advocates
of "termination" sought to eliminate Indian people's limited sovereignty,
abrogate treaties, and extend state jurisdiction over Indian lands. Senator
Arthur Watkins, a Utah Republican, argued that the IRA represented a
deviation "from . . . accustomed policy" of assimilation and that federal
policy should "return to the historic principles of much earlier decades,"
including allotment, Christian missionary activity, and an extension of
American citizenship. Termination's advocates supported the creation of
the Indian Claims Commission in 1946, a body dedicated to resolving
ongoing land disputes arising from the allotment era, as a means to resolve all treaty claims as a necessary precursor to the ethnic and territorial incorporation of Indian peoples.[29] In short, termination's advocates,
who gained increasing power in Congress in the late 1940s and through
the 1950s placed the forceful assimilation of Indian people and incorporation of Indian land at the forefront of federal policies.[30]

The programs outlined in *The Navajo* were designed, Interior officials
insisted, to accomplish such goals. New roads would allow greater access to consumer goods, enabling Navajos, Warne explained, "to experience the American standard of living." Building infrastructure would also

serve as an educational process. "Every single road camp we set up where these men are employed in putting these new roads through," Warne recommended, "ought to have night classes in English and all of the various and sundry things that it will be advantageous for these people to know." Once Navajos had received that education, they would be prepared to move off the reservation, Warne continued. "If we follow . . . our work with an appropriate off-the-reservation employment program, we can put small groups of them at satisfying and pleasurable employment for them, in road building and elsewhere in the Southwest."[31]

Indeed, moving Navajos away from the reservation became perhaps the central object of *The Navajo*'s rehabilitation program. Elsewhere in the Southwest, the BIA believed Navajos could learn skills suited to the "modern American economy," in order to "change their standard of living away from subsistence agriculture." *The Navajo* presented the Poston War Relocation Center as a site to learn irrigated agriculture, despite troubling questions from anthropologist Alexander Leighton, who had performed fieldwork in both locations. "Is it known that the temperature during the summer months here goes to 128 in the shade?" Leighton asked in a letter to the AAIA that was copied to the BIA's Navajo Agency. "Are small children expected to move down there from the temperate plateau of Arizona?"[32] While the Poston project was relatively small-scale, involving five hundred Navajo families, the Navajo Placement Service (NPS) sought to move Navajos permanently to labor camps throughout the Southwest. Navajo superintendent James Stewart, the creator of the NPS, described the labor camps as potential "neighborhoods" that could serve the same purpose as "Chinatowns" and "Little Italys" had in urban America, "points of departure from which the individual and his children could learn the language and customs of America and ultimately assume his place in our national life."[33] Stewart suggested that cultural aspects of relocation were as important as material ones. It was only through permanent relocation that Navajos' attachment to the reservation could be broken. William Warne suggested the need for such relocation was simple. "Even with full development of the reservation resources, however, there will still remain some 27,000 Navajos with no adequate means of making a living. . . . Even using adequately the resources of the area . . . we will still not be able to take care of all of them."[34]

Relocation, then, would accomplish both acculturation and modernization. BIA officials were not subtle about the latter point. As Warne told Congress, "the Navajos are passing through a stage of development that the rest of American society experienced fifty to one hundred year[s] ago."[35] Warne and Stewart suggested that the camps of the Navajo Placement Service could, in a sense, speed the wheel of history by introducing Navajos to semi-industrial work discipline and the world beyond the reservation under controlled circumstances in which federal officials could foster their development. Employers too had a role in modernization. Regional BIA directors warned growers participating in the Navajo Placement Service that "the Navajo is in general a primitive sort of individual, the wide world is foreign to him, he doesn't feel any happier than we would feel in the Navajo world." William Zeh, a local BIA director, asked for growers' help closely supervising Navajos, aiming to "keep them on the job longer," so the lessons of acculturation would take.[36]

Navajos did, indeed, abandon the agricultural camps in large numbers. In part, mobility represented a rejection of the poor conditions they frequently found in camps originally built as temporary homes for seasonal *bracero* laborers.[37] It also, however, reflected Navajos' particular history with wage labor. Using wage work as only one element of a broader subsistence economy, Navajos did work differently than workers fully reliant on wages. They insisted on, in Colleen O'Neill's words, "working the Navajo way," regarding wage work as temporary, a means to contribute to a family income or to acquire funds for purchasing livestock.[38] Sam Ahkeah, tribal chairman from 1947 to 1954, for example, worked as a laborer on ranches near Alamosa, Colorado, in mines near Telluride, and as a construction foreman at Mesa Verde National Park. With his wages, he gradually purchased a substantial herd of 550 sheep at which time he abandoned off-reservation wage work.[39] While BIA officials hoped the NPS would transition Navajos to life off the reservation, Navajo workers themselves regarded it largely as a means to support reservation life.

Zeh's evaluation of "the Navajo" as "a primitive sort of individual," as well as *The Navajo* as a title itself, signaled the BIA's understanding of the fungibility of individual Navajos. Stuck in a primitive stage of development, "the Navajo" were essentially identical in their isolation from modern life and their need for experts to help them along the course of development. This understanding also enabled the exclusion of Navajos from rehabilitation planning. In late 1947, William Warne wrote to a colleague that "We must guard against the possibility of undue delay which might result from referring to the Indians various administrative and operational decisions and procedures which are properly the function of the government."[40] Anthropologists reacted with alarm, and Navajo leaders with irritation. Dorothea Leighton, coauthor of an influential 1946 ethnography, wrote to the president of the Association of American Indian Affairs, worrying that BIA plans threatened to repeat the dynamics of stock reduction. "Is it going to be the old story of just telling them or presenting them with tailor-made schemes that turn out to be hopeless misfits? Or is the idea of making the Navajo responsible for himself going to begin at the grass-roots by inviting him in at the planning stage?"[41] Navajo leaders objected along similar lines. In a 1949 letter to the chairs of several Senate and House committees considering the Rehabilitation bill, tribal chairman Sam Ahkeah complained that the tribal council had been granted two days to approve *The Navajo*'s proposals before congressional consideration. "Even if someone kindly offers to paint one's house and improve one's property," Ahkeah acidly wrote, "we are sure that almost any man would wish to state his preferences as to color and consider the present alterations."[42]

When Navajo political leaders were asked for input, they gave clear direction. They sought programs that promised opportunity on the reservation. In 1948 the tribal council had quickly endorsed a proposal by Max Drefkoff, an industrial consultant hired by the Department of the Interior, to create eleven "industrial villages" on the reservation where Navajos could manufacture furniture, shoes, leather goods, and other consumer items. While Drefkoff's proposal still contained the paternalist language of "teaching Navajos to work," it promised to create enduring institutions on the reservation itself. "Getting industry here to serve all Navajos should be our goal," Councilman Ronald Begay of Crownpoint told the council.[43] Drefkoff's plan fizzled largely because he proposed funding it through new taxes on trading posts, whose prices he found "unconscionable." Smelling government regulation, the Pulliam press and other Southwestern papers denounced Drefkoff for introducing "Communist-style" controls on private enterprise. Drefkoff's plan would, in the words of one *Los Angeles Times* reporter, "set up among the 61,000 Navajo Indians the first Russian-style 'Soviet' on the American continent." Breathless reports in the *Times* and *Arizona Republic* told of "Attempt to 'Sovietize' Navajo Tribe" and to establish "a stringent and bankrupting set of 'price controls' and strangling red tape" that would lead to "Russian-type 'co-operatives.'" The papers repeatedly described Drefkoff, a native of Poland, as "Russian-born" and pictured him in shadowy photos. The BIA soon caved, repudiating Drefkoff and canceling consideration of his program, despite the Navajo Tribal Council's endorsement.[44]

Even after Drefkoff's proposal was repudiated, Navajo officials offered a dramatically different portrait of their reservation. Sam Ahkeah suggested the NPS was creating "brain drain": "We already have a lot of young people off the reservation, those who are more highly educated, and they got their training and left the reservation. . . . We need to find ways to keep those highly educated people on the reservation. So they can be teachers and lawyers and managers on the land where their people live."[45] And tribal leaders suggested the reservation was not poor, but potentially wealthy. As Joe Duncan testified, "We have an immense reservation which we feel should be utilized. After we have exhausted every effort on the reservation, then it will be time for us to send our Navajos somewhere else, but we have not done that yet."[46]

Ahkeah and other leaders placed the blame for Navajo poverty and social problems solidly on the BIA. Not only had stock reduction robbed Navajos of their property, Duncan testified, but the BIA had failed to develop a consistent educational response. "The Department educators," Duncan explained, "start something among the Navajos, 'Here is the way you should make a living,' and then before the man has finished the course . . . they change the course and start something else again. In that way we are all confused about just what is the right thing to do."[47] Ahkeah expanded on Duncan's point, claiming that BIA education prepared Navajos for little more than "digging ditches." Instead, he insisted on a full-bore economic development of the reservation driven by professionalized Navajo workers, "We need thousands of young lawyers, doctors, dentists, accountants, nurses and secretaries. We need young men and women who have majored in business administration. We don't want them to get an education and take jobs off the reservation. We need them here!" Concluding his testimony, Ahkeah issued a challenge, "The Department educators need to teach modern skills so our people can become true Americans."[48]

The passage of the Navajo-Hopi Rehabilitation Act in 1950 realized some of these goals. At the time of its passage, the reservation had 52 miles of paved road. One decade later, it had 652 miles. Roads ran through the reservation's center, reaching communities like Ganado, Kayenta, and Tuba City, where previously, in Peter Iverson's words, "the possibilities for inconvenience only slightly exceeded the chances for disaster."[49] The Rehabilitation Act also tripled the reservation's number of day schools. By the late 1950s, almost 80 percent of Navajo children attended elementary school. The act funded air-transportation facilities, telephone- and radio-communications infrastructure, and a new tribal hospital. It also appropriated $250,000 for mineral surveys to determine whether the reservation's supposedly worthless lands contained any minerals in profitable quantities.[50] It did little, however, to ensure the long-term economic development Navajo leaders hoped to achieve. Sam Ahkeah and Joe Duncan imagined a reservation where Navajo professionals could live and thrive. While the Rehabilitation Act provided improved infrastructure that enabled commerce, it provided little capital to generate new business development and no programs to attract non-Indian industries. Improved roads made it easier for Navajos to work beyond the reservation's boundaries, speeding back in one of the soon ubiquitous pickup trucks to visit family, tend small sheep herds, or attend ceremonies or dances. The reservation remained a center of Navajo cultural life. But the question of whether it could be an economic base remained open. Indeed, two years before the Bureau of Reclamation's *Study of Future Transmission for the West* portrayed the Colorado Plateau as rich in energy supplies, the word "coal" appeared nowhere in *The Navajo* or the testimony of its advocates.

LAND FREEDOM

The *Arizona Republic* expressed annoyance at one facet of the Rehabilitation Act. After its passage by Congress in 1949, President Truman vetoed the law, concerned that an amendment inserted by New Mexico congressman Antonio Hernandez extending state jurisdiction over tribal lands violated the principle of "tribal self-determination in matters of local government."[51] For Eugene Pulliam, the veto reflected a continued pattern of looking to the federal government, rather than the states, as the main agent of Indian development. The veto, he complained, "blasts away the bridge across which 70,000 indians might have crossed to a new life." For Indians to avoid "ignorance, disease and despair," Pulliam suggested, they would need to be "assimilated eventually into the white man's world." Given this necessity, he asked, "why should the Indians not become subject to the same laws and courts as the people of that world?"[52]

Barry Goldwater offered a similar sentiment to John Howard Pyle the year after Pyle's election as Arizona's first Republican governor since 1930, a campaign that Goldwater himself had managed. "One of your first and most important measures should be to unlock the natural resources known to exist on the reservations," he told Pyle. "In mineral wealth alone there is enough in reserve within the reservation boundaries to make our so-called Indian problems simple enough."[53] Goldwater sensed, as did an increasing number of Arizonans, that mineral development could answer both the state's demand for resources and the poverty of its Indians.

After the election of 1952, a number of Arizonans proceeded into governing positions where they could put such ideas to the test. Pyle's election represented only a hint of the growing power of the Republican Party in a state where registered Democrats had outnumbered Republicans four to one in 1948. In 1952, efforts to increase registration and rebuild the Republican Party, driven by Republican members of Charter Government, bore fruit. Dwight D. Eisenhower won Arizona's four electoral votes. Pyle won a second term as Arizona's governor. And Goldwater stunned Ernest MacFarland, the Senate minority leader, by becoming Arizona's junior senator. While Goldwater later said he believed the election was a fifteen-to-one long shot, his campaign had effectively attacked MacFarland as a tool of President Truman and a Washington insider.[54] Goldwater, by contrast, was a native Arizonan. His highway signs read, "Mac Is for Harry / Harry's All Through / You Be for Barry / 'Cause Barry's for You."

Goldwater also attacked the expansive power the federal government held over Arizona's lands, asking audiences, "Do you believe in expanding federal government?" and "Do you want federal bureaus and federal agencies to control Arizona's lands?"[55]

Goldwater was not the only Phoenician to move to Washington following the election. While attending Eisenhower's inauguration, Orme Lewis discovered he was to be appointed Assistant Secretary for Public Lands, William Warne's former position. Lewis's appointment reflected the challenges Republicans faced after twenty years out of executive power. With few party members possessing executive-branch experience, they tapped local officials, lawyers, and businessmen from across the West to fill positions in the Interior Department. While Interior Secretary Douglas McKay had been Oregon's governor, all six of his assistants, including Lewis, came from the private sector. As Lewis said later, "As a partner in a law firm in Arizona, I had handled many legal matters involving the Department of the Interior, but I certainly had little expectation of being tapped for public service on that trip to Washington."[56]

As a lawyer in a state where the federal government owned 75 percent of the land, Lewis had experience with federal land law. He had represented cattlemen challenging new grazing regulations put in place in the 1930s. He had defended timber companies whose harvests in Coconino National Forest had been limited. He had represented traders on the Navajo Reservation challenging price controls. He had served as pro bono council for several irrigation districts that fought for greater water appropriations.[57] In almost all of these cases, Lewis opposed, and deposed, federal authorities, reflecting a long-standing history of local anti-Washington sentiment regarding the jurisdiction and development of public lands in the West.[58] By the time he was appointed assistant secretary, he had developed particular views about federal resource policies. His opening statement at his confirmation hearing before the Senate Committee on Interior Affairs read, in part, "I would like to see the Government get out of ownership of lands that do not benefit everyone." His testimony differentiated between federal lands with broadly public interests, such as national parks, and lands that contained primarily economic resources. The former should, of course, continue to be federally managed. But on the latter, he argued, private enterprise could produce the greatest public good. Policies existing since the beginning of the New Deal that regarded public lands as federal property in perpetuity did more to stymie economic growth than to protect the national interest. And preference policies for the purchase of electric power pointed "in the direction of the nationalization of power."[59] As he wrote in an article soon after taking office, "the Federal government is not the sole and only competent manager of our resources." Indeed, Lewis claimed that policies permanently withdrawing public lands from private sale went against the historic purposes of public lands. "Sometimes our lands are more valuable in private hands, contributing more to the national economy, than in those of the federal government. This was the thinking which guided Congress into the enactment of laws by which individual Americans could acquire lands and homes and futures in the public domain."[60]

Lewis was not alone in these views. Conservationists soon dubbed the new interior secretary "Giveaway McKay" for advocating the private takeover of public power systems and for permitting an Alabama mining company to harvest large swaths of timberland in Oregon. Even before Eisenhower's election, Laurence Lee, the president of the U.S. Chamber of Commerce, had also insisted that the privatization of public lands would benefit the national interest. Dubbing the policy "land freedom," Lee argued before the National Lumber Manufacturer's Association in November 1952 that large-scale federal landholding was tantamount to the collectivist policies of the Soviet Union. In the journal *American Forests*, he called on Congress to conduct an inventory of all public lands. "All property which, in the public interest, is best adapted to private ownership," Lee declared, should "be offered as soon as possible" and placed "in productive use by private enterprise" to create new jobs and enrich local tax rolls. Like Lewis, Lee suggested that federal land policy should focus on the dispersion of land into the private sector, rather than on the ongoing management and regulation of potentially productive resources.[61]

Conservationists and their supporters criticized Lewis's outspoken advocacy for what Lee had described as "land freedom." In their *Washington Post* column, Joseph and Stewart Alsop labeled Lewis a potential "trouble maker" in the new administration, writing "Orme Lewis has testified that the public lands . . . should ultimately be turned over to 'private citizens.' This is hardly what Theodore Roosevelt had in mind. . . . President Eisenhower is clearly going to have to ride the executive branch on very tight rein." Lewis wrote later that "extreme conservationists" who held that "use is abuse" targeted him for their ire, accosting him at dinner parties for considering proposals to build a gondola on Mount Rainier or disputing plans for a dam in Dinosaur National Monument as he flew to Europe.[62] Indeed, many historians trace the origins of modern environmental politics to McKay's (and Lewis's) time in Washington, as groups like the Sierra Club began to organize against excessive development of public lands.[63]

Lewis's support for "land freedom" had much more support among advocates of termination. By the early 1950s, termination legislation had come to focus on the abolition of reservation boundaries and the extension of state jurisdiction over Indian lands. Echoing Laurence Lee, termination's advocates used the language of freedom, believing such steps would free Indian people from the shackles of tribalism.[64] Introducing House resolution 108 in 1953, which declared it federal policy to end supervision of Indian tribes as soon as possible and to extend state jurisdiction over Indian lands, Senator Arthur Watkins of Utah proclaimed, "Following the footsteps of the Emancipation Proclamation . . . I emblazon the letters of fire above the heads of the Indians—these people shall be free!" As Interior's liaison with Congress, Lewis managed bills terminating federal supervision over the Klamath and Menominee tribes. While these tribes faced land loss and social dislocation in the years following termination, the termination era also had far-reaching effects on tribes that never faced such legislation. The era saw changes in leasing terms, opening of resource lands, and formation of the American Indian Research Fund, a private five-member committee that produced surveys of reservation resources, chaired by Laurence Lee. Lee's presence made the committee's dynamics, as well as the termination era's at large, clear. Termination was land freedom for Indians.[65]

For Navajos, these dynamics became most clear in the proposals made by a separate committee. Shortly after his appointment, Lewis suggested Walter Bimson head a survey report authorized by the House Interior Committee, charged with implementing federal withdrawal from Indian affairs and cutting the BIA's budget. Bimson's Valley National Bank had a long-standing interest in Indian affairs. It had been the main lender to Apache Tribal Enterprises, a tribal corporation of the San Carlos Apache tribe created to pursue commercial cattle ranching in the late 1940s. Since that time, the bank had maintained an Indian Affairs office that surveyed the state of Indian economics. While the records of Bimson's federal panel could not be located in the National Archives, the contemporaneous records of Valley Bank's Indian Affairs Division provide suggestions of the thinking that informed Bimson's federal panel, which recommended broad revisions to both federal leasing policy on Indian land and the spatial organization of BIA offices.

Sometime in early 1953, Tom Shiya, the director of the bank's Indian Affairs Division, received a letter from an unknown Arizona tribal leader who had recently visited Phoenix. It read, in the portion of the letter Shiya quoted, "Living in an isolated area and taking things as they come, then suddenly realizing that isolation is fast evaporating and things are changing faster than one realizes for the moment leaves one rather stunned. Questions pop up faster than you can answer, questions like: Why are we so far behind?" Shiya's response to the writer is unknown. He did, however, use the question as an opportunity to draft a five-page memorandum, copied to Bimson and to Orme Lewis at the latter's Phoenix law office.[66]

The memo argued that the source of the economic problems facing the state's Indians did not arise primarily from overpopulation, erosion, or a confrontation with modernity. Rather, it lay in the political economy of the reservation. Shiya argued in particular that the IRA had raised new barriers between reservations and the regions in which they lay. While efforts to empower tribal governments may have been well-meaning, combined with the heavy hand of federal authority, they had transformed reservations into, Shiya wrote, "islands of sovereignty under federal trusteeship." While this spatial division offered the illusion of autonomy, it severely hampered Indian economic development by discouraging capital investment. "The free flow of economic transactions is hindered, problems of legal jurisdiction complicate normal legal business," Shiya continued, "and there is an artificial barrier between Indians and non-Indians in social and political interaction." In short, federal policy left reservations uncharted territory amid the currents of capital transforming the Southwest.[67]

Shiya suggested these islands would remain undiscovered so long as they abided by the "economic fallacy" that reservations could be governed independent of their surrounding regions. The overlapping jurisdictions that resulted from federal and tribal authority discouraged potential investors, Shiya argued, "[T]hree areas of redtape or government regulation must be hurdled—federal trusteeship, tribal government, and the already top-heavy redtape burdening private enterprise." The legacy of the IRA did not only discourage investment, it also harmed Indians, instantiating a "reservation-isolation psychology" in Indian people that hampered them as they confronted the region's competitive ethos. "The normal incentives and values in a competitive society do not exist on the reservation," Shiya wrote in his report. "In fact, everything mitigates against them."[68]

William Kelly, an anthropologist who directed the University of Arizona's Bureau of Ethnic Research, echoed Shiya's analysis in an August 1953 memorandum sent to Bimson, Lewis, and Richard Harvill, the president of the university. "The effective deterrent to the adjustment of most Indian tribes is no longer cultural difference but economic depression," Kelly wrote. Depression had fostered "attitudes of dependence" among Indians, producing "social maladjustment" as well as economic inequality. While Kelly remained somewhat more sympathetic to Indian authority, writing of the need to bridge the gap between "the white demand that the Indian conform to the American social and economic system, and the Indian demand that he be permitted to choose his own way of life," he also asserted that the confusing welter of federal and tribal jurisdiction meant that "the free flow of economic transactions is hindered, problems of legal jurisdiction complicate normal legal business . . . and there is an artificial barrier between Indians and non-Indians in social and political interaction."[69]

Kelly and Shiya agreed that the problem facing Indians lay not in the issues of acculturation or "stages of development" that the BIA had emphasized. Rather, the primary issue lay in political barriers that prevented capital from transforming both reservation lands and Indians themselves. Neither advocated the abolition of tribal governance for any Arizona tribes, like the most ardent terminationists. Shiya, however, suggested severe limits on the ability of tribal governments to shape economic affairs. "Indian economics," Shiya wrote, "must be surgically separated from tribal government and all other considerations of the reservation people." He argued that potential investors would be scared away from reservations if they perceived the tribe might meet social-welfare needs directly through taxation or other transfer payments. If "government becomes all things to all the people—in other words, applied socialism, actually," industry would never find Indian lands attractive. Shiya, in short, advocated that the ethos of competitive growth politics' deference to business interests be extended to Indian lands.[70]

Bimson's committee contained echoes of Kelly's and Shiya's analysis. Policy recommendations took three directions. First, it recommended the expansion of programs relocating Indians away from reservations. Relocation represented, Bimson wrote to Senator Carl Hayden, "the cheapest possible way to lessen the cost to the government and to get them assimilated in non-Indian society."[71] Rather than programs like the NPS, however, which had relocated Navajos to scattered agricultural camps across the Southwest, Bimson's committee recommended the programs focus on relocation to urban areas. "There," Bimson's letter continued, "they can learn to fit into this nation's modern economic life." And where the NPS had concentrated on acculturation in camps compared to "neighborhoods," Bimson's committee focused on relocation as a form of economic integration, in which reservation Indians could find a proper "fit" in the American economy.[72] Lewis moved quickly to implement this suggestion, developing a program that eventually relocated thirty thousand Indians to Chicago, Denver, Seattle, Phoenix, and Los Angeles in the 1950s. The effort to cut costs, however, quickly gave these programs a bad reputation among Indians for finding housing in "skid row sections" and "slum areas," and for placing Indians in unskilled jobs. As one relocated individual in Denver commented, "Heck, if I wanted to work in a junkyard, I could've stayed at home."[73]

Second, Bimson's panel suggested most BIA authority be delegated to regional offices located in the same cities that hosted relocated people. From those locations, the committee's report stated, "the area office directors can best make decisions about economic integration, the capacity for independence, and the development of reservation resources."[74] This shift would allow BIA officials to locate jobs and housing for Indians as they entered the metropolitan economy. BIA agents could also interact with local businessmen to understand how best to place Indians in new jobs. As Bimson wrote to Lewis, "One of the great benefits of such reorganization will be the opportunity for connections between BIA officials and those of us working to attract industry and commerce."[75] Bimson's report envisioned a fundamental spatial reorientation of Indian policy away from Washington and to the regional level with an aim toward linking Indian economies with metropolitan areas. Lewis enthusiastically endorsed the report, writing that its changes would allow "Indians to participate fully in our free enterprise system."[76] BIA Commissioner Glenn Emmons, however, convinced Lewis the reorganization would be costly to administer and it was eventually scrapped.

Finally, the report recommended changes in policies for leasing tribal lands. Bimson's panel argued that extending the standard leasing terms from five to twenty-five years would act as an incentive to draw businesses to reservations, insuring them against changes in federal policy or tribal governance. It also recommended easy renewal terms, with determination left largely up to the lessee, unless violations of the lease's terms had occurred. Congress acted shortly after receiving the report in early 1954, amending the Navajo-Hopi Rehabilitation Act's standard lease terms to twenty-five years for "business purposes, including the development or utilization of natural resources in connection with operations of such leases." The following year, Public Land Law 255 extended those terms to all Indian tribes. While the laws granted preferences for hiring "qualified Indians" on reservation leases, as Lewis wrote to Goldwater in reference to the terms of the Rehabilitation Act, "The decision as to who is a 'qualified Indian,' however, necessarily has to be left to the individual contractor."[77] The changes to leasing law represented, in many ways, the flip side of relocation programs. Instead of relocating Indians to metropolitan areas, they sought to bring metropolitan capital to Indian land. And following the practices that surrounded efforts to locate capital in space across the metropolitan Southwest, those changes granted capital owners generous terms in establishing their operations and broad authority once established.

Lewis's term as assistant secretary and the height of the termination era coincided. Both were also brief. By the late 1950s, termination faced increased criticism for the failures of urban relocation and the exclusion of Indian tribes from deliberations over their fate. At the same time, Indian-led social movements and Supreme Court rulings began to erect a new era in which Indian sovereignty gained greater protection. Self-determination became the central political project of Indian politics. No tribe faced congressional termination following the California Ranche-ria Termination Act in 1958. Lewis's term was even shorter. Passed over for promotion to undersecretary of the interior in late 1954, he resigned from the Interior Department early the next year. On his way out of federal service, he penned a somewhat comic, somewhat bitter article for the *Saturday Evening Post* about the absurdities faced by a modern businessman serving as "caretaker for all our human and all our natural resources." In "I Was the Great White Father," Lewis explained that "it was the all too human resources that gave me the most trouble." Lewis wrote of being besieged Polynesians, Virgin Islanders, and Indian "strong men" who confronted him "like Gen. George Custer at the Little Bighorn River." He concluded that he had gained insight into "the psychology of people who are used to being taken care of by the Government. You furnish a certain service to people," Lewis wrote, "and after a period, that service becomes a possession."[78]

Lewis began his otherwise sardonic article by stating that "the power I had staggered me." His experience indicated the new, and unfamiliar, scale he worked at. Accustomed to the levers of power available at the local level to reshape tax and zoning policy, the power to reshape land law and Indian policy in the nation at large proved surprising. Both levers of power, however, had long-term spatial manifestations. In Phoenix, they resulted in new manufacturing plants. On federal lands, they created a new landscape of private development of which power lines were only a part.[79]

"Divine Providence"

The changes that Lewis precipitated helped create the Navajo Nation. Since the 1920s, energy development had never contributed more than $30,000 to tribal coffers in a single year. Encouraged by burgeoning de-mand for oil and natural gas, short supplies in West Texas, the comple-tion of a natural gas pipeline from northern New Mexico to Southern California, and the policies of the Interior Department, however, wild-catters and established oil and natural-gas companies began exploratory drilling in the northeastern portion of the reservation in the early 1950s. In 1953, Shell Oil completed an extensive oil and gas survey, and recom-mended the company bid on 214 tracts. That same year, fourteen other companies, including small independent outfits and major ones, such as Continental Oil and Texaco, paid the Navajo Tribe more than $104,000 in bonus payments alone for exploratory leases. In 1955, Texaco made a major oil discovery near Aneth, in the Utah portion of the reservation. Over the following seven years, companies paid the tribe $76.5 million for resource exploration and development. These discoveries led tribal chairman Paul Jones to thank, in 1959, the "Divine Providence" that had brought "unexpected wealth" from "natural resources not known to be there in our earlier history."[80]

Continuing earlier patterns of eschewing per capita payments, which would have amounted to $425 per tribal member, the Navajo Tribal Council used the money to increase the size and capacity of tribal government. A year after the Aneth oil strike, the tribe established a Department of Social Services, responsible for providing food, clothing, and relief money to destitute Navajos, and a tribal scholarship fund. Tribal leaders also used returns from energy resources to develop reservation infrastructure, funding further road building and the construction of chapter houses in 47 out of the Navajo Reservation's 110 chapters. It also used oil income to create a new bureaucracy, hiring a permanent tribal secretary and increasing the salary paid to council members and tribal officials. Tribal budgets increased exponentially across the course of the 1950s, from $1 million in 1954 to $13 million by 1958. By that time, 23 percent of wages earned on the reservation came directly from tribal government. Indeed, as Peter Iverson writes, many Navajos refer to the 1950s as the era in which the Navajo Tribe became the Navajo Nation because of the increased presence of tribal government in daily life.[81]

Paul Jones, elected tribal chairman in 1954, drove many of these changes. Born in 1895, Jones had traveled east, like Jacob Morgan, with a missionary family, attending high school in Englewood, New Jersey, and beginning college at Calvin College in Grand Rapids, Michigan. After a stint in the army during World War I, Jones returned to Grand Rapids and completed a degree at McLaughlin's Business College. After working for a decade in Chicago as a shipping clerk, he returned to the reservation during the Depression to become the BIA's chief interpreter. Like his predecessors, Morgan and Sam Ahkeah, then, Jones had experience working off the reservation. Where Morgan worked as a missionary, and Ahkeah as a wage laborer, however, Jones had experience in urban business culture. He saw the reservation developments that occurred during his early chairmanship as a means to begin to advance the reservation toward that standard. Indeed, Navajo tribal government began funding housing developments that replicated the clustered style of contemporary subdivisions, including one by Allied Homes, a medium-sized home builder in Phoenix. Such development also represented a means of cushioning the tribe against what Jones believed to be the inevitability of the withdrawal of federal support and possible termination. Energy development represented a key element of this strategy. As he explained in a 1956 speech, "We are not going to let our people starve. We will give them as decent a living as we can within our power. That is the reason for the various projects, to get industry and drilling for gas and we are able to do this."[82]

To create a government that could both protect and provide for Navajos, Jones believed that the tribe needed to become more directly involved in energy development. The process of mineral leasing in the early 1950s weighed against tribal involvement. The Indian Mineral Leasing Act of 1938 set fixed rent and royalty payments of $1.25 per acre and 12.5 percent of the market price, respectively, with bonus payments being the only variable on competitively bid tracts. Tribal officials played little part in a process that began with a prospector requesting that a tract be offered for bids and only involved tribal officials after bids had been let. These patterns appear to have held until 1956. Few letters from tribal officials appear in the files at the National Archives concerning oil and gas leasing. Tribal correspondence increased in 1956, however, and remained constant thereafter.

Much of this correspondence related to the tribal government's efforts to protect Navajos from the dangers that energy development introduced to the reservation. Virginia Benally's eye injury provides a prime example. Playing near her house on June 18, 1955, four-year-old Virginia, of Sweetwater, New Mexico, found a dynamite cap left by drillers who had been exploring for natural gas nearby. The cap exploded, sending fragments of rock into her face, and blinding her right eye. Virginia's father, Fred Benally, contacted the Navajo tribal attorney, who put him in touch with Mark Reno, a legal advisor employed by the tribe. In December 1955, Reno began negotiating with an adjustment company in Farmington, New Mexico, that represented the driller most likely responsible, the National Geophysical Company. After months of negotiation, Reno reached a settlement of $6,250 for the loss of Virginia's vision and an injury to her brother's hand. After the agreement, however, an agent for Traveler's Insurance, who underwrote the Farmington adjustment company, approached Fred Benally and offered him $4,000 cash on the spot to settle the claim. When word of Traveler's cost-cutting maneuver reached the tribal attorney and tribal chairman's office, Jones was furious, believing an impoverished Navajo man who had suffered family tragedy had been taken advantage of by an offer of quick cash. Jones insisted that Traveler's no longer be allowed to underwrite policies for companies doing business on the reservation. While R. B. Clay, the area director of the BIA's Navajo Agency doubted "that sufficient justification is at hand to eliminate the Travelers Insurance . . . Company from the U.S. Treasury list of acceptable surety on bonds," he admitted that "the fact remains that the Navajo Tribe will refuse a lease if the subject company appears" on the lease materials.[83]

Navajo tribal government under Jones did not only seek to regulate the companies involved in energy development. It also sought to garner greater profits. Jones and other tribal leaders grew increasingly frustrated with the limited 12.5 percent royalty the tribe received from oil and gas leasing. In 1957, the Tribal Council called for a moratorium on future leasing and negotiated an agreement with the Delhi-Taylor Oil Company, without receiving BIA approval. In the agreement, Delhi-Taylor gained sole exploration and drilling rights to 54,000 acres of unleased lands near Aneth, in return for a 50 percent share of the profits from the operations. Dehli-Taylor also agreed to institute a management training program for Navajo workers. Rather than merely being a landowner drawing rent from operations, the tribe sought to become a partner in the business operations. New Mexico senator Clinton Anderson reacted favorably, telling Jones in a hearing on the course of rehabilitation, "When you have a large amount of money, and the Navajos are in prospect of having that by these oil leases, you are in a position to do a little gambling that you otherwise would not do, if you anticipate unusually fine returns from it."[84] Expressing reservations that the agreement exposed the tribe to unnecessary risk, and likely peeved at being not told of the negotiations, BIA officials quashed the plan. Tribal secretary Maurice McCabe reacted angrily while testifying before Congress, "In other words, the Great White Father in Washington is better able to say what is good for us than we ourselves. How can we be considered ready to participate in government when we are not considered capable of knowing our own best interests?"[85] While this episode showed the continuing legal force of the BIA's trust responsibility, it also demonstrated the dissatisfaction of Jones and other Navajo leaders with the tribe's lack of agency in energy development. Rather than accepting a position as a recipient of rents and royalty payments, Jones and other Navajo officials in the 1950s acted as bullish advocates of energy development, seeking arrangements that allowed greater potential financial returns and enabled tribal members to move into management positions.

It was with this interest in protection and provision that the Navajo Tribe received Utah International's interest in coal deposits on the northeastern portion of the reservation in 1956. As in the case of oil and gas development, Utah International initiated the process, requesting that a tract of land of more than 24,000 acres be opened for exploration for a potential coal strip mine. BIA and Navajo officials reciprocated the interest. BIA estimates held that oil and gas reserves would run out in fifteen years, leaving the tribe without its main source of income. The extensive work required in mining coal, even with modern machinery, promised to employ more Navajos than the relatively small, expert crews that drilled for oil and gas. Furthermore, the heavy transportation costs of coal weighed in favor of use on the reservation. Indeed, the lease, as the chapter's opening indicated, pledged cooperation of the Navajo Tribe and Utah International in enticing a utility that would build a nearby power plant. Coal, unlike natural gas and oil, seemed to promise possibilities for the tribe beyond rentier status.

Coal differed from gas in two other ways, however, that worked to the tribe's disadvantage. First, coal leases had no standard payment rate. Unlike natural-gas leases, which granted royalties of 12.5 percent on gas's sales price according to the terms of the Indian Mineral Leasing Act of 1938, coal payments were set in negotiations between energy companies and the BIA, acting as agents for the tribe.[86] Second, where natural-gas exploration was at its midcentury height, coal exploration was at its nadir, despite the Bureau of Reclamation's enthusiasm for coal as the West's energy future. With railroads converting to diesel, homes using oil and natural gas for heating, and industry largely turning to electricity, American coal production hit its lowest point of the twentieth century in 1954, when only 392 million tons of coal were extracted, off more than 200 million tons from its earlier peak. The low price of coal reflected this ebb in production. Indeed, lease rates for coal had been declining 1.2 percent annually since the end of World War II.[87] While later critics charged that the rates the BIA negotiated with Utah International, in which the tribe was paid fifteen cents for coal used on the reservation and twenty cents for coal used beyond its borders, were unconscionably low, those rates actually compared favorably with contemporaneous leases on non-reservation land. Still, Utah International paid no bonus, and payments from coal mining remained low.[88] Where oil and gas leases brought almost $80 million to the tribe in the late 1950s and early 1960s, the Utah International lease brought $8 million in the twenty years after 1957, despite that fact that the mine became the energy source for the largest power plant in the region during that time, Four Corners Power Plant.[89]

Other lease terms were advantageous to Utah International as well. Lease rates were fixed across the term of the contract, without a scheduled renegotiation. Because the IMLA allowed for the automatic renewal of leases as long as minerals were recovered in paying quantities, this failure to insert a renegotiation clause essentially fixed the payment rates at the historical nadir of coal prices.[90] While the contract contained a clause pledging the company to "make special efforts to work Navajo tribal members into skilled, technical, and other higher level employment," the clause did not include any goals, timelines, or quotas. Interior officials' belief in the ultimate authority of employers in hiring decisions—encapsulated in Orme Lewis's statement to Barry Goldwater that "the decision as to who is a 'qualified Indian,' however, necessarily has to be left to the individual contractor"—also weighed against Indian job advancement. Still, the lease represented an attempt to create mineral development that not only brought royalties, but employment, to reservation workers. It was not only in the mine itself, however, that Jones and tribal leaders hoped Utah International's lease would expand possibilities for Navajos on the reservation.

"Two Light Bulbs in Every Hogan"

"We need power, cheap power, as cheap as possible and lots of power if we are going to bring industry onto the reservation," Martin Bennett told the Navajo Tribal Council in August 1960. Bennett, a consultant for the Navajo Tribal Utility Authority, argued that the ability to attract industry made it worthwhile to overlook the potential shortcomings of an agreement with Arizona Public Service to build a 175-megawatt coal-fired power plant near Utah International's Navajo Mine. Council members initially balked at the utility's reluctance to fund construction of local distribution lines and questioned whether the employment practices that characterized Navajo Mine, where Utah International had imported workers from Utah and Arkansas to work large drag shovels, rather than training Navajos to operate them, would hold at the power plant as well. They also likely had in mind the failure of previous outside industries on the reservation for reasons that seemed to have little to do with power supply. Still, APS did agree to sell wholesale power to the newly created tribal utility for thirty years, and the promise of "lots of cheap power" would, Bennett assured the council, draw new industries.[91]

By 1960, the tribe had tried for five years to draw manufacturing industry to the reservation, following the creation of a BIA industrial-development program in 1955. The program was the brainchild of Glenn Emmons, commissioner of the BIA through the 1950s. A banker from nearby Gallup, Emmons's experience dealing with Navajos had convinced him that federal oversight created dependency among Indians. Though he agreed with Lewis about the generally deleterious effects of federal supervision, he worried that Interior officials threatened to push termination too aggressively, instituting it before Indians were prepared for economic citizenship. Unlike earlier programs under the Rehabilitation Act, which had created a revolving credit fund to enable the formation of tribally owned businesses, Emmons sought to draw businessmen to the reservation, using the new twenty-five-year, renewable leases as a means of assurance. Familiar with the competitive growth politics that increasingly characterized the national economy, Emmons advised companies that tribes would provide lucrative inducements, including rent-free buildings, free land, tribally sponsored job-training programs, and labor costs far below prevailing wages.[92]

Phoenix's business establishment assisted with these efforts at industrial development. Beginning in 1956, the Arizona Commission on Indian Affairs (ACIA) began hosting economic development conferences for the state's tribal officials. Chaired by Tom Shiya of Valley Bank and an APS executive, the ACIA was an effort to bring tribal leaders, business executives, and state politicians together to chart a state-oriented Indian policy. Its economic development conferences presented to Indian leaders the economic and political ideas underlying Phoenix's growth. During one representative conference in February 1958, forty officials from Arizona tribes traveled to Phoenix for a banquet dinner with 120 "representatives of business, industry, and agriculture," followed by a keynote address by Shiya explaining how business recruitment might serve to bridge the gap between Indian economies and the state's dynamic center. The following day, the tribal leaders received a bus tour of the Valley of the Sun, including stops at John Jacob's irrigated farms in northern Phoenix, Ocotillo Power Plant in Tempe, and the headquarters of Valley Bank, where Walter Bimson explained, according to Shiya's later report, "the basics of our labor and taxation principles." For Phoenix's businessmen, the conferences likely represented an opportunity to understand particular Indian reservations where they might redirect inquiries from industries "inappropriate" for Phoenix, as they did with other Chambers of Commerce around Arizona.[93]

Jones and other Navajo leaders apparently took eagerly to the BIA's program and the ACIA's suggestions. Advised by Interior geologists that the tribe's oil and gas deposits would be exhausted in ten to fifteen years, Jones saw that it was imperative to quickly draw industry to the reservation. The Navajo Tribal Council appropriated $300,000 in December 1955 to pay for plant construction and job training for potential manufacturers. At Jones's request in 1957, Congress allowed the tribe to extend business leases far beyond the twenty-five-year term instituted in 1955, to ninety-nine years. Most indicative of the influence of the ACIA, the Tribal Council passed a right-to-work law in 1958 far harsher than Arizona's, forbidding unions on tribal lands and threatening hard labor, imprisonment, or expulsion from tribal land for any union members working to organize Navajos on the reservation. When the D.C. Circuit Court struck the law down three years later, the tribal council's press release announced "Unions to Invade Reservation Land," attempting to impress upon potential businesses the tribe's continuing hostility to union labor.[94]

Despite such policies, the industrial recruitment efforts brought few tangible benefits in the late 1950s. Several manufacturers located operations on reservation land, but their promised benefits soon proved ephemeral. In June 1956, the Baby Line Furniture Corporation of Los Angeles agreed, after a $200,000 tribal subsidy, to create Navajo Furniture Industries, a new subsidiary located in Gamerco, New Mexico, that would manufacture furniture, shutters, and similar products. In November of the same year, Lear, Inc., of Santa Monica, opened Lear-Navajo near Flagstaff to manufacture electrical components. Despite BIA fanfare, both plants failed to meet the employment targets of one hundred workers apiece that the BIA had established. Eighteen months after opening, Navajo Furniture Industries employed only ten workers, while Lear-Navajo fell victim to the recession of 1957 and ceased operations altogether.[95]

Navajo leaders hoped APS's interest in building a mine-mouth plant would avoid these earlier failures. In 1958, APS had agreed in principle to purchase 4,200 tons of coal per day from Utah International at a price of $2.50 per ton. With power from the plant, scheduled to produce 175 megawatts of electricity, BIA commissioner Emmons suggested that aerospace and electronics firms could likely be enticed to the area. Martin Bennett, the consultant for the Navajo Tribal Utility Authority (NTUA) who told the tribal council that "We need cheap power," concurred, arguing the NTUA could offer very competitive prices. And NTUA general manager Philip Vanderhoof promised that inexpensive electricity would allow more comfortable indoor temperatures in the summer and better lighting that would allow schoolchildren to study at home in the evening.

Vanderhoof's promises, as well as those of the tribal utility for which he worked, signaled that Jones and other Navajo leaders hoped APS's plant would enable not only reservation industrialization but residential modernization. Established in 1959 and claiming 15,000 potential customers, but only 250 actual consumers, the Navajo Tribal Utility Authority represented a response to tribal frustration at power companies that requested rights-of-way for high-voltage transmission lines through reservation lands but showed little interest in providing service to scattered Navajo customers. The NTUA also promised to give Navajo workers experience as electrical linemen and service workers. Mostly, however, it sought to bring electrification to areas of the reservation outside of population centers in Window Rock, Fort Defiance, Tuba City, and Shiprock. While private utilities like APS had extended service to certain areas of the reservation, they had maintained high fees for extending distribution lines to any potential customers living more than five thousand feet from existing power lines. The NTUA, by contrast, sought to distribute electricity broadly to Navajos who lacked service. By extending power lines across the reservation, the utility promised material improvements in the lives of Navajos. "The Navajo family, whether they are living only in a summer shelter, in a Hogan, or in a modern house, our people want to have the benefits of modern living with electricity," Councilman Howard Gorman stated. "People who have these facilities seem happier. They seem to have better health where they have modern facilities." The celebration of the first electrified home in Ganado, a small town thirty miles west of Window Rock, featured a ceremony in which tribal officials presented Mr. and Mrs. Henry Spake an electric radio, hot plate, and iron. The gifts symbolized Vanderhoof's larger plans. "We want to put an electrical outlet and two light bulbs in every Hogan. . . . This would ensure the user of an outlet for a radio and a small refrigerator, if they could afford to buy them."[96]

The NTUA suggested the subtle ways in which doctrines of sovereignty manifested themselves in Navajo politics and society amid the energy boom of the late 1950s and early 1960s. When local utilities balked at providing service to tribal members, the tribe formed its own utility. The need to create the utility revealed the blindness of Thomas Shiya's vision of Indian incorporation. Shiya had imagined that with political barriers reduced, reservations would soon be incorporated into the broader economic structures of Arizona. The terms by which the state's private institutions were willing to incorporate the reservation, however, proved unworkable, leading tribal officials to turn inward, creating new institutions. On a larger scale, reservation sovereignty was the story of Navajo modernization in the 1950s and 1960s. Envisioning the end of federal services, Navajo officials began fashioning a social service infrastructure that could protect and provide for tribal members, making the tribal government a daily presence in Navajo lives. In part, these developments show the real effects that termination policy had on those tribes that never faced formal termination. Even beyond the effects of termination, however, these leaders worked to fashion an explicitly Navajo vision of modernity. Seeing the economic growth and demographic explosion occurring in the postwar Southwest, tribal leaders sought ways for Navajos to be included in the region's prosperity and to escape the antimodernity imposed on the tribe by *Arizona Highways* and other Southwestern image makers.

Paul Jones articulated this vision of the sovereign growth of a self-sufficient Navajo Nation at the dedication of Four Corners Power Plant. Announcing that the plant would provide "a better life for all our people," he explained that the plant's power would, "we hope, attract many industries," creating new jobs for Navajo workers. Jones detailed the future he envisioned the plant creating for all Navajos. "I can visualize ultimately a grid of power lines throughout Navajoland, electric power in Navajo dwellings and with the advent of such power, the acquisition of electrical appliances, including refrigeration." This modern development, this "great stride forward in the progress of the Navajo people," would create the reservation as another growing metropolis. The reservation's growth would indeed be "coupled with the further development of Phoenix, Tucson, and other cities." In Jones's vision, the Navajo Nation would rise as the successor to Phoenix in the industrialized and electrified modernity of the postwar Southwest.[97]

The sovereignty of the late 1950s only went so far, however. In its negotiations with the Navajo Tribe, APS secured terms that limited Navajo control over their operations. APS feared, in part, that bond investors might be scared away by possible complications involving BIA and tribal jurisdiction. To avoid such complications, APS secured lease terms ensuring that US district courts would have jurisdiction over any lawsuits related to its contract. Furthermore, the contract established the legal jurisdiction as New Mexico, not the Navajo Nation. The company also wrote into the contract a protection against objections to pollution. APS's list of matters to negotiate read, in part, "The lease of plant site should state that it is for use by a coal-burning power plant and that it is recognized such plant in its normal operation will give off some stack gas and fly ash." APS also negotiated the right to discharge wastewater into a wash that led to the San Juan River and right-of-ways for power lines across reservation land.[98]

Negotiations of these issues were contentious, with Navajo leaders pushing especially for more extensive line construction. They were concluded to APS's satisfaction only when the utility announced a plan to build a second coal-fired plant on private land just south of the reservation near Winslow. Fearing that they might miss out on the electricity central to their development plan, the Jones administration agreed to lease terms for building Four Corners Power Plant next to the Utah International lease, just west of Fruitland, New Mexico, on the eastern edge of the reservation. The tribe would receive rental payments of $25,000 per year, Navajo preference in hiring, donations to a tribal scholarship fund and sale of wholesale power to the NTUA.

With the opening of Four Corners and Cholla Power Plants, Arizona Public Service began drawing nearly half its power off of a landscape far from where it was used. This new geography drew energy from the Colorado Plateau to Phoenix and increasingly placed decisions about the land and people of the Colorado Plateau in the hands of utility companies dedicated to producing an insatiable consumer demand. Much as Bernard DeVoto had described the relationship between the West and the nation in 1934, the Colorado Plateau rapidly became Phoenix's "Plundered Province."[99] In 1963 that relationship remained localized in Arizona. As the next chapter will show, the place of the Colorado Plateau and the people living upon it changed again as electricity generated on the Colorado Plateau began to cross both state lines and lines that had divided public and private utilities.

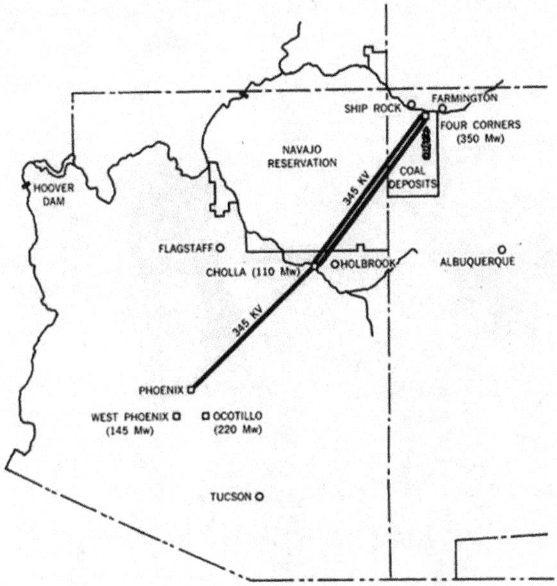

FIGURE 4.4. Map of power lines linking Four Corners Power Plant with Phoenix. Utah Construction Company/Utah International Collection. Image courtesy of Special Collections Department, Stewart Library, Weber State University, Ogden, Utah. 1962.

By the time Four Corners Power Plant opened in August 1963, the landscape surrounding it had undergone a tremendous transformation. At Navajo Mine to the plant's east, a 40-cubic-yard electric dragline, the largest such machine in the world, dug into the earth, stripping away the soil that covered the coal. Within the pit itself, miners blasted the exposed coal with dynamite charges and loaded 4,200 tons of it a day onto conveyors that led to waiting trucks. North of the plant, a giant pipe reached from the San Juan River to a new lake, created by an earthen dam almost 1.5 miles across and 110 feet high. Two 15,000 horsepower pumps had worked for thirteen months to fill the lake to its 39,000-acre-foot capacity. Two more pumps on the lake's opposite shore took water out of the lake and pumped it into the plant to cool and condense steam for reuse. The plant thus represented the point where supplies of energy long stored beneath the Colorado Plateau intersected with Phoenix's demand for electricity.

Within the plant, coal's chemical energy was transformed into electrical energy that entered a network reaching from the plant outward to Albuquerque, Salt Lake City, and Phoenix. The plant was much what the

FIGURE 4.5. Navajo Sheep appear before a strip-mine drag shovel. Utah Construction Company/Utah International Collection. Image courtesy of Special Collections Department, Stewart Library, Weber State University, Ogden, Utah. 1962.

Bureau of Reclamation had envisioned in its study of future transmission needs. The power lines, however, were not. Instead of public lines interconnecting Reclamation's dams with mine-mouth power plants, they were the property of Arizona Public Service, private lines connecting private utilities across the West. In the coming years those boundaries, too, would begin to disappear.

Other boundaries already had. As APS's power lines reached far beyond the Valley of the Sun to supply Phoenix's demand, the Navajo Reservation and Colorado Plateau became, in a sense, a vital part of urban space. Those lands and the lives of people who lived near them, would be deeply shaped by the urban demand for electricity growing relentlessly in the early 1960s, part of a more generalized search for growth that reached from the levels of local government all the way to the Council of Economic Advisors. At the same time, the fact that these boundaries had disappeared was visible to few people who did not live on the Navajo Reservation, which continued to appear in *Arizona Highways* and in John Ford's films, such as 1962's *How the West Was Won,* as a space out of time from the modern world. The new source of electricity was not apparent in Phoenix, either. In the homes of Phoenix, electricity continued to run air conditioners, stoves, and outdoor lighting, exactly as it had when its energy had come from falling water or burning gas.

CHAPTER 5

Integrating Geographies

THE NAVAJO AQUIFER LIES 2,500–3,000 FEET BENEATH BLACK MESA, where water percolates within a band of Entrada and Navajo sandstone. 90 percent of the aquifer's water was deposited between 10,000 and 25,000 years ago, "fossil groundwater," in the words of one geologist. For the span of human residence on Black Mesa, water seeping from the Navajo aquifer provided the main source of drinking water in a landscape that receives less than eight inches of rain annually.[1] In 1968, following negotiation of new mining contracts with the Navajo and Hopi Tribes, negotiations in which the Hopi Tribe's main lawyer was also secretly on retainer for Peabody Coal, contractors began drilling wells deep into the Navajo Aquifer.[2] Following the terms of the contract, they allowed local residents to draw water from the new wells to drink and water their stock. Most of the water, however, was mixed in equal proportions with pulverized coal from Peabody's new Black Mesa Mine, forming a slurry that was fed into a pipeline that stretched 238 miles across the Colorado Plateau and terminated at Mohave Generating Station, a new power plant built by Southern California Edison on the western shore of the Colorado River, near Bullhead City, Nevada. Over the course of a year, the pipeline carried almost 150,000 tons of coal and 4,085 acre-feet of water, an amount of water roughly 500,000 times the annual rainfall that fell on Black Mesa.[3]

Within Mojave Generating Station, the slurried coal replicated the process that occurred at Four Corners. It produced steam, spun turbines, and generated electricity, which was transmitted through high-voltage power lines. When the electricity left the plant, however, it underwent a significantly different journey than the electricity from Four Corners had six years earlier. Rather than shooting directly to a substation in Phoenix, the electricity from Mojave Generating Station entered a massive pool from which multiple Southwestern cities drew their electricity. In this pool, the electricity from Mojave Generating Station mingled with electricity from other nearby coal-fired generating stations. It also joined with electricity from other sources—natural-gas-fired power plants surrounding Phoenix and Los Angeles, and hydroelectric power from Glen Canyon, Hoover, Parker, and Davis Dams. Within the pool, the electricity passed over a network of private and public lines but its destination was indefinite. It might flow south to Phoenix, west to Los Angeles, east to Four Corners and Albuquerque, north to the farms of the Central Utah Project, or even to far-off homes in the Pacific Northwest.

The indefinite journey of electricity from Mojave Generating Station suggests the dramatic changes that occurred out of view of many Southwesterners during the 1960s. Early in the decade, the electricity that reached consumers in Phoenix had come entirely from generation located within Arizona or owned by Arizona utilities.[4] That electricity was also rigidly divided along public and private lines. With some research, a curious consumer in Phoenix could have determined, with a degree of certainty, the source of his or her electricity. By the late 1960s, the certain connection between production and consumption no longer existed. In the intervening years, public and private utilities jointly built a new system of power plants and electrical lines that pooled the electricity of the entire region, making it impossible to trace electricity back to its specific origin point. Instead, the electrical power used by consumers in Los Angeles and Phoenix emerged from a nebulous pool that combined public and private, coal, natural gas, and hydropower, into a totally fungible commodity whose origin could not be located.

At the same time as the specific source was abstracted however, the general location of electrical generation became clear. With the construction of Mojave Generating Station, and the expansion of Four Corners Power Plant from 230 megawatts to over 1,000 megawatts in the late 1960s, the landscape of the Colorado Plateau, and specifically the landscape of the Navajo and Hopi Nations, became the broad origin point for most of the electricity used by consumers in the Southwest. Even as this power opened up new possibilities for high-tech manufacturing industries and climate-controlled lifestyles in the region's metropolitan areas, its production increasingly structured and defined the lives of those people living on the Colorado Plateau. These changes in geography remade space in the Southwest, rendering the Colorado Plateau in many ways the center of the region's economic development.

PUBLIC AND PRIVATE CONFLICTS

During the 1950s, APS expanded its service area throughout the state and interconnected its system with SRP. Even as the two utilities agreed to coordinate power plant development and sell power to each other, other lines dividing the recipients of public and private power in the region became more rigid. With the expansion of its generating capacity and its interconnection with private utilities in neighboring states, APS required less and less power from Bureau of Reclamation facilities. At the same time, Reclamation pursued plans to expand its generating capacity and to develop a system of federally owned transmission lines that would link its far-flung public customers into a "strong transmission system" that aimed to ensure reliable service to the rural irrigation districts and municipal systems that relied on Reclamation power.[5] As public and private utilities pursued these plans simultaneously, they developed dual and competing transmission systems in the Southwest that revealed conflict between the private utilities' grow-and-build strategy and policies governing the generation and transmission of federally generated electricity.

At the founding of the Bureau of Reclamation in 1902, electrical power had been considered a useful by-product of its primary tasks: the control of Western rivers' seasonal cycles and the transformation of the desert lands of the West into agricultural acreage. Initially, Reclamation built dams primarily to prevent floods and to irrigate farm fields. As land adjacent to available water sources became "reclaimed" and transformed into farmland, farmers farther and farther from rivers began demanding assistance from Reclamation. While some of these farms were supplied via long irrigation canals, many more used electrical irrigation pumps to water their fields. In this way, electrical power became central to the mission of Reclamation. Increasingly, its role in the reclamation of arid lands involved not building irrigation ditches to carry water from reservoir to field but powering pumping systems that lifted water from aquifers lying deep below the surface of the earth.[6]

Because the National Reclamation Act limited the agency's authority to dam construction, dams remained central to Reclamation's agriculturally oriented mission. Reclamation officials had interpreted the Act as forbidding the agency from building any steam-generating plants, an interpretation that the region's private utilities had heartily endorsed to avoid the competition federally generated steam power would have represented. Even though Reclamation customers were using electricity rather than water, Reclamation could only generate that electricity using the energy of falling water. While water would never be diverted from Lake Powell or Lake Mead directly onto a farm field, the water in the reservoirs would indirectly irrigate farm fields by generating electricity. Furthermore, Reclamation used the proceeds from power sales to pay back the cost of the dams over the course of sixty years. Until the changes of the early 1960s, then, Reclamation customers used hydroelectrically generated power almost exclusively to irrigate farm fields.[7]

This interpretation of Reclamation's mission meant that the divide between public and private power also represented a divide between hydroelectric power and steam-generated power. The language in the enabling legislation for most dams strengthened this divide, as it directed Reclamation to give first priority for sale of electricity to "preference customers," public utilities that mainly consisted of agricultural irrigation districts and municipally owned utilities. Furthermore, it directed Reclamation to transmit this power using the lowest cost method possible. This method invariably promoted the federal construction of transmission lines. While the construction of such lines required high up-front costs, these costs could be repaid at low rates over sixty years, keeping the end cost to "preference customers" lower than if customers paid fees (called wheeling costs) to private utilities in order to transmit electricity over their existing lines. While these decisions made sense economically to preference customers, and politically to Reclamation, they limited the integration of regional electrical systems, effectively creating two different systems throughout much of the Southwest.[8]

Until at least the early 1960s, the Bureau of Reclamation's program focused primarily on the development of agriculture. While Reclamation on certain exceptional occasions had explicitly worked to transmit electricity to urban residents (most notably during the power shortages that marked the early days of World War II), its preference customers remained almost exclusively agricultural, with the great exception being the mostly self-sufficient Salt River Project, which essentially split its electrical load between agricultural and other customers.[9] Reclamation had only once ventured into a broader effort at regional planning with its 1952 *Study of Future Transmission in the West*, an initiative that the region's private utilities and their supporters in the region's newspapers had met with widespread disdain and dismissal.[10]

The split between public and private power thus represented a larger divide in the Southwest—between rural and urban land—that did not fall into the familiar narrative of declining farms and ascending cities; both these sectors of the Southwestern economy underwent tremendous economic growth during the postwar era. Until the early 1960s, however, these geographies remained unconnected. Investor-owned companies generated the vast majority of power for the regions' metropolitan areas, using natural gas and coal-fired power plants. At the beginning of the 1960s, each growing metropolitan area also had its own discrete geography that remained relatively isolated from other such areas: Arizona Public Service served Phoenix, Southern California Edison served the suburbs of Los Angeles and Orange County, the Public Service Companies of Colorado and New Mexico, respectively, served Denver and Albuquerque.

In contrast, farms drew their power largely from the Bureau of Reclamation's dams and from smaller, publicly owned power plants. Reclamation used federal loans to build these dams and used proceeds from the sale of power as a financing mechanism. Rural cooperatives, irrigation districts, Indian reservations, and municipally owned utilities were, by law, the only entities that could contract with Reclamation for "firm"

power—electricity guaranteed to be delivered. These preference customers were scattered throughout the region, connected by a messy assort-
ment of federal and private transmission lines. When receiving power
sent over private lines, the preference customer would pay, as mentioned
above, "wheeling" fees to the private line owner, fees for carrying electricity that raised the cost of delivery typically two mills per kilowatt-hour.[11]
Since wheeling over private lines raised the cost of electricity, Reclamation aimed to extend its network of transmission lines as much as possible to achieve the lowest possible price to the preference customer.[12] Even
as APS located its generation facilities far from Phoenix, Reclamation
sought to build transmission lines to serve preference customers throughout the Southwest. As the 1960s began, these two geographies intersected
and came into conflict.

Electricity generated at the Colorado River Storage Project served as
the precipitating cause. CRSP was designed to promote farmland irrigation in the states of Utah, New Mexico, and Colorado and to store water
for the river's Upper Basin states through the construction of multiple
dams on the Upper Colorado River.[13] After a contentious fight between
the Sierra Club and the Bureau of Reclamation, which eventually blocked
a dam planned for Echo Park within Dinosaur National Monument, Reclamation settled on a location in Glen Canyon as the site of CRSP's key-
stone project, Glen Canyon Dam.[14] The water of Lake Powell, Glen Canyon Dam's reservoir, would not be used directly for irrigation; instead,
the sale of the dam's power would finance both the cost of its construction and $1 billion of irrigation projects in Upper Basin states. The dam
would serve as a cash register, providing funds for all subsequent CRSP
projects, including additional dams on the Upper Colorado River. Like
other postwar Reclamation projects, CRSP's initial plan limited supply of
the dam's firm power (power contracted for in advance) to public utilities. And the CRSP guidelines mandated that power be delivered to these
public systems over federally owned transmission lines.[15]

Prior to CRSP's authorization in 1956, most private power companies
in the Southwest had achieved a measure of peace with Reclamation. Public and private utilities had pursued at least limited interties (connections
between electrical systems), linking their systems with Reclamation transmission lines, as was the case with APS's interconnection at Parker Dam.
System operators for both Reclamation and private utilities used these
interconnections to stave off emergency blackouts. CRSP's so-called all-
federal system, however, proposed an extensive network of transmission
lines stretching outward from Glen Canyon Dam into Arizona, Utah, New
Mexico, and Colorado. Endorsed by Eisenhower's secretary of the interior, Fred Seaton, in August 1957, the all-federal system projected the construction of twenty-seven high-voltage transmission lines and seventeen

transmission substations at a cost of somewhere between $150 million and $176 million. This newly built system would allow Reclamation to deliver power directly to its preference customers, eliminating the need to pay wheeling fees to private utilities for carrying its power. While most of this system connected isolated rural customers to electricity from Glen Canyon Dam, several of the planned transmission lines appeared to aim straight at the metropolitan consumers served primarily by private utilities. Reclamation planned construction of three 230-kilovolt lines from Glen Canyon Dam to Phoenix and two similar lines connecting Glen Canyon to Albuquerque. Furthermore, Reclamation sought to use CRSP power lines to link the multiple Bureau projects across the Southwest in an extensive power grid. The all-federal system proposed the interconnection of the new CRSP system with the existing federal lines reaching outward from Parker and Davis Dams, which would, in theory, allow Reclamation to transmit excess power from Glen Canyon to Southern California. In Colorado, CRSP's transmission lines would tie in with the Bureau's Curecanti Project and the Missouri Basin Project in eastern Colorado and Wyoming. The all-federal system thus planned a much greater federal involvement in not only the generation of power but in its transmission across the West. It represented a new geography that seemed to compete directly with private utilities.[16]

And such utilities reacted to these plans with alarm. Some private officials chose to attack the entire preference customer system; E. M. Naughton, president of Utah Power and Light, stated, "There must be no giveaway to preference customers. Power must be sold to whomsoever will pay the highest price."[17] Most power executives were, however, satisfied with the ruling reserving firm power to preference customers. The ambitious building plans of private utilities such as APS had alleviated their need for the dam's firm power, and they had little interest in supplying small collections of rural customers. On the other hand, private utilities saw Reclamation's plan to build power lines to heavily populated areas as a strike at the heart of their business. They feared that power from Glen Canyon Dam would allow small rural systems located close to metropolitan areas to begin competing with private utilities for customers. The all-federal system had the potential for constraining the future growth of private utilities' customer bases, endangering the build-and-grow strategy that formed the basis of their business plans. Private utilities launched Red-baiting attacks on "socialistic power interests," including one mailing, entitled "Public Power's Red Roots," sent to utility customers and members of Congress that traced the history of socialized power from the current proposals back through the TVA to the writings of Karl Marx.[18]

The utilities offered more than just opposition. They offered their own alternative plan. In October 1959, five private utilities (Arizona Public

Service, Utah Power and Light, the Public Service Companies of Colorado and of New Mexico, and Pacific Power and Light of Wyoming) offered to spend $100 million to build transmission lines to carry power to Reclamation's preference customers. Under the private plan, Reclamation would spend only $52 million to build lines connecting Glen Canyon Dam with Four Corners Power Plant, and Four Corners with a major federally owned substation in Salida, Colorado. Private utilities would build the additional lines interconnecting CRSP projects and carrying Reclamation power to load centers. As part of the plan, the private utilities would charge preference customers the current established rate for wheeling power across their lines. According to the utilities' estimates, the plan would save the federal government over $100 million while protecting Reclamation's financing mechanisms.[19]

This plan set off a furious political battle between public and private power interests that extended from the last year of the Eisenhower administration into the early years of the Kennedy administration. Kennedy's appointment of Stewart Udall as secretary of the interior only exacerbated the political struggle. Udall, a native of St. John's, Arizona, and, until his appointment, Tucson's representative in Congress, had been a longtime public power advocate and, like almost all politicians from the state, a supporter of Reclamation's plans to bring Colorado River water to central Arizona.[20] At the same time, Udall's former constituents pressured him to follow the low tax, "business friendly" policies promoted by the states' boosters. As one letter stated, "I am surprised. . . . [Y]ou appear to have become a rubber stamp on what the Kennedy Administration wants instead of what the people of Arizona want. Arizona has an outstanding record nationally, to reject excessive spending by the Federal Government. . . . I still wish you would reconsider and permit the investor owned utilities to build the transmission lines."[21]

The political battle over the CRSP power lines in many ways replicated past disputes between public and private power. Public-power advocates portrayed the private utilities as greedy parasites attempting to usurp the public's power for their own profit. After Reclamation issued a report in April 1960 comparing the two systems, concluding that the all-federal system would transmit power more inexpensively (6 mills to 6.57 mills per kwh),[22] public-power advocates claimed that the private plan would end up costing preference customers $253,808,000 over the course of CRSP's 86-year repayment schedule, expenses that federal supporters likened to "perpetual rent."[23] Questioning utility executives' contention that Reclamation did not have the know-how to properly build transmission lines, Udall acerbically responded, "The Bureau has been trusted to construct and operate some of the world's largest dams and powerplants. Surely it can and must be trusted to construct necessary transmission lines in order to market the power produced at those powerplants."[24] Public-power advocates also attacked the geography of the private utilities' plan, charging that they had offered to build only the lines that could turn a profit, leaving unprofitable lines to be built at the government's expense. As Udall stated in a congressional circular, "The private utilities do not offer to build *all* the transmission lines. They want to build only those lines that are lucrative to them and give them control of the entire power system. . . . They are willing to let the Government build the least profitable lines as apparently this is not Government interference."[25]

For their part, the utilities and their supporters repeated arguments that Reclamation's plan represented a dangerous socialist infringement on private industry. As the utilities sent their circular to congressmen tracing the Marxist roots of the Bureau of Reclamation, Representative Craig Hosmer, Republican from California, denounced the plan as a waste of government funds: "Private power companies stand ready, willing, and able to build every inch of needed transmission lines for this system at no cost whatever to the federal taxpayers. . . . Not one cent of federal funds need be spent to accomplish any objective listed by the secretary as the reason for federal construction of these lines." Seeing little practical reason for building the lines, Hosmer hinted at darker motives: "There must be other reasons for his proposal. The principle [*sic*] reason, in my opinion, being that Fabian-minded reclamation bureaucrats again have propelled Udall into an egghead shaped orbit calculated to end in the transfer of control of the Upper Colorado basin states from the local people to power hungry civil servants."[26]

Hidden within this long-standing debate over public and private power, however, was a new dispute over the proper structure of power networks that did not break along the same lines. While the public-private power debate captured most of the rhetorical heat, this second debate proved far more influential in settling the CRSP power-line dispute. In developing its conception of the all-federal network, Reclamation placed the connection of its own transmission networks as its highest priority. Reclamation posed this development as a logical step in system development. As Udall stated in support of the project, "It's simply the Government connecting its property together. In this manner the full benefits of the project can flow direct [*sic*] to the preference customers without any middlemen taking shares."[27] Their main stated concern with the private plan was that the utilities would become the de facto owners of the power and could control its flow. Reclamation thus conceived a network in which electrical power would remain continuously within its own transmission lines. This system would maintain rigid separation between public and private utilities.[28] In Reclamation's plan, farmers in the Vernal (Utah) Irrigation District using CRSP power would know not only that the electricity that powered their irrigation pumps originated at Glen Canyon Dam but could trace the precise path from origin to consumption.

Private utilities attacked the premises of this division, claiming that they rested on archaic understandings of power systems. Reclamation's cost estimates had evaluated the private plan without taking into consideration the effect of interconnections with privately owned power plants. While Reclamation claimed this was necessary to achieve a fair comparison between the two wheeling systems, the private utilities ridiculed the report's assumption that preference consumers needed to receive the *actual* electricity generated at Glen Canyon Dam. Instead of precisely matching production with consumption, the private utilities proposed to satisfy the demands of preference customers through electricity generated at their power plants while offsetting that use with power from Glen Canyon. In this plan, the utilities treated electrical power as fungible. In their estimates, it mattered little whether the farmers in Vernal received power from Glen Canyon or Four Corners as long as the electricity was there when they turned on their pumps.[29]

In this understanding of power as a fungible commodity, the private utilities had an ally in the Federal Power Commission, the federal agency regulating the interstate transmission of electricity. Throughout the late 1950s and 1960s, the FPC continually pushed for the maximum possible interconnection of utilities. In its periodic surveys of the nation's electrical facilities, the Commission warned that electrical networks in much of the nation remained dangerously isolated. Pointing to the Soviet Union, which was in the process of developing a nationally interconnected power grid, the FPC cautioned that the U.S. system, with its divisions between public and private, left the nation at a dangerous disadvantage to the Soviets. "Without greater interconnection between systems," the 1960 *National Power Survey* warned, "an enemy attack could disable electrical systems in many western states and cripple essential military production."[30] While the FPC officially favored a federally built and managed system, they stressed that all potential opportunities for interconnection should be pursued.

While the FPC seemingly favored the "all-federal" plan, the Commission's understanding of electrical power favored the ideas held by private utilities. A national grid would strengthen electrical networks not, as Reclamation officials held, because it connected separate government properties; rather, it strengthened those networks by better allowing electricity to flow to where it was demanded, regardless of its source. A national grid would allow utilities to reduce their need for reserves by permitting them to sell excess capacity to neighboring areas with demand for electricity. Utilities realized this benefit particularly, the FPC pointed out, with interconnections that linked areas across time zones, as usage regularly peaked at 5:00 P.M., and across climactic zones; cold climates used more electricity

BENEFITS OF INTERCONNECTED POWER SYSTEMS

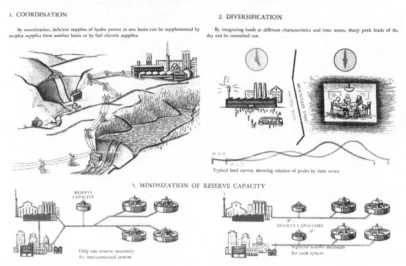

FIGURE 5.1. Benefits of Interconnected Power Systems. Source: Bureau of Reclamation, *A Study of Future Transmission in the West* (Government Printing Office, 1953).

in the winter while hot climates used more in the summer. More important to the FPC than efficient use, interconnections would protect national security, allowing the quick management of disruptions in generation caused by attack or sabotage. If shortages or outages occurred, a national grid would allow the problem to be rectified simply by transferring power from other generating plants. The idea that electrical power was fungible remained central to these notions of interconnection. Electricity could be used whether a public or private agency supplied a consumer or whether coal, natural gas, or water generated the electricity.[31]

In managing the dispute over CRSP's power lines, Udall was therefore faced with conflicting priorities. Reclamation, concerned with ensuring ownership and control of the power it generated, sought all-federal transmission lines that would enable its properties to form a region-wide network. Reclamation would treat interconnection with private utilities as, at best, a marginal concern. The FPC, concerned with ensuring the strongest and most reliable transmission system possible, sought extensive interconnection between public and private systems. This interconnection would make it virtually impossible to know who owned or had generated any of the power within the system at any one time. While

Udall's secretarial papers contain little detailed information about the deliberations over this conflict, Udall's eventual decision left little doubt which priority prevailed.

On February 20, 1962, Udall announced new agreements between Reclamation and five private utilities in four states. These five utilities agreed to work with Reclamation to transmit CRSP power and eventually to interconnect their systems. The agreement, negotiated by Reclamation commissioner Floyd Dominy, was far from the utilities' initial offer to build the vast majority of necessary transmission lines. Private utilities would build and own only $27 million of CRSP transmission lines while Reclamation would still spend $151 million building transmission lines. However, the agreement did begin to link the Upper Basin states in the kind of strong grid that the FPC had urged.[32]

Advocates of both the all-federal and the mostly private systems objected to the system. Representative Hosmer denounced the limited number of power lines that private utilities would build as "a cynical and deceptive attempt to perfume a stinking socialistic power grab" and "a $151 million raid on the federal treasury."[33] The American Public Power Association, the nation's leading public-power advocacy group, registered its "sharp disappointment" that the Department of the Interior had "decided to abandon important aspects of the all-Federal system" for agreements with private utilities "that are vague in many respects, and leave serious doubts as to whether the new arrangements will provide all of the benefits to the government and to the consumer-owned electrical systems that would have been made available from the all-Federal system."[34] Despite these objections, Reclamation officials and the five private utilities appeared relatively happy with the compromise they had struck.

Two types of agreement linked the public and private systems. In one, Reclamation contracted with a private utility to reserve space in a transmission line until demand dictated the construction of a new power line. Reclamation would pay for the new line and would then share use and operation of the transmission system. For example, the Public Service Company of New Mexico (PSC-NM) agreed to dedicate 140 megawatts of transmission capacity for CRSP needs in its existing high-voltage line from Farmington to Albuquerque at a cost of no less than $300,000 annually. Once CRSP transmission requirements exceeded 140 megawatts, Reclamation would build its own line from Farmington to Albuquerque, and it would operate that line jointly with PSC-NM to serve both public and private consumers.[35] In the second type of agreement, Reclamation and a private utility agreed to develop an interconnected transmission system immediately. In Colorado, Reclamation agreed to build two lines linking Fort Lupton with Beaver Creek, and Midway with Denver, and to operate these lines jointly with the Public Service Corporation of

Colorado (PSC-Colorado), using both Reclamation and PSC-Colorado power interchangeably. As the agreement stated, "Maximum advantage will be taken of exchanging power, both at generating plants and at loads, in order to utilize the Company's existing system as long as possible, thereby delaying Reclamation line construction, and to reduce ultimate transmission investment for both parties."[36]

The agreements between Reclamation and private utilities, all of which concluded with eventual agreements to operate the resulting systems co-operatively, dissolved the lines between public and private power in the Upper Colorado Basin states. The agreements worked to link consumers primarily to the closest power source. To take one example, Reclamation had several preference customers in northeastern Colorado with contracts for CRSP power. The nearest CRSP power source, however, was a dam on the western slope of the Rockies, more than two hundred miles away. With its interconnection agreement, Reclamation could turn the job over to nearby PSC-Colorado generating plants. In return, Reclamation power would serve PSC-Colorado customers in the San Luis Valley of southern Colorado. These connections were not fixed. In the cases of power short-ages or disruptions from downed power lines and transmission failures, power from public or private sources would flow through the intercon-nected network to answer the endangered demand. Since the agreements eventually resulted in interconnected systems, rather than wheeling con-tracts, there was no need for an elaborate accounting system to trace the path of power. Payments for power from the two partners could be based on the amount of power put into the system at a particular time of day.[37]

The interconnection agreements had the further advantage of using different types of generation to their best ability to meet demand. Coal-fired plants produced inexpensive electricity if they ran constantly, but they became significantly less efficient if their output required constant adjustment. Therefore, it made sense to run coal-fired plants continu-ously, producing a regular base level of electrical power. Hydroelectric dams, however, were quite easily regulated. They had no boilers that needed time to heat up; power began flowing as soon as water passed through a dam's turbines. They could therefore best be used to meet peaks in usage. As this peaking power was considerably more expensive and inconvenient to produce than the base power generated at the coal-fired plants, the private utilities welcomed interconnection as a means to avoid building peaking plants that would sit idle most days. Reclamation officials, in turn, welcomed connection with private utilities that allowed it to meet the demands of preference customers without the immediate need to build and maintain power lines.[38]

While the agreements of February 1962 created broad connections be-tween the Bureau and private utilities in the Upper Basin states, Reclamation and APS remained at odds. Though private utilities in the Upper Basin had reduced their wheeling prices to a price equivalent to Reclamation's cost for building new lines, APS's lowest offer would still have left Reclamation paying $650,000 more annually than the cost of building lines from Glen Canyon Dam to Phoenix, where they would supply SRP, the one major preference customer in the Lower Basin states (Arizona, California, and Nevada). It is unclear why APS refused to lower its offer as the Upper Basin utilities had, but two possibilities exist. With Four Corners about to come on line, APS may have seen little use for the power that would have entered its system. The evidence suggests, however, that APS feared that interconnection with Reclamation lines would put it at a competitive disadvantage with SRP. In theory, power from Glen Canyon Dam would leave SRP needing less power from Four Corners and Cholla Power Plants, complicating APS's plan to run the plants at maximum capacity by selling excess power to SRP. In short, APS was unwilling to allow Reclamation electricity to enter the power market in central Arizona on terms that would prove advantageous to its public competitor.[39]

The disputes between Reclamation (and SRP) and APS intensified in the year after the agreement with the Upper Basin utilities. As interconnections took shape in the Upper Basin's system, APS and public power advocates skirmished over who would develop new transmission facilities in the state. APS conducted an aggressive public-relations campaign, once again claiming SRP gained unfair advantages from its tax-free status. Editorials and political cartoons in the conservative *Arizona Republic* portrayed APS as carrying an excessive tax burden, which it passed on to consumers, while SRP skated by tax free. APS also encouraged its customers to write letters to Udall, pointing out that SRP did not pay taxes, allowing it both to infringe on APS's business and to increase the tax burden on Arizonans. "The rascals [SRP] don't even pay something in lieu of taxes," one letter read,

> which would certainly lessen our individual tax burdens. The other utility here, which is private, paid $13,403,000 in federal, state, and local taxes in 1960; that helps build a lot of schools and roads. I point this out to show that the combination plan would contribute tax relief to all taxpayers in the basin area. I object to my tax dollars going to a few un-regulated preference utilities in an area where private enterprise is willing to help build the overall system.[40]

Not to be outdone, the Department of the Interior, on behalf of Reclamation, searched for ways to more extensively regulate APS's construction of transmission lines. In late 1962, Interior officials proposed new rules for granting rights-of-way for transmission lines crossing federal lands that would grant the secretary of the interior veto power over rights-of-way if they were deemed "inconsistent with Federal power marketing policy." Furthermore, they empowered public power producers to utilize any excess capacity in transmission lines crossing federal lands. As APS was still in the process of building new transmission lines from Four Corners to Phoenix, this change would have allowed SRP to receive CRSP power through APS lines.[41]

APS officials predictably responded with outrage to the new rules. In a letter to the Bureau of Land Management and all of Arizona's congressional representatives, APS president Walter Lucking denounced the rules, claiming that they threatened the essence of the utility's business. The veto power, Lucking feared, would subordinate APS construction plans to Reclamation's needs. "Possibly, the construction of plants or transmission lines . . . could be deemed inconsistent with these future plans of the department. . . . Laying aside the questions of whether there is or should be a Federal power marketing policy, [the veto power] is a vague standard which would give the Secretary wide discretion to approve or disapprove power transmission and interchange between electric utilities." The line-usage rules would force the utility's capital resources to be used by their central competitor. As Lucking wrote, "That to give the government the one-sided right to use our excess capacity to wheel power for distributors serving in competition with us is to make our customers second class citizens, whose interests are to be subordinated to the interests of the customers of rival distributors preferred by the government."[42]

Lucking recognized that the new Interior rules were aimed to take advantage of APS's build-and-grow strategy. Since APS built transmission lines with excess capacity, Reclamation could easily wheel all of SRP's preference power across APS's lines. The proposed rules would thus use the utility's very growth strategy against it. As Lucking wrote, "The very nature of the utility business requires it to look to the future in the interests of its consumers. By the proposed regulations the Department would deprive the utility-owner of this essential tool for expansion." In concluding his objections to the policy, Lucking made an argument that would become dominant years later in the legal interactions between federal authority and owners of private property: "As we read the regulations, there is no compensation for potential increase in capacity. This amounts to the taking of property without due process of law."[43]

Lucking's and APS's legal-takings argument never saw the inside of a courtroom. Arizona representatives John Rhodes and George Senner stalled the new rules in committee for the balance of 1964. APS, however, was experiencing the dangers that small utilities had always faced; they had to continue growing or interconnect with another utility. Without continual growth, they had no way to finance new power plants and retire inefficient older ones. Without increasing efficiency, investors became skeptical of their future prospects, and attracting capital became more difficult. APS had never faced this problem; they had been the largest utility in a growing state in an era when private utility territory had stopped at state lines. The increased cooperation between public and private utilities in the Upper Basin states threatened this secure position and removed the need for neighboring private utilities to interconnect with APS. It endangered their ability to sell off excess power from Four Corners Power Plant. It even threatened to strengthen public power to the point it could mandate the involuntary transmission of power. In short, the public-private partnership in the Upper Basin threatened to leave APS an isolated and stagnant exile from the structure that linked the region.

WEST ASSOCIATES

On September 22, 1964, D. W. Reeves, president of the Public Service Company of New Mexico, stood before reporters, smiled broadly, and introduced what he called "the largest regional electrical power development program ever planned anywhere in the world." Newspaper photos of the event show Reeves gesturing toward a map of the western United States, which read, "WEST Associates: 36,000,000 new kilowatts by 1985." Upon that map, a great circle reached from Los Angeles to eastern Colorado, encompassing almost all of Nevada, Utah, Colorado, Arizona, and New Mexico.[44]

In his statement to the press, Reeves explained that WEST (an acronym for Western Energy Supply and Transmission) Associates was a new organization composed of ten investor-owned utilities throughout the Southwest dedicated to fostering cooperation and connection among the region's private power systems. During the twenty-one years from 1964 to 1985, the ten members of WEST planned to spend $10.5 billion in order to generate 36 million kilowatts of electricity, more than twice the amount of power its member utilities currently possessed or planned to build. WEST's plan also called for construction of a series of extra-high-voltage transmission lines that would link the utilities, allowing them to share electricity. The proposed system would create a series of connected power plants with three times the capacity of the TVA. And unlike the federally run TVA, private utilities would own and control WEST. As Reeves emphasized, WEST would not include power projects run or financed by the federal government.[45]

WEST's plan represented private utilities' response to concerns that Reclamation would dictate the terms of the interconnection of Southwestern transmission systems. While the plans private utilities had negotiated with the federal government in the Upper Basin would continue, WEST called for the transmission lines connecting the Lower Basin states—private utilities in Southern California, Nevada, and Arizona—to be privately owned and unconnected with the existing federal system. To meet demand in these growing states, WEST utilities planned to jointly finance and build large-scale power plants to deliver base power throughout the region. With a stress on the generation of large amounts of power from the cheapest available fuel source, these power plants would almost certainly be coal fired. And while Reeves speculated to reporters that WEST might explore the construction of a nuclear plant that could both produce electricity and desalinate ocean water (thus providing private solutions to the region's power and water shortages), the expansion of Four Corners Power Plant was the only project WEST announced at its inaugural press conference; five utilities agreed to build two new generating units capable of producing almost 1,600 megawatts (1,590,000 kilowatts) of electricity.[46]

In many ways, WEST's plan replicated the system that the Bureau of Reclamation had called for a little more than ten years earlier in its *Study of Future Transmission in the West*. Like that system, WEST's plan would utilize mine-mouth power plants connected with multiple metropolitan load centers by a series of extra-high-voltage power lines. In WEST's case, the new generating units at Four Corners would be connected not only to APS in Phoenix, but also to the PSC-NM's main load center in Albuquerque and to Southern California Edison's huge market in metropolitan Los Angeles.[47] To ship "coal by wire" to Southern California more efficiently, WEST planned to build a 500-kilovolt transmission line across northern Arizona, connecting to Southern California Edison's system just south of Hoover Dam.[48]

The expansion of Four Corners demonstrated the novel joint-financing arrangement that WEST utilized to finance power plants. Previously, single utilities had built and financed power plants, almost always within their service area. The utility used electricity generated at that plant primarily to satisfy the needs of its customers and only secondarily sought links with other utilities to sell off excess capacity. For a utility like APS, whose customer base was growing but remained a relatively small 750,000 people, relying primarily on their own customers meant forgoing the massive economies of scale available from the newest generators, capable of generating up to 1,000 megawatts apiece. A utility like APS would simply have no ability to sell that much electricity and would lose the benefits of its lower costs because of its inability to run the generator to its maximum capacity.[49]

WEST's plan allowed Southwestern utilities to escape this dilemma by sharing generation among multiple utilities. WEST members invested a percentage of the total capital cost of a power plant in proportion to the percentage of the energy they were entitled to as firm (guaranteed) power, the utility managing the plant's operation receiving an additional 5 percent of the electricity. For example, Southern California Edison provided 50 percent of the capital for the expansion of Four Corners Power Plant. The utility thus owned 48 percent of the power from the new units installed at the plant, with the extra 2 percent of electricity going to APS, which operated the plant. Participating utilities were free to exchange or sell excess power to other participating utilities.[50] The joint investment in power plants by multiple utilities thus allowed the construction of far larger generating units than a single utility's customer base could have sustained. With these larger generating units, the cost of electricity declined, as inexpensive coal-fired base power could make up a greater and greater proportion of each utility's electrical load. Furthermore, as transmission technology improved to allow the construction of 500-kilovolt lines, the cost of shipping electricity long distances declined accordingly.[51]

The utilities within WEST remained separate entities. They maintained their separate service areas and their separate distribution systems for bringing electricity to consumers. The agreement, however, dramatically altered the geography of electricity in the Southwest by combining the utilities' generating capacity into a single pool. The original Four Corners Power Plant had been built in a geography where the generation, transmission, and distribution of electricity occurred mostly in discrete networks with interconnections providing emergency backup. The expanded Four Corners would exist in a very different geography. Utilities would maintain their discrete local distribution systems. Generation and transmission capacities, however, would be shared, with multiple utilities drawing electricity from the same source, allowing for electricity to be produced much more inexpensively, but also making much more intensive use of energy sources. Where Phoenix had been the main population center for the original Four Corners plant, it became just one of several major centers served by the expanded plant. Southern California Edison, in fact, financed one of the 750-megawatt generators for its sole use.[52]

The expansion of Four Corners was not the only WEST project. Three months after Reeves's press conference, Southern California Edison announced plans to build a massive 3,000-megawatt plant on the Nevada shore of the Colorado River, two miles south of Davis Dam. The plant, which would be named Mohave Generating Station, would have four 750-megawatt generators and would be jointly owned by Nevada Power and Sierra Pacific Power Companies along with Southern California Edison. The fuel source for this plant remained uncertain. However, Southern California Edison announced they were in negotiations with Peabody Coal to utilize coal from lands just leased on Black Mesa, at the intersection of the Navajo and Hopi Nations.[53] Coal from Black Mesa would also eventually be used to power Navajo Generating Station, a 2,250-megawatt plant located on Navajo land adjacent to Glen Canyon Dam. The following chapter will examine the construction of Navajo Generating Station separately to explore the effect the emerging environmental movement would have on politics of electrical generation in the Southwest. For now, however, Mohave, Navajo, and Four Corners Power Plants illustrate a separate point. A central element of WEST's plan involved locating most of the Southwest's base power generation in the Navajo Nation. While utilities would retain their existing, mainly gas-fired power plants, they would increasingly look to use them for peaking power, drawing most of their base power from the jointly built coal-fired plants on the Colorado Plateau.

The formation of WEST, thus, intensified energy development on the Colorado Plateau and the Navajo Nation. The Colorado Plateau and Navajo Nation had become, by the early 1970s, the center of power production for a growing metropolitan Southwest located on its periphery. WEST's plan concretized the vision that Phoenix's boosters had of modern manufacturing centers with open skies. The ability to locate base power production far away from centers of consumption created new center-periphery relationships in the Southwest. This geography reversed traditional center-periphery geographies; while power flowed out of this center, political decision-making power was not retained there. Instead, it remained within the peripheral metropolitan areas that benefited from those resources, and as these grew more powerful, they increasingly controlled the landscape that made up the center of the modern Southwest.

Public and Private Systems Revisited

It was not only private utilities that created this new geography. By 1966, Secretary Udall was describing the federal government as "a non-member member of WEST" while D. W. Reeves was hailing "a new era of cooperation between private utilities and the government."[54] Seemingly overnight, the relationship between federal public power officials and the private utilities involved in WEST had gone from stark antagonism to mutual respect. In 1965, federal officials and utility executives began the interconnection of WEST's private transmission system and the public system of the Bureau of Reclamation. By the winter of 1968, power from Four Corners Power Plant streamed not only to Phoenix but also to Los Angeles, Albuquerque, and far northward to heat homes in the Pacific Northwest over lines built by both private utilities and the federal government. Why did this new cooperation between the federal government and private utilities occur? And what did it mean for people living on the Colorado Plateau?

Initially, Udall was not thrilled with the formation of WEST. Coming in the wake of the agreements with the Upper Basin utilities, he seemed to have expected the Lower Basin utilities to gradually seek interconnection largely on Reclamation's terms, as had the Upper Basin states. Following Reeves's announcement, Udall expressed surprise that the federal government was not included in the talks. "I was a little bit disappointed—I had regrets—that they did not choose to sit down and have some talks with us about it, to see whether we might try to coordinate overall efforts."[55] That the utilities driving the formation of WEST—primarily Southern California Edison and APS—chose to avoid negotiations with the Bureau of Reclamation and federal government demonstrated their lack of interest in the kind of arrangements negotiated between the Bureau and the Upper Basin utilities. Those deals had resulted in widespread federal ownership of major transmission lines and the interconnection of the Bureau of Reclamation and investor-owned utilities.

Utilities in Arizona and California were not interested in such arrangements for several reasons. First, APS resisted any changes that might supply SRP with inexpensive electricity. This point demonstrates a larger difference between the Upper and Lower Basin states. Public power entities in the Upper Basin were almost exclusively geographically isolated, small rural cooperatives that were costly to serve. SRP had begun as such a cooperative but had evolved into a major metropolitan utility because of the suburban growth on Phoenix's periphery. APS feared that the Project's lower residential and commercial prices would act to limit APS prices and lead to more rapid development in areas served by the Project.[56] Second, WEST utilities in the Lower Basin had little interest in sharing capacity with the federal government given the Interior Department's transmission right-of-way policy. WEST's plan to cooperate in the use of power lines represented an ingenious way around Interior's rule that the federal government could use excess capacity in transmission lines crossing federal land. Lines used by a single utility would undoubtedly have significant excess capacity, as transmission lines were built in advance of demand according to the dictates of the grow-and-build policy. If the lines were jointly used by multiple utilities in a single network, however, little excess capacity would exist in the lines on any reliable schedule. WEST utilities thus could make the most of the lower cost advantages of extra-high-voltage transmission lines without allowing the federal government to use them.[57] Finally, the decision to exclude the federal government indicated private utilities' interest in dictating the course of electrical development. They might pursue interconnection with the Bureau of Reclamation or other federal agencies, but only if they could dictate the terms.

By 1965, WEST's terms appeared more and more palatable to power officials in the Department of Interior. By then, Udall's rhetoric had changed dramatically from three years prior when he had labeled private utilities greedy profiteers who were attempting "to erect tollbooths" on CRSP transmission lines. Even with his initial pique at the formation of WEST, Udall's rhetoric never returned to the stark divisions between public and private power that had marked the CRSP transmission-line controversy. Following the formation of WEST, Udall began referring to interconnection between the consortium and Reclamation as inevitable and beneficial for both parties, even if it occurred largely on WEST's terms. Asked in the wake of Reeves's announcement whether WEST posed a "challenge to the federal system," Udall responded that he foresaw extensive cooperation in generating power between public and private systems: "I think that there are a lot of reasons why we should try to coordinate our plans and cooperate to the fullest extent." Udall stated that in his ideal situation private coal-fired generating units would produce the region's base power while the Bureau of Reclamation's dams could provide a reliable supply of inexpensive peaking power.[58] Udall was, in many ways, extending WEST's vision of the pooling of electricity. His proposal foresaw all electricity consumers drawing power from a single pool of electricity undivided by public and private terms. Because this pool would be produced from a variety of sources—coal, natural gas, and hydropower—each of these sources could be used in their most efficient manner. Coal power could provide constant low-cost base power while hydroelectric dams and natural gas plants could be used to meet high-usage peaks.

There are several reasons for this rapid transition in federal policy from rigidly separated electrical systems to the pooling of public and private power. First, agricultural customers demanded increasing amounts of Reclamation electricity. During the 1950s and 1960s, agricultural use of electricity across the Southwest rose at two times the rate of residential consumers.[59] While Reclamation's preference customers did not generally face the same population increases that private utilities did (the SRP being the major exception), this increasing rate of electrical usage strained Reclamation's ability to ensure supply to its preference customers in the foreseeable future. According to Reclamation estimates, preference customers would exhaust the supply of CRSP power sometime around 1970.[60]

In addition to the pressure from this increased usage of electricity, the Bureau of Reclamation had nearly exhausted the available dam sites on the Colorado River, the only river in the Southwest with a large enough water volume to enable the building of major power-producing dams. Following the completion of Glen Canyon Dam, the only remaining dam sites on the main stream of the Colorado were downstream at Marble and Bridge Canyons. As chapter 6 will detail, potential dams at these sites were already under attack by the Sierra Club and other environmental groups because of the risk they posed of impinging on Grand Canyon National Park. Other possible dam sites upriver at Echo Canyon had already been blocked in Congress due to the strident opposition of the Sierra Club.[61] With an impending crunch between supply and demand, interconnection with steam-fired plants seemed the inevitable cost of meeting demand and would also have the benefit of allowing Reclamation to draw greater revenue from its generating capacity if it was sold as peaking power. As Udall stated, "As far as electric power is concerned in the West, the federal system is a hydro-electric system. . . . [H]ydro-electric power is going to be more and more valuable as peaking power to be used only at times of greatest demand on a power system—usually in the early evening."[62] While some linking could be made with publicly owned steam-fired plants, only a few public utilities had the financial capacity to build such major plants, leaving the Department of Interior to turn to connection with WEST.

The FPC's increasing stress on creating a "strong grid" was another concern driving linkage. Prior to the formation of WEST, the FPC had urged interconnection during the 1962 CRSP power-line controversy and had registered its disapproval of Interior's right-of-way rules that threatened to retard transmission-line construction.[63] The formation of WEST coincided with the publication of the FPC's *National Power Survey* for 1964. The *Power Survey*, an overview of the nation's electrical system, contained a grave warning about the potential for failure in some regional systems. "Many regional systems, especially those in the Southwest and upper Midwest, remain dangerously isolated and prone to failure and extended outages." The FPC's solution was "interties anywhere, by any systems, in the interests the systems, their consumers, the area they serve, and the country."[64] In the survey, the FPC harshly criticized the right-of-way rules, suggesting they may have adversely affected the economic growth of states with public lands by preventing interties.[65] While this recommendation carried no force, it did represent the official policy recommendation of the federal agency charged with regulating interstate power transmission, and Udall's actions in the wake of WEST's formation followed its recommendation.

These two rationales for interconnection convinced the Department of Interior to pursue further negotiations with WEST. In June 1965, these negotiations produced an agreement to connect the two systems. These agreements not only pledged the Bureau of Reclamation and WEST facilities to intertie their lines and share electricity; they also broke down the last vestiges of the separation of public and private power. Thus they went further than earlier interties in the Southwest, which had treated interties as emergency backups for systems that remained essentially separate. Instead of this arrangement, the agreements of 1965 essentially merged the two systems.[66] At the same time Udall announced the cooperative agreements, SRP announced it had joined WEST.[67] With this addition, WEST's pledge that facilities run or financed by the federal government would be excluded was essentially voided, but on WEST's terms. When SRP joined WEST, it agreed to cease plans for any developments that would compete with APS and to introduce its generating load, including the significant amount of peaking power from Glen Canyon Dam into WEST's system.

Udall's subsequent public statements indicated that the agreement represented more than just a response to the problems posed by Reclamation's limited potential for new generation and the FPC's pressure for new interconnections. Instead, the statements revealed a greater interest in regional economic development within the Department of Interior. Since Reclamation's creation, its power had been earmarked explicitly for the benefit of the region's farms. During those years, Reclamation had played a peripheral role in economic development strategies that had located the region's metropolitan areas as the driving force in the Southwest's economic future. With the announcement of the interconnection agreement, the Department of Interior moved toward the booster vision of the Southwest as a national center of energy-intensive high-tech industries. Where earlier public statements about the Bureau of Reclamation had always emphasized a rhetoric of "making the desert bloom," Udall's statements about the interconnection agreement echoed the boosters' emphasis on the region's lifestyle possibilities and business-friendly policies. Speaking at Arizona State University's 1965 commencement, Udall prophesied, "If we can perfect this new and unique partnership to produce low-cost electrical power for all, it will be the best region in the nation both to live in and work in." Some of this rhetoric, no doubt, was the product of Udall speaking before his home-state audience; however, it also spoke to the Department of Interior's new perspective.[68]

By focusing on regional economic development, Udall papered over the long antagonism that had existed between public and private utilities. At the dedication of the expansion of Four Corners in 1966, Udall appeared arm in arm with D. W. Reeves and Walter Lucking. Addressing the WEST officials gathered for the dedication, Udall envisioned a new harmonic relationship between the former antagonists: "If we plan and work together on a regional basis, we can achieve for consumers the economics of modern, large-scale electric technology without sacrificing the independence and integrity of the many electric utility systems, public and private, which serve the region."[69] Achieving this cooperation, however, entailed abandoning the Bureau's social mission of enabling agriculture in the West's arid lands. Replacing this social mission was a new technical mission for the Bureau of ensuring the efficient flow of water and electricity from source to consumer. "Our main job is engineering, integrating transmission lines, and deciding where to build a plant for the best result economically. You don't build competitive lines."[70] Rather than pursuing a social vision of promoting agriculture in arid lands, the interconnection agreements refocused the Bureau as a technical agency responsible for helping private utilities to knit together the region's disparate electrical systems. In this change, of course, the Bureau had bought into a separate social vision, one that regarded as paramount the economic interests of the region's metropolitan consumers and industries in low-cost, efficiently delivered electricity.

The new system for managing the flow of electricity demonstrated this dedication to technical competence. To direct the daily operations of this new integrated system, WEST and the Department of the Interior agreed to turn the administration of the region's electricity over to an independent system operator, the Western Systems Coordinating Council (WSCC). The WSCC's central responsibility was to manage the electrical load of the entire region. It would receive information on how much electricity each base plant could produce on any given day. The engineers at the WSCC would then inform peaking plants and hydroelectric dams when to start producing electricity and when to cut off production as peak demand declined. In popular technology magazines, such as *Popular Mechanics*, WSCC became a symbol of the region's modernity. System operators at the WSCC's headquarters in Salida, Colorado, were portrayed as technical wizards, sitting before an enormous electronic map tracing the high-voltage lines that linked the West, and "ensuring that the lights stay on."[71] The map looming above the heads of WSCC's engineers was the ultimate symbol of the pooling of the Southwest's power and of the new bonds that linked the entire region.

In 1967, these bonds became even more extensive as power began flowing along the Pacific Northwest–Southwest Intertie. The Intertie linked the publicly owned transmission system of the Bonneville Power Authority with the public-private WSCC system and allowed power to flow north in the winter and south in the summer, making up the power deficit caused respectively by electric heating and air conditioning in the West's cities. The cost of the transmission system was almost equally split between public and private monies, with WEST utilities plus Pacific Gas and Electric and Portland General Electric contributing $330 million, the Bureau of Reclamation contributing $300 million, and the Los Angeles Department of Power and Water paying $70 million. The Intertie, capable of carrying 4,500 megawatts (enough electricity to meet the combined demand of cities the size of Chicago and Philadelphia), consisted of four transmission lines connected to the Bonneville Power Authority's system at Round Butte Dam in central Oregon that took two paths south. One passed through the coastal range of Northern California and into the Central and San Joaquin Valleys, supplying San Francisco and then Los Angeles, where it linked up with WSCC lines. The second followed a path east of the Sierra Crest through Nevada, linking up with Hoover Dam and then south to Phoenix, where it also linked up to WSCC's transmission system. The Intertie thus finally brought Hoover Dam power to Phoenix.[72]

More important, it linked the electrical systems of most of the American West together into a single system. What had been a series of discrete electrical networks only five years earlier—New Mexico separated from Arizona separated from California, urban space separated from agricultural districts—had been merged into a single, seamless pool of electricity. The advantages of this pooling to utilities and consumers seemed so great that several commentators remarked that "almost everybody wins" in the arrangement. In *Newsweek*, Raymond Moley heralded "A New Electric Age." Moley, a former New Deal official who had split with the New Dealers over power policy and moved steadily rightward in his *Newsweek* column, hailed the formation of WEST and its pooling agreements as the death of the dispute between public and private power. As he wrote, "Technological progress has always had a way of sweeping aside old political shibboleths." The new pooling and interconnection agreements, Moley wrote, succeeded in meeting the paramount consumer demands, "good service and reasonable rates." That WEST was moving to satisfy these needs revealed its true nature to Moley. "These private companies are public servants, too, just as dedicated and more efficient than any government operation."[73]

To a degree, Moley was correct. The interconnection and pooling agreements did represent "A New Electric Age." It was a situation in which "almost everybody wins" in the Southwest. With the extensive interconnections between the Pacific Northwest and the Southwest, utilities could build fewer power plants that would run at less than full capacity for the summer months. With the need for new construction reduced, consumers would see lower prices as the private utilities would have reduced amounts of public debt they needed to satisfy. Service would be more reliable as the electrical systems had multiple backups. As the next chapter will show, even the rising number of people who considered themselves environmentalists could claim the new system as a victory for their cause.

One area, however, bore the brunt of this new geography in which *almost* everybody won. A 1971 map of the Southwest's electrical system showed the Colorado Plateau and the Navajo Reservation ringed with

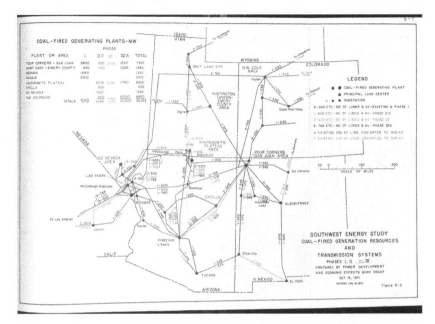

FIGURE 5.2. By 1970, coal-fired generation had made the Colorado Plateau the center of electrical production for the metropolitan Southwest. The lines represent extra-high-voltage transmission lines. A series of six such transmission lines can be seen running off the left side of the map toward Los Angeles. Source: U.S. Department of the Interior, Southwest Energy Study (Washington, D.C., 1971).

coal-fired power plants. To the west sat Mojave Generating station; to the east the expanded Four Corners; to the south Cholla Power Plant; and to the north Navajo Generating Station. While the new geography allowed utilities to build fewer power plants, it required them to run the power plants that they built to their maximum capacity. The effect of this system could be seen from space; as the Mercury astronauts reported that the two man-made entities they could see from space were the Great Wall of China and the plume streaming forth from Four Corners Power Plant.[74]

The 1971 map revealed another truth about the new geography. On the map, high voltage transmission lines crisscrossed the Colorado Plateau, heading to Phoenix, Albuquerque, Los Angeles, Salt Lake City, and the Pacific Northwest. All these metropolitan areas, however, existed at the periphery of the map. That geography located the Colorado Plateau as the new center of the modern Southwest. Like other geographical centers, power flowed out from the center toward the periphery. Unlike most other systems, the economic, political, and social power of the periphery determined the organization of the center. It was the periphery's capital that reorganized the center. It was the periphery's society that created great new sources of unmet demand for electricity that could be met by supplies in the center. And it was the periphery's political influence that determined where power plants would be built and how the lives and landscape of those living in the center of this new region, the modern Southwest, would change because of the massive peripheral demand for electricity. At the heart of this system, where the Navajo and Hopi Reservations intersected, lay Black Mesa Mine, sending its coal to Mojave Generating System. Soon Peabody Coal would send more Black Mesa coal to Navajo Generating Station, a power plant built to save the Grand Canyon.

PART IV

Protest

CHAPTER 6

The Living River

THE *NEW YORK TIMES* LEAD EDITORIAL ON MAY 18, 1966, WORRIED about "The High Cost of Arizona." Reading the editorial's lede, Phoenix's boosters must have hoped it would not be as bad as the title suggested. It did, after all, lay out Arizona's appeal, and the difficulties it faced: "With its magnificent scenery and attractive climate, Arizona has a fast-growing population and a worsening water shortage." The editorial went downhill quickly, however, as it turned to "the state's breathtaking political audacity in trying to seize hold of national resources and put them to its own use." The *New York Times* not only challenged the long-held claims of Arizona officials that their state was entitled to a portion of the Colorado River by rights, a claim recently upheld by the Supreme Court. The paper also argued that Arizona's attempt to realize those claims endangered the Colorado River and the Grand Canyon itself. The core of the editorial focused on two dams planned outside the boundaries of Grand Canyon National Park. Dismissing arguments that the resulting reservoirs would lie unseen from the canyon's rim and that they would actually make the canyon more accessible to Americans, the *Times* claimed that, by destroying the river's ability to work, the dams would indelibly alter the meaning of the river itself. "One of nature's master workmen flowing freely, moving thousands of tons of silt every day, and cutting canyons," the editorial lamented, "would do its work no more." Moreover, the paper claimed that the dams were not even necessary for Arizona's water claims to be realized; instead, "they are merely intended to generate hydroelectric power which will be sold at a profit." Transforming the flowing energy of water into flowing electricity, the *Times* suggested, in great contrast to the words Franklin Roosevelt had spoken just over thirty years earlier, was not in the national interest. "Arizona has to have water," the editorial argued, but "the state's needs" must be balanced "in terms of national priorities." Given those priorities, "the violation of the Grand Canyon is too high a price to pay."[1]

The *Times* editorial suggested how national priorities, as well as the perceived value of high dams, had changed in the thirty years following the completion of Boulder Dam. The paper gave little mention of the productive labor the dam would make possible elsewhere. Nor did it speak of the recreational possibilities realized by millions of people since the creation of Lake Mead and Lake Powell, upstream from Glen Canyon Dam. Instead, it spoke of the "free-flowing" river as valuable, not dangerous, and claimed the dams would subvert its "ecology." Finally, it suggested that growth, particularly Arizona's, came with significant, potentially irreversible costs.

Such critiques of Arizona's growth emerged in the wake of the Interior Department's development of the Pacific Southwest Water Plan, a plan designed in 1963 to realize Arizona's Colorado River claims. The critiques emerged from several different conservationist groups, but most powerfully from the Sierra Club, which was gradually changing the description of its politics from "conservation" to "environmentalism" and assuming a far more public voice in disputes over the proper use of public lands. In newsletters, congressional testimony, letter-writing campaigns, and, most effectively, large-format photo books that displayed the Colorado River bottoms in vivid color and striking detail, the Sierra Club contested the wisdom, and the legality, of damming the Colorado River. Its arguments helped introduce into the nation's political dialogue new ideas about nature: that Americans had the right to visit undeveloped nature, that nature, at least in some places, had rights to protection, and that metropolitan claims to resources, and metropolitan growth itself, endangered these "natural rights." Phoenix, with its explosive postwar growth and sprawling physical layout became, in many ways, the poster child for irresponsible growth. Arizonans vigorously fought against these depictions of their state's growth as well as for the water and power resources that would enable its continuation. By the late 1960s, however, public opinion on the national level had turned against the dams, and they were eliminated from the plan.

The Sierra Club's fight against the Grand Canyon dams has become one of the signal events in the story of the rise of environmentalism as a political movement. And indeed, the Sierra Club's public efforts shifted Eastern media outlets like the *New York Times* to critique in new terms metropolitan growth's impact on the natural world. The public fight also helped increase the Sierra Club's membership fourfold over the course of the 1960s. And the Club's public stance helped turn public opinion against dam building. The Club's efforts to create public controversy were not the only way its members fought the dams, however. They also offered a solution that was much less critical of the needs of metropolitan growth, a solution involving the new geography of interconnected power lines and pooled generating capacity developed by public and private utilities in the mid-1960s. This system, Sierra Club officials suggested, could power the key elements of the Pacific Southwest Water Plan (PSWP), eliminating the need for the dams. While this negotiating strategy was successful, it required electricity to come from elsewhere. That elsewhere was Navajo Generating Station, built near Page, Arizona, in the early 1970s. It was also Black Mesa, where new strip mines began operations in the same year.. The power plant's construction in the early 1970s suggested that the Sierra Club's public critique of development did not go as far as it promised. Indeed, the battle over the PSWP resulted in both the protection of Grand Canyon *and* the intensification of energy development on the Navajo Reservation, furthering the environmental inequalities of the modern Southwest.

PACIFIC SOUTHWEST WATER PLAN

On January 21, 1963, Stewart Udall and Floyd Dominy stood before reporters and made two announcements. First, they reported that workers at Glen Canyon Dam had closed a steel gate sealing the last diversion tunnel. With this done, the Colorado River began filling the canyon and climbing the upstream face of the dam. In six months, the waters of Lake Powell begin flowing through the intake tunnels of the dam's power plant. At the dam's base, the generators in the power-plant would begin spinning, sending electricity across the maze of public and private power lines to Colorado River Storage Project customers.

After announcing the successful completion of CRSP's signature project, Udall made the second announcement. Declaring the "need to ensure a reliable supply of water to the arid Southwest," Udall unveiled the Bureau of Reclamation's newest project, the Pacific Southwest Water Plan. The project encompassed dozens of dams, aqueducts, and canals, but three projects formed its vital center. First, the Trinity River would be diverted from Northern California through a series of aqueducts to metropolitan Los Angeles. Second, Colorado River water would be drawn from the Colorado River at Lake Havasu and pumped over the Buckskin Mountains into the Valley of the Sun, creating Arizonans' long-awaited Central Arizona Project (CAP). Finally, two new dams on the Colorado River at Bridge and Marble Canyons, dams bracketing the Grand Canyon, would generate electrical power both to pump water and to finance the other developments.[2]

Stuart Udall envisioned the PSWP as making the Colorado River more productive. It placed dams at likely the last available dam sites on the lower Colorado in order to bring water to Arizona. In so doing, he reinforced metropolitan preferences that had governed Interior policy since Boulder Dam, which held that ensuring economic growth in metropolitan areas was consistent with Interior's mission. This broad aim meshed well with the utilitarian philosophy of the Bureau of Reclamation. As Herbert Hoover had long earlier emphasized, "every drop of water that runs to the sea without yielding its full commercial returns to the nation is an economic waste." Any water not used in irrigation, any dam sites left unbuilt, represented lost productivity.[3]

Udall also envisioned the plan as the best way to realize his home state's long-lived attempts for their own Reclamation project on the Colorado River. Before the PSWP, Reclamation projects had bypassed Arizona. While SRP could purchase power from Glen Canyon Dam, that project was intended for the upper basin's development. In the lower basin, the Bureau's utilitarianism and emerging eye for metropolitan consumers had, at first, sent water and power streaming toward Los Angeles. In the following years, California's congressional power had protected that appropriation, repeatedly blocking Arizona's efforts to authorize CAP.[4] Editorial cartoons in Arizona newspapers portrayed the state as hypnotized, bullied, and swindled by both California and federal officials.

In 1963 those deceits appeared sure to end. Eleven years earlier, Arizona's attorney general, assisted by the law firm of Lewis and Roca, had turned to the courts to demand Arizona's share of the Colorado. The result was the longest-running lawsuit in the nation's history. Lawyers for both states litigated *Arizona v. California* before a special master assigned by the Supreme Court for eleven years, with testimony from 340 witnesses and arguments by fifty separate lawyers, all debating whether California had fulfilled the divisions of the river established in the 1922 Colorado River Compact. In 1963 the Court's special master, Simon Rifkind, finally decided, upholding Arizona on almost every count. California, Rifkind ruled, had taken water in excess of its allocation. Arizona was entitled to 2.8 million acre-feet of Colorado River water. Arizona's victory was stunning, endangering a large portion of Los Angeles's water supply.[5]

Hearing advance word of the special master's decision, Stewart Udall and the Bureau of Reclamation began working on the PSWP, aiming to bring water to central Arizona without leaving Southern California dry. The plan reorganized water management for the entire region. The PSWP would take 1.2 million acre-feet of California's Colorado River allocation for the CAP. To make up Southern California's water loss, new dams in Northern California would divert the Trinity River south through a series of canals and tunnels, and develop plans to potentially divert water from the Columbia River to Southern California.[6] To finance the construction costs of the entire project, the PSWP called for the construction of dams 2.5 miles upstream from the headwaters of Lake Mead at Bridge Canyon, and at Marble Canyon, 12.5 miles upstream from the border of Grand Canyon National Park. The headwaters of Marble Canyon's reservoir would reach the tailwater of Glen Canyon dam, while the headwaters from Bridge Canyon's reservoir would abut Grand Canyon

National Park for thirteen miles along its downstream border, and reach into Hualapai Canyon, in the park's boundary.[7]

Park boundaries had gained new importance for Reclamation projects. In the early negotiations over CRSP, the Sierra Club managed to block a proposed dam in Dinosaur National Monument, arguing it would violate the National Park Service's duty to preserve land within its jurisdiction in a relatively unchanged state for the enjoyment of future Americans. The PSWP's impoundment of water into the border of Grand Canyon National Park, however, did not appear legally problematic to Udall. The park's 1919 legislation creating Grand Canyon National Park allowed for the future use of the park's territory for federal reclamation projects. In addition, Udall's aides assured him studies had shown that Bridge Canyon Dam's reservoir could not be seen from any point from the rim above.[8]

Udall's regional plan was designed to placate obstinate political demands. Senator Carl Hayden desired a "clean" CAP bill, without any other projects. The Arizona Power Authority had gone as far as proposing in 1961 that the state itself fund the dam without federal assistance, a proposal denied by the Federal Power Commission.[9] In a 1963 letter to Hayden, Udall wrote that California legislators would never allow a stand-alone CAP. "The old Central Arizona Bill will stir up a major controversy in the House that will almost certainly defeat it," Udall advised. Any attempt by Arizona to build the project on its own would certainly be blocked by the Federal Power Commission once again. Instead, Udall pitched the regional PSWP as a means to create a favorable coalition, satisfying home-state interests without risking the ire of Southern California's representatives.[10]

The PSWP's plan, also, represented Interior's recognition of Arizona's new metropolitan status. While acknowledging some urban growth, earlier Bureau of Reclamation reports portrayed Arizona as primarily an exporter of natural resources and agricultural products. The PSWP, by contrast, categorized the state as urban and industrial. The Pacific Southwest contained, the report stated, "the metropolitan centers of Los Angeles, San Diego, Phoenix, Tucson, and Las Vegas, which are the fastest growing cities of the United States." In what must have been music to Phoenix Chamber of Commerce director Lewis Haas's ears, the report explained that the region was vital to national defense, containing "a new industrial complex . . . in the now-dominant missile, space, and nuclear fields." The region had also been "the national leader in economic growth rate during the decade from 1950 to 1960." The report's authors saw the 1950s as the beginning, writing, "Impressively, this phenomenal growth shows no signs of abating." The report predicted the region would have

260 percent more people in 2020 than it had in 1960; Arizona alone was predicted to increase 640 percent. Throughout, the report contained predictions of exponential growth, in population, manufacturing, and home construction, and, in a sense, represented the moment Reclamation recognized Phoenix as entitled to the types of metropolitan preference Los Angeles had received since the Boulder Canyon Act. Recognizing the region as "the most critically water-short region of the Nation," the PSWP promised to provide "an adequate water supply" to ensure that region's future growth.[11]

This focus on metropolitan growth raised a sticky legal issue. By law, Reclamation projects had to provide irrigation water. The PSWP report did mention that the region's agricultural valleys were "centers for the production of winter vegetables and specialty crops." However, the report largely charted a future in which farmland gave way to industry and subdivisions. In fact, that future had already begun, "In metropolitan Phoenix, 50,000 acres of irrigated land were shifted from crop production to housing and industrial sites during the 50's." Arizona was not alone in this practice of converting agricultural water to residential use, which the report considered the future of urban water development: "Urban developments throughout the West are demanding water supplies which, in many cases, can only be obtained by condemning agricultural water rights."[12] The report, then, cited CAP as necessary to replace irrigation waters that had been converted to urban uses. There was nothing, however, that prevented the eventual conversion of CAP water to the same use. The provision of irrigation water was essentially a temporary matter, assuring a water supply for the continued expansion of metropolitan Phoenix and Tucson.

Arizonans thus came to understand the plan and its dams as central to future metropolitan growth. Furthermore, given the special master's ruling in *Arizona v. California*, CAP would carry water that most Arizonans believed was theirs by right. Newspaper editorials in the *Arizona Republic* and the *Phoenix Gazette* continually referred to "our water" or "Arizona's water" as the state's rightful possession, its reward for achieving metropolitan status.[13] As one editorial written even before the announcement of the PSWP stated, "All of us in Arizona have worked too hard to make this state the best place in the country to live to have bureaucratic fighting prevent us from receiving the water that is, by right, ours."[14] In this view the PSWP would not so much make the desert bloom as protect the rights of Phoenix's farmers, its homeowners, and its boosters, to the water that was their property by right.

The PSWP's warnings about short water supplies also led many Arizonans to view water shortage as the only factor that might inhibit the entire region's continued growth. Imagination of water shortage was imagination of economic and social catastrophe. "When water fails, the economic base fails," one correspondent wrote to the *Tucson Daily Star*. "When the economic base fails, schools, churches, family life, and many other things suffer."[15] Given these increased divisions, little potential for compromise seemed possible. It was in this context that the Sierra Club began its fight against the Grand Canyon dams.

BATTLE BOOKS

"After a while, one begins to wonder about the sense of it all," Francois Leydet wrote. "Would Arizona be a better place to live with six times its present population? Must Phoenix become another Los Angeles?"[16] In the pages surrounding Leydet's words, in a "battle book" named *Time and the River Flowing*, vivid photos from the shores of the Colorado River within the Grand Canyon showed the places threatened by Arizona's continued growth: slot canyons with sandstone whorls, delicate desert flowers, rippled sand dunes, and riffles on side streams. All, Leydet emphasized, would cease to exist if Marble and Bridge Canyon Dams were built. David Brower, the Sierra Club's president, cast blame in the book's introduction. For thirty years, he explained, the Bureau of Reclamation's vision of an orderly, managed river had slowly choked the life from the Colorado. Just the year before, Reclamation's most recent dam had destroyed the natural landscape that lay "upstream and unmarred . . . the exquisite beauty of Glen Canyon." The latest plan represented the critical moment for the river and its most sacred landscape. "The same bureau has proposed to build dams in Grand Canyon itself," Brower wrote, "to end the living river's flowing for all this civilization's time."[17]

Since the early twentieth century, when its founder John Muir campaigned against the construction of a dam in Yosemite National Park's Hetch Hetchy Canyon, the Sierra Club had challenged attempts to build dams in national parklands. The Club's political efforts had intensified in the decade before *Time and the River Flowing* was published in 1964 as its leaders became increasingly involved in the politics of the Colorado River.[18] In the early stages of CRSP, the Club had challenged plans to build a dam at Echo Park within Dinosaur National Monument. While Walter Huber, the organization's postwar president, initially suggested that a such dam in Echo Park would have little effect other than to drown sandstone and sagebrush, David Brower, named the club's executive director in 1952, brought the Club into a seventeen-organization coalition called the Citizens Committee on Natural Resources, which had been formed by Howard Zahnziner of the Wilderness Society and was dedicated to the proposition that properties governed by the National Park

Service—national parks and national monuments—should be excluded from reclamation projects. In the campaign against Echo Park, the Sierra Club played a dual role. First, its members, Brower particularly, joined a legion of conservationists who became increasingly expert about the operation of reclamation projects in the terms defined by the Bureau of Reclamation. In Brower's most dramatic testimony, he calculated, using a blackboard and chalk, that a CRSP built without a dam at Echo Park but with a higher dam at Glen Canyon would both store more water and cause less evaporation. In offering such expert testimony, conservationists challenged the idea that Reclamation officials were the only ones who could judge the propriety of the agency's projects.[19]

Second, and more importantly, the Sierra Club rallied public support against the dam. Sponsoring float trips through Dinosaur beginning in 1953, the Club exposed large numbers of its membership, which had previous alpine experience, to the beauty of the canyon country. Reaching far more people in 1955, the Club produced *This Is Dinosaur* in cooperation with Alfred Knopf, the publisher and chairman of the Interior Department's Advisory Board on National Parks. Containing dozens of black-and-white and color photos of Echo Park and edited by Wallace Stegner, the book professed to demonstrate "what the people would be giving up, what beautiful and instructive and satisfying things their children and their grandchildren and all other Americans from then on would never see."[20] The Club, in effect, simultaneously helped create the idea that Dinosaur National Monument's landscape was irreplaceable and that its loss was imminent. The resulting public uproar led to a flood of letters running 80–1 against the dam besieging congressional representatives. It also led an Austrian pilot to corner Orme Lewis, then Assistant Secretary for Public Lands, and question him for two hours during a flight across the Alps, an encounter with an "extreme conservationist" that Lewis later huffily recounted in his *Saturday Evening Post* story, writing that "I still feel that amateur European conservationist had no right to be intrigued with our Echo Park dam issue, particularly on Lewis' vacation."[21]

The Echo Park battle revealed significant spatial boundaries to conservationists' critiques of development. Focused on protection of National Park Service properties, Brower had advocated the compromise of building a higher Glen Canyon dam, inundating 186 miles of canyon upstream. Brower later came to believe he had made a grave mistake. After visiting Glen Canyon on the eve of its inundation, he discovered a landscape that he believed to be the most beautiful on the Colorado and mourned his role in its flooding, later writing "Glen Canyon died in 1963 and I was partly responsible for its needless death."[22] Brower's guilt was so extreme that friends worried that he might commit suicide.[23] After the "tragedy" of Glen Canyon, the Sierra Club and other conservation organizations came to see dam building, in general, as problematic.

By the early 1960s, the Club also began to use a new language to speak about the parks. Previously, the conservation groups that made up the Citizens Committee on Natural Resources had emphasized that reclamation projects violated the enabling legislation of the National Park Service, which charged the agency with "conserving the scenery and the natural and historic objects and the wild life therein." Pointing out that the Federal Power Act of 1920 had forbidden private companies from developing projects in national parks and monuments, they asked that government agencies be held to the same standard. By the early 1960s, however, the Sierra Club began to shift away from this argument about competing interests within the Interior Department to suggest that reclamation projects that impinged on national parklands also impinged upon the individual rights of all Americans. In a legal brief written for the Sierra Club in 1963, Robert W. Jasperson, the general counsel for the Conservation Law Society of America, claimed that individual Americans possessed a legally protected right to experience national parks in an unchanged natural state. Jasperson emphasized a different part of the NPS's enabling legislation, not the charge to conserve scenery, but the charge "to provide for the enjoyment of the same in such manner and by such means as will leave them unimpaired for the enjoyment of future generations." Jasperson's brief contended that the dam portion of the PSWP was fundamentally incompatible with the NPS's enabling legislation because it would "preclude the rights of current and future generations to obtain enjoyment through use of the river." The brief argued for the existence of individual rights to enjoy parkland that superseded regional demands for use of the resources contained within the park. In short, the Sierra Club argued that the right to experience nature in the Grand Canyon trumped Arizona's needs for development.[24]

What, however, did an individual right to obtain enjoyment and experience in nature mean? The completion of Glen Canyon Dam confronted opponents of the PSWP's dams with an unexpected problem. In its first year of existence, Lake Powell drew 500,000 visitors. People waterskied in flooded slot canyons, took cruises to see Rainbow Bridge, and jumped off cliffs, not into the abyss of the canyon, but into the standing water forty feet below. Recounting the recreational amenities on Lake Powell, dam proponents contended that public enjoyment of the natural parks and the development of their resources were not incompatible. The two, in fact, went hand in hand. Even the National Park Service, which opposed the dams proposed by the PSWP, admitted that at least half a million people would visit the reservoirs behind Bridge and Marble Canyons to boat, water-ski, fish, swim, and camp in a "unique and spectacular setting."[25] Dam supporters took this argument even further, arguing that anyone opposing the dams was simply an elitist, determined to keep most Americans out of the Grand Canyon. As Rich Johnson, president of the Central Arizona Project Association, wrote, "The Sierra Club represents the right of the 400 people who 'shot the rapids' by boat . . . in 1962, and opposes the right of the 500,000 people whom the park service believes would enjoy the area each year."[26] In this sense, dam opponents were doubly guilty; they wanted to deny both people's rights to water and their rights to recreation.

Promoting a right to access nature within the Grand Canyon was thus insufficient to the Sierra Club's task. Countering the arguments of dam supporters required a contrast between the individual experience of a dammed and of a free-flowing river. In short, dam opponents required an explanation of why the right to experience nature required a flowing river. If accessing nature merely meant riding a boat on Lake Powell or standing at the rim of the Grand Canyon, then the dams would do little to impede this right (and in the former case, would enable it). Therefore, dam opponents set out to change the way in which people imagined and experienced the Grand Canyon. Most centrally, they portrayed the river as alive and real, as opposed to the lifeless, manufactured experience to be had on a reservoir.

The "living river" became the central motif of the Sierra Club's two large-format photography books published in 1963 and 1964. *The Place No One Knew* examined the doomed world of Glen Canyon while *Time and the River Flowing* explored the threatened Grand Canyon. Both, however, focused on the river's energy as the vital living force that had created the canyon country and continued to give it life. Focusing almost all their images on the river bottoms, the books altered the normal view, from above, of the Colorado River canyons. They contained no panoramas of the open spaces of the canyon country reaching off into the distance. Instead, they focused entirely on the river itself. After the initial two photos in *The Place No One Knew*, the sky was never visible in a single photograph, other than when reflected off the river. Instead, the book offered tightly shot perspectives of the minute life-forms in the canyon. The book contained fifteen different photographs of flowering plants growing out of cracks in the canyon's sandstone walls, hanging gardens on the walls of the canyon, and tamarisk growing on the river's shores. It contained forty-eight photos of moving water or the natural forms produced by it: riffles on side branches of the Colorado, recesses in the sandstone carved by moving water, nearly vertical slot canyons and delicate sand dunes. *Time and the River Flowing* extended this portrait to the animal life in the Canyon and to the flow of the river itself. Philip Hyde's photograph,

Vasey's Paradise, showed water coursing from a spring in the canyon's wall, passing through several tiers of vegetation bright green against the red of the canyon walls, before flowing through the foreground of the photo. Leydet's narrative on the page opposite imagined the fate of this life if the dams were not stopped. "I saw Vasey's Paradise lost, the candy-striped walls obliterated, the graceful beaches buried, the native plants and animals evicted or drowned, the living river, with its varied moods of fury and tranquility, replaced by the monotony of a reservoir lake."[27] Together the photos and text of the books combined to tell stories about the unique web of life that existed below the Canyon's rims; a web that would be lost if the river were dammed.

Francois Leydet, the main author of *Time and the River Flowing* placed the Sierra Club's legal argument about an individual right to access natural landscapes in place, implicitly challenging Arizona's leaders' arguments about the Colorado River's waters being a state right. "The Grand Canyon was one of the glories of the Nation," he wrote, "and should *belong* to the nation and be preserved by it unblemished for the inspiration of the present and future generations of Americans."[28] Leydet took the argument further, however, arguing that the life-filled canyon that photographs portrayed possessed rights of its own. "As a National Park, it is your property," he wrote. "Or to be exact, *almost* your own. For that raven, soaring out there contemptuous of the void, those pretty ground squirrels . . . have property rights that precede yours. Only in the National Parks, unfortunately, is the wildlife's *Lebensraum* given recognition, and their territorial rights awarded full protection of law."[29]

Combined, the two books told stories about "the living river." They showed the river's dynamic, ever-changing landscape; they showed an environment that was full of life. The fact that these were visual stories made them even more effective. The photography in *The Place No One Knew* froze time in the canyon before its damming, displaying forever the costs of Glen Canyon Dam. By creating a limited spatial vision of the dam's effects, the photography drew attention away from the social ends toward which the dam was built. Viewers did not see farms in central Utah or new houses in Arizona. They only saw a frozen moment of a landscape on the verge of death.[30] The photos were thus artifacts of an ongoing tragedy, what Eliot Porter portrayed as wildness's slow death. "As the waters creep into the side canyons, enveloping one by one their mirroring pools . . . a fine opaque silt settles over all, covering rocks and tress alike with a gray slimy ooze. Darkness pervades the canyons. Death and the thickening, umbrageous gloom take over where life and shimmering light were the glory of the river."[31]

If *The Place No One Knew* was an elegy, it was also a call to arms. As Brower concluded his introduction, "In Glen Canyon, the people never knew what the choices were." *Time and the River Flowing*, which followed a year after *The Place No One Knew*, sought to make those choices clear. Again, "the living river" acted to personify the river. "The dams would destroy not only the living river," Leydet wrote, "but also the unique life forms that through the ages have come to depend on the river's life. The major part of the canyon walls would still be there, but the pulsing heart of the place would be stopped." Even at low flow as Lake Powell filled, he suggested that the river continued to transform the Canyon. "In spite of the extremely low flow, the river was still working; it still had its tools and its pulse. . . . The river swirled and murmured and sang . . . continued to chisel at what might lie below the schist. . . . While it lived, so would the canyon."³²

Using photos from the slow flooding of Glen Canyon and from the headwaters of Lake Mead, *Time and the River Flowing* was able to portray the river's "death" in a way the previous book had not. Its epilogue, titled "Remember These Things Lost," reprinted some of the most striking photos from *The Place No One Knew*, placing them side by side with images of the same places a year later. Tamarisk and reflecting pools in Music Temple were replaced with flat, dull water rising against sandstone. The book demonstrated the effects of flooding on the downstream end of Grand Canyon as well. The headwaters of Lake Mead showed a gray landscape of mud flats. The narrative of Leydet's journey through the canyon ended with images of his rafting expedition in these mud flats, in one case showing an unnamed man literally crawling out from the mud in which he had fallen. The photos of silt piled up on the canyon walls, cracked mud flats, and sink holes made a dramatic contrast to the vibrant, colorful landscape of the Canyon. The message was clear: the dams would kill the sacred, living space of the Grand Canyon.

The Sierra Club worked hard to spread the books' message. It sent copies of both books to every member of Congress, and Brower asked for the books to be entered into the official records of the congressional committees hearing testimony on the PSWP. The Book-of-the-Month Club chose *Time and the River Flowing* as one of its monthly selections, sending it to its forty thousand subscribers.³³ The Sierra Club also sent copies to the editorial boards of the nation's fifty most widely circulated papers. Fairly quickly, the Sierra Club's language and arguments began appearing in the editorials of the *New York Times* and *Washington Post*. In December 1964, shortly after publication of *Time and the River Flowing*, the *New York Times* published an editorial entitled "Grand Canyon Not for Sale!" which conveyed the Sierra Club's arguments against the dams virtually word for word, concluding, "much has been said by the dam proponents of how small an area of the total canyon would be affected by these dams and reservoirs. Yet it is the very heart, the most significant force that gives meaning to the canyon scenery, that would be destroyed. That is the living river."[34]

DEFENSIVE LOCALISM

Russel Werneken was angry. For two years, he had read the Sierra Club's criticisms of the Marble and Bridge Canyon Dams from his home in Scottsdale. He had read claims that the dams would flood the Grand Canyon, that people would no longer be able to enjoy nature, and that the dams had no redeeming value. Sitting before his typewriter, composing a letter to the *Arizona Republic*, Werneken asked who the Sierra Club really represented. Why was the Sierra Club, Werneken asked, challenging "the golden formula for the opening of all the arid lands of the Southwest"? Why were they so set against reservoirs like Lake Powell, where hundreds of thousands of people now boated and played? His answer came forth in a torrent of anger at elitists. "What they really want," Werneken typed, "is to keep people like you and me away from 100 miles of spectacularly beautiful riverway that they are hoping to retain as a private little reserve for themselves and their millionaire friends." This elitism, he wrote, would have broad social consequences if successful. What would happen, he asked, to "the 23 million people of the Colorado River Basin states who need water for their prosperity."[35] For Werneken, the PSWP represented not only the realization of Arizona's water rights, but the value of metropolitan growth itself. It was vital to ensure that Arizona received its water supply, he argued, because metropolitan growth had broad social benefits. In attacking Arizona's ability to realize its water rights, Werneken believed the Sierra Club was attacking the metropolitan growth that had transformed Arizona into a modern region.

Werneken was far from alone. The *Arizona Republic* filled its editorial page with angry letters denouncing the Sierra Club for violating the principles of conservation, for selfishly limiting use of the canyon, and for depriving Arizonans of their water rights. One letter writer wrote that the Club's publications "vigorously oppose everything else that conservation has stood for and accomplished for the last hundred years. . . . Conservation still means man's skillful and far-sighted management of natural resources for the greatest good for the greatest number."[36] Another attacked Club members for seeking to preserve "for a handful of people natural resources that millions have a right to use."[37]

Arizona's politicians and newspapers united, attempting to turn attacks on the dam into attacks on the state itself. Tucson's *Daily Sun* questioned how residents of "the Grand Canyon State" could possibly be understood as wanting to harm the canyon. "Arizona is the Grand Canyon

State—it has boasted such on motor vehicle license plates for nearly three decades. The Grand Canyon is its principle tourist asset. For Arizona to damage the beauty of the Grand Canyon or to destroy its scenic splendor is unthinkable to Arizonans."[38] Arizona politicians claimed their local standing granted superior knowledge of the canyon. Speaking at a forum sponsored by Reader's Digest on the fate of the Grand Canyon, Goldwater said, "I know this river better than most people, and I love it as much as anyone here. This canyon is the greatest natural beauty we have in Arizona . . . but I believe a dam at Bridge Canyon would enhance the canyon."[39]

Closing the circle of this argument, dam supporters portrayed the Sierra Club as outsiders who were unfamiliar with the Canyon. Questioning David Brower at a 1965 hearing on the dams, Morris Udall contended that 90 percent of the photos in *Time and the River Flowing* showed riverscape that would be unaffected by the dams. The Sierra Club's photography, according to this argument, was an example of its "irrational emotionalism" that valued primroses over people. Filled with photography of lost landscapes and personal experiences with the river, the Sierra Club's books represented sentimental attempts to stir action among, as the *Arizona Republic* stated, "Eastern readers who know little about the river."[40] As Rich Johnson, president of the Central Arizona Project Association, stated, the Sierra Club intended "to arouse emotional reaction among people who are poorly informed or misinformed concerning the need for and the true nature of the dams."[41]

Arizona newspapers began to assign ulterior motives to the Sierra Club. The state's press wondered why a relatively small organization— "about one-eighth the size of Tucson's population," in the Tucson paper's account—received so much attention. They quickly focused on California. The *Republic* suggested, "The Sierra Club is an organization of some 40,000 individuals, living mostly in California but also in other states, with headquarters in San Francisco. It has few members in Arizona."[42] Echoing such claims, the *Daily Star* announced that "Human Beings are Valuable Too," and suggested the Sierra Club "was all Californians who have never loved Arizona or Arizonans and probably never will."[43] Other accounts found the Club's opposition beyond reason, representing "such a reactionary and selfish interest that their noise should be discounted."[44] The *Republic* declared the organization's members "rabid and senseless and irresponsible."[45] The headline writer for the *Arizona Republic* simply declared them "Fanatics to Subdue."[46]

Arguments that met ready audiences in Arizona, however, found less purchase nationally. Reports in Arizona newspapers of the importance of the dams to metropolitan growth confronted broader counterarguments about the costs of growth being asked in the nation at large. As Adam

Rome has shown, writers like William Whyte as well as suburbanites themselves launched a broad critique of suburban development for polluting water, consuming open space, and generally destroying the natural amenities that suburban landscapes were supposed to provide. The two Sierra Club books articulated a similar critique, suggesting that in addition to the Bureau of Reclamation, contemporary ideas of progress were to blame for the canyon's plight. "Grand Canyon will go the way Glen Canyon did," David Brower wrote, "unless enough people begin to feel uneasy about the current interpretations of what progress consists of— unless they are willing to ask if progress has really served good purpose if it wipes out so many of the things that make life worthwhile." And nowhere was this question more pressing, the books suggested, than in Arizona and the arid Southwest, a land of limits where incessant demand had created incessant crisis. "Arizonans in positions of influence and power were . . . hypnotized by the fool's gold of Growth," Leydet wrote, "and there is every reason to believe they would use the additional Colorado River water, *and* continue to overpump their groundwater . . . until another Federal plan is devised to bail them out again."[47]

The Sierra Club's attack on Southwestern growth thus represented an attack on the central tenets of the boosters' vision of Phoenix and the Southwest. The boosters had portrayed Phoenix as the nation's last frontier, a place where an individual could escape the confines of Eastern government and bureaucracy in order to make life on his own. In contrast, the Sierra Club showed the Southwest to be essentially dependent on the federal government. Far from an independent frontier, the Sierra Club's Southwest was a dependent province incapable of caring for itself. The boosters had also portrayed the Southwest as a region where people could "have it all," where they could enjoy both modern life and natural splendor. The Sierra Club's campaign made it clear that the space of modern life in central Arizona did not exist independent of the natural spaces that provided solace from modern life. Instead, its growth endangered an American birthright, the Grand Canyon. Instead of benefiting the nation, regional growth imperiled it. As Brower wrote of these multiple costs of Southwestern development, "Are the citizens of the whole nation prepared to subsidize the growth of the Southwest to that extent?"[48]

National newspapers began to articulate similar critiques of Phoenix. "The High Cost of Arizona," the editorial mentioned in the first paragraph of this chapter, suggested that the city's growth was damaging the nation at large. Such critiques also appeared in paid ads in the pages of the *Times, Washington Post,* and other papers reaching Eastern audiences, arguing that Arizona's claims to control the space of the Grand Canyon violated a sacred obligation to preserve the Grand Canyon for the enjoyment of all Americans. The Club's advertisements were striking. Ridiculing the statements by Floyd Dominy, Barry Goldwater, and others that the dams would "improve" the Canyon, an advertisement ran on August 27, 1966, in the *New York Times, Washington Post, San Francisco Chronicle,* and *Los Angeles Times,* asking simply, "SHOULD WE ALSO FLOOD THE SISTINE CHAPEL SO THAT TOURISTS CAN GET NEARER THE CEILING?" The advertisement was so memorable that many popular accounts of the dam controversy credit it, to the exclusion of any other event, for the defeat of the dams.[49] While this exaggerates the ad's influence on a complicated political process, it did provide an additional rhetorical tool for attacking the dams. Damming the Grand Canyon, the ad suggested, represented not only the destruction of a natural landscape, but blasphemy against the nation's sacred spaces.[50]

The influence of the Sierra Club's "living river" and "sacred space" arguments was also evident in the language of individual citizens opposing the dams. Stewart Udall's papers contain numerous letters opposing the dams in language deeply influenced by the Sierra Club. An entire box of them contains little but letters objecting to the dams. A short sampling demonstrates the pervasiveness of the Sierra Club's language: "We are not concerned only with the view from the rim of the canyon but also with the effect on the flora and fauna of the canyon bottom." "When we finally succeeded in getting Grand Canyon declared a national park and monument we felt that it would be safe for all time. . . . It means that the government would be breaking faith with the people." "Why does the government want to take away my right to raft the Canyon?"[51] These letters existed separate from various forms the Sierra Club encouraged their members to send to the Department of Interior and to their senators and congressmen. One such campaign in 1966 flooded the Interior Department with over fifty thousand letters clipped from a Sierra Club newspaper advertisement.

The Interior Department came up with at least six different forms that could be personalized in order to respond to the objections of dam opponents. The forms generally tried to convey understanding of the intense emotions raised by the issue; one went so far as to state, "So much has been said and so many emotions aroused that I am afraid it is impossible to discuss the facts logically." That particular form went on to plea for understanding: "The decisions were not made lightly, and while we respect your right to dissent, we would appreciate your accepting our sincerity in making these statements to you."[52] The limited responses available to these letters suggest that no such understanding was forthcoming. Ethel Selbo, a resident of North Hollywood, was apparently so upset by the letter she received from Orren Beaty, Stewart Udall's assistant, that she marked up the letter with her objections and returned it to him. Her objections are telling. She underlined a passage Beatty had written, assuring her that no point in the park existed from which "tourists could even see the water." She responded below, "Mr. Beaty, I am not interested in what tourists can or cannot see. I am interested in keeping the Grand Canyon *as it is!*" She doubly underlined a phrase that stated the dams were the only projects contemplated "at this time," responding "I understand only one thing. The *first* dam is the beginning of the end of this wilderness area. If one dam is built, soon there will be 2, then 4, and eventually the ruination (by *people*) of one of the wonders of the world. It is a *CRIME* to begin it!"[53]

The Place No One Knew and *Time and the River Flowing* helped to convince a sizable portion of the American public that the PSWP entailed both the destruction of nature in the Grand Canyon and a threat to individual rights. The books allowed their readers to see an intimate view of the nature of the Canyon that had rarely been seen and linked their photographs to a larger story of nature imperiled by ill-considered development. They also created a new environmental enemy, the growing cities of central Arizona, especially Phoenix. In ensuing years, many environmentalists would come to see Phoenix as representing all the problems of uncontrolled growth; they would liken the city to a cancer, a tumor, and a blob.[54] Increasingly, many Americans—members of the Sierra Club, the *New York Times* editorial board, subscribers to *Readers Digest*—became likely to view the growth of the Southwest as benefiting Arizona but harming nature and, in the case of the dams, the nation itself.

Even as it helped launch this critique of Phoenix, however, the Sierra Club offered a means to solve its water shortage. This solution occurred not in the nation's print culture, but in the political spaces of congressional hearing rooms. The solution still insisted that the dams be removed from the CAP legislation, but suggested that the Bureau of Reclamation could find a ready replacement in the coal deposits on Black Mesa.

"Is a Dam Ever Necessary?"

Floyd Dominy was confused. Testifying before the House Subcommittee on Irrigation and Reclamation in May of 1966, Congressman John Saylor had asked him to explain why the dams at Marble and Bridge Canyon were necessary. Even more perplexing was his follow-up question. "Actually, can you tell us why any dam built only to generate power is ever necessary, given the ability of atomic energy or coal to generate electricity far more inexpensively?" Ignoring the second question, Dominy grudgingly admitted that the CAP was "theoretically feasible" without either of the dams.[55] Saylor's second question, however, demonstrated how quickly the ground had shifted beneath Dominy's feet. In 1963 the PSWP had seemed the logical next step in the Bureau's development of water and power resources. While the dams retained strong support in the Southwest, many Americans had come to see them as destroying some of the most sacred spaces in the nation.[56]

Dominy had weathered such challenges before. In the debate over the CRSP, he had lost the Echo Park dam site, but he still built Glen Canyon Dam. Saylor asked more disturbing questions. He did not object just to the location of a particular dam; instead, Saylor suggested that dams themselves were unnecessary. This question reflected, in part, Saylor's support for environmental legislation. A Pennsylvania Republican, Saylor was an early supporter of the Wilderness Act of 1964 and the Wild and Scenic Rivers Act of 1968.[57] The question also reflected the increasing number of challenges the Bureau of Reclamation faced to its authority over Western water and power resources. Public pressure from the Sierra Club was only one of these challenges. Reclamation officials also faced new critics within the executive branch as well as from Congress and experts on the electric utility industry. Saylor's question also, however, reflected the changes that occurred in the Southwestern electrical grid between 1963 and 1965. As the political barriers that had divided public and private utilities began to dissolve, as the region's private utilities formed WEST Associates to coordinate their operations, and as the new consortium rapidly expanded its coal-fired generating capacity, the logic underlying building "cash-register" dams meant to fund systemic development collapsed. These changes also suggested a new possibility, a public-private partnership between WEST's utilities and the Bureau of Reclamation.

Federal economists advising Lyndon Johnson were the first actors within the federal government to broadly question the PSWP. In April 1964 the Council of Economic Advisers applauded the plan as "a commendable advance in water resource planning and development" but responded with major concerns about the plan's economic logic. First the Council concluded that the Bureau of Reclamation had dramatically overvalued the need for agricultural irrigation. Even though metropolitan development was rapidly consuming farmland in the Southwest, the Council argued that there was little need to create agricultural sprawl to partner metropolitan sprawl. In fact, the Council stated, "There is not present *economic* justification for the creation of additional farm lands or for their intensification through irrigation when the Nation's agriculture already has an excess capacity of at least 8 or 9 percent of production annually." Even if additional farmland would be an asset to the nation, the Council stated, "it could be obtained in other parts of the US for substantially less than the cost of creating this capacity in the arid West." The Council, in effect, claimed that the Colorado River water rights Arizona had gained through *Arizona v. California* were not absolute but needed to be justified in relation to their effects on the nation's economy.[58]

The Council's second objection appeared even more troubling to the plan's supporters, given the arguments that environmentalists were making about the Grand Canyon. The Council questioned the ability of water from Northern California to provide adequate water for Los Angeles, especially given a recent proposal by the Interior's Bureau of Outdoor Recreation to preserve "some of these streams as 'wild rivers' for recreational purposes." While this objection said nothing about the protection of the Grand Canyon, it did pose recreation as a valuable use of water. And, challenging the dam supporters' notions of the recreational benefits of a reservoir, it focused on the recreational amenities of "wild rivers."[59]

Finally, the Council raised questions about the financing of the PSWP. It claimed that in its economic evaluation of the proposal, the Bureau of Reclamation had used an artificially low interest rate, with little relation to existing market conditions.[60] While the Council merely recommended that the Bureau recalculate its cost estimate using a higher interest rate, this objection signaled that the various component projects of the PSWP would be evaluated by criteria other than merely their benefit to the Southwest. While this point seems obvious, it signaled a shift within the federal state away from the ideology that held that regional economic development was automatically a boon to the nation. The Council on Economic Advisors took pains to point out that while the PSWP would undoubtedly be of tremendous benefit to the Southwest, its current version ran counter to the national economic interest.[61]

Many Eastern congressmen, Saylor among them, echoed the Council's concern that the dams provided little benefit to the nation. These congressmen, who would come to be known to dam supporters as "the economy bloc," viewed Bureau of Reclamation spending as having purely local benefits.[62] The economy bloc thus challenged the importance of regional economic development to the nation's overall economic health. The Council on Economic Advisors' report on the plan's questionable financial details only fueled the economy bloc's suspicions that the PSWP was a boondoggle.

Western congressmen had overcome similar concerns to pass CRSP legislation in the 1950s by forming a broad Western coalition. The early legislative attempts to pass the PSWP, however, demonstrated that Southwestern growth had fractured this coalition. In the preliminary deliberations over the PSWP, congressmen from other regions of the West voiced concern that a water-hungry Southwest would endanger their own regional futures. Congressmen from Northern California objected to efforts to divert the Trinity River to Southern California. Wayne Aspinall of

Colorado, chairman of the House Subcommittee on Irrigation and Reclamation, opposed any plan that threatened the water supply of his district on the western slope of the Rockies. Henry Jackson of Washington State, chairman of the Senate Interior Committee, promised to block any plan that even investigated diverting water from the Columbia River. In effect, Phoenix had come to provoke the same fears of a bottomless demand for water that Los Angeles had always raised in the minds of Westerners.[63]

Carl Hayden and Morris Udall, who had won Arizona's second congressional seat after his brother's nomination as Interior Secretary, introduced two different versions of the plan in 1964 and 1965, adapting the bill each year to respond to the various objections of Western congressmen. Each bill contained the CAP and either Bridge or Marble Canyon Dams. And each year, their proposals failed to garner enough support to be voted out of committee because of regional Western concerns.[64] Morris Udall's legislative memoranda to John Rhodes, the representative from Arizona's first congressional district, in early 1966 demonstrated the various interests dam supporters had to navigate. Udall identified thirteen different political "power centers," five of whom were "indispensable," who "simply must be *for* the bill . . . if it has any chance to pass." This group included Senator Hayden, Congressman Aspinall, Senator Jackson, and Senator Clinton Anderson of New Mexico, along with "the Johnson administration." While Udall listed "the conservation organizations and their spokesmen, including the *New York Times* and *Washington Post*" as a power center, he also wrote that "in the right circumstances we could pass a bill over their objections." Focusing on powerful Western legislators, Udall argued for resuscitating the consensus that dams held broad benefits for the West as a region. The key to the bill's passage, he wrote, was "that the plan not appear to be a local project. . . . [W]e must take a regional approach."[65]

The 1966 Colorado River Basin Project (CRBP) represented Stewart Udall's attempt to recreate this coalition of Western legislators. Working with his brother, he designed the bill to avoid antagonizing any Western interests. One dam would be authorized at Marble Canyon, and Bridge Canyon would be "studied for potential authorization should the need arise." The bill limited the CAP to 1.2 million acre-feet of Colorado River Water, far below the 2.8 million acre-feet that *Arizona v. California* had recognized as Arizona's legal right. Southern California would lose only 0.7 million acre-feet of water. The new plan also included five new water projects in Colorado, attempting to reassure Aspinall that Upper Basin water rights would be protected. Avoiding any mention of the Pacific Northwest, the bill's language spoke of finding sources of water for the Pacific Southwest from "outside of the Colorado River system." While the federal government's initial appropriation for the project would be

$1.3 billion, editorial writers across the West reminded their readers that the project "would pay for itself" through the sale of power to metropolitan consumers.[66]

Udall's and Hayden's efforts to recreate the pro-dam Western congressional coalition collapsed, however, largely due to a third set of critics: experts from the electrical power industry. The Bureau of Reclamation had long employed economists to develop the financing mechanisms for their projects. Expert testimony, however, proved a tenuous tool to use in support of federal programs. On their own, experts provided powerful support for Bureau policies. If their conclusions were called into question by competing experts, however, the authority of expert testimony was severely discounted, as congressmen and their aides were left to make sense of arguments that featured competing expertise. Congressmen with memories of CRSP also had reason to doubt the veracity of Reclamation's calculations. Indeed, David Brower had revealed that the agency had miscalculated the amount of evaporation from an expanded Lake Powell due to a simple subtraction error.[67]

Challenges to the CRBP came from a different direction. In a 1966 report to the House Irrigation Subcommittee, faculty from the California Institute of Technology raised two troubling issues. First, they questioned the project's financing. The faculty members—an economist, a hydrologist, and an electrical systems engineer—claimed that the Bureau had used artificially low interest rates to calculate the long-term cost of the dam, the same practices that the Council of Economic Advisors had earlier criticized. Even worse, they evaluated alternatives using higher interest rates. Where the cost of privately financed alternatives for the dam had been evaluated using a 6 percent interest rate, the Bureau calculated the dam's cost using "the artificially low interest rate of 3.2%," a calculation that amounted to "a hidden subsidy" for the Bureau of Reclamation. Such an unbalanced comparison, the researchers argued, served only to inflate the value of the dams. As they stated, "The economic evaluation of alternative projects, whether public or private, should reflect as nearly as possible the true costs to society for given benefits." When they readjusted the costs of Marble Canyon Dam to take account of the hidden subsidies, they found that a comparable nuclear power plant could be built for $91 million and produce electricity at 3.1 mills per kilowatt hour, as compared to $239 million and 6.5 mills for the dam.[68] In testimony before the Subcommittee, other expert witnesses reinforced these conclusions. Alan Carlin, an economist for the Rand Corporation, testified that coal-fired plants could be built for even less money than the nuclear plants suggested by the CalTech faculty members.[69]

Second, the CalTech faculty suggested the new power plants that WEST was building on the Colorado Plateau eliminated the need for dams altogether. As the CalTech researchers wrote, "There are trends in the power business which the Bureau of Reclamation has not fully taken into account, chief among them the interconnection of generating facilities and the rapid increases in demand."[70] In doing so, they directly questioned Reclamation commissioner Floyd Dominy's understanding of the ongoing changes in electrical power in the Southwest. While admitting in previous testimony that dams would be unnecessary for base-load power, Dominy argued the new dams would provide essential peaking power to meet spikes in demand during the day: "I do not care whether we have thermal power by atomic energy [or] by coal. . . . [H]ydropower will still fit into it masterfully as peaking power," he had argued, explaining the flexibility that dams provided: "I was at a powerplant when the noon hour was reached. The operator just pulled the switch and cut the generating units off for an hour to save water—because the factory shut down, and the peak use was closed out for one hour. . . . You cannot do that with steam."[71]

In the judgment of electrical industry experts, Dominy failed to grasp the vast size and scope of the new electrical networks in the Southwest. Dominy's example of an isolated factory and dam connected immediately to each other, in which the supply and demand of electricity existed in isolation from other generating facilities or sources of demand, struck the utility experts as quaint. Dominy described a system with such limited demand that the closing of one factory would affect the system to such an extent that electrical generation would be stopped. The electrical experts thought in terms of vast, interconnected electrical systems that reached out to multiple metropolitan areas. Interconnected facilities could merely exchange electricity to meet spikes in demand, rather than regularly turning generators on and off. In addition, the need for peaking power itself was in decline. The increased use of electricity in the home for heating and air conditioning had reduced large differentials between peak and regular demand. With lower spikes in demand, an electrical system could rely more and more on base-load plants fueled by coal or atomic energy. The peaks that did exist could easily be met by exchanging electricity between utilities. As the researchers from CalTech wrote, "There will simply not be so much need in the future for large hydropower capabilities to meet sudden changes in power demand."[72]

Large hydroelectric dams had been essential for electrical utilities' ability to meet sudden changes in demand in the 1950s. Before that, they had been used to generate large amounts of inexpensive base power at rates far below fuel-fired plants. Those days were past, the experts suggested, ended by technological change. One expert offered a comparison: using hydroelectric dams to produce the constant base power needed for pumping water was akin to asking Ford Motor Company to produce

Model-Ts in 1966. Even if the peaking power from the dams would be marginally useful within the larger pool of electricity, the marginal gain did not offset the $1.3 billion cost to build one of the dams, especially when the same electricity could be generated far more inexpensively using other fuels. Changes in the geography of power had, in a sense, made the Colorado River Dams—the engineering marvels of the 1930s, 1940s, and 1950s—obsolete.[73]

If this new geography made dams obsolete, it also made the CAP possible. Following the failure of Congress to pass the CRBP, Stewart Udall requested a complete reevaluation of CAP proposals by the economic and engineering analysts in the Department of the Interior's Water and Power Division.[74] These analysts evaluated thirty-four different plans—varying the number of dams, changing the height of the dams, and including, for the first time, analysis of a CAP powered by a coal-fired plant. The subsequent report concluded that there were two options. The first cost $1.2 billion and represented "the traditional approach to reclamation." The Bureau of Reclamation would build Hualapai Dam—the Department of Interior's preferred name since 1966 for Bridge Canyon Dam in order to emphasize its benefits for the Hualapai and Havasupai Tribes—to provide all of the necessary power for CAP.[75] The Bureau of Reclamation favored this option as it operated according to the same terms as all other postwar Reclamation projects. Sale of excess power from the dam would provide funding for the construction of CAP's canals and pumps. To mitigate environmentalists' inevitable objections, the plan would expand the boundaries of Grand Canyon National Park upstream to include Marble Canyon. It would also include projects in Aspinall's district while avoiding any mention of diverting water from the Pacific Northwest. In a memorandum to President Johnson, Stewart Udall admitted that the case for building even one dam on the Colorado River was more a political measure than an engineering necessity. The dam, Udall wrote to Johnson, "has the most political appeal for members of Congress from the Colorado Basin." The case for building even one dam had become mainly symbolic. It would satisfy Arizonans notion that their state "had finally made it" in the words of one constituent writing to Morris Udall.[76] In January 1967, Udall forwarded this plan, as the recommendation of the Bureau of Reclamation, to the 90th Congress.

Even as he passed the Bureau's recommendations to Congress, Stewart Udall had decided on the second plan, which had less symbolic appeal for Arizonans, but, in Udall's words, "would be the least costly and, from a national point of view, the least controversial plan." It called for the Bureau of Reclamation to purchase 425 megawatts of electricity, enough to power the CAP's pumps, from a coal-fired power plant built by private utilities in Arizona. Irrigation works would be financed from revenue from Hoover, Parker, and Davis Dams, which would soon be generating budget surpluses. The proposal would lower the total cost of the project by $500 million. And such a power plant was already in the planning stages. In late November 1966, Walter Lucking, president of APS and chairman of WEST Associates, wrote to Udall and informed him that WEST was considering building a new power plant near Page, Arizona, using coal from Peabody's mine on Black Mesa. Udall quickly responded, informing Lucking about the Bureau's interest in potentially purchasing electricity from the new plant. In absence of a specific plan, Lucking offered a general assurance of cooperation but, afraid of appearing to be against the dam, steered far away from the controversy over the Grand Canyon Dams. "So there will be no misunderstanding, if we are asked to comment on other proposals on the Lower Colorado which involve hydro development," Lucking wrote, "we would also state our intention to cooperate. . . . I would expect the utilities would be pleased to undertake joint studies concerning the marketing of power produced from any hydro development power features that may be adopted."[77]

Nevertheless, Udall's interest in purchasing electricity from the plant provided advantages to WEST's proposed power plant. It guaranteed a long-term payment for a steady, sizable load of electricity. With such constant demand, the power plant could be run more constantly at maximum capacity, lowering the cost of electricity for all utilities drawing power from the plant. In effect, CAP would not support a publicly built dam, but would help WEST's plant achieve a better economy of scale.

On February 1, 1967, with Floyd Dominy conveniently flying overseas to examine hydroelectric facilities funded by the U.S. Agency for International Development, Udall announced that Hualapai Dam was off the table along with the projects in Aspinall's district. Instead, the Bureau of Reclamation would build the CAP, powering it with 425 megawatts of firm power purchased from WEST's new power plant at Page, Navajo Generating Station.[78] The Bureau would purchase roughly one-quarter of Navajo Generating Station's electrical power, with the remainder going to five other member utilities of WEST.[79] The Interior Department agreed to facilitate negotiations between WEST and the Navajo Tribe to secure a lease for the plant site, 34,000 acre-feet of the tribes' Colorado River water to cool the plant's boilers, and rights-of-way for a railroad from Black Mesa Mine to Navajo Generating Station. The Bureau of Reclamation and WEST agreed to cooperate on the construction of new shared transmission lines. All documentation about the agreement referred to the Bureau's involvement as a "prepayment purchase of pumping power," to avoid the impression that the public Bureau of Reclamation was investing in a privately owned generating plant.[80] Of course, this was exactly what the plan did. It created a public-private partnership in all aspects of the electric utility industry other than the final distribution of electricity to consumers. After the first unit of Navajo Generating Station went online in 1974, the lines dividing the production of public and private power would be dissolved completely in the Southwest. Electricity from the power pool shared by WEST Associates and the Bureau of Reclamation would pump water, light homes, cool offices, and run assembly lines.

Udall's proposal provoked a good deal of opposition. Dominy told a friend, "My secretary turned chickenshit on me."[81] Public power advocates denounced the plan because of the cooperation with private utilities. "Secretary Udall," the American Public Power Association stated, "has killed public power forever." Aspinall vowed on the day of the announcement that Udall's plan "never would live to see the light of day." California representative Craig Hosmer questioned how the project would be financed without extra revenue from the sale of power: "Possibly Secretary Udall will next propose two large gambling casinos at Las Vegas as a substitute for Hualapai and Marble Canyon dam revenues." Arizona legislators were outraged, claiming that Udall had "double-crossed his own state" by "caving in to the ultra-conservationist Sierra Club." Even Morris Udall came out against the proposal, stating he was standing by the Hualapai Dam proposal.[82]

Despite this opposition, Udall had garnered key supporters for the bill. Even before announcing it, he had briefed Senators Hayden, Jackson, and Anderson—all three key members of the Senate Interior Committee—and convinced them that the bill was the only possible measure that could pass Congress. All three senators promised to rally support in their own state caucuses and to pressure Aspinall to pass the bill out of the House Subcommittee on Irrigation and Reclamation. Equally as important as the legislative politics behind a coal-powered CAP, the plan satisfied the electric utility experts and economic analysts who had expressed skepticism about the dam-based CAP plans. The utility experts saw the plan as increasing interconnections and thus strengthening the Western grid as well as utilizing the most cost-efficient fuel for base power generation. The financial analysts simply preferred the lower cost of the coal-fired CAP. Unlike Western congressmen who held on to the fiction that the dams paid for themselves, they had long realized that the repayment plans did not work unless they were calculated with abnormally low interest rates.[83]

Udall's plan also satisfied the Sierra Club. Despite the Club's rhetoric about the danger of Southwestern growth, Brower and other Sierra Club leaders had long supported coal or even atomic energy as alternatives to the Grand Canyon Dams. Aware of the use of coal at Four Corners, David Brower began promoting coal-fired plants as an alternative source of power in 1963, almost immediately after the announcement of the plans to build the dams. In *Time and the River Flowing*, he wrote, "The states of the Upper Basin of the Colorado contain a major part of the earth's coal reserves. The development of these resources is in the doldrums—and they are a much longer-lived source of energy than the short-lived reservoirs planned for the silty Colorado."[84] Francois Leydet echoed Brower's support for coal-burning plants and added that nuclear power plants provided another alternative: "Not only have steam plants burning conventional fossil fuels become increasingly efficient over the years, but the day may be near when atomic energy will begin to produce really inexpensive electricity." Leydet also foresaw the possibility of hydrogen fusion plants that could power desalination plants, which would "thereby obviate the need for complicated, astronomically expensive and scenery-damaging transfers of water from one watershed . . . to another."[85] Throughout the campaign against the dams, the Sierra Club continued to maintain support for mining and burning coal. In 1966 testimony before Aspinall's subcommittee, Brower stated that the Club would "support as many coal plants as is necessary to make the CAP viable."[86]

The Sierra Club's continuing advocacy for coal and nuclear plants demonstrated two facets of the Sierra Club's opposition to the dams. First, the Club's officials and authors retained a tremendous faith in the ability of technology to solve problems. While they appeared to question the entire developmental ideology of the boosters, they maintained faith that changing technology would eliminate the need for dams.[87] The changes occurring in the electric utility industry as they wrote *Time and the River Flowing* bore out this faith. The increasing capacity of coal-fired generators and extra-high-voltage transmission lines along with the increasing cooperation between public and private utilities proved dams unnecessary for the generation of electricity. Because of the fungible nature of electricity, water did not have to be used to move water; instead, coal could move water even more efficiently and effectively.

Second, the advocacy for coal or nuclear plants indicates the Sierra Club continued to focus primarily on the preservation of "sacred" landscapes. While the Sierra Club used the language of ecology in speaking of "the living river" and called on people to rethink their relationship with the world around them, their political goals did not reflect that ecological thinking. Their statements, such as Leydet's denunciation of "scenery-destroying" water projects, and their promotion of the coal-fired plants indicate that protecting specific places remained far more important than ecological concerns with pollution and soil and water contamination. Long after many environmentalists began expressing concern about pollution and other environmental health hazards, the Sierra Club continued promoting coal-fired plants as a harmless means to resolve the Southwest's water needs. Instead, their goals emphasized the preservation of the Grand Canyon for individual experience. Given that focus, the Sierra Club found a solution in the spatial reorganization of the Colorado Plateau into what we might think of as sacred and industrial spaces. After the passage of the Colorado River Basin Project in 1968, the Grand Canyon became protected, sacred space. The Navajo Reservation, slightly to the east, became increasingly industrial.

The Eastern press hailed Udall's decision to build a coal-powered CAP as a major victory for the Sierra Club. The *Washington Post* framed Udall's proposal using the Sierra Club's language, his compromise representing a "victory for all those who have fought to protect the Grand Canyon from desecration."[88] The *New York Times* proclaimed "Victory for Grand Canyon" on its editorial page, writing that Udall's decision bore out the Sierra Club's logic that "there are feasible alternatives to the Grand Canyon dams if the will exists to seek those alternatives." The *Times* viewed the settlement as a masterful compromise—"making it possible for fast-growing Arizona to get the water it needs while preserving the irreplaceable glories of the Grand Canyon"—that left all parties satisfied.[89] The reaction in Arizona was less enthusiastic. The *Arizona Republic* warned, "The nation will be in danger if a small number of people who love nature more than people can prevent needed progress." Nevertheless, the *Republic* admitted, "If, at long last, Arizona receives the Colorado River water that is its right, the new plan will be acceptable."[90] In almost all these editorials, the concerns of actors within the state were boiled away in favor of a struggle between the Sierra Club and the Bureau of Reclamation.

This struggle between the Sierra Club and the Bureau of Reclamation formed the dominant public memory of the controversy. Philip Hyde, a Sierra Club photographer, suggested twenty years after the fact that the decision marked a critical turning point in Western history: "The environmental movement's chief purpose was to fight the Grand Canyon dams. The Bureau of Reclamation lost that fight, and they went into decline after that."[91] John McPhee's *Encounters with the Archdruid* portrayed the struggle as a personal battle between David Brower and Floyd Dominy. The third section of McPhee's book recounts a rafting trip through the Grand Canyon and a power boat ride on Lake Powell taken by Brower and Dominy in 1970. In Hyde's and McPhee's account, stark divisions characterize the narrative of the battle over the dams: divisions between Brower and Dominy, between the flowing river of the Grand Canyon and the still waters of Lake Powell, and between sacred and productive visions of nature.[92]

Two main changes exist in the space between these oppositions. First, the changes to the organization of electricity in the Southwest that occurred before and during the controversy led to the elimination of the dams. The construction of Mojave Generating Station and the expansion of Four Corners Power Plant revealed the economies of scale possible through a new generation of coal-fired power plants. The interconnection of power lines across the Southwest reduced the need for the dams' potential peaking power. The merging of public and private transmission systems allowed not hydropower, but any electricity to power CAP. All these changes proved effective weapons to fight the dams. In a very real sense, dam opponents used the new geography of electricity to prevent the dams' construction. These changes also bridged the gap between nature and culture. As WEST and Reclamation built power lines to connect Navajo Generating Station to the Southwestern power pool, natural energies flowed to meet the demands of consumers in Phoenix and Los Angeles. They also flowed to the pumps of the CAP, finally completed in 1978, using coal to move water.

If these stories overlook the intersection of nature and culture, they also overlook the landscape where production occurred. While Navajo Generating Station preserved the landscape of the Grand Canyon, it dramatically intensified the production occurring on the Colorado Plateau. The stories of battles between Dominy and Brower, or between the Sierra Club and the Bureau of Reclamation, largely ignore this second landscape. The opening of Navajo Generating Station meant far heavier production at Black Mesa Mine, which now supplied Mojave and Navajo Generating Stations with four hundred tons of coal per day. The Sierra Club, however, did not entirely forget about this landscape. In the early 1970s, many Club members came to regret the compromise that pushed production onto the Colorado Plateau. Seeing pictures of Black Mesa Mine in the *Sierra Club Bulletin*, they began a campaign to block additional strip mining. Using the tactics they had learned during the earlier struggle, Sierra Club members besieged congressmen with letters, appealed to the national press, and placed full-page advertisements in the *New York Times*, *Washington Post*, and *Los Angeles Times* denouncing the strip mining of Black Mesa. "Should we also tear apart St. Peter's to get at the marble?" the ad asked. While several critical national profiles of the mining appeared, they had no effect on it. Partially, this ineffectiveness represented a failure to rally public support for a landscape with which few Americans were familiar. More than that, though, it reflected the importance of time. By the time the Sierra Club launched these challenges, WEST Associates was already building Navajo Generating Station and its transmission lines. They represented capital fixed in space. As the following chapter will explore, once the material aspects of the geography of power came into existence, resistance to development became much more difficult.

CHAPTER 7

A Piece of the Action

BLACK MESA IS LOCATED NEAR THE CENTER OF NAVAJO TERRITORY, AT THE point where the Navajo and Hopi Nations intersect. The mesa, a broad plateau covered in ponderosa pine rises steeply above the Chinle Valley to its north. In the early 1960s, scattered settlements of Navajo shepherds grazed their sheep and goats on the mesa. The ground beneath Black Mesa is shot through with veins of coal up to sixty-five feet thick, making it one of the richest coal deposits in the United States. In 1964, seeing the successful development of coal at Navajo Mine, Peabody Coal, the largest industrial mining company in the United States at the time, negotiated a lease of almost 65,000 acres with the Department of the Interior and the Navajo Tribal Council to strip-mine coal on two different sites on Black Mesa. Two years later, Peabody signed an agreement with a consortium of Southwestern utilities to provide coal to two new power plants located near Page, on the western end of the Navajo Nation and in Bullhead City, Nevada, near Las Vegas. Shortly thereafter, SRP leased five hundred acres near Page to build the new Navajo Generating Station.

While some Navajos later charged that the Tribal Council never received an opportunity to truly evaluate and debate the leases, few complaints appeared publicly at the time the leases were signed in 1964. Five years later, however, the leases were the hottest topic of discussion in the *Navajo Times* and *Diné Baa-Hani*. Almost every week, letters attacked the Tribal Council and Chairman Raymond Nakai as corrupt, treacherous, and worse. The leases on Black Mesa became the key example in a widely voiced critique of the Navajo place within the Southwest. For those voicing this critique, Peabody's strip mine was vivid proof of the tribe's colonial status within the Southwest. The tribe would not overcome this status, young radicals argued, until Navajos wrested control of their land from the outside forces that currently controlled it. Navajos would remain subordinated within the Southwest until they *acted* like a sovereign nation, rather than merely calling themselves one.

Navajo nationalism represented the main language by which Navajos sought to alter the dynamics of energy development in the Southwest. It arose in critiques by young Navajo activists that claimed energy development represented the colonization of Navajo land and the destruction of

Navajo culture and assumed new form during the tribal chairmanship of Peter MacDonald, who envisioned Navajo control, management, and production of energy resources as leading to new tribal power. These conflicting visions of nationalism and energy development came to a head in the mid-1970s in a conflict over the construction of new coal gasification plants near Burnham, forty miles south of Four Corners Power Plant. While MacDonald supported the plants as giving the tribe "a piece of the action," most younger nationalists opposed them for endangering local communities.

Energy development was not merely an issue that Navajos debated; it was constitutive of the versions of Navajo nationalism that developed in the early 1970s. Metropolitan demand for energy produced the new spatial structures that previous chapters have explored, a system in which resources on Navajo lands provided the fuel for the growth of the modern Southwest. At the same time, the effects of the changing geography of energy development were not limited to their material manifestations in power plants and transmission lines. This geography also created new understandings among Navajos of their land's value. By making the natural resources of the Navajo Nation central to its expansion, the metropolitan Southwest created a new vision among Navajos of the power they could have if they could control this wealth. The new process of wealth and energy production spanning the Southwest resulted in debates within the Navajo Nation over the character of Navajo nationalism.

At the same time, the existence of energy production led to both the particular critiques of the Navajo place in the Southwest that characterized the discourse of Navajo nationalism and the visions of the nation that Navajos produced. Metropolitan demand produced the notion that Navajos possessed massive mineral wealth, and this allowed young activists to imagine the Nation as space colonized by the greedy cities of the Southwest. It allowed Peter MacDonald to imagine the Navajo Nation as a mineral-rich "emerging" nation equivalent to the OPEC nations rising to global power at the same moment in history. The value created by metropolitan demand allowed MacDonald to imagine the formation of a Navajo state powerful enough to control the distribution of power in the region.[1] Moreover, all versions of Navajo nationalism recognized that metropolitan growth depended on the resources located on their land. Navajo nationalists attempted to manipulate the Southwestern cities' dependence on Indian resources to produce meaningful power within the region. Navajo nationalism thus attempted to alter the spatial dynamics that subordinated Navajo claims to control their land to metropolitan demands for inexpensive power.

THE NAVAJO NATION IN THE 1960S

By the late 1960s, Paul Jones's vision of Navajo industrial modernity seemed to be proceeding apace. Navajos formed a majority of the work force in both Navajo and Black Mesa Mines. The 210 Navajo miners earned between $41 and $50 a day. In a single day, those miners earned almost half the per capita annual income of the reservation twenty years earlier. At Four Corners Power Plant, 800 Navajos worked to complete the plant's expansion. Upon its completion in 1968, Arizona Public Service employed 123 Navajos at the plant. While most of these workers occupied the lower employment rungs at their respective work places, they represented some of the best-paid jobs on the reservation. Increasing numbers of Navajos pursued higher education, either at nearby state institutions, their educations funded with scholarships underwritten by proceeds from oil and natural-gas development, or after 1969, at Navajo Community College at Chinle. The Navajo Times, a tribally managed newspaper begun during Jones's administration in 1957, flourished, gaining fifteen thousand subscribers, and helping to convey a sense of a shared Navajo community. Jones's vision of a powerful Navajo Tribe, growing in concert with the metropolitan Southwest, appeared bright.[2]

Jones had not witnessed these changes from office. In 1962, he was defeated in his bid for a third term as tribal chairman by Raymond Nakai, a radio broadcaster with a popular Navajo-language program on Flagstaff's KCLS. Nakai took advantage of the radios that became increasingly omnipresent in the reservation's pickup trucks and electrified homes to convey a populist message that Jones's administration had become remote from the people and too dependent on outside experts. The message apparently resonated. Nakai defeated Jones and a third challenger, Sam Billison, with a plurality of 40 percent of the votes cast. In his inaugural, he promised a new direction. "I will spend less money in my administration on monuments and white elephants and more for the direct and lasting benefit of the Navajos in the hogans," Nakai promised. "I will seek advice from our non-Indian consultants, but not take orders from them. . . . I will engage economists to give economic advice, engineers to give engineering advice, and lawyers to give legal advice. For political advice, I will go to the people." Suggesting a tighter link between tribal government and the Navajo people in the government of their homeland, Nakai insisted that tribal officials refer to the "Navajo Nation" rather than the "Navajo Reservation."[3]

Despite this rhetoric, Nakai extended Jones's initiatives more than he challenged them. While he did fire tribal attorney Norman Littell in a bruising fight that created political rifts on the tribal council, he continued to broadly back energy development and seek reservation industrialization. Nakai endorsed the two leases negotiated between the BIA and Peabody Coal early in his chairmanship and supported the agreement to build Navajo Generating Station, though, as had been the pattern during Jones's administration, Navajo officials were largely excluded from negotiations.

The Fairchild Semiconductor plant at Shiprock represented the crown jewel of Nakai's administration. By the mid-1960s, BIA industrial-development efforts promoted reservations as providing ready supplies of low-cost labor in a western region where, as one BIA memo from 1966 stated, "rising labor costs and employee transience increasingly trouble western industries." Navajos' "ready dexterity" and "attachment to place" made them ideal workers for textiles, electronics, and other forms of light manufacturing, while "available land and ample energy supplies from nearby power-plants," the memo argued, made the reservation an ideal plant site.[4] The BIA began negotiating with Fairchild Semiconductor, a Silicon Valley firm whose scientists had invented the silicon semiconductor and whose engineers had devised a low-cost manufacturing process, in July 1966. BIA officials resisted initial locations beyond the reservation's borders proposed by Fairchild's representative. Instead, they insisted any plants employing Navajo workers be built on the reservation. With that stipulation, however, the BIA proved generous. It agreed to fund plant construction out of tribal funds, with costs repaid over the course of forty years with 5 percent interest. During that time, Fairchild could vacate the plant without completing payments, making only two years of continuing payments. NTUA would provide electricity at a rate only 1 percent above its wholesale cost. In return, Navajos would receive preference in hiring and would be promoted into plant management after completing a training program. The September 1966 contract between the tribe and Fairchild represented Navajos' first success in the competitive growth politics that increasingly defined the American economy.[5]

Nakai hailed the agreement as the centerpiece of his first term during his second inaugural address, held in February 1967, after his second defeat of Paul Jones. "Industrial plants, like people," Nakai told the crowd assembled at the Navajo Tribal Fairgrounds, "grow in places where they feel wanted and needed." The results of the Navajo Tribe's welcoming attitude toward industry were evident in the growing community that lay ninety miles to the north of the Navajo Nation's capital. "The Shiprock area has become a hub of economic development," Nakai explained, "electric power production, oil and gas production and refining, electronic parts manufacturing, coal mining, irrigation and helium and uranium processing, all hiring Navajos." Nakai stressed that, unlike his predecessor's attempts to develop reservation resources, which had brought only royalties, his efforts had brought jobs to ordinary Navajos in the eastern reservation, with the initial employment of eight hundred Navajos at the Fairchild plant expected to increase to two thousand people. Fairchild proved a model for the reservation at large. "Almost any area on the reservation has a potential for electric parts manufacture if the people are willing to make the sacrifice of seeing that the companies' needs are met for roads, housing, water, sewer, and other requirements."[6]

The pages of the *Navajo Times* over the following two years contained evidence of the ongoing transformation of the reservation. The paper reported that firms as well known as General Electric, RCA, and Honeywell were interested in locating plants on the reservation alongside reports about the expansion of coal mining on Black Mesa and Navajo Mine, "the largest coal mining operation in the country," the paper boasted.[7] They also could be seen on the reservation landscape. In Shiprock, new roads, power lines, and dormitories to house Fairchild workers, joined the 60,000-square-foot plant built on the outskirts of the small community as new features of the landscape. Twenty miles east, Utah International's operations at Navajo Mine expanded steadily as Four Corners Power Plant's expansion demanded 4,200 tons of coal per day. On Black Mesa, one hundred miles to the west, new drag shovels began digging into the earth, removing overburden to get at the coal seams below; at the same time, workers began laying tracks Glen Canyon Dam for a new electric railway connecting Black Mesa to Navajo Generating Station. And crisscrossing the reservation's lands, power lines carried "coal by wire" to Phoenix, Los Angeles, and elsewhere in the metropolitan Southwest.

As all of this became visible in the landscape, letters to the editor in the *Navajo Times* began challenging the wisdom of industrial development, the legitimacy of the tribal government, and the broader alignment of power that electrical transmission lines represented. Instead of words like "modern," "progress," and "growth," the authors of those letters used words like "exploitation," "colonialism," and "ruin." They warned that energy development brought short-term profits but threatened the destruction of Navajo culture itself. And they pointed an accusatory finger at the BIA, at the cities that used Navajo power, and at tribal government itself as the source of the people's subordination and oppression.

NATIONALISM AS CULTURAL PROTECTION

"We the Navajos of Black Mesa area never surrendered to Kit Carson and never even left our land to walk to Fort Sumner," declared a seventy-three-year-old resident of Black Mesa. One of his neighbors, Florence Leonard, voiced incomprehension at the destruction of pastureland her family had used for generations: "We don't like what is going to be done to our land. Why do they have to do this to our land?" Many Mules Daughter sounded the most plaintive sentiment. "Where they are mining now is my land," she explained. "My father is buried there. His grave was torn up in the strip mining." "All the chapter leaders have to say," the unnamed writer reported, "is 'that there will be more work for men.'" Jobs were not enough, the article argued, a position made clear by the article's headline: "We Will Not Surrender Black Mesa."[8]

The October 1970 headline appeared in *Diné Baa-Hani*, a newspaper founded the year before by members of the National Indian Youth Council (NIYC) who posed "the people's press" as an alternative to the tribally owned *Navajo Times*. By the late 1960s, the paper's suggestion that energy development brought unbearable costs to Navajo people had become a central part of Navajo political culture. Headlines in *Diné Baa-Hani* warned, "You Are Being Robbed!!," "The Sacred Mountain Will Die," and "Clean Up Your Act, Honkey," while its cartoons portrayed "The Rape of Black Mesa for $$$" and depicted a giant death's head rising from the combined emissions of Four Corners, Navajo, and Mojave Generating Stations.[9] At the same time, the tribally managed *Navajo Times* ran statements, manifestos, and angry letters from members of Dineh for Justice, the Coalition for Navajo Liberation, Indians Against Exploitation, the Committee to Save Black Mesa, the American Indian Movement, and Navajos unaffiliated with any of these newly formed organizations.

Within these documents, young activists formulated a new language of Navajo nationalism that would become increasingly influential in the late 1960s and 1970s. Unlike Jones's and Nakai's belief in tribal growth within the contours of the Southwestern economy, these new nationalists saw Navajos as fundamentally oppressed within the region. Navajos, they argued, existed as a colonized people, and the Navajo Nation as colonized territory within the broader geography of the Southwest and the United States.[10] Energy development represented the prime example of these colonial bonds. And fighting this colonialism would require challenging not only the BIA but also tribal officials who acceded to energy development and the metropolitan consumers whose electrical demand was ultimately responsible for Navajo subordination. In their vision, nationalism would be directed not only toward asserting tribal sovereignty, but also toward protecting the people and places central to "traditional" Navajo culture from the energy production that endangered both.

Navajo nationalists' protests against energy development represented a manifestation of the broader politicization of young Indians in the late 1960s. The National Indian Youth Council stood at the center of this process. Founded in 1961 as a result of discussions among young Indians at the American Indian Chicago Conference for the purpose of introducing Indian voices into federal policy making, the NIYC grew slowly,

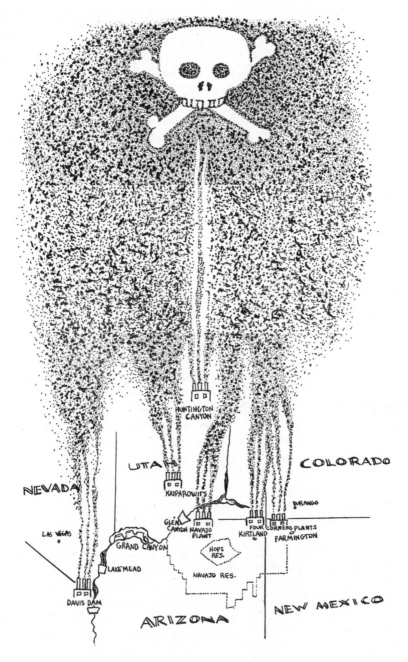

FIGURE 7.1. The editors of *Diné Baa-Hani* portrayed the power plants that ringed the Navajo Reservation as a destructive force. *Diné Baa-Hani*. November 1971.

possessing only 120 members as late as 1964. As a result of its successful direct actions at fish-ins in the Pacific Northwest in the mid-1960s
and a subsequent recruitment campaign among high school and college
students, the intertribal organization grew to over 5,000 members by
1970 and 15,000 by 1972. On the one hand, the NIYC benefited from
changes in Indian education such as the formation of Navajo Community
College, whose curriculum incorporated Navajo language, history, and
cultural studies, broadly emphasizing the importance of protecting Indian culture. On the other, it benefited from the continued cruelty of the
boarding schools where many Indian students still received high school
educations. Intermountain School, in Brigham, Utah, which housed approximately seven hundred Navajo students, employed coercive practices similar to boarding schools in the early twentieth century, including handcuffing and shaving the heads of disobedient students, enforcing
Mormon religious observance on Native students, and even, reportedly,
administering the powerful tranquilizer Thorazine to particularly recal-
citrant students.[11]

The NIYC presented such students with a broader framework in
which to understand their collective experiences as a result of an ongoing
history of oppression and conquest. While the NIYC carried out the goals
that had dominated intertribal politics for thirty years—the protection
of treaty rights, the quest for sovereignty and self-determination, and the
preservation of Indian culture—the NIYC pursued these goals through
direct-action campaigns such as the fish-ins and through rhetoric intended
to mobilize young Indians. "This is a real war," NIYC founder Mel Thom
stated in 1964. Winning it, Thom argued, would require young people to
take the lead in "rally[ing] our Indian forces" and pursuing education to
gain a "full understanding of the present American system."[12] Knowledge
of politics and law, the NIYC hoped, would provide a means to protect
Indian culture and particularly those elders who preserved Native traditions. This knowledge of the American system would be paired with new
attention to tradition among young Indians, dismissing the lessons of assimilation urged by BIA and some tribal officials. As Herbert Blatchford,
a Navajo founder of the NIYC, explained in 1967, "It started with the
old people. . . . [T]he youth, when they get together now, always meet on
Indian land, always with the old tribal people."[13]

NIYC members provided a clear message about the people and forces
most responsible for endangering these elders and the cultural endurance
they represented. As NIYC president Clyde Warrior told the Presidential
National Advisory Commission on Rural Poverty in 1967, "For those
of us who live on reservations . . . choices are made by federal administrators, bureaucrats, and their 'yes men,' euphemistically called tribal
governments." Two points are vital. First, tribal governments, in the eyes

of NIYC leaders, looked suspiciously like local agents for broader forces of cultural destruction, or, as they were derisively called, "Uncle Tomahawks" or "Apples." Second, the activists of the NIYC aimed their politics at protecting the wisdom of tribal elders and extending it into a new generation's experiences on and off reservations.[14] As one Navajo group formed in 1968 explained,

> Some of us have gone to college, but our education, if it was a good one, has pointed out to us that we do not want and will not live the life of an ulcerated white, middle-class Christian suburbanite. We are learning to take the material aspects of the Anglo world just as we are listening with pride to our elders for advice on the spiritual aspects of our world. . . . We do not want to hold back the times—we merely want to clarify that we are grateful to our elders for enriching us with a heritage, unique and secure, in this time of chaotic and rapid change.[15]

The NIYC also provided institutional mechanisms to introduce young Indians into both theories of oppression and practices of political organizing. Charlie Cambridge, a Navajo student at the University of Colorado, first encountered NIYC members at a Southwestern Youth Council meeting in Durango, Colorado, in 1967. Shortly thereafter, he enrolled in the Workshop on American Indian Affairs, a six-week crash course on federal Indian policy, social theory, and native history that was designed by the NIYC and the National Congress of American Indians for the purpose of training young activists. After completing his education at Boulder in 1969, he relocated to Shiprock where he joined with James Nez, who was a NIYC member and former president of the University of New Mexico's Kiva Club, to form *Diné Baa-Hani*.[16]

Diné Baa-Hani demonstrated just one instance of the way in which broader patterns of Indian youth politics assumed local form on the Navajo Nation. While some local activism remained explicitly intertribal— the American Indian Movement attracted enough Navajo members by 1974 to have a regular column in the *Navajo Times*—most groups associated themselves specifically with Navajos as a distinct people. Groups almost always indicated their tribal status in their names: Dineh for Justice, the Coalition for Navajo Liberation, the Committee to Save Black Mesa. Such names may have partially reflected a strategic decision by the NIYC in 1970 to encourage members to pursue local issues under the NIYC's broader umbrella. More importantly, however, it reflected the political mobilization of many young Navajos in opposition to the ongoing changes that energy development brought to tribal land and Navajo society.

These groups adapted the NIYC's broad description of Indian oppression to the particular conditions facing Navajos. The manifesto of

Dineh for Justice, published in the *Navajo Times* in 1968, demonstrated the three main culprits Navajo nationalists generally blamed for their people's subordination. First, the manifesto indicted the Bureau of Indian Affairs for "playing god with our lives just because they were given some power." Second, it blamed Navajo leaders who profited from their positions: "We disrespect any one Indian who attempts to superimpose his will on the majority of us . . . who gets fat jobs, drives big cars from his payoffs, and forgets the welfare of the people." Finally, it broadly pointed to "the whiteman who attempts to superimpose his culture on ours . . . who attempts to use the Navajos to his own advantage . . . who come[s] to our reservation and leave[s], without a backward glance, with money in their pockets." While Dineh for Justice's manifesto borrowed NIYC's broad indictment of the BIA and tribal government, it added economic exploitation by "the whiteman" and payoffs to tribal leaders as key elements of Navajos' "colonial status." Indeed, "colonialism" was considered of far more economic and material significance in this manifesto than in the NIYC's usual depictions of Indian oppression. Navajo nationalists' understanding of colonialism was, in short, marked not only by the BIA's control of Navajo people but also by exploitation of tribal land and resources by outside forces.[17]

To be sure, Navajo nationalists targeted issues other than energy development. The highest-profile political actions during the early 1970s involved protests against the Gallup Ceremonial, an annual festival of Indian arts, crafts, and dancing that trafficked in the type of objectification portrayed in *Arizona Highways*. The Ceremonial allowed local officials to claim Gallup as "the Indian Capital of the United States," a moniker that proved lucrative to local merchants. Indians Against Exploitation, formed in 1969 by students from the University of New Mexico's Kiva Club, charged that the Ceremonial's performances made a mockery of Indian culture and that Gallup businesses "rechannel[ed] only an insignificant amount of public services for Indians."[18] Criticism of BIA boarding schools, as well, filled the pages of *Diné Baa-Hani*. Its editors objected not only to the often violent treatment of Navajo students but to the curriculum they were offered. *Supernavajo*, a recurring satirical cartoon, denounced BIA schools for ignoring the educational needs of Navajo students ("They have great cliché's, such as 'education must fit the needs of the people,' yet they'll teach you only their ways") and for foisting upon them an Anglo-American past ("You'll begin with their history and study it from the beginning of man until the present! If there's anything concerning your people, you can bet it'll be biased. For example, if they win, it's a victory, if you win it's a massacre"). BIA education intended, the cartoon suggested, to turn Navajos away from their cultural identity and imbue them with the beliefs of Anglo society.[19]

Protest against the exploitation of Indians at the Gallup Ceremonial and in BIA boarding schools fed into a broader critique of the inequalities inherent in the BIA's vision of Navajo development. At least since the Long Range Rehabilitation Act, the BIA's model of economic development had implied that the Navajo Tribe was experiencing gradual progression along a linear path that led from subsistence agriculture to modern industrial development. According to the social-scientific beliefs that underlay not only the BIA's vision of Navajo development but modernization theory more generally, resulting economic inequities resulted primarily from the discrepancy between Navajos and the modern industrial economy of the surrounding society. In contrast, the Navajos writing in *Diné Baa-Hani* or joining Dineh for Justice largely saw economic inequalities, like other inequalities, as resulting from the subordination of Navajo interests to the demands of the regional economy. The BIA's assumption that Navajo resources should be developed for the benefit of the regional economy rather than for the benefit of the Nation itself represented, in their eyes, a fatal decision that both robbed Navajos of control over their own land and revealed BIA beliefs about the fundamental incapacity of Navajos to act in their own interest.

This critique of the political economy of the Southwest extended beyond the reservation's borders and beyond the BIA's policies. In 1969, *Supernavajo* portrayed the BIA's area director, Samuel Smith, repeating what William Warne had said to Congress twenty years earlier, that "The Navajos are going through a stage now that rural America went through fifty years before." *Supernavajo*'s author, "Navajo John," responded caustically by comparing Navajo progress to the fate of the nation's other minority groups, "The reservation will be exactly like the rest of America in 50 years. . . . [T]he Blacks and Raza are living in equality with the rest of America. After all, they've been dealing with the U.S. for the last 150 years and longer."[20] The cartoon thus suggests that some Navajo activists joined the broader critiques of America, offered by Chicanos and black nationalists, as a terminally racist society that exploited its internally colonized people. In this portrait, the regional and national economy possessed a dual structure in which the economic interests of people of color were exploited by the larger racist structure of Anglo society. Within this economy, nonwhites living in ghettos, in barrios and farm labor camps, or on reservations faced colonial exploitation.[21]

This critique dismissed the BIA's explanation of Navajo poverty as determined by the process of economic modernization. Instead, young activists argued that the Navajo reservation and the urban Southwest occupied the same position in time. Both spaces were modern, but the colonial relationship between the urban Southwest and the Navajo Nation maintained Navajo underdevelopment in order to ensure metropolitan growth. Many Navajo activists rejected the central concepts of modernization theory: the division of the world between primitive and civilized nations and the ability of objective social science to bring about "modernization" through the economic development of non-Western nations. Increasingly, they began to speak in the language of non-Western intellectuals, denouncing the BIA as "neocolonialists" and the Black Mesa Mine as the "pseudo-capitalist exploitation of a spiritual shrine."[22] The embrace of this language by young college-educated Navajos was the ironic product of the BIA's and Navajo leaders' quest for modernization, both of which had believed that higher education would produce a Navajo managerial class; instead, it produced an organic anticolonial intelligentsia.

While young Navajo activists' attacks on the BIA were sustained, they vacillated on Navajo tribal government's role in creating structures of colonialism. Tribal leaders like Raymond Nakai as well as the Navajo Tribal Council received praise for helping establish Rough Rock Demonstration School and Navajo Community College, whose curricula reflected Navajo students' hopes to include Navajo language, culture, and history into educational structures. Nevertheless, the tribal council had repeatedly endorsed energy development. Throughout the late 1960s and early 1970s, Diné Baa-Hane and letters in the Navajo Times debated whether tribal leaders were naive dupes giving away valuable resources or greedy parasites growing fat off energy contracts. The gentlest treatment of the tribal government primarily blamed the BIA for the leases, portraying the tribal council as acceding to its recommendations without gaining necessary information. In Diné Baa-Hane, Orville McKinney quoted Navajo council members' recollections that BIA representatives had brought completed contracts to council meetings and told the council to approve them without deliberation. "It is apparent," McKinney concluded, "that the Navajo tribal council signed the lease without a complete understanding of the ecological damage that these power plants could do to the land, air and water. This pressure came through its favorite whipping boy—the BIA." The blame for unequal lease terms, environmental damage, and the lack of information about leases in McKinney's portrait rested primarily on the BIA. At the same time, he implicitly criticized the tribal council for trusting the BIA, for failing to manage land in the interest of the Navajo people, and for neglecting to even conduct a debate over energy development.[23]

Many Navajos shared this conception of the tribal government as politically powerless and inept in the face of federal pressure. Letters to the Navajo Times blamed tribal officials for agreeing to inequitable contracts. Most also indicated that federal officials and energy companies manipulated the tribe into accepting unfair leases. Esther Patrick, a resident of

Gallup, responded to a tribal decision allowing Navajo Generating Station to use Navajo water by writing, "Here we go again. The vultures of a non-Indian society are pulling the strings in Washington. The Four Corners Area is licking its chops to see where the stupid Indians can give in to some kind of political pressure." The agreement contradicted the tribal governments' stated goal of developing a self-sufficient industrial economy, she wrote. "I would like to know if the tribal council knows that if water is decreased or cut off there will not be any type of industry. We are getting peanuts when we should be getting billions."[24]

While Patrick stopped there, other writers went further, charging that the tribal government and its officials were themselves corrupt. In this view, tribal officials had abandoned the interests of "the people" for their own monetary gain. Caleb Johnson, a member of the Hopi Tribe and frequent presence on the letter page of the *Navajo Times*, charged that both the Hopi and Navajo Tribal Councils had abandoned their public trust in the face of financial offers. "This is an irresponsible form of government because a moral government is responsible to the land as well as to its people. The trend in these two tribal governments is for more and more profits at the expense of the land of all the people. But, I have yet to see in what way the Hopis and Navajos have been helped."[25]

Raymond Nakai had run for tribal chairman promising "to go to the people." Increasingly, however, energy development symbolized to many Indians in the Southwest the insular nature of tribal government. While residents of the affected areas lost rights to land so mining could commence, the tribal governments used the money to create "a self-supporting bureaucracy." Profits of energy development thus failed to help "common people" and enriched only government officials. In this account, tribal government exchanged land resources that a broad range of tribal members had relied on, for royalty payments that benefited only those within a growing tribal bureaucracy. Tribal leaders were to blame for agreeing to this exchange and for forcing it upon an unwilling people. For these critics, attitudes toward development represented a clear dividing line in attitudes toward the Navajo people. They viewed concern for Navajo people and Navajo culture as the essence of Navajo nationalism while seeing support for energy development as incompatible because it destroyed Navajo culture. This version of nationalism saw nondevelopment of Navajo land as the key to the preservation of Navajo cultural identity. In this ideology, leaders who supported energy development were the pawns of larger forces antithetical to and destructive of Navajo culture.[26]

Increasingly, Navajo nationalists saw the Southwest's cities as the ultimate agents and beneficiaries of colonialism. Consumers in Los Angeles and Phoenix, who "destroyed our land so they can use electric can openers and tooth brushes," as one letter in the *Navajo Times* argued, represented the primary force constraining possibilities for Navajo people and unalterably changing their land. In a 1970 letter, Douglas Dunlap asked why the wishes of people living on Black Mesa were ignored to supply electrical power to Arizona, Nevada, and California. "Why weren't the plants planned for California?" The uneven power dynamics illustrated by Navajo nationalists framed his answers. "People there didn't want pollution. So we got it. Is it worth it? Only a fool would say poisonous air was worth it." Similarly, William Beaver denounced a speech given to the graduates of Navajo Community College by Arizona governor Jack Williams for obscuring both the differences and the connections between Phoenix and the Navajo Nation. Williams, Beaver wrote, gave the "same speech as given to the great white middleclass children of the Phoenix area, even though they are sustained by water stolen from the Navajos. APS has grabbed at the Navajo Reservation too." For some writers, like Michael Gruber, the vices of white society were at extreme odds with the virtues of Navajo society. He wrote, "The Whiteman will do anything for money and greed. His cities have dirty, filthy air. We Indians used to have clean air and no traffic jams and noise of the city." The cities of the Southwest became the rhetorical counterpoint to the Navajo Nation, a space of irresponsible resource use and wasteful, meaningless lives upon which many young Navajos built their sense of their own nation.[27]

The economic and ecological imbalances of these material relationships formed the heart of Navajos' critique of the colonial bonds between their land and the metropolitan Southwest. In response to a series of SRP advertisements in the *Navajo Times* touting the environmental safeguards and economic benefits of Navajo Generating Station, *Diné Baa-Hani* ran photos of the vast gashes of Black Mesa Mine and smokestacks of Four Corners. Text superimposed on the photo pointed to the fundamental spatial inequalities of energy production, "The coal that fires their power plants to produce electricity for them will be returned to you in the air you breathe. The water that was yours will be turned to steam to power their generators. It will no longer feed the land. The land will no longer feed you. They will make $750,000,000. They will give you 1.6% of this amount. They will take 98.4% of it." In captioning the photo, *Diné Baa-Hani*'s editors warned that the colonial power of outsiders to determine the future of Navajo land threatened the spiritual and cultural relationship between Navajos and their land. With the land no longer feeding Navajos, with their air and water taken, the termination era, within which the plants and coal mines were negotiated, seemed more than a discrete moment in federal policy. Rather, the infrastructure created in that era threatened the survival of Navajos themselves.

FIGURE 7.2. Navajo protester poses with shotgun before a Peabody Coal drag shovel at Kayenta Mine. "Navaho Power," *Diné Baa-Hani.* 1970.

Our water and our land resources will be drained, taken out of the reservation, and in exchange we get a handful of jobs and a small payoff. What will be left of our way of life? No resources! No pastures for our sheep! No jobs when the Mesa is gone! They say the Indians must join the market economy, but they force us into a colonial economy. This is not economic development. This is economic termination.[28]

To be sure, these various anticolonial critiques and those offering them were not universally accepted among Navajos. As long as the official tribal position remained, that Navajo Generating Station and the Black Mesa Mine were financially vital, *The Navajo Times* maintained its editorial support for them. As a 1970 editorial stated,

There is something tragic in the pleas of the traditionalists, whose fears may be valid. The white man, indeed, seems bent on a course of destroying the very earth that sustains him. . . . However, the other side of the coin is the more realistic side. The coal mining operation will provide income that is badly needed by the Navajo Tribe, which has been faced with steadily declining revenues for the past several years.[29]

Reducing the concerns of the anticolonialists to concern with environmental protection allowed the paper to dismiss the projects as a necessary evil. Those Navajos who worked on the Black Mesa Mine frequently went further in letters to the paper, defending the mine as the only employment on the reservation that brought a reasonable amount of income. As one worker at the Peabody Mine stated, "I want to know where I will earn a living if Peabody leaves. These 'radicals' are going to destroy the very people they say they want to save."[30] Other Navajos were turned off by the identification of many young activists with the wider changes in American youth culture. As Betty Boyd wrote, "Our leaders are turning out to be leaders in the world of the hippies, not the world of the Navajo."[31]

Many Navajos, however, looked to the ongoing rebellions among young African Americans and Chicanos as something to emulate. As Louis Rogers wrote to *The Navajo Times*, "The Navajo tribe recently celebrated 100 years of progress but where is it? . . . The Negroes have their rebellion. It's time for a Navajo Rebellion."[32] If there was to be a Navajo rebellion, however, many questions were left unanswered. What would a postcolonial Navajo Nation look like? How should it balance tradition and economic development? How should it interact with the metropolitan areas that surrounded it? And finally what should be done about energy development? Should the tribe try to take advantage of energy development, or should it be stopped? Navajo anticolonialists lacked clear answers to these questions. In the years after 1970, Peter

MacDonald, the new tribal chairman elected largely on the votes of those dissatisfied with energy development, would attempt to provide them.

NATIONALISM AS STATE BUILDING

January 6, 1971, dawned clear but bitterly cold in Window Rock. The temperature remained below zero at noon when Peter MacDonald's inauguration as chairman began. MacDonald ascended a platform built in the rodeo ring of the tribal fairgrounds wearing a long coat and his trademark outfit—a turquoise necklace over a velvet shirt. While the cold drove some of the 7,500 people gathered around the rodeo ring of the tribal fairgrounds indoors, those who remained heard the new chairman promise "a new day for the Navajo" in his address. Midway through his speech, he announced three imperatives that echoed the anticolonial rhetoric of the young militants: "First, what is rightfully ours, we must protect; what is rightfully due us we must claim. Second, what we depend on from others, we must replace with the labor of our own hands and the skills of our own people. Third, what we do not have, we must create for ourselves."[33] Hearing these comments, the crowd erupted in such applause that MacDonald had to wait several minutes before finishing his address. The applause, however, did not last. In the early years of his tenure as tribal chairman, MacDonald searched for some way to make his goals of self-determination and self-sufficiency manifest within political and legal structures that had historically allowed Navajos little control over the energy resources that powered much of the metropolitan Southwest.

At first glance, Peter MacDonald seemed an unlikely figure to embrace the rhetoric of Navajo anticolonialism. Born in 1928 near Teec Nos Pos, in the New Mexican portion of the reservation, MacDonald left home in 1943 to enlist with the Marine Code Talker battalion and would not permanently return for more than twenty years.[34] Discharged from the marines in 1946, MacDonald moved to Oklahoma to attend Bacone High School, a missionary school on Creek land, and then the University of Oklahoma, where he earned a degree in electrical engineering in 1957. After graduation, MacDonald took a job as a project engineer and then project director with Hughes Aircraft in suburban Los Angeles. He returned to the Navajo Nation in 1963 to join the New Mexico state economic advisory board and to head the Navajo Nation's Management, Methods, and Procedures Division. Two years later he became head of the Office of Navajo Economic Opportunity, a Great Society agency. In a way, MacDonald shared the professional attributes—aerospace engineer, white-collar worker, federal employee—of many of the middle-class migrants who flocked to Phoenix during the postwar years.[35]

Despite this background, MacDonald embraced the nationalist rhetoric of young activists throughout his election campaign and his first two administrations. In the 1970 campaign, he denounced Nakai for caring more about securing money from energy companies than protecting the "the people," turning his opponents' populist rhetoric from the 1962 campaign against him. In office, he openly talked of the Navajo Nation as an American colony and referred to "the colonial relationship between the Navajo Nation and the cities of the Southwest." He displayed his difference from Nakai sartorially as well, wearing ribbon and velvet shirts, cowboy hats, and silver and turquoise jewelry, while Nakai wore mostly suits. Despite (or because of) his time away from the Navajo Nation, MacDonald emphasized his support for the "traditional" Navajos, having his photo taken with his family's sheep and near their hogans in Teec Nos Pos. the *Navajo Times* articulated these differences, saying that Mac-Donald "probably speaks more for the young people in the Navajo Nation" and "is more of a nationalist" than Nakai, whom, it wrote, "is more of the voice of the establishment."[36]

Speeches posing energy development as a manifestation of colonialism seem to have greatly contributed to MacDonald's election in 1970. Mac-Donald emphasized the dilemmas of energy development particularly in speeches on the western portion of the reservation, which included both Navajo Generating Station and Black Mesa Mine. MacDonald criticized Nakai for subordinating the interests of "the people" to demands made by energy companies and for turning control of Navajo land over to outsiders. MacDonald sounded similar broad themes in speeches in the eastern portion of the reservation, but mixed his critique of Nakai's connection to energy companies with calls for the improvement of education and economic development on the reservation.[37] The results of the 1970 campaign demonstrated the success of this campaign. MacDonald and Nakai ran fairly even in the eastern portion of the reservation. However, MacDonald swamped Nakai in the western portion, winning a convincing victory, 18,334–12,069.[38]

Upon assuming office, MacDonald continued to utilize rhetoric that emphasized the exploitation of Navajos to off-reservation audiences. Speaking to the Phoenix Community Council, MacDonald boldly stated, "Economically, our reservations are in a colonial relationship with the rest of the United States."[39] While energy development was not the only facet of this colonial relationship, it formed the most frequent referent in MacDonald's speeches and involved the explicit comparisons between the exploitation and deprivation of Navajo land and the consumer excesses of the surrounding cities. Speaking to officials from western states and power companies in Albuquerque, MacDonald stated, "For too long we have seen unfair contracts for the exploitation of our resources and our people. We have seen our land scarred by mine sites . . . so that the giant cities of our country can be too cool in summer and too warm in winter and choked with smoke from unnecessary automobiles."[40]

Black Mesa represented, in MacDonald's speeches, the starkest case of the inequality that lay at the heart of the modern Southwest. "Think for a minute about how it feels to be a Navajo shivering through a cold winter on Black Mesa in a Hogan without electricity or gas or water, while at the same time you watch well-paid anglo workers assemble a ten or fifteen million dollar drag line only a few hundred yards from your front door," MacDonald demanded of lawyers attending the Rocky Mountain Mineral Law Foundation's 1973 meeting in Tucson. "It is obscene for energy to be produced on Indian lands and yet see our own people deprived of the very barest necessities of civilized life."[41] MacDonald used the people of Black Mesa, then, to portray energy development as a crude exploitation of primitive people.

In posing energy development in these terms, MacDonald played not primarily to Navajo audiences, though they could read his speeches in the pages of the *Navajo Times*. Rather, he played to an emerging national concern over the exploitation of both Indians and nature. MacDonald took office in the historical moment when Earth Day was invented and environmental legislation began moving through Congress, when *Bury My Heart at Wounded Knee* became a best seller and "anti-Westerns" like *Little Big Man* drew large audiences. As the broader antigrowth sentiment that animated the debate over the Grand Canyon dams took root, and as Indians came to represent a people with a connection to the land that suburbanites lacked, reporters for national and regional newspapers and magazines found the strip mining of Black Mesa and the construction of Navajo Generating Station potent examples of these two forms of exploitation. In 1970 alone, *Life*, *ABC Nightly News*, and *KNBC–Los Angeles*, all ran stories portraying energy development projects as damaging pristine reservation landscapes.[42] The *Kansas City Times* ran a series of articles on the mine and power plant with titles such as "Navajo Learns of Ecology from White Man's Smog" and "Navajo Oppose Strange Smoke Signal." As the titles suggest, these articles framed their stories in the tropes of primitivism and isolation, explaining how, "on this lonely mesa in northeastern Arizona the Navajos are discovering the white man."[43]

Judging from Barry Goldwater's constituent correspondence, such articles did, however, produce a steady flow of concern about energy development on Indian land to Arizona's politicians. A woman from a Kansas City suburb wrote Goldwater to ask, "Why must those poor people be routed from their land and homes? Haven't we whites done enough to them?" A couple from Chicago wrote that "For too long Americans have shown no respect to our land or to the Indians. We can not further hurt the Indians by building a electrical plant on their land, especially [*sic*] when the people who will benefit most live hundreds of miles away." A "member of your national constituency" from New York asked, "Are a few short term dollars for the Navajos worth strip mining? I'm sure you know what strip mining does to the land and how ineffective repair is. How about the low-grade coal electrical generating plant? Remember when the sky was a bit cleaner in downtown Phoenix?" And one of Goldwater's actual constituents in Flagstaff questioned, "Must we cheat the Indians of their land and heritage for the sake of electricity for Los Angeles and other cities? Must we rob the Arizonan of his birthright—a tough, rugged, often hostile (yet clean) environment that demands his strength, independence, and energies to survive?" Playing to Goldwater's rhetoric of individualism, he declared that "Challenge builds character. Too much dependence on power and utility companies, appliances, electric toothbrushes, etc., make the individual dependent, weak, and flabby." Overall, the letters in Goldwater's public papers ran 438–5 against the power plants.[44]

In the *Kansas City Times* articles, MacDonald struck a defiant stance. "We will no longer succumb to the white man who comes along and says, 'Oh, you poor Navajo. You are so poor. By the way you have some coal or oil or something else I want. Here is a penny for it.' Those times are past." In laying out the dynamics of the new age, however, MacDonald revealed his differences from the young nationalists' whose rhetoric he embraced. He told the reporter that the tribe demanded lease renegotiations, royalty increases, profit sharing, and joint ownership. "I'm not against electrical power," MacDonald told the reporter. "But we will do it right."[45]

"Doing it right" entailed not the cessation of energy development on tribal land that some nationalists demanded, but new relationships with energy companies. This search for a new relationship can be seen, in part, in the locations where MacDonald critiqued energy development: forums on Southwestern development that included local and federal government officials along with business leaders and energy executives. In these speeches, he critiqued the dynamics of the existing relationships but held back from directly criticizing energy companies for their role in creating this inequality. Where young nationalists had pointed to the tribal government, energy companies, and the BIA as agents of colonialism, MacDonald focused only on the BIA. He did not denounce Peabody Coal or Arizona Public Service. The main goal of these speeches was not to repudiate energy development, but to critique the BIA officials that had allowed energy contracts that failed to take the long-term needs of the Navajo Tribe into consideration.

In many different forums, MacDonald charged the BIA with failing to maintain its trust responsibility, largely because of conflicts of interest within the Department of the Interior. Testifying at a Senate hearing in early 1972, MacDonald charged that the BIA "is so enmeshed in conflicts of interests that . . . it usually compromises Indian interests to competing claims by the Bureau of Reclamation, the Bureau of Wildlife, Sports, and Fisheries, the mining industry, the electrical power industry, and other interest groups." Even worse, MacDonald told Congress, the Navajo Nation had almost no role in negotiating the terms of development: "Industry determined what minerals were to be exploited and where; the government determined the regulations under which the minerals were to be exploited. . . . The Navajo Nation was to be subjected to this exploitation and paternalism for nearly fifty years."[46] The terms MacDonald used in describing the role of the BIA—"subjected" and "enmeshed in conflicts of interest"—demonstrate a characterization of the agency as both neglectful and incompetent. MacDonald also objected to the contract terms the BIA negotiated. Like Navajo officials in the late 1950s, he felt the BIA too often settled for contracts (such as the contracts with Peabody and Utah International) that gave the tribe a fixed return based on the volume of coal mined, rather than realizing coal's market value. "The Navajo people were told to accept this exploitation and be content with the royalties provided for them."[47] Such contracts, according to MacDonald, made the interests of the tribe antagonistic to those of the energy companies, when they could have been partners. To rectify this situation, MacDonald sought tribal authority over economic development, relegating the BIA to an advisory status. MacDonald sought, in short, to sideline the BIA and create new partnerships between the Navajo Tribe and energy companies.

MacDonald thus rejected younger nationalists' contention that energy companies were automatically agents of colonialism; rather, he came to view energy development as the potential source of Navajo self-determination. Free from the constraints imposed by the BIA, he claimed, the tribe could make its own decisions about energy development with their own interests in mind. This difference between MacDonald and younger nationalists largely arose from different understandings of "Navajo nationalism" and "self-determination." Should those concepts emphasize the protection of cultural and religious traditions, and the landscapes central to them? Or should they be primarily matters of political economy, of a self-determination through tribally controlled economic development? In short, was the Navajo Nation primarily an ethnic nation whose land and traditions required protection or was it a nation-state that should direct development of the resources contained in its territory for the economic benefit of its citizens?[48]

Both the 1972 energy crisis and the increasing power of OPEC led MacDonald to believe the tribe occupied a particularly advantageous position. While the crisis occurred due to a combination of factors—

long-standing increases in demand for gasoline and electricity, federal price controls and depreciation policies that encouraged the overproduction of domestic oil and natural-gas supplies, and eventually the oil embargoes of 1973—it created conditions of energy scarcity within which MacDonald envisioned new power.[49] National energy policy, MacDonald told an audience of Western governors in 1972, had dramatically shifted "from the disposal of abundance to the rationing of scarcity." It need not be so, he suggested. "The Navajo Nation has many of the ingredients to help solve the energy crisis." Any solution, MacDonald warned, would have to take place on Navajo terms, however. "It must be clearly understood that it will no longer be accepted practice to sell the reservation off by the ton or by the barrel. From now on the Navajos want a piece of the action."[50]

The influence of OPEC's model of energy ownership and state power was evident in MacDonald's imagination of "a piece of the action." Formed in 1960, the cartel had, by the late 1960s, devised a strategy to shift control of energy resources from multinational corporations to national governments. OPEC mandated increased participation of nationals in all phases of energy development and distribution, with the eventual goal of reducing foreign companies to minor partners or licensed contractors. The OPEC nations, as Fernando Coronil has argued, viewed increased state control over energy pricing and development as "intimately related to their political consolidation as sovereign states in the domestic and international areas and to the development of specific state capacities."[51] For MacDonald and other Indian leaders whose tribes owned significant mineral resources, these actions demonstrated how energy resources could be used as a political tool to give relatively powerless nation-states the ability to dictate to the nations that had once colonized them. Soon, MacDonald and other Navajos began drawing comparisons to their own situation. "Navajos, Arab-Style, to Cash in on Resources," read the title of a 1974 letter to the *Navajo Times*, stating, "From now on the Navajos intend to use the same kind of tactics that oil-rich Arabs have employed. Our goal is the same: a bigger take from our desert Kingdom."[52]

MacDonald told Western governors that the tribe would pursue "joint ventures" with energy companies. These partnerships, however, came with three main stipulations. First, Navajos must be business partners, rather than just passive suppliers of resources. Agreements needed to ensure that the tribe received a percentage of profits from energy developments, not merely fixed royalties. This arrangement reflected, in MacDonald's view, the mutual capital investment involved in energy development. The tribe would provide capital in the form of land and minerals while corporations provided investment capital and technical assistance. These partnerships were designed to end. MacDonald aimed for the right to displace the non-Indian developer as tribal members gained technical expertise. "As in the third world, this includes the right to buy out the non-Indian developer with revenue bonds which are based upon the continued successful operation of the mineral development."[53]

Second, tribal members would be employed as managers, not merely manual laborers. In part, this stipulation responded to the failure of previous leases to force energy companies to institute meaningful training programs. MacDonald aimed to place Navajos in administrative and management positions. And he sought for these latter positions to not be limited to the areas surrounding the mines. "It is not enough for Peabody Coal Company to train Navajos to be administrators on Black Mesa. Our people must also have the opportunity, if they choose, to become administrators in St. Louis," the site of Peabody's corporate headquarters, he argued. The goals of employment and partnership thus came together in MacDonald's vision, with the non-Indian developer providing the training that would allow Navajos to assume total control of the business venture.[54]

Third, MacDonald's vision required energy companies to abide by tribal laws when doing business on tribal land. The question of whether tribes retained jurisdiction over non-Indians had been one of the continuing legal issues since the Supreme Court had ruled (in *Williams v. Lee*) that tribal governments retained "unique and limited sovereignty" over their reservations. Since the ruling in 1959, several lawsuits had reached the Supreme Court attempting to clarify which subjects were encompassed within the legal doctrine of "measured separatism" that guaranteed tribes internal rule over their own affairs but kept them subject to overriding federal power.[55] Arizona Public Service had explicitly placed language in the 1961 lease for Four Corners Power Plant stating that Navajo courts had no legal authority to adjudicate disputes over the lease. MacDonald compared this situation to the European economic colonization in "China 40 or 50 years ago in which there were special courts for Europeans." MacDonald argued that ultimate tribal jurisdiction was simply a matter of equity: "If our laws and justice are good enough for our own people, then it has to be good enough for people who choose to do business on our lands. If companies don't want our laws, then they shouldn't want our minerals either."[56]

MacDonald thus imagined tribal control of development as the solution to the problems of past development. The problem with past development, in MacDonald's view, lay primarily in the unfair returns that existing leases had brought and the paternalistic manner in which they had been negotiated. "The DOI and BIA signed perpetual leases which gave companies the right to extract all of our coal at 15 cents per ton for as long as it lasted. Why?" he asked. "Because we lacked the expertise, the knowledge, the information, and the sophistication necessary to protect ourselves. We also lacked the legal ability to do it because we were wards of the federal government, presumably incompetent to act on our own behalf."[57] Joint ventures would allow Navajos to develop new expertise as well as economic development, self-sufficiency, and meaningful sovereignty. Nationalism for MacDonald thus entailed strengthening the state power of the tribe and encouraging national development.

This view was evident in his second inaugural. In the speech, titled "The Emerging Navajo Nation," MacDonald made a direct historical analogy between the Navajos and the new power of decolonized nations in OPEC, in the nonaligned movement, and in the United Nations. The speech stressed that, like those nations, the Navajo people were currently poor because of the past actions of colonial powers. "I know that our people are poor now because they have been exploited in the past. Navajo resources have been used to make others rich. Navajo trust has been rewarded by greed. Navajo people have been regarded as commodities to be used and abused and discarded." Promising that "these practices will end," MacDonald announced a program that would move beyond his first-term's goal of self-sufficiency. The goal of his second term was power. He promised to "fully develop the Navajo Nation as an important economic, social, and political force in the Southwest." The development of resources, in accord with Navajo interests, would be the engine that could produce a powerful and independent Navajo Nation: "We must protect the land which we love and which sustains and nourishes us. At the same time, we know that we must use our land since it is necessary to our very existence. As an emerging nation, we know well the value of our resources."[58]

The search for joint ventures, however, did little to address the objections of Navajos living on Black Mesa or their sympathizers writing in *Diné Baa-Hani*. Like MacDonald, they objected to the inequity and paternalism in the past leases negotiated by the BIA. More than that, however, they objected to energy development itself. They objected to the changes it created in the landscape and to the displacement of "traditional" tribal members. Furthermore, as MacDonald explicated his vision of nationalism, they began to object to his philosophy that held the state power of the tribe above the protection of individual Navajos. To them, any participation of the tribe in energy development contradicted the very idea of being Navajo. These disputes remained latent until MacDonald announced a new agreement for a new mine and plant at Burnham. Then they flared into the open, revealing the multiple limitations on the Navajo Tribe's ability to transform the modern Southwest.

LOCAL POWER

In September 1975, the U.S. Commission on Civil Rights embraced the colonial critique that young Navajo activists and Peter MacDonald's administration had advanced. The bold title of their 1975 report announced Commission's conclusion: *The Navajo Nation: An American Colony.* Within its pages, the report contained a litany of the objections that both activists and MacDonald had voiced about their current place in the Southwest. The report stated, "Development as it occurs under the tribe's current status . . . is no more than exploitation, with profits flowing off the reservation to the majority, non-Indian population" and "The BIA is a 19th century colonial institution which, as structured, is wholly out of step with the requirements of a new era of self-determination." The report also endorsed some of MacDonald's key reforms, including dramatically scaling down BIA oversight and favoring joint ventures over royalty-only leases.[59] The report, however, did not signal any new momentum toward achieving MacDonald's goals. Rather, it stood as a sign that the general acknowledgment of the Navajo's colonial position within the Southwest did little to resolve the increasing conflicts over the proper solution to the Navajos' colonial dilemma.

Nothing demonstrated these conflicts better than the five-year struggle for approval of multiple coal gasification plants on tribal land at Burnham, New Mexico. Proposed by El Paso Natural Gas and WESCO (an energy services company) in November 1972, coal gasification represented a response both to shortages of natural gas in the Southwest and to calls for the transformation of coal into clean fuels in the wake of increasing controversy over coal-fired power production.[60] Coal gasification combined coal with oxygen and steam to produce a crude form of methane, which could then be purified into synthetic natural gas. The initial proposal called for nine plants using coal from Utah International's Navajo Mine. The synthetic natural gas produced by the plants would be shipped via pipeline to the natural-gas trunk lines near Gallup and from there to Phoenix and Los Angeles, with most of the gas ending up at Fry Mountain Power Plant, near Barstow, California.[61]

Burnham was in many ways analogous to Black Mesa; it was a small community of between 1,200 and 3,500 Navajos (depending on the report) that relied mainly on raising sheep and migratory wage work. Other than two generators used to power the local school and trading post, Burnham was without electrical power or running water. The new plants promised to dramatically change the area. They would employ three thousand workers during construction, and another one thousand workers when operational. The plants would require massive changes in infrastructure—new roads, electrical wires, and homes—and potentially a new strip mine if the El Paso plants were built. Opponents of the plants estimated that the plants would bring an additional sixty thousand people to Burnham.[62]

Unlike the case at Black Mesa Mine, the negotiations for the coal gasification plants at Burnham were carried out quite publicly. From their proposal in 1972 to their eventual abandonment in 1977, the *Navajo Times* ran more than two hundred pieces reporting on the projects and the approval process, including letters from supporters and opponents, and longer investigative essays. Contained within these articles were lengthy debates over the goals of energy and economic development for the Navajo people, the proper role of the tribal government, and the nature of Navajo culture. All of these became key points in which different visions of the Navajo Nation were worked out.

MacDonald retained a neutral public pose toward the plants, but it appears quite clear that he favored them and worked behind the scenes to gain approval for them. While he made repeated public statements portraying himself as an impartial public servant—"If the people do not want gasification, we will not have it"—he almost always followed such statements by stressing the goals of his economic development program. "We also seek new ideas, new influences, new opportunities. That is why we solicit industry. Industry to help reduce our rate of unemployment. Industry to help better our living standard. Industry to provide reservation employment that keeps our people here, at home."[63] He warned that the alternative to pursuing development of tribal resources was "to withdraw from the rest of the world and live in mutual poverty."[64] In Washington to lobby Congress on behalf of a bill guaranteeing federal loans for coal gasification plants, MacDonald was more openly in support of the plants. "As pragmatists," he told the House Science and Technology Committee," we know that wishing we had clean industry and wishing that we had mineral treasures that were somehow 'cleaner' than coal will hardly help alleviate the real problems we do have." Coal gasification was a necessary evil—the only option, as he told the committee, for "getting needed employment and revenue."[65]

Tribal officials also attempted to convince Navajos that the plants would bring broad benefits to the tribe. They argued that returns from current lease deals were declining due to inflation, threatening to reduce the value of current leases by 30 percent between 1975 and 1985. In the face of this decline in revenue, the projects promised to help the tribe's finances. El Paso's promise to renegotiate their existing coal lease would bring in $5.6 million immediately and an estimated $300 million over forty years. The WESCO deal, which would use coal from Navajo Mine, was seen as "one way to make the best of a bad deal," bringing $200 million from increased coal development over the course of the deal in addition to revenue from leasing land for the plants.[66] As well, Mac-Donald argued, the plants did not represent the continuation of the bad lease deals of previous administrations. Instead, they represented gains for the nation in employment and in sovereign power. While the leases did not contain the possibility of tribal ownership or joint venture that MacDonald had previously advocated, WESCO agreed to hire at least an initial work force that was minimally 52 percent Navajo, a number that would eventually rise to 90 percent. Furthermore, the company agreed to institute a training program to introduce Navajo employees to skilled work and potential plant management. To ensure that Navajos would be eligible for construction jobs when the plants were being built, the tribe's Labor Relations Board entered into an agreement with the AFL-CIO to train Navajos as apprentices in building-trades unions. Additionally, WESCO and El Paso agreed that the Navajo courts would have jurisdiction over disputes involving employment and workplace disputes, a concession that MacDonald portrayed as a significant victory for the tribe's goals of sovereignty and self-determination.[67]

MacDonald also launched a campaign to convince tribal members to see approval of coal gasification as consistent with Navajo tradition. "Traditionally," MacDonald wrote in the *Navajo Times*, "we have always followed a plan of strategy. We have never used force or acted rashly without applying our minds and our plans to the task." MacDonald constructed a narrative of Navajo history in which negotiation with non-Navajos had allowed Navajos to control their own destiny. "Our past leaders have negotiated the release of our people from the bondage at Fort Sumner, and this is how our predecessors increased our land base . . . and this is how the livestock reduction was stopped. We have survived these great challenges, not because we are powerful, but because we have appealed to the rationality of men." Citing "economic strangulation, the forces of poverty, and the lack of education and training" as the forces that endangered the Navajo, MacDonald appealed to Navajos to consider coal gasification rationally as the necessary evil that would allow contemporary Navajos, as had their predecessors, to surmount the challenges facing them.[68]

In contrast, opponents of the projects focused only marginally on the "national" importance of the plants. When they did focus on the arguments proponents had made about the necessity of the plants for the tribal treasury and tribal employment, they hoisted MacDonald on his "joint venture" petard. With MacDonald's talk about the tribe acting as an equal partner in development, the new proposals, in which payments were based on the coal royalty foundation that MacDonald had criticized, seemed like an abandonment of principle and another example of exploitation by energy companies. John Redhouse, head of the local NIYC chapter, embraced MacDonald's rhetoric of economic self-determination, writing in the *Navajo Times* that "We should seek to develop our resources ourselves and receive a greater portion of their true value." The projects at Burnham, however, did not meet those goals. Instead, they repeated the patterns established in the 1960s. "The big companies think that Indians are easily manipulated and that they will be able to make us turn over our land to be a resource colony for Southern California. They want us to sacrifice our land, our air, and our water for a short term monetary gain."[69] The Committee for Navajo Development, formed to fight the proposals, asked, in a full-page statement in the *Navajo Times*, why the proposals could not follow MacDonald's prescriptions for tribal development. "The gasification plants cannot be built without our coal and our land. Why can't the Navajo Tribe have controlling interest of the gasification plants? . . . It is plain stupidity to allow others to benefit more than the Navajos from the use of Navajo resources." To ensure the point was not missed, the statement was headed with an illustration of a bulldozer advancing on a corral and hogan while power lines extended away toward Phoenix and Los Angeles.[70]

Opposition to coal gasification, however, focused more centrally on the local community in Burnham. Where MacDonald had posed the developments as a necessary evil that would provide for the greater good, the opponents portrayed them as an almost criminal violation of Navajo tradition. Unlike MacDonald, who connected sustaining Navajo tradition to maintaining the health of the tribe, gasification opponents emphasized the close connections between people and their immediate landscapes. As one letter to the *Navajo Times* explained, "Our land is more valuable than your money. It will last forever. It will not even perish by the flames of fire. As long as the sun shines and the water flows, this land will be here to give life to man and animals—we cannot sell the lives of men and animals. Therefore we cannot sell this land."[71] Testifying before the Federal Power Commission, Richard Hughes, a Navajo lawyer claimed Burnham residents "stand to lose all they have, including the intangibles of a culture deeply rooted in the land. . . . The Navajo culture in large parts of northwestern New Mexico," he argued, "faces obliteration."[72]

At times, fears of cultural destruction became attacks on Navajos leaders for abandoning tradition. Coalition for Navajo Liberation blamed Navajo leaders who "gave up their own land a long time ago . . . who decided to take a job with a corporation or the BIA or even the tribal government" for endangering Burnham and Navajo tradition.[73] Coal gasification appeared to simply be a repeat of Black Mesa, and opponents returned to their original portrait of the tribal government as an exploiter of everyday Navajos, equivalent to the BIA or energy companies. As Harris Arthur said at one of WESCO's presentations, "Tribal officials have too often succumbed to pressures from outside exploiters for political expediency. . . . When this happens, it is the grassroots people at the chapter level who are the innocent victims." Tribal officials, in this view, had abandoned the thing most central to Navajo culture, close connection to the land. As one letter to the *Navajo Times* put it, "You would never go to another area and tell those people how to live or tell them that you were going to bring in some kind of industry for their own good. . . . Who would ever do something like that? The answer is simple: The Navajo Tribal Government."[74]

Opponents argued that the influx of people to build the plants would change the character of the area in ways that eliminated the "traditional" lifestyles. Harold Foster, writing to the *Navajo Times* warned of "unmanageable boom towns" in which the interests of existing residents would quickly be swamped by those of outsiders.[75] The Coalition for Navajo Liberation argued that of Anglos who would move to Burnham, "many have a racist attitude" and "will not for one moment stand for any Navajo right to pursuit of happiness and equality."[76] Coal gasification, these opponents warned, threatened to import patterns of racist attacks on Navajo culture from the metropolitan Southwest to the Navajo homeland.

These different versions of coal gasification's potential impact on the Navajo future confronted one another not only in the pages of the *Navajo Times*, but also in the Burnham chapter house. In a marked difference from practice ten years earlier with the Black Mesa lease, energy companies took their plans before the people they would most affect and attempted to convince them of their value. El Paso Natural Gas and WESCO hosted numerous barbecues, informational sessions, and public meetings in Burnham between 1973 and 1976. At these meetings, they assured Burnham residents that they were different from Peabody Coal or Utah International. Unlike those companies, WESCO and El Paso promised Navajos employment and would pay "substantially strong penalties" if they failed to meet those targets. To demonstrate their good faith, general manager of WESCO, Bob Rudznik, promised that enforcement of these employment provisions would lie in the hands of Navajo regulators. "The tribe can take us to court if necessary. Individual Navajos who feel they haven't had a fair deal in hiring could appeal directly to the office of Navajo Labor Relations. If necessary they can take us to tribal courts." To allay fears of environmental despoliation, the WESCO officials brought photos of coal gasification plants in South Africa showing animals grazing and crops growing nearby. They assured the audience that they were willing to pay residents for any land they needed: "We will pay a fair amount and in any way they want it."[77]

These attempts, however, fell flat in a community threatened by dramatic change. Three times in 1973 and 1974, the Burnham chapter voted in regard to approval of the coal gasification plants. The first two votes unanimously rejected the plants; the third vote came back 114–14 against. Tribal officials attempted to sway Burnham residents by appealing to their tribal loyalty. Reinterpreting previous energy development as freely embraced by local communities, Andrew Benally, director of the tribe's Department of Economic Development, urged the people of Burnham to "accept your responsibility to add money to the Tribal treasury as the residents of Black Mesa and the Aneth area have so willingly done." Ignoring Benally, the Burnham chapter forwarded a petition calling on MacDonald to cease negotiations and on the tribal council to reject any resolutions permitting coal gasification. While some officials blamed the overwhelming opposition of the chapter on "outside agitators," the votes demonstrated the increasing divide that existed between MacDonald's supporters and a coalition of local communities facing energy development and the young activists who supported them.[78] While MacDonald believed that the dynamics of energy development could be manipulated to bring the Navajo Tribe into a position of influence, authority, and power, the residents of Burnham and the young activists saw inequalities as fixed and unsurmountable.

As debate over Burnham continued, militants began taking matters into their own hands. On October 13, 1974, armed members of the American Indian Movement marched past the security guards at Black Mesa Mine No. 1 and sat down before one of the mine's massive drag shovels. When the operator refused to stop the shovel, one AIM member fired at him, the bullet lodging in the cab of the shovel. The occupiers issued a set of demands, most of them revolving around Peabody's lack of attention to local concerns—grazing land destroyed without compensation, sheep and dogs killed by Peabody trucks, and Peabody officials who refused to listen to local complaints. While MacDonald called the incident "a case of the chickens coming home to roost" and attempted to serve as a mediator, the AIM protesters had little good to say about his administration, stating "we have little time for tribal governments that don't protect their people" and refusing to allow uniformed tribal police into their camp. After a week and concessions by Peabody involving payments to local shepherds who had lost sheep, a moratorium on new road construction, and the creation of a board of local residents and tribal officials that would meet monthly with Peabody officials to resolve any disputes, the AIM members relented and left the mine. But they left with an increased reputation for standing up for the interests of local Navajos and demonstrating that energy development could, at least temporarily, be halted.[79]

The perceived successes of the Black Mesa occupation quickly led to a second occupation, which clarified their target was not Peabody in particular but any economic development controlled by outsiders. Six months after the Black Mesa occupation, forty armed AIM members occupied the Fairchild Semiconductor Plant in Shiprock, ostensibly to protest the layoffs of 140 workers. During 1974 and 1975, Fairchild cut back on production in response to defense cuts, laying off half of the work force. In seizing the plant, AIM demanded not only that the laid-off workers have their jobs restored but also that there be far reaching changes in the environmental and employment policies at Four Corners Power Plant and Navajo Mine. Fairchild, Four Corners, and Navajo Mine were tied together, in the eyes of the protesters, as outsiders that did not have the best interest of "the people" in mind.[80]

The outcome of the Fairchild occupation differed from that at Black Mesa. Unlike Peabody, Fairchild quickly refused to negotiate as long as the AIM members remained inside the plant. Furthermore, they refused to reconsider the layoffs and threatened to close the entire plant if the situation was not resolved quickly. This stance put MacDonald and the tribal government in the awkward position of being Fairchild's main negotiator. With Fairchild removed from the negotiations, the occupation crumbled after a week. AIM received concessions only the tribal government could grant—immunity from prosecution (as long as they pursued no further occupations) and an inspection of the plant for unsafe working conditions. This latter concession became moot when Fairchild closed the plant, citing the difficulty of doing business in the Navajo Nation.[81] The different outcomes reflected not primarily strategies for responding to protest, but the different locational nature of both enterprises. Peabody's operations were fixed in place by the location of coal beneath the earth's surface. Fairchild, however, existed in the world of competitive growth politics, in which troublesome local issues could be simply remediated by relocating operations elsewhere.

Both occupations put MacDonald in an awkward position. He was accustomed to playing a politics of opposition at home, telling Navajos that the unequal geography of energy development in the Southwest was the key driver of inequality. At the same time, he courted development from energy companies to accomplish his vision of the Navajo Nation as an economic force in the region. In this balancing act, MacDonald attempted to manage these two worlds separately: He played the politics of opposition among his constituents while portraying the Navajo Nation as ready, willing, and able to do business if companies would meet its terms. This strategy could work as long as these two worlds remained separate. As long as a majority of Navajos saw MacDonald and his tribal government as their representative fighting the energy companies, MacDonald could denounce them at home and court them away from the reservation. When Navajo militants took direct action against energy companies—

energy companies MacDonald had claimed were responsible for their exploitation—MacDonald found himself between the two, trying to balance the concerns of each. Forced to negotiate with other Navajos on behalf of outsiders, he and the tribal government increasingly came to be seen as allied with outside companies rather than with the "local" Navajos both he and the militants claimed to be representing.

This perception left it politically impossible for MacDonald and his supporters to pursue the gasification projects. The issue of Burnham damaged MacDonald politically among the supporters of so-called traditional Navajos and may have had a good deal to do with an the emerging land dispute between the Navajo and Hopi Tribes. While consideration of the complex Navajo-Hopi Land Dispute is beyond the scope of this book, the dispute, in which MacDonald ardently defended "traditional" Navajos at Big Mountain from federal relocation efforts, came to a head at a time when MacDonald was most under attack for "selling out" local Navajos in Burnham.[82]

Local opposition was not the only reason for defeat of the Burnham proposals. That defeat owed much to both the new political power of environmentalists and the new environmental regulations that structured development in the Southwest. The gasification plants drew attention from environmentalists across the Southwest who lent their expertise and support to the Shiprock Research Center, the Black Mesa Defense Fund, and other groups allied with Navajos opposed to energy development. The new environmental laws passed in the early 1970s also dramatically affected the course of the proposals. The National Environmental Policy Act's requirement to file Environmental Impact Statements (EIS) regarding development on federal land both slowed the process and forced its details into the open. It took two years for the gasification plants' EIS's to reach draft review status, and that review provided ammunition for both local and regional opponents of the plants. The reports predicted massive changes to the local economy ("within months the local economic environment would evolve from a traditional livestock, crafts, and unskilled labor base to a specialized mining construction and industrial occupational mix") to local health ("It is possible that rates of alcoholism, suicide attempts, divorce and mental health problems would increase . . . as well as potential adverse direct and indirect effects from relatively low level, but long term stack emissions")—and to "traditional" culture ("The Indian people, especially those who desire to maintain traditional lifestyles, will be severely stressed by the close proximity of a work force oriented to industrial employment").[83] These environmental developments were not separate from local efforts to block gasification plants. Opponents skillfully used them to demonstrate the breadth of their objections, demonstrating that these were not isolated objections that applied only to Burnham but that they could apply to anyone living in the Navajo Nation if the plants went forward.

Burnham marked the last time new energy developments were seriously considered by the Navajo Nation under Peter MacDonald's leadership. The episode demonstrated the ability of concerted local opposition to block development, even if it was favored by the tribal government. That impasse led to a change in policy within the tribal government. From 1977 onward, when Navajo politicians focused on redressing the unequal geography of the modern Southwest, they no longer spoke of joint ventures or getting "a piece of the action." Instead, they focused on taxation, passing a business activities tax in 1978 on "all goods produced, processed or extracted from the Navajo Nation" at 5 percent. Peabody Coal, Utah International, and APS began paying the tax in 1983 after the Supreme Court ruled in *Merrion v. Jicarilla Apache* that businesses operating on tribal land were subject to tribal taxation. The tax represented a repudiation of MacDonald's ideas of economic development; with taxation, the Navajo Nation took an alternative route to economic development than had the boosters in Phoenix.

In many ways, the turn to taxation represented a victory for the tribe. Their sovereign power to regulate the industry that operated on their land was upheld. At the same time, it represented a capitulation to the inequality that the infrastructure of energy development had fixed in space. The tribal government could work around the margins of that geography; it could draw marginal capital from limited regulation of the development that occurred on their land. It could not, however, change the dynamic by which demand for electricity from the metropolitan Southwest caused the transformation of Navajo landscapes. By the time Navajo people came to view the strip mines, power plants, and power lines as dangerous, it was too late. Concerted political action could stop new development; but it could not reverse existing exploitative development. By the time the political ability to do that had cohered, the unequal geography of the modern Southwest had taken the form of capital fixed in space. It could not be reversed, it could only be regulated.

"Good Bye, Big Sky": Coal and Postwar America

JACK NEARY, THE AUTHOR OF AN ARTICLE THAT APPEARED IN *LIFE* ON April 16, 1971, six days before the one-year anniversary of Earth Day, opened with an appeal Southwestern boosters had been making since the end of World War II. "When I first came out here from the East a dozen years ago it was like having the bandages taken off after an eye operation." Neary wrote that the region's clear skies and far-reaching vistas had rejuvenated his sense of self, giving him a genuine understanding both of himself and of the world in which he lived. "Folks back home who'd never been here, I realized sadly, grew up and died without ever having really *seen*."[1]

The photos that accompanied Neary's story, however, told not of the power of this vision, but of its death. The opening page showed the smokestacks of Four Corners Power Plant spewing emissions. As the article proceeded, it became clear that Neary's account, like *The Place No One Knew*, was an elegy for a lost world. Beneath black-and-white photos of smog hanging low over the Sangre de Cristo Mountains, Neary lamented the pollution that had obscured the region's grand vistas and introduced the nation's environmental troubles to its last pristine region, thereby destroying the unique character of the Southwest. "This morning the mountains were just a silhouette in ink wash, a vague gray somberness, like the mountains in Pennsylvania or West Virginia . . . that same darkening of tone you can see looking from the Atlantic toward Long Island and New York City—a shadowy, smudgy cobweb of smog lying on the horizon." Neary portrayed the pollution of the Southwest as representing the final closing of the American frontier. Once, the sky had been clear from coast to coast, now the "dark miasma" of "soot and dirt and ash and photochemical smog" stretched all the way from the Atlantic to "the Pacific ashtrays" of Los Angeles and San Francisco. The pollution from Four Corners, Mojave, and Navajo Power Plants had destroyed the last remnant of that frontier. As he pondered the pollution from those plants, Neary wrote, "Now you know that the last stretch of wide-open space we had left, the American Southwestern skyscape, is gone, too." *Life*'s editor captured Neary's funereal sentiments in the article's title: "Good Bye, Big Sky."[2]

Two months before Neary's article appeared in *Life*, a very different headline appeared in the *Financial Analysts Journal*, a magazine aimed at stockbrokers and investment professionals. "Coal: The Giant Revived," the headline proclaimed. The article explained that the coal industry, so central to the industrial economy of the late nineteenth- and early twentieth-centuries, had steadily recovered from its postwar collapse. Following the nadir of American coal production, 392 million tons in 1954, mining activity had seen a dramatic resurgence. A single industrial sector accounted for this revival. While use of coal in railroads, manufacturing industry, and home heating continued to decline during the 1960s, "a very sharp increase in utility coal use," an increase of 77 percent, drove overall coal production to 563 million tons by 1969. In future years, the *Financial Analysts Journal* predicted a 50 percent increase in coal use by electrical utilities by 1975 with "much higher levels by 1980." "The major coal companies," the journal predicted, should see steady income growth and "will be in a position to borrow funds to open new mines, and utilities will obviously be more willing to sign long term contracts now that they have learned how unreliable and costly the installation of nuclear plants can be." Indeed, economic conditions, the journal reported, "now favor coal as the primary source of energy" for the nation at large.[3]

Read together, "Good Bye, Big Sky" and "The Giant Revived" told a story of coal's rise as the fuel of postwar America and the cost of that transition. "The Giant Revived" explained how American electrical utilities found coal to be an inexpensive alternative to natural gas and nuclear power that could meet the nation's burgeoning demand for electricity. This demand drove a revival of the coal industry. By 1970, demand from utilities had tripled the amount of electricity generated by coal since 1956. In the 1960s alone, utilities had built 328 coal-fired power plants.[4] In the Southwest, the transformation was even starker. In 1954, the year Utah International negotiated a mineral exploration permit for territory on the eastern portion of the Navajo Reservations, utilities in the region generated no electricity by burning coal. By 1975, coal from the Navajo and Hopi Reservations, transported by truckload, rail line, and slurry pipeline, fed furnaces at Four Corners, San Juan, and Cholla Power Plants and Navajo and Mojave Generating Stations. Collectively, they generated almost 8,000 megawatts of electricity, almost 65 percent of the electricity consumed in Arizona, New Mexico, and Southern California.[5] "Good Bye, Big Sky" suggested the costs of coal's new place as the nation's dominant source of electricity. With Four Corners alone releasing approximately 46,000 tons of nitrogen oxide and 35,000 tons of sulfur dioxide, the two main chemical components of smog, as well as 50,000 tons of fly ash annually, the resulting air pollution obscured vistas and suggested the Southwest's unique nature had come to an end.[6]

Those stories, like all stories, contained gaps. "Coal: The Giant Revived," presented the resurgence of coal as purely a function of economic demand. It contained no mention of the politics that had encouraged the development of coal deposits. It also gave no sense of spatial and geographic change, of the immediate connection coal-fired electrical generation forged between peripheral resources and metropolitan consumers. For its part, "Good Bye, Big Sky" looked only to the skies of the Colorado Plateau to see coal's costs. In portraying his concern at the loss of environmental experience—the disappearance of "the last stretch of wide-open space we had left, the American Southwestern skyscape"—Neary avoided more material environmental changes occurring on the ground: the transformation of grazing lands into tailing piles, of water holes into acidic ponds, and of Ram Springs into Area Four of the Navajo Mine. Writing in 1970, Neary had no reason for concern over the approximately 16,000,000 tons of carbon dioxide—carbon emissions equivalent to 2.8 million passenger cars—that issued from Four Corners annually.[7] Neary's article also ignored the debates, ongoing at the moment he wrote, among Navajos about the future place of coal mining and power production in their immediate lives. Those debates, more than any other critique, illustrated the deep regional connections, connections that were simultaneously political and environmental, that coal-fired energy production had forged in the Southwest.

Those connections would have surprised Americans earlier in the twentieth century. Coal was not supposed to be the fuel of modernity, in either the Southwest or the nation at large. Writing as Boulder Dam was being completed, the social critic Lewis Mumford described coal as an unwelcome artifact of an earlier "paleotechnic era." In Mumford's view, coal served as the engine of the industrial revolution's "upthrust into barbarism." Wrenching coal from the earth required the simultaneous exploitation of labor and nature. Coal's stored energy allowed ceaseless industrial work, exhausting workers, and placing near limitless demands on their time. Coal produced, according to Mumford, "a befouled and disorderly environment," nature's exhaustion evident in abandoned mine shafts, tailing piles, and the pallor of smoke that hung in the air. The associated human exhaustion lay evident in the foul cities despoiled by the aftermath of coal's combustion. In Mumford's eyes, it was electricity that would finally bury the "maggoty corpse" of the Paleotechnic Era. "With electricity the clear sky and clean waters come back again," Mumford suggested. Electricity would serve as the engine of a "neotechnic era" characterized by garden cities, alloyed metals, and "flowing energy." While he held out particular hope for the hydroelectric projects being built on the Colorado, Columbia, and Tennessee Rivers—"democratic pyramids," in his estimation—he celebrated electricity in general as a liberatory force. By removing the necessity of locating cities near the waterways where coal was easily transported, electricity would free human work from the constraints of place, allowing people to work in "the more salubrious seats of living."[8] Mumford was far from alone. Hopes that electrification could produce social modernization that would be distributed widely across space also instantiated themselves deeply in New Deal programs: in the Greenbelt towns of the Resettlement Administration, in the Rural Electrification Administration, and perhaps most powerfully in the Tennessee Valley Authority.[9]

Those visions were partially realized. In the years after World War II, industry decentralized. Americans decamped in great numbers for seats of living they considered more "salubrious": the Mediterranean climate of Southern California, the dry air of the desert Southwest, and the temperate winters of the American South. And electricity became realized in every facet of American life. As boosters celebrated "clean industry," home builders competed to create "Gold Star Electric Homes," and electric utilities told consumers of the ability to "live better, electrically," portions of Mumford's vision of industrial and residential life freed from the despoliation of the natural world appeared to exist in the suburban landscape that surrounded Phoenix and other Southwestern cities, a consumer's paradise with all the comforts of modern life but easy escape into the spaces of nature that surrounded.

By the early 1960s, however, that consumer's paradise had come to rely on the very fuel that Mumford had described as responsible for the environmental and social maladies of an earlier age. In a sense, Mumford's vision of social and economic liberation from coal was undermined by the ever increasing demand for electric power. By 1952, the Bureau of Reclamation realized its dams could never provide the amount of electricity the burgeoning population of the Southwest would soon demand. Its search for a reliable, ready fuel that could supply the needs of the swelling metropolitan population federal policies were helping to create quickly turned to the West's coal deposits, deposits sufficient to last "more than 1,000 years," according to the estimates of Reclamation officials. Enthusiastically embraced by investor-owned utilities seeking both their own secure supply of fuel and the ability to preclude the construction of a Tennessee Valley Authority West, coal returned as the engine of modern development.[10]

The coal mining and electrical generation that occurred on the Colorado Plateau from the 1950s onward recapitulated many of the maladies Mumford had highlighted. The process of strip mining disrupted already unstable environments, leaving deep holes and new mountains of displaced earth where, despite efforts at range reclamation, little flora took root. Mercury, chromium, and sulfurous compounds, the by-products of coal combustion, became lodged in places near the mines and plants, contaminating water holes and seeping slowly into deep aquifers. The Navajo Nation experienced political and economic maladies from coal production as well. The long-term, inflexible contracts that characterized energy development in the 1950s and 1960s meant that most of the profits from coal mines and power plants were realized in places far distant from the reservation. Those contracts also meant that, even as court cases affirmed tribal sovereignty and federal policy moved away from the termination era and toward Indian self-determination in the late 1960s and 1970s, the Navajo Nation possessed extremely limited authority over the most valuable resources within its borders. Finally, Navajos by and large failed to receive the material benefits of the high-energy society being created upon their lands. Despite the Navajo Tribal Utility Authority's hopes in the 1950s that Four Corners and other projects would lead to "a light bulb in every hogan," almost 40 percent of Navajo homes remained without electricity in 2010.

These conditions reflect the failure to achieve the broad spatial distribution of modernity's benefits that New Dealers had imagined in the 1930s. Instead, electrical power, like postwar modernity's other benefits, was developed in a manner both uneven and unequal, inequalities that, as urban historians have noted for a decade, were products of New Deal policies themselves. In underwriting new housing construction and the proliferation of consumer credit, those policies spurred the creation of a new suburban America. The inequalities of this system did not exist merely within metropolitan political boundaries, however; they stretched far beyond them as both public authority and private capital reorganized the countryside to fuel the metropolitan consumer society created by public policy since the 1930s.

The experience and ideology of postwar metropolitan growth has made the inequalities that exist beyond the metropolis difficult to appreciate. While Michael Harrington worried about the increasing isolation of suburbanites from urban poverty within the metropolis in his 1962 *The Other America*, he admitted that "middle-class women coming in from Suburbia on a rare trip may catch the merest glimpse of the other America on the way to an evening at the theater" or that "the business or professional man may drive along the fringes of slums in a car or bus."[11] Urban racial inequality, as Thomas Sugrue brilliantly detailed, remained a spatialized presence in the lives of middle-class residents of the metropolis, a constant counterpoint and imagined threat to their own security. Non-urban inequality has been different. With metropolitan America imagined as the engine of economic growth, it became easy to imagine that the economic struggles of those people living beyond metropolitan borders arose from a lack of integration into the metropolitan economy.

Diagnosed as "backwardness" or a "missing out on modernity," such understandings of rural underdevelopment missed the fundamental connections that metropolitan development had forged between growing cities and the spaces beyond. Unequal connections between city and country have long characterized capitalism, of course, but they intensified in the years after World War II as increased interurban competition for mobile capital put new pressures on peripheral resources and as the sheer scale of metropolitan growth led multiple growing cities to forge regional connections that drew peripheral resources in multiple directions. These connections have been particularly difficult to appreciate when they involve Indian peoples. Long represented as the antithesis of modernity, Indian people's continued place in modernity's development, both culturally and materially, has remained hidden to many Americans.[12] Indeed, even as electricity began streaming from Four Corners Power Plant to Phoenix, *Arizona Highways* magazine was advising people to "turn from the great, wide, slick, speedy arteries of travel and go forth ten, twenty, a hundred miles into Navajoland and you will find the people as they were a decade, two decades, a half century ago."[13]

The primitive imaginary contained in "Navajoland," or in the native arts and crafts many in the Southwest used to decorate their homes, made it difficult to appreciate the industrialization of the Navajo Nation in the postwar years and the connection of that industrialization to the growth and prosperity of Phoenix. So too did the product. Beamed into homes from distant, unseen sources, electricity allowed the freedom to light the night, to surmount the desert heat, and increasingly to call entire electronic worlds into life. Produced in locations the vast majority of consumers never saw or experienced, it was easy to assume that electricity was not produced, that it existed naturally, and that its costs were minimal. Staring at the lights of Phoenix from the southern slope of Camelback Mountain night after night, such assumptions were, and are, easy to make, in Phoenix and elsewhere in metropolitan America.

Such assumptions have proven a boon to the nation's coal industry. As the *Financial Analysts Journal* predicted, demand for electricity led to booming coal production in the forty years after 1970. Even as the American economy became postindustrial, as the federally funded high-tech industries of Silicon Valley and the eager consumers in metropolitan America combined to create the Information Age, coal-fired electrical production in the United States nearly tripled. By the late 2000s, more than 1.9 trillion kilowatt-hours of electricity were generated annually from burning coal. Since 1970, 594 new coal-fired power plants have been built. Today, coal generates more than 40 percent of the nation's total electrical power, and electrical generation consumes 93 percent of the nation's coal production. While few of these plants are located on

Indian lands or are as large as Four Corners, Navajo, or Mohave Generating Stations, most have similar locational characteristics. Sitting distant from the metropolitan areas they serve, near coal deposits or on easy transportation corridors, on land made available by local governments eager for jobs and tax revenues, they generate the inexpensive electricity that became the expectation of modern metropolitan life in the years following World War II. The plants stood, in short, as evidence of the power of metropolitan growth, both the economic demand that accompanied it and the political forces that placed it at the center of postwar economic policy, to reshape politics, economies, and ecologies of people and places far from metropolitan centers. They indicated, in stark form, the new regional inequalities that accompanied postwar metropolitan growth and the devil's bargains that faced Navajos, and other people living on the metropolitan periphery, as demand for the resources that made metropolitan growth possible revalued the places they called home.

The presence of the rich fossil fuel deposits upon which residents of the metropolitan Southwest depended, deposits that Paul Jones had once described as a gift from "divine Providence" and that Peter MacDonald had seen as the key to allowing the Navajo Nation to seize "a piece of the action" have continued to present Navajos with such devil's bargains into the 2000s. In 2003 a Houston-based energy company, Sithe Global Power, partnered with Diné Power Authority, an entity created by the tribal government in 1985 to manage Navajo energy resources, announced plans to build a 1,500-megawatt coal-fired power plant, named Desert Rock Power Plant, in Burnham, where MacDonald had envisioned the construction of coal gasification plants in the 1970s. In many respects, Desert Rock represented the realization of MacDonald's desire for the tribe transition from an owner of resources collecting royalties to a developer collecting profits. The plan for Desert Rock called for the tribe to own half of the plant and to ship electricity to metropolitan markets through its own 500-kilovolt transmission lines, collecting wheeling fees from local utilities in the process. David Lester, executive director of the Council of Energy Resource Tribes and a member of the Muskogee Creek Tribe, praised the agreement as a rejection of "that old paradigm [that] left us with all the social and environmental costs and none of the economic benefits." Other proponents, including the United Mine Workers local in Window Rock, praised the project's potential creation of four hundred permanent jobs that would allow young Navajos to remain "at home" as well as annual revenues that would meet one-third of the tribe's yearly budget. George Hardeen, spokesman for Navajo president Joe Shirley, explained: "It's going to provide jobs that are needed on Navajo—people are getting poorer, and Navajos want jobs."[14]

Much as they had when MacDonald pursued coal gasification near their homes in the 1970s, many people living near Burnham responded by looking at Four Corners. "We won't benefit from it. We'll get the trash, the smoke and the dirt," said Sarah White, president of Dooda (No) Desert Rock, a group formed shortly after the proposal of the power plant. "I really want to believe that this is something that will work, but when I look at . . . Four Corners, I see nothing but broken promises." They also looked toward the unequal connections to the metropolitan West and modern life that the plant represented. After lamenting that only 61 percent of Navajo homes possessed electricity, Lori Goodman, a member of Diné-CARE (Citizens Against Ruining Our Environment) told a reporter that "Navajos are going through hardship just so someone in Los Angeles can run their lights day in and day out."[15] And many responded with laments about how energy development altered connections to particular places that had developed over the course of their lives. "This is my birthplace, a place where my father raised us, a place where my father sang his blessing songs and said his prayers for us and his grandchildren. His livelihood still remains. The places he herded sheep are still alive with memories," one female Burnham resident explained to a local ethnographer. "My life remains here and on the farm where I also live. . . . I lost five of my female cows . . . from drinking contaminated water in the mining area. The energy company creates hopes and dreams it does not keep."[16]

As in the 1970s, organized local activism and the regulatory apparatus put in place in the wake of the National Environmental Protection Act of 1970 proved a powerful combination for Navajos opposed to energy development. Members of local groups such as Dooda Desert Rock and Diné-CARE mounted public actions against the project, physically blocking equipment sent to survey the proposed site, distributing information about the proposal, and organizing speakers at the ten public hearings on the Draft Environmental Impact Statement for the project held on the Navajo Nation. Those hearings displayed both the effectiveness of the political mobilization by Dooda Desert Rock and Diné-CARE as well as the general mistrust Navajos continued to hold for energy development. At the hearings, 95 percent of the speakers spoke against the proposal, a percentage repeated in the 54,000 public comments sent to the Bureau of Indian Affairs following the hearings.[17]

The opposition to Desert Rock did not, however, merely recapitulate events that had occurred in Burnham thirty years earlier. Diné-CARE, in particular, went beyond opposition of the power plant to propose its own vision of energy development. A reservation-wide, decentralized organization that was formed in 1987 after an attempt to locate a toxic-waste incinerator west of Window Rock, Diné-CARE pursued campaigns protesting timber harvesting in sacred portions of the Chuska Mountains and advocating for Navajo uranium miners, campaigns that created new connections between Indian activists and environmental and land-use experts off the reservation. In the campaign against Desert Rock, members of Diné-CARE collaborated with an environmental consulting group, Ecos Consulting of Durango, Colorado, to write a renewable energy proposal in 2008. *Energy and Economic Alternatives to Desert Rock* proposed a new energy regime embedded amid the transmission technology built in the 1960s and 1970s. The report suggested that the Navajo Nation contained the potential for over 11,000 megawatts of wind-powered electrical generation as well as spaces for solar development that were "proximate to existing transmission lines" that "dwarf the amount of energy available from excavating and burning Navajo coal over the coming century." The report spurred new interest in the potential benefits of renewable energy. In 2009 the Navajo Nation Council established the Navajo Green Energy Commission (NGEC), tasked with studying the possibility for renewable energy development. In one sense, the report and the commission demonstrated the continuing power of the spatial organization of energy in the modern Southwest that took shape in the postwar years. Both broadly accept a role for the Navajo Nation as a site of electricity production for export to metropolitan centers. At the same time, it envisioned a form of Navajo-owned energy development without the ecological consequences of coal-fired development that could nevertheless meet the essential economic role that the jobs and royalties from coal mining and power plants have assumed on the Navajo Nation. As Wahleah Johns, a member of the NGEC, suggested to Curtis Yazzie, a resident of Black Mesa, "Maybe we can use [reclaimed mine lands] for solar panels to generate electricity for Los Angeles, to transform something that's been devastating for our land and water into something that can generate revenue for your family, for your kids." Yazzie responded favorably, before a *New York Times* reporter, reasoning "Once Peabody takes all the coal out, it'll be gone. Solar would be long-term. Solar and wind, we don't have a problem with. It's pretty windy out here."[18]

The Navajo Nation faces other imminent pressures to find alternatives to coal. On January 1, 2006, Mohave Generating Station ceased operations after failing to meet the terms of a 1999 consent decree reached with the Sierra Club, Grand Canyon Trust, and National Parks Conservation Association that required Southern California Edison to install stack scrubbers and other pollution controls to alleviate haze in the Grand Canyon. Navajo environmental groups, organized as the Just Transition Coalition, opposed efforts to reopen the plant, fearing that its coal slurry line would continue to deplete the N-aquifer beneath Black Mesa. In 2009 Southern California Edison decommissioned the plant, and in February 2013 the California Public Utilities Commission created a $10 million revolving credit fund to pay development deposits for renewable energy projects that would benefit the Navajo Nation and Hopi Tribe, using revenues from the sale of sulfur dioxide allowances.[19] In October 2012 APS announced plans to purchase Southern California Edison's stake in Four Corners Power Plant and to shut down three generating units.[20] The decommissioning of Mohave and proposed reduction of Four Corners generating capacity come amid both new environmental regulations on coal-fired power-plant emissions of sulfur compounds and carbon dioxide and the boom in natural-gas supplies that began in the late 2000s. In the years 2011 and 2012 these changes helped produce the first reduction in coal production for electrical power generation since the 1950s.

While cheered by environmental groups, this reduction in coal use alarmed many Navajo officials, reflecting the 50 percent share of annual tribal revenue generated from mineral royalties. Appearing before the a subcommittee of the House Appropriations Committee, tribal president Ben Shelly attacked EPA proposals to regulate carbon emissions, stating that "the Navajo Nation faces many regulatory burdens placed on us in our energy development by the EPA's negative view towards further coal development." Attempts to force reductions in coal-fired electrical generation by American utilities threatened, Shelly argued, Navajo efforts "to create a sustainable economy that will reduce our dependence on the federal government." Speaking to the Republican-led panel, Shelly asked for help to "clear the path for Indian energy independence and innovation by reducing regulatory burdens."[21]

Efforts to reduce "dependence on the federal government," however, revealed other dependencies. Even as Shelly attacked the EPA's proposed new regulations, BHP Billiton, an Australian mining conglomerate that had acquired Utah International in 1984, announced plans to close Navajo Mine once its original lease reached its fifty-year term in 2016, citing high taxes and uncertainty over coal's future as an energy source. Navajo officials feared that the closing of Navajo Mine could lead to the shuttering of Four Corners Power Plant and the elimination of eight hundred jobs for tribal members as well as a dramatic loss in tribal revenue. In May 2013 the tribal council voted to create the Navajo Transitional Energy Company (NTEC), a limited liability company authorized to negotiate with BHP Billiton over the future of Navajo Mine.[22] After the resulting negotiations, NTEC agreed to purchase Navajo Mine from BHP Billiton for $85 million, assuming ownership on December 1. The newly formed company also completed an energy supply agreement with APS that would provide coal to Four Corners Power Plant until 2030. On October 31, 2013, the Navajo Tribal Council ratified the agreements.

Navajo president Shelly celebrated the agreements not only for preserving eight hundred jobs, but also as a fulfillment of the efforts to use energy resources to benefit the tribe that had begun in the 1950s. "The coal mine purchase," he announced, "secures our economic future, strengthens our Navajo Nation Energy Policy, and the portfolio of the Nation." The contracts, however, came with significant costs. BHP Billiton insisted on a waiver of liability against past, present, and future damages from mining. APS demanded that any disputes or arbitration fall under the jurisdiction of New Mexico state courts, rather than the Navajo tribal court system, and be adjudicated in Santa Fe, rather than in the two judicial districts that lay closer to the mine. Opponents of the deals attacked the legal immunity given to BHP Billiton and the jurisdictional protection offered to APS as violations of tribal rights, signs of the continuing ways in which energy corporations constrained Navajo political possibilities, even after, in the case of BHP Billiton those corporations abandoned the reservation itself. Duane Yazzie, chapter president for Shiprock, stated that the tribal council's decision "to waive our sovereignty" in both cases represented "a very serious and flagrant violation of our sovereign rights."[23]

Many critics of the purchase articulated a further dependency that the deal extended, a dependency on coal itself. While the enabling legislation for the NTEC requires 10 percent of the profits of Navajo Mine to be used for research and development of "renewable and alternative" energy technologies, the chairman of NTEC's board, Steve Gunderson, has stated that "alternative" energies could include clean coal technology and coal gasification plants like those defeated in Burnham during the 1970s. Gunderson confidentially told an interviewer that "Coal, broadly speaking, will probably always have a future in the U.S." Critics argued otherwise. Protesters outside the Navajo Nation Council Chamber held signs that read, "Don't Spend My Money on a Dying Coal Mine," while Andrew Curley wrote in the *Navajo Times* that the Navajo Nation's ownership of Navajo Mine occurred "at a time when the resource is at its most uncertain and contentious. . . . But we know the Navajo Nation is betting on it.[24]

That the Navajo Nation's wager on coal occurred at the historical moment in which coal's future value appeared deeply unstable represents the present-day manifestation of inequalities the development of the modern Southwest had located in space. Decisions by utility and mining executives, state and local officials, federal bureaucrats, Navajo officials, and millions of metropolitan consumers combined to develop Phoenix and other metropolitan spaces at the expense of the land and people of the Navajo Nation. There is another story embedded in the decision by the tribe to purchase Navajo Mine, however. In the pages of the *Navajo Times*, in newsletters, in blogs, and in protests, Navajos debated both the

Navajo Nation's, and the American nation's, energy future. People like Sarah White and Lori Goodman asked whether the employment made possible by coal mining should outweigh the protection of local places and the demands of local people. People like Curtis Yazzie contemplated the difference between coal and solar-energy development near his home. That the nation's energy future is most hotly debated in places far from the nation's metropolitan centers should not be surprising. If it is, it is because Navajos, and other Indians, have too easily been thought of as isolated from the political and economic changes occurring in the world around them. Instead, Navajos have long explored, debated, and experienced in daily life the broad-scale transformations that the post–World War II years have wrought. If any people have lived isolated from the consequences of those transformations, it has been the residents of metropolitan America, who have, for generations, consumed inexpensive electrical power produced far from their daily lives with little knowledge or thought about the changes it created. That ignorance abetted the practices of utilities that drove electrical demand ever higher, intensifying demand on resources far from the point of consumption. It also created a style of modernity reliant on ready and inexpensive energy, a style that developing nations across the world have aimed to replicate. In an era of unprecedented global climate change, that style, and the ignorance that has accompanied it, must become an artifact of history.

Abbreviations of Sources and Collections

NEWSPAPERS AND MAGAZINES

ADS *Arizona Daily Sun* (FLAGSTAFF, ARIZONA)
AR *Arizona Republic* (PHOENIX, ARIZONA)
DBH *Diné Baa-Hani* (FORT DEFIANCE, ARIZONA)
HCN *High Country News* (LANDER, WYOMING)
LAT *Los Angeles Times*
NT *Navajo Times* (WINDOW ROCK, ARIZONA)
NYT *New York Times*
PG *Phoenix Gazette*
SEP *Saturday Evening Post*
USN *US News and World Report*

ARCHIVAL COLLECTIONS

AHF   Arizona Historical Foundation, Tempe, Arizona
AHS-TEMPE   Arizona History Society, Tempe, Arizona
BMG   The Personal and Political Papers of Senator Barry M. Goldwater, AHF
FSP   Frank Snell Papers, AHF
MKU   Morris K. Udall Papers, Special Collections, University of Arizona, Tucson, Arizona
NNM   Navajo Nation Museum, Window Rock, Arizona
OLP   Orme Lewis Papers, AHF
OMP   Otis "Dock" Marsdon Papers, Huntington Library, San Marino California
PHP   Phoenix History Project, AHS-Tempe
SLU   Stewart L. Udall Papers, Special Collections, University of Arizona, Tucson, Arizona
VNB   Valley National Bank Papers, AHS-Tempe

Notes

INTRODUCTION: BEYOND THE CRABGRASS FRONTIER

1. John Long Oral History 2000, PHP-AHS. List of appliances taken from "Phoenix Home Show," *AR*, 2/14/1952, III, 5.

2. Staggs-Bilt Homes, "Northeast Village" advertisement, *AR*, 2/23/59, V, 4.

3. In 2003, Arizona's State Board of Geographic and Historic Names changed the name of Squaw Peak to Piestewa Peak, in honor of a Hopi woman killed in the Iraqi War, following a decade of protest by native groups. Connie Sexton, "Squaw Peak Officially Piestewa Peak," *AR*, 4/10/2008, 1.

4. Population figures taken from Bureau of the Census, *U.S. Census of Population and Housing: 1960*, Census tracts, Phoenix, Ariz. Table P-1. General Characteristics of the Population, by Census Tract, 1960, 13–25.

5. For the federal subsidy for suburban home building, see Kenneth T. Jackson, *Crabgrass Frontier: The Suburbanization of the United States* (New York, 1985), Adam Rome, *The Bulldozer in the Countryside: Suburban Sprawl and the Rise of American Environmentalism* (New York: Cambridge University Press, 2001), and David Freund, *Colored Property: State Policy and White Racial Politics in Suburban America* (Chicago: University of Chicago Press, 2010). For "growth machine" as a concept in urban development, see Harvey Molotch, "The City as a Growth Machine: Toward a Political Economy of Place," *American Journal of Sociology* 82 (Sept. 1976): 309–32; and John Logan and Molotch, *Urban Fortunes: The Political Economy of Place* (Berkeley, University of California Press, 1997). The literature on racial inequality in postwar urban development is vast; see in particular Freund, *Colored Property*, Thomas Sugrue, *Origins of the Urban Crisis: Race and Inequality in Postwar Detroit* (Princeton: Princeton University Press, 1996); Ira Katznelson, *When Affirmative Action Was White: An Untold History of Racial Inequality in Twentieth Century America* (New York: Norton, 2006); Kevin Kruse, *White Flight: Atlanta and the Making of Modern Conservatism* (Princeton: Princeton University Press, 2006); and Robert Self, *American Babylon: Race and the Struggle for Postwar Oakland* (Princeton: Princeton University Press, 2003). "Possessive investment in whiteness" is from George Lipsitz, *The Possessive Investment in Whiteness: How White People Profit from Identity Politics* (Philadelphia: Temple University Press, 1999). For postwar consumer culture, see Lizabeth Cohen, *A Consumer's Republic: The Politics of Mass Consumption in Postwar America* (New York: Vintage, 2003), and Elaine Tyler May, *Homeward Bound: American Families in the Cold War Era* (New York: Basic, 1990). For military Keynesianism, see Ann Markusen, et. al., *The Rise of the Gunbelt:*

The Military Remapping of Industrial America (New York: Oxford University Press, 1991); Roger Lotchkin, *Fortress California, 1910–1960: From Warfare to Welfare* (New York: Oxford University Press, 1992). For political identity as "tax payer, home owner, school parent," see Matthew Lassiter, *Silent Majority: Suburban Politics in the Sunbelt South* (Princeton: Princeton University Press, 2006). For other treatments of suburban political identity, see Lisa McGirr, *Suburban Warriors: The Origins of the New American Right* (Princeton: Princeton University Press, 2001); Darren Dochuk, *From Bible Belt to Sunbelt: Plain-Folk Religion, Grassroots Politics, and the Rise of Evangelical Conservatism* (New York: Norton, 2011); Michelle Nickerson, *Mothers of Conservatism: Women and the Postwar Right* (Princeton: Princeton University Press, 2012); Kruse, *White Flight*; Self, *American Babylon*; and the articles collected in *The New Suburban History*, Kruse and Sugrue, eds., (Chicago: University of Chicago Press, 2006). "Dream Homes by the Dozen," is taken from a 1954 article in *Arizona Highways* magazine, *AH* (Feb. 1954), 12–18. Edward Abbey, "The Blob Comes to Arizona," *NYT* 5/16/1976, 184.

6. Carl Abbott, *The Metropolitan Frontier: Cities in the Modern American West* (Tucson 1993); Joel Garreau, *Edge City: Life on the New Frontier* (New York, 1991); and Jackson, *Crabgrass Frontier.*

7. Gerald Nash, *The American West in the Twentieth Century: A Short History of an Urban Oasis* (Albuquerque: University of New Mexico Press, 1977).

8. Frederick Jackson Turner, "The Significance of the Frontier in American History," (1893) *Rereading Frederick Jackson Turner: "The Significance of the Frontier" and Other Essays,* John Mack Faragher, ed. (New Haven: Yale University Press, 1994). Debate over the advantages and shortcomings of "frontier" as historical narrative was central to the rise of the new Western history in the 1980s and 1990s. That scholarship contains the best critique and defense of frontier narratives. For two different perspectives on use of the frontier, see Patricia Nelson Limerick, *The Legacy of Conquest: The Unbroken Past of the American West* (New York: W. W. Norton, 1987), esp. "Introduction: Closing the Frontier and Opening Western History;" and William Cronon, George Miles, and Jay Gitlin, "Becoming West: Toward a New Meaning for Western History," in *Under an Open Sky: Rethinking America's Western Past,* Cronon, Gitlin, and Miles, eds. (New York: W. W. Norton, 1993).

9. For treatments that emphasize the suburbs as the boundary to urban space, see Carl Abbott, *The Metropolitan Frontier: Cities in the Modern American West* (Tucson 1993); Joel Garreau, *Edge City: Life on the New Frontier* (New York, 1991); and Kenneth T. Jackson, *Crabgrass Frontier: The Suburbanization of the United States* (New York, 1985).

10. Henri Lefebvre, *The Production of Space*, trans., Donald Nicholson-Smith (Oxford: Blackwells, 1991), 93.

11. This narrative map is based on the author's experiential tracing of the electrical transmission lines of northern Phoenix by physically following power lines from Glenview and Tenth to Pinnacle Peak Substation.

12. John Shaw, *Forest Resources of the Tonto National Forest* (Ogden: USDA, 2004).

13. Many Navajos refer to themselves as "Diné," or "the people." As that name is largely used by Navajos self-referentially, I will use "Navajos." I avoid use of the singular "the Navajo," which has a history of colonialist uses. I will generally use "Navajo Reservation" to refer to Navajo political spaces before 1962, when tribal chairmen began referring to the "Navajo Nation." For the colonialist roots of "the Navajo," see Erika Bsumek, *Indian-Made: Navajo Culture in the Marketplace, 1866–1940* (Lawrence: University Press of Kansas), esp. ch. 1, "Creating the Navajo." For a broader examination of the politics of Navajo history and naming, see Jennifer Nez Denetdale, *Reclaiming Diné History: The Legacies of Chief Manuelito and Juanita* (Albuquerque: University of New Mexico Press, 2007).

14. Original Navajo names taken from Dana Powell and Daláin Long, "Landscapes of Power: Renewable Energy Activism in Diné Bikéyah," in *Indians and Energy: Exploitation and Opportunity in the Southwest*, Sherry Smith and Brian Frehner, eds. (Santa Fe: SAR Press, 2010).

15. The best description of the landscape surrounding Four Corners is Abbey, "The Second Rape of the West," in *The Journey Home: Some Words in Defense of the American West* (New York: Dutton, 1977).

16. David Nye, *Consuming Power: A Social History of American Energies* (Cambridge: MIT Press, 1999). For an interpretation of energy as grounding for historical change, see Vaclav Smil, *Energy in World History* (Boulder: Westview Press, 1984).

17. Salt River Project Ad, "Electric Valentine," *AR* 2/10/1957, V, 8; Hallcraft Homes, "Note to the Ladies," *AR* 2/16/1959, V, 12.

18. Quote from "Arizona: Air-Conditioned Desert," *SEP*, 6/17/1961, 31; Harold Martin, "The New Millionaires of Phoenix," *SEP*, 9/30/1960, 24–31; "Big Boom in the Desert," *USN*, 10/11/1957, 78. For the proliferation of air conditioning in the United States, see Gail Cooper, *Air Conditioning America: Engineers and the Controlled Environment* (Baltimore: Johns Hopkins University Press, 1998); and Marsha Ackerman, *Cool Comfort: America's Romance with Air Conditioning* (Washington, D.C.: Smithsonian Institution Press, 2002). Air conditioning stands as a prime example of an emergent technology that was enabled by and served to extend "high-energy society," pointing to the key role that consumption played in deepening the instantiation of electrical networks into American social life in ways suggested by Ruth Schwartz Cowan in both *More Work for Mother: The Ironies of Household Technology from the Open Hearth to the Microwave* (New York: Basic Books, 1983) and "Consumption Junction: A Proposal for Research Strategies in the Sociology of Technology," in *The Social Construction of Technological Systems*, Wiebe Bijker, Thomas P. Hughes, and Trevor Pinch, eds. (Cambridge: MIT Press, 1987).

19. Arizona Public Service Company, *Industry Views* (Phoenix: Arizona Public Service, 1961).

20. Henry Adams, "The Dynamo and the Virgin," *The Education of Henry Adams* (Boston: Houghton Mifflin, 1918), 383.

21. David Nye, *American Technological Sublime* (Cambridge: MIT Press, 1994) pp. 143–98, 150–51, 192.

22. For such visions, see Sarah Phillips, *This Land, This Nation: Conservation, Rural America, and the New Deal* (New York: Cambridge University Press, 2007).

23. See, in particular, Sugrue, *Origins of the Urban Crisis*; and Self, *American Babylon*. For an account that introduces greater class diversity and stretches suburban development earlier than the New Deal while still emphasizing postwar suburban protectionism, see Becky Nicolaides, *My Blue Heaven: Life and Politics in the Working Class Suburbs of Los Angeles* (Chicago: University of Chicago Press, 2002).

24. Samuel Zipp writes that postwar economic policy makers "believed that increased government spending and private consumption would ward off another depression and push the economy to ever-higher levels of growth. The unprecedented tax revenue surpluses such growth produced . . . could be reinvested in the social programs that had previously been underwritten by direct federal spending during the New Deal." Zipp, *Manhattan Projects: The Rise and Fall of Urban Renewal in Cold War New York* (New York: Oxford University Press, 2010), 22–23. See also Cohen, *A Consumer's Republic*, ch. 3, and Robert Collins, *More: The Politics of Economic Growth in Postwar America* (New York: Oxford University Press, 2010).

25. For variants of this argument, see, in particular, the essays in *Sunbelt Rising: The Politics of Place, Space and Region*, Darren Dochuk and Michelle Nickerson, eds. (Philadelphia: University of Pennsylvania Press, 2011); Elizabeth Shermer, *Sunbelt Capitalism: Phoenix and the Transformation of American Politics* (Philadelphia: University of Pennsylvania Press, 2013); and Bethany Moreton, *To Serve God and Wal-Mart: The Making of Christian Free Enterprise* (Cambridge: Harvard University Press, 2009). For a broader argument about the Sunbelt's emergence as part of a broader pattern of regional dominance associated with changes in the nation's political economy, see Philip Ethington and David P. Levitus, "Placing American Political Development: Cities, Regions, and Regimes, 1789–2008," in *The City in American Political Development*, Richard Dilworth, ed. (New York: Routledge, 2009). For the vital role of local growth machines in creating urban transformation, see Logan and Molotch, *Urban Fortunes*.

26. For the particular dilemmas of tourism, and more general analysis of the position of peripheral communities vis-à-vis metropolitan change, see Hal Rothman, *Devils Bargains: Tourism in the Twentieth Century American West* (Lawrence: University of Kansas Press, 1998), ch. 1.

27. A burgeoning scholarship on the history of urban Indians has challenged these assumptions. See Coll Thrush, *Native Seattle: Histories from the Crossing-Over Place* (Seattle: University of Washington Press, 2007); and Nicolas Rosenthal, *Reimagining Indian Country: Native American Migration and Identity in Twentieth-Century Los Angeles* (Chapel Hill: University of North Carolina Press, 2012). For the political movement for Indian sovereignty, see Charles Wilkinson, *Blood Struggle: The Rise of Modern Indian Nations* (New York: Norton, 2005) and Daniel Cobb, *Native Activism in Cold War America: The Struggle for Sovereignty* (Lawrence: University Press of Kansas, 2008).

28. Quotation in Peter Iverson, *Barry Goldwater: Native Arizonan* (Norman: University of Oklahoma Press, 1998), 180–81.

29. For the suburban roots of environmentalism, see Rome, *Bulldozer in the Countryside*, and Christopher Sellers, *Crabgrass Crucible: Suburban Nature and Environmentalism in Post–WWII America* (Chapel Hill: University of North Carolina Press, 2012). For a case study of the place of environmentalism in metropolitan politics, see Lily Geismer, "Don't Blame Us: Grassroots Liberalism in Massachusetts, 1960–1990," (Ph.D. diss., University of Michigan, 2011).

30. Abbey, "The Blob Comes to Arizona." For an account of environmental limits and the prospects for sustainability in Phoenix, see Andrew Ross, *Bird on Fire: Lessons from the World's Least Sustainable City* (New York: Oxford University Press, 2011).

31. For ecotechnological systems, see Thomas Parke Hughes, *Human-Built World: How to Think about Technology and Culture* (Chicago: University of Chicago Press, 2004). In emphasizing the place of the intersection of nature and technology in the development of contemporary metropolitan space, I build on an increasingly vast literature that demonstrates the centrality of nature to the creation of modern social and economic life. See William Cronon, *Nature's Metropolis: Chicago and the Great West* (New York: Norton, 1991); Richard White, *The Organic Machine* (New York: Hill and Wang, 1995); Fernando Coronil, *The Magical State: Nature, Money, and Modernity in Venezuela* (Chicago: University of Chicago Press, 1997), particularly ch. 1; Sara Pritchard, *Confluence: The Nature of Technology and the Remaking of the Rhone* (Cambridge: Harvard University Press, 2012); Matthew Klingle, *Emerald City: An Environmental History of Seattle* (New Haven: Yale University Press, 2007); Richard Walker, *The Country in the City: The Greening of the San Francisco Bay Area* (Seattle: University of Washington Press, 2007).

32. Phillips, *This Land, This Nation*, 83–107.

33. "Black Mesa Mine, Peabody Coal Co," Arizona Ephemera Collection (AHF).

34. Allen Dieterich-Ward and I have elaborated this argument at greater length in "Beyond the Metropolis: Metropolitan Growth and Regional Transformation in Postwar America," *Journal of Urban History* 35 (November 2009).

35. As Thomas Hughes has argued, in their incipient phases large technological systems are highly manipulable by human actors. As they achieve "technological momentum," however, they increasingly act to shape human action rather than to be shaped by it. See Hughes, "Technological Momentum," in *Does Technology Drive History? The Dilemma of Technological Determinism*, Merrit Roe Smith and Leo Marx, eds. (Cambridge: MIT Press, 1995).

36. In emphasizing infrastructure as a form of capital set in place, I draw upon David Harvey's broader ideas about urbanization in general as a form of capital accumulation that further facilitates the economic processes of urban life. See Harvey, "The Urbanization of Capital" in *The Urbanization of Capital: Studies in the History and Theory of Capitalist Urbanization* (Baltimore: John Hopkins University Press, 1985). For the uneven development of nature as a key element of capitalist development, see Harvey, *Justice, Nature and the Geography of Difference* (London: Blackwells, 1997).

37. The Clean Air Task Force estimates that emissions from Four Corners Power Plant alone are responsible for forty-four premature deaths and eight

hundred asthma attacks annually. Clean Air Task Force, "New Mexico State Profile of Exposure to Coal-Fired Power Plants"; http://www.catf.us/resources /factsheets/files/Children_at_Risk-New_Mexico.pdf. For uranium mining and its effects on Navajo public health, see Robert Roscoe et. al., "Mortality Among Navajo Uranium Miners," *American Journal of Public Health* (1995), 535–41; Valerie Kuletz, *The Tainted Desert: Environmental Ruin in the American West* (New York: Routledge, 1998); Barbara Rose Johnson, Susan Dawson, and Gary Madsen, "Uranium Mining and Milling: Navajo Experiences in the American Southwest," in *Indians and Energy Development*. The 1990 Radiation Exposure Compensation Act (RECA) provided payments to residents exposed to fallout from atomic-weapons testing in Nevada and uranium miners who worked before 1971, when uranium became a commodity saleable to entities other than the Atomic Energy Commission. As Gabrielle Hecht suggests, "RECA offered reconciliation for the sins of the Cold War, not capitalism." Hecht, *Being Nuclear: Africans and the Global Uranium Trade* (Cambridge: MIT Press, 2012), 180. There has been no large-scale epidemiological study of asthma on the Navajo Reservation. The one small-scale study that exists traces high asthma rates to the indoor combustion of wood and other biofuels. While such heating efforts have been long-standing parts of Navajo life, however, Navajos living near both Four Corners and Black Mesa Mine report that familial asthma has increased dramatically since the early 1970s. For such anecdotal accounts, see Adella Begaye, "Coal Plants Make Navajo Suffer," *Albuquerque Journal*, Apr. 12, 2012 http://www.abqjournal.com /main/2012/04/12/opinion/coal-plants-make-navajo-suffer.html; Marley Shebala, "Protesters Air Complaints about Peabody," *NT*, Apr. 26, 2010 http://navajo times.com/news/2010/0410/042610peabody.php. For the relationship between Navajo childhood asthma and indoor combustion, see L. F. Robin et. al., "Wood-burning Stoves and Lower Respiratory Illnesses in Navajo Children," *Pediatric Infectious Disease Journal* 15(10) (Oct. 1996): 859–65.

38. Brett Walker, *Toxic Archipelago: A History of Industrial Disease in Japan* (Seattle: University of Washington Press, 2010).

39. For the history of uranium mining on the Navajo Reservation, see Peter Eichstaedt, *If You Poison Us: Uranium Mining and Native Americans* (New York: Red Crane Press, 1994); *The Navajo People and Uranium Mining*, Doug Brugge, Timothy Benally, and Esther Yazzie-Lewis, eds. (Albuquerque: University of New Mexico Press, 2007); Judy Pasternak, *Yellow Dirt: An American Story of a Poisoned Land and a People Betrayed* (New York: Free Press, 2010); and Michael Admundson, *Yellowcake Towns: Uranium Mining in the American West* (Boulder: University Press of Colorado, 2004).

40. I have found only one mention of "Sunbelt" in relation to Phoenix before the mid-1970s. A 1940 promotional study recounting the resources of the "Valley of the Sun" stated that "Phoenix lies in the Sun Belt." Arthur Horton, *An Economic, Political, and Social Survey of Phoenix and the Valley of the Sun* (Phoenix: Southside Progress, 1941), 94.

41. Kevin Phillips, *The Emerging Republican Majority* (New Rochelle: Arlington House, 1969). For examples of these uses, see Luci Mouat, "Frost Belt Sees Its Federal Funds Sink Slowly in West," *CSM*, 9/9/1981, 1; Kirkpatrick Sale, *Power Shift: The Rise of the Southern Rim and Its Challenges to the Eastern*

Establishment (New York: Random House, 1975); and Bernard Weinstein and Robert Firestine, *Regional Growth and Decline in the United States: The Rise of the Sunbelt and Decline of the Northeast* (New York: Praeger, 1978).

42. In using "organized worlds of meaning" to define place, I borrow Yi-Fu Tuan's definition. Philip Ethington has written provocatively that place should form a central analytic of historical scholarship. Ethington argues that human action always occurs in both place and time and that human history can be read in the layered places created in the past. As he writes, "The past is the set of places made by human action. History is a map of those places." In emphasizing mapping, Ethington both attempts to provide a richer sense of the role of past places on human place-creation than Tuan's emphasis on experiential place making and to connect place to the essential practices of history as a discipline. As he writes, "The incalculable volume of historical writing on all subjects should be thought of as a map because the past can only be known by placing it, and the way of knowing places is to map them." Here, I argue that the Sunbelt came to exist as a particular place in the 1970s, as people began to use it to organize their spaces by creating new maps. Uses of "Sunbelt" to refer to human experience earlier refer to a place that did not yet exist. Ethington, "Placing the Past: 'Groundwork' for a Spatial Theory of History," *Rethinking History* 11 (Dec. 2007), 465, 486–87. For Tuan's understanding of place, see Yi Tu Fuan, *Space and Place: The Perspective of Experience* (Minneapolis: University of Minnesota Press, 1977), 8–19.

43. Horton, *Survey of Phoenix*, 160.

44. Valley of the Sun Club, "Arizona's Valley of the Sun is the perfect spot to combine business with pleasure," *Fortune* (Jan. 1948), 211.

45. For similar claims made by Chicago's nineteenth-century boosters, see Cronon, *Nature's Metropolis*, 31–45.

46. Jones quoted in Marshall Tome, "Coal Mine Will Help Navajo Tribe," *NT*, July 27, 1957, 1, 22.

47. "Opposes Leasehold Tax: Pete Talks in Phoenix," *NT*, March 4, 1971.

48. William Beaver, letter to the editor, *NT*, June 4, 1970.

49. See Ethington, "Placing the Past," 465.

50. Horton, *Survey of Phoenix*, 125.

51. "Roads Through the Indian Country," *AH* 29 (June 1953), 12.

52. Philip Vanderhoof, general manager of Navajo Tribal Utility Authority, quoted in Leah Glaser, *Electrifying the Rural American West: Stories of Power, People and Place* (Lincoln: University of Nebraska Press, 2009), 168.

53. Michael Benson, letter, *NT*, March 28, 1968.

54. For work arguing that human and natural systems are connected by the flow of energy, see White, *The Organic Machine*; Edmund Russell et al., "The Nature of Power: Synthesizing the History of Technology and Environmental History," *Technology and Culture* 52 (April 2011); James Williams, *Energy and the Making of Modern California* (Akron: University of Akron Press, 1997); John McNeill, *Something New Under the Sun: An Environmental History of the Twentieth-Century World* (New York: Oxford University Press, 2000); Elliot West, *The Contested Plains: Indians, Goldseekers, and the Rush to Colorado* (Lawrence: University Press of Kansas, 1997); and Thomas Andrews, *Killing for Coal*.

55. In using "Sunbelt" loosely, too many historians suggest that the postwar growth of Houston, Atlanta, Orange County, Phoenix, and other fast-growing places was the result a shared ideological project that linked local officials and businessmen in those cities. Labels such as "Sunbelt strategy" or "Sunbelt synthesis" misrepresent parallel strategies to attract capital that occurred within cities in similar structural positions in the American political economy as shared regional strategies to create growth. While cities across the South and West did employ similar tactics to draw capital—largely low personal and corporate tax rates, minimal regulation, and anti-union laws—they did so in a climate of fierce interurban competition and federal subsidies for growth that formed the key components of the postwar political economy. Historical uses of "Sunbelt" to explain the rise of modern conservatism also all too often involve, in Matthew Lassiter's words, "a teleological approach in which the tropes of the triumph of conservatism or the rightward turn become the narrative climax of broader developments with more diverse causes and consequences," particularly the broader processes of metropolitan development that were national in scope. Indeed, the "metropolitan preferences" that *Power Lines* charts suggests that postwar politics in general should narrate the disputes between liberals and conservatives amid the developing consensus that economic growth should privilege metropolitan development, particularly on the suburban periphery, over other forms of social policy. Lassiter, "Political History beyond the Red-Blue Divide," *Journal of American History* (December 2011), 761. This argument is similar to that made by Bruce Schulman, emphasizing that federal economic policy in the South developed "place" over "people." I add emphasis that the places developed lay largely on the metropolitan periphery and growth occurred at the expense of other places throughout the region. Schulman, *From Cotton Belt to Sun Belt*.

56. My understanding of regions emerging as distinct spatial formations in the practices of daily life, in attempts by political and economic actors to impose order, and in the representations of those spaces as distinct regions is heavily influenced by Lefebvre's *Production of Space*. For an excellent account of how these three levels of practice intersect, see Richard White, "What Is Spatial History?" Spatial History Lab: Working paper; Feb. 1, 2010. https://www.stanford .edu/group/spatialhistory/cgi-bin/site/pub.php?id=29.

57. For an analysis of how some recent histories of energy have elided differences in social power, see Bruce Stadfeld, "Electrical Space" (Ph.D. diss, University of Manitoba, 2001).

58. See particularly Cronon, *Nature's Metropolis*; Worster, *Dust Bowl* and *Rivers of Empire*.

59. "Indian Tribes Must Get Fair Return for Resources," *NT*, April 22, 1976.

Chapter 1: A Region of Fragments

1. Thomas Treanor, "Million Give Wild Ovation as Hoover Dam Lights City," *LAT*, 10/10/1936, 1.

2. For Americans' responses to Boulder Dam, see Nye, *American Technological Sublime*, 136–41. For details of the dam's construction, see Michael Hiltzik, *Colossus: Hoover Dam and the Making of the American Century* (New York: Free Press, 2010).

3. For the renaming of Hoover Dam, see Hiltzik, *Colossus*, 311.

4. Chester Hanson, "Awed Thousands See Hoover Dam Dedicated," *LAT*, 10/1/1935, 1.

5. Franklin D. Roosevelt: "Address at the Dedication of Boulder Dam," 9/30/1935. Online by Gerhard Peters and John T. Woolley, *The American Presidency Project*. http://www.presidency.ucsb.edu/ws/?pid=14952.

6. Donald Berman, *Arizona Politics and Government: The Quest for Autonomy, Democracy and Development* (Lincoln: University of Nebraska Press, 1991), 161; Norris Hundley, *The Great Thirst: Californians and Water, 1770s–1990s* (Berkeley: University of California Press, 1991).

7. Richard White, *Roots of Dependency: Subsistence, Environment, and Social Change among the Choctaws, Navajos, and Pawnee* (Lincoln: University of Nebraska Press, 1983), 258.

8. Robert Wiebe, *The Search for Order, 1880–1920* (New York: Hill and Wang, 1968), 1.

9. Roosevelt, "Address at the Dedication of Boulder Dam."

10. Donald Baars, *The Colorado Plateau: A Geologic History* (Albuquerque: University of New Mexico Press, 1983).

11. Alan Graham, *Late Cretaceous and Cenozoic History of North American Vegetation*; Scott L. Wing, et al., "Implications of an Exceptional Fossil Flora for Late Cretaceous Vegetation," *Nature* 363 (5/27/1993).

12. For an account of coal's formation, see Barbara Freese, *Coal: A Human History* (New York: Penguin, 2004).

13. Guillermo Rein, "Smouldering Fires and Natural Fuels," in *Fire Phenomena in the Earth System—An Interdisciplinary Approach to Fire Science*, C. Belcher, ed. (New York: Wiley and Sons, 2013).

14. Baars, *The Colorado Plateau*, 161–75. For another historical account of the coal beds created on these shores, see Andrews, *Killing for Coal*.

15. For further explication of "the wealth of nature," see Cronon, *Nature's Metropolis*, and Coronil, *The Magical State*, ch. 1.

16. Baars, *The Colorado Plateau*, 85.

17. John Wesley Powell, *The Exploration of the Colorado River and Its Canyons* (Dover Publications: New York, 1895), 29.

18. Victor Polyak et al., "Age and Evolution of the Grand Canyon Revealed by U-Pb Dating of Water Table-Type Speleothems," *Science* 319 (3/8/2008), 1377–80.

19. Donald Baars, *The Colorado Plateau: A Geologic History* (Albuquerque: University of New Mexico Press, 1983), 224–25.

20. Philip Fradkin, *A River No More: The Colorado River and the West* (New York: Knopf, 1981), 182.

21. Barry Goldwater, *Delightful Journey Down the Green and Colorado Rivers* (Tempe: Arizona Historical Foundation, 1970), 104.

22. Marsha Weisiger, *Dreaming of Sheep in Navajo Country* (Seattle: University of Washington Press, 2009), 140–41.

23. Michael Scott et al, "The Structure and Functioning of Riparian and Aquatic Ecosystems of the Colorado Plateau," USGS, Southern Colorado Plateau Network Phase Three Supplement III Riparian and Aquatic Ecosystems Model, http://science.nature.nps.gov/im/units/scpn/Documents/Supplements/SuppIII _Riparian_Aquatic_Model.pdf. 1998.

24. On Navajo migrations, see David Wilcox, "The Entry of Athapaskans into the American Southwest—The Problem Today," in *The Protohistoric Period in the North American Southwest, A.D. 1450–1700*, David Wilcox and Bruce Masse, eds. (Tempe: Arizona State University Press, 1981).

25. Imperial Irrigation District, "The Colorado River and Imperial Valley Soils," quoted in Michael Hiltzik, *Colossus*, 31–32.

26. Michael Logan, *Desert Cities: The Environmental History of Phoenix and Tucson* (Pittsburgh: University of Pittsburgh Press, 2006), 18.

27. James Bayman, "The Hohokam of the American Southwest," *Journal of World Prehistory* 15 (Sept. 2001), 257–311.

28. Duppa quoted in Horton, *Survey of Phoenix*, 15.

29. For tourist development of the Grand Canyon, see Rothman, *Devils Bargains*, ch. 2; for Dodge's salon, see Flannery Burke, *From Greenwich Village to Taos: Primitivism and Place at Mabel Dodge Luhan's* (Lawrence: University Press of Kansas, 2008); for "Indian-made" goods, see Bsumek, *Indian-made*; Leah Dilworth, *Imagining Indians in the Southwest: Persistent Images of a Primitive Past* (Washington: Smithsonian Press, 1996), 5.

30. James Snead, *Ruins and Rivals: The Making of Southwestern Anthropology* (Tucson, University of Arizona Press, 2001), 69–74, 91.

31. Charles Fletcher Lummis, *The Land of Poco Tiempo* (London: Low, Marston & Company, 1893), 3.

32. For Lummis's role in shaping this image of Los Angeles, see Lawrence Culver, *The Frontier of Leisure: Southern California and the Shaping of Modern America* (New York: Oxford University Press, 2011), ch. 1.

33. Quotes from Greg Hise, "Industry and Imaginative Geographies," and Mike Davis, "Sunshine and the Open Shop," both in *Metropolis in the Making: Los Angeles in the 1920s*, William Deverell and Tom Sitton, eds. (Berkeley: University of California Press, 2001), 19, 138.

34. For Los Angeles's appropriation of the Owens River, see Hundley, *The Great Thirst*.

35. Scattergood and Mulholland quoted in Hiltzik, *Colossus*, 100–103.

36. The literature on the creation of the National Reclamation Act is vast. For three separate perspectives, see Donald Worster, *Rivers of Empire: Water, Aridity, and the Growth of the American West* (New York: Oxford University Press, 1985), 127–88, which emphasizes the act as a manifestation of western conquest and as the emergence of a federal "power elite"; Hundley, *The Great Thirst*, 113–20, which argues the act reflected Western consensus over use of water; and Donald Pisani, *From the Family Farm to Agribusiness* (Berkeley: University of California Press, 1985), 283–381, and *To Reclaim a Divided West: Water, Law, and Public Policy, 1848–1902* (Albuquerque: University of New Mexico Press, 1992),

which argues the act emerged out of an attempt to resolve Western political fragmentation.

37. Donald Pisani, *Water and American Government: The Reclamation Bureau, National Water Policy, and the West* (Berkeley: University of California Press, 2002), 123–53.

38. Hundley, *The Great Thirst*, 122–26.

39. Chandler had invested much of his fortune in the 860,000-acre Colorado River Land Company, located just south of the U.S.-Mexico border, land irrigated by a canal below the border that flowed north into the United States and Imperial Valley. Control of water had sent land prices on the company's property soaring from 60¢ an acre to $280. The proposal of construction of the new "All-American Canal" as part of the Boulder Canyon Project threatened to break Chandler's control over the river's water and thus devalue his land. Hiltzik, *Colossus*, 59–60.

40. Kevin Wehr, *America's Fight over Water: The Environmental and Political Effects of Large-Scale Water Systems* (New York: Routledge, 2005), 96.

41. Household electrical consumption surveys began in 1945. That year, domestic consumer use for both Southern California Edison and the LADPL (by then the LADPW) averaged slightly less than of 1,500 kwh annually. The dam's initial generating capacity was 1,344 megawatts. The estimate of 800,000 homes is thus conservative. The division of the dam's power was a contentious matter. Concerned mainly with guaranteeing repayment, Interior Secretary Ray Wilber initially split it between Edison (25 percent), the LADPL (25 percent), and the MWD (50 percent). After severe criticism, Wilber revised his decision. Arizona and Nevada retained 18 percent shares, purchasable at the power plant's switching yard only for use within those states, amounts that remained largely unused. The cities of Glendale, Pasadena, and Burbank gained the right to purchase 4 percent of the dam's power. The MWD received an allocation of 36 percent of the dam's firm power and the right of first refusal on any power unclaimed by Nevada and Arizona, which initially gave the district as much, if not more, electricity than the initial apportionment. The LADPL received 15 percent of the dam's firm power, and secondary rights to Arizona's and Nevada's power. Southern California Edison appeared, at first glance, to be the biggest loser, as it saw its share of firm power reduced to 9 percent and held only tertiary rights to unclaimed power. However, many of the smaller public recipients of Boulder Dam power—the cities of Glendale, Burbank, and Pasadena—elected to pay Edison rather than the LADPL to transport their preference power fearing the Power Trust less than subordination to Los Angeles's municipal utility. Pisani, *Water and American Government*, 135; Hiltzik, *Colossus*, 152–54.

42. Pisani, *Water and American Government*, 152.

43. Hiltzik, *Colossus*, 119.

44. Cronon, *Nature's Metropolis*, 41–45; David Scobey, *Empire City: The Making and Meaning of the New York City Landscape* (Philadelphia: Temple University Press, 2003).

45. Hanson, "Hoover Dam," *LAT*, 9/30/1935, A4.

46. "The Gateway of Empire," *LAT*, 10/1/1935, A6.

47. Horton, *Survey of Phoenix*, 153.

48. George Hunt, *Why I Oppose the Colorado River Compact* (1923), 1, GWH.

49. An acre-foot is an amount of water sufficient to cover one acre of land one foot deep.

50. Norviel's position was based on the calculations of Arizona's chief water engineer, James Girand, who also claimed that Arizona was entitled to 92 percent of the river's power, based on a polemical interpretation of the river that began calculating its power head not at the origin of the Green River in Utah or the Colorado (which he referred to as the Grand) in Colorado, but at the junction of the two, just upstream from the Arizona State line in Utah. Norviel was not the only delegate to produce state's rights claims highly favorable to his own state. Colorado deputy state engineer Ralph Meeker argued that since 85 percent of the river's water originated in the upper basin, those states should retain that amount. Girand's and Norviel's arguments appear in Horton, *Survey of Phoenix*, 103. For the various arguments made by other state representatives, see Norris Hundley, *Water and the West: The Colorado River Compact and the Politics of Water in the American West* (Berkeley: University of California Press, 1995, 2009), 222. Hundley's book remains the best history of the Compact.

51. John Goff, "George W. P. Hunt," in *The Arizona governors, 1912–1990*, John Myers, ed. (Phoenix: Heritage Publishers, 1989), 7–17.

52. Horton, *Survey of Phoenix*, 139.

53. Patrick Hamilton, *Resources of Arizona* (San Francisco: A. L. Bancroft & Company, 1884) 30–31. On river fluctuations during the 1890s, see Karen Smith, *The Magnificent Experiment: Building the Salt River Reclamation Project, 1890–1917* (Tucson: University of Arizona Press, 1986).

54. Smith, *The Magnificent Experiment*; Luckingham, *Phoenix*, 46–49.

55. Bureau of Reclamation History Program, *Salt River Project* (1997) BuRec. Pisani, *Water, Land, and Water in the West: The Limits of Public Policy, 1850–1920* (Lawrence: University Press of Kansas, 1996).

56. Worster, *Rivers of Empire*, 131.

57. Barry Goldwater, "A Good Reclamation Project," *LAT*, 4/18/1961, B4

58. Horton, *Survey of Phoenix*, 18.

59. Kotlanger, "Phoenix, 1920–1940" (Ph. D. diss., Arizona State University, 1983), 35–50.

60. Ibid., 40–45.

61. Horton, *Survey of Phoenix*, 102.

62. The Central Arizona Light and Power Company charged upward of $1,000 per mile for line extensions beyond Phoenix, reflecting the belief that rural residents consumed far less electricity than the cost of extending service to them warranted. Line-construction policies contained in CALAPCO, *Annual Report*, 1923. For the general belief about rural consumers, see Ronald Tobey, *Technology as Freedom: The New Deal and the Electrical Modernization of the American Home* (Berkeley: University of California Press, 1995), 29–35.

63. Steven Shadegg, *Century One: The Story of Man's Progress in Central Arizona* (Phoenix: Salt River Project, 1969), 14.

64. Shadegg, *Century One*, 18. I am grateful to SRP historians Shelly Dudley and Dan Killoren for explaining the details of this agreement.

65. Horton, *Survey of Phoenix*, 125.

66. Shadegg, *Century One*, 25. Ruth and Myrtle Staley Oral History, PHP.

67. Horton, *Survey of Phoenix*, 125.

68. Quoted from Logan, *Desert Cities*, 86.

69. Shadegg, *Century One*, 31.

70. The Boulder Dam Power Transmission Association of Arizona, "Boulder Dam Power for Arizona," Bureau of Reclamation Project Files, Hoover Dam, Box 42, RG 75, NARA-D.

71. N. D. Houghton, "Problems of Public Power Administration in the Southwest: Some Arizona Applications," *Western Political Quarterly* 4 (March 1951), 123.

72. Bryant quoted in Weisiger, *Dreaming of Sheep*, 18.

73. Weisiger's *Dreaming of Sheep* represents the best account of stock reduction in the broad context of Navajo history. For other accounts, see White, *Roots of Dependency*, 212–314; and Donald Parman, *Navajos and the New Deal* (New Haven: Yale University Press, 1975).

74. Weisiger, *Dreaming of Sheep*, 105–128. For relationships between Navajos and Puebloan peoples from the fifteenth through the nineteenth centuries, see James Brooks, *Captives and Cousins: Slavery, Kinship and Community in the Southwestern Borderlands* (Chapel Hill: University of North Carolina Press, 2001).

75. Weisiger, *Dreaming of Sheep*, 123. On energy economy of domestic ungulates more generally, see Elliot West, *The Contested Plains: Indians, Goldseekers, and the Rush to Colorado* (Lawrence: University Press of Kansas, 1998), xxi, 331–32.

76. Weisiger, *Dreaming of Sheep*, 64.

77. Peter Iverson, *Diné: A History of the Navajos* (Albuquerque: University of New Mexico Press, 2004), 153–54.

78. Daily care for their animals also maintained hózhó, the idealized state of harmony with all life that represents the central spiritual goal of Diné cosmology. When hózhó was established, livestock would provide protection not only from hunger but of a world out of harmony. If Diné failed to provide care, the entire world could fall out of balance. For more about hózhó, see Weisiger, *Dreaming of Sheep*, 55–57; Colleen O'Neill, *Working the Navajo Way: Labor and Culture in the Twentieth Century* (Lawrence: University Press of Kansas, 2005), 38; and Milford Muskett, "Identity, Hózhó, Change, and Land: Navajo Environmental Perspectives" (Ph.D. diss., University of Wisconsin, 2003).

79. Jennifer Nez Denetdale, *The Long Walk: The Forced Navajo Exile* (Philadelphia: Chelsea House Publishers, 2007).

80. Quoted in White, *Roots of Dependency*, 216.

81. Iverson, *Diné*, 93–96.

82. For a survey of this era of Indian history, see Frederick Hoxie, *A Final Promise: The Campaign to Assimilate the Indians, 1880–1920* (Lincoln: University of Nebraska Press, 2001). On Navajo boarding-school experience, see Iverson, *Diné*, 117–25.

83. For Chee Dodge's stockholdings, Weisiger, *Dreaming of Sheep*, 125. For rug manufacture, see Bsumek, *Indian-Made*; and O'Neill, *Working the Navajo Way*, 55–80.

84. Steven Stoll, *Outliers and Savages: The Ordeal of the Agrarian Household in the Atlantic World*, unpublished manuscript, ch. 1.

85. Weisiger, *Dreaming of Sheep*, 101.

86. Ibid., 123. For climatic fluctuation as an agent of historical change, see Joseph Taylor III, "El Nino and Vanishing Salmon: Culture, Nature, History, and the Politics of Blame," *Western Historical Quarterly* 29 (Winter 1998).

87. O'Neill, *Working the Navajo Way*, 35–38.

88. Paul Rosier, *Serving Their Country: American Indians and Patriotism in the Twentieth Century* (Cambridge: Harvard University Press, 2010), 65.

89. Collier quote from Weisiger, *Dreaming of Sheep*, 15. For Collier's association with Luhan, see Burke, *From Greenwich Village to Taos*.

90. Paul Rosier, *Rebirth of the Blackfeet Nation, 1912–1954* (Lincoln: University of Nebraska Press, 2001), 82.

91. Representatives of the numerous Navajo clans did meet every two to four years for ceremonials called Naach'id, which aimed to maintain hózhó. The Naach'id aimed to settle any disputes between clans and selected Hashkééjí Naat'ááh, a war chief who protected individual Navajos from harm as they moved away from hózhó, and Hózhóójí Naat'ááh, a peace chief who assisted clans to maintain their relationships with all creation. Iverson, *Diné*, 23.

92. Robert Young, "The Rise of the Navajo Tribe," in *Plural Society in the Southwest*, Edward Spicer and Raymond Thompson, eds. (New York: Interbook, 1972), 192.

93. O'Neill, *Working the Navajo Way*, 36–43.

94. James Allison, "From Survival to Sovereignty: 1970s Energy Development and Indian Self-Determination in Montana's Powder River Basin," *Environmental Justice* 5 (October 2012).

95. John Collier, "Indians at Work," *Survey Graphic* 23, (June 1934), 261.

96. Quotes from White, *Roots of Dependency*, 251.

97. Parman, *Navajos and the New Deal* has the best details about the mechanics of stock reduction. See esp. ch. 5.

98. Kathleen Chamberlain, *Under Sacred Ground: A History of Navajo Oil, 1922–1964* (Albuquerque: University of New Mexico Press, 2000), 73.

99. This misunderstanding forms Weisiger's central analysis of stock reduction. *Dreaming of Sheep*, 4–12.

100. Chamberlain, *Under Sacred Ground*, 76.

101. Ibid., 74.

102. Iverson, *Diné*, 155–65.

103. Ibid., 168–72.

104. Weisiger, *Dreaming of Sheep*, 224–25; White, *The Roots of Dependency*, 309–14.

105. This interpretation of Collier's actions, that his actions during the stock reduction era reflected not primarily an interest in protecting Boulder Dam but in protecting Navajos from the political fallout of the perception that their land-use practices endangered the dam, that stock reduction would be, for Collier, a demonstration that Navajos could be responsible land users, reflects Marsha Weisiger's recent argument about Collier's intentions. Where Richard White ar-

gued earlier that Boulder Dam had served as the catalyst for stock reduction, Weisiger contends that Collier had expressed concern about overgrazing for years and "used the dam as leverage" to gain funding for erosion-control programs on the reservation. Weisiger, *Dreaming of Sheep*, 24, 252n20.

CHAPTER 2: THE VALLEY OF THE SUN

1. Census reports listed 166,638 people moving from the North or West, out of 197,343 people who had moved to Phoenix from outside the area. U.S. Census Bureau, *U.S. Census of Population and Housing: 1960*, Census tracts, Phoenix, Ariz. Table P-1. General Characteristics of the Population, by Census Tract, 1960, 13–25.

2. Raymond Carlson, "Frontier," *AH* (November 1948), 1.

3. "Dream Homes by the Dozens," *AH* (February 1954), 12–18.

4. Carlson, "Happy Land," *AH* (January 1948), 18.

5. "Roads Through the Indian Country," *AH* (June 1953), 12.

6. For another work that shows the role of local businessmen in reshaping core-periphery relations, see Gray Brechin, *Imperial San Francisco: Urban Power, Earthly Ruin* (Berkeley: University of California Press, 1999).

7. Frank Snell Oral History, Box 3, Folder 37, VNB.

8. Sam Mardian Oral History, July 2, 1978, PHP, AHS.

9. Frank Snell Oral History, Dec. 7, 1978, PHP, AHS.

10. William Jervey, Jr., "When the Banks Closed: Arizona's Bank Holiday of 1933," *Arizona and the West* 10 (Summer 1968), 131, 133. Bimson's position at Harris Trust, in which he financed cotton shipment and organized bond offerings for the SRVWUA, made him familiar with Phoenix's economy.

11. Don Dedera, "Walter Reed Bimson: Arizona's Indispensable Man," *AH* (April 1973); Larry Schweikert, "A Record of Revitalization: Financial Leadership in Phoenix," in *Phoenix in the 20th Century*, Wesley Johnson, ed. (Norman 1993), 124; Frank Snell Oral History, Box 2, Folder 37, VNB; Keith Monroe, "Bank Knight in Arizona," *American Magazine* (November 1945).

12. Snell Oral History, PHP.

13. Carl Bimson Oral History, Oct. 8, 1985, Box 2, Folder 25, VNB.

14. G. Wesley Johnson, "Generations of Elites and Social Change in Phoenix," in *Community Development in the American West: Nineteenth and Twentieth Century Frontiers*, eds. Jessie Embry and Howard Christy (Provo, 1985), 98.

15. Frank Snell Oral History, PHP.

16. Orme Lewis Oral History; Johnson, "Generations of Elites," 96–102.

17. Johnson, "Generations of Elites."

18. Walt Lockey, "Banking on Progress: The History and Future of the Valley National Bank Buildings in Phoenix," at http://www.modernphoenix.net/vnb /bimson.htm.

19. Haas quoted in Tim Kelly, "The Changing Face of Phoenix," *AH* (March 1964), 10.

20. Bimson speech at Western Area Development Conference "Opportunities for Business Leadership in Area Development," 11/17/54, Box 29, Folder 235, VNB.

21. Luckingham, *Phoenix*, 102–104.

22. Kotlanger, "Phoenix, 1920–1940," 230.

23. Frank Snell Oral History, VNB.

24. Phoenix Chamber of Commerce, Advertising Committee Minutes, 10/10/49, Box 10, Lewis and Roca and Phoenix Chamber of Commerce Collection, 1949–63, AHS-Tempe.

25. "Promotional Committee Reports," *Phoenix Action*, September 1960, 3.

26. "Fun in Sun City," *Holiday* (January 1958), 45–51; "It's Fun to Live in Phoenix," *Better Homes and Gardens* (February 1957); "Big Boom in the Desert," *US News and World Report*, October 11, 1957, 78; Prentiss Combs, "What It's Like to Live in Arizona," *Better Homes and Gardens*, February 1962, 90–98.

27. "Phoenix in the Valley of the Sun," *Holiday*, March 1953, 62.

28. Mrs. David Prouty, in Combs, "What It's Like to Move to Arizona."

29. "Sands of Desert Turn Gold," *Life*, March 12, 1956, 79; "Phoenix Architect Designs His Own Home," *Architectural Record*, Sept. 1951, 131.

30. "Arizona's Fashions," *Better Homes and Gardens*, March 1958, 65–73.

31. John Cowan, "Baptism by Sunset," *Vogue*, January 15, 1966, 128.

32. Combs, "What It's Like to Live in Arizona," 93.

33. Circulation figures from "Understatement in the Southwest," *Fortune* 38, July 1948, 114; "People Like Pictures," *Time* 58, September 24, 1951, 75; and "Frontpiece," *AH* 28, December 1952. "A Look Inside the Business of Arizona Highways," *AH* 39, July 1963, 2–5.

34. "Phoenix: City in the Sun," *AH*, February 1951; "You'll Like Living in Phoenix," *AH*, April 1957; "Phoenix, City on Wings," *AH*, January 1962.

35. Peter Iverson, *Barry Goldwater, Native Arizonan*, 42–43.

36. Joyce Rockwood Muench, "Pilgrimage into Spring," *AH*, February 1955, 28.

37. "Colorful People," 10.

38. "Roads Through the Indian Country," *AH* (June 1953), 12.

39. "Operation Snowbound Successful," *Los Angeles Times*, February 8, 1949, 12. Alison Bernstein, *American Indians and World War II: Toward a New Era in Indian Affairs* (Norman: University of Oklahoma Press, 1991), 157.

40. White, *Roots of Dependency*, 327.

41. "Big Boom in the Desert," *US News and World Report*, October 11, 1957, 78.

42. David Freund, "Marketing the Free Market: State Intervention and the Politics of Prosperity in Metropolitan America," in Sugrue and Kruse, *The New Suburban History*, 15.

43. Jackson, *Crabgrass Frontier*, 203–5.

44. As Freund has shown, such language was intentionally chosen to obscure the new role of the state in stabilizing the construction industry even as the FHA's lending practices fueled debt-driven economic growth in newly created residential spaces. Freund, "Marketing the Free Market," 26.

45. Carl Bimson Oral History, VNB.

46. Schweikert, "A Record of Revitalization," 125. Schweikert writes it is likely, though unproven, that Walter Bimson's former employer, Harris Trust of Chicago, provided Valley Bank with the capital that allowed the nearly insolvent bank to begin initiating federally insured loans during the Depression years.

47. Valley National Bank, *President's Annual Report to Stockholders*, 1947–70 (years 1953, 1957, 1958 missing), Box 75, VNB; Carl Bimson Oral History, VNB.

48. John Long Oral History (2000), AHS.

49. Ibid.

50. Price of agricultural land in 1954 Phoenix taken from Ralph Staggs Oral History, May 18, 1977, PHP. Construction costs and housing details in John Long Oral History (2000), PHP.

51. John Long Oral History (2000), PHP.

52. Respectively, Nelson Dunham, New Brunswick Saving Institution, New Brunswick, New Jersey; B. C. Nichols, Maine Savings Bank, Portland, Maine; and William Livingston, City and County Savings Bank, Albany, New York, "Dream Homes by the Dozens," *AH*, February 15, 1954.

53. Jason LaBau, "Phoenix Rising: Arizona and the Origins of Modern Conservative Politics" (Ph.D. diss., University of Southern California, 2010), 74.

54. Interest calculated at 3.77 percent, the prime commercial rate for 1954. Obviously, if Valley Bank required Long to pay interest above prime, given the perceived risk of the loan, the bank's return on its investment would have been higher.

55. U.S. Census Bureau, *U.S. Census of Population and Housing: 1960*, Census tracts, Phoenix, Ariz. Table P-1. General Characteristics of the Population, by Census Tract, 1960, 13–25. U.S. Census Bureau, "Phoenix, Arizona, by Census Tract and Blocks, 1960," map included in *U.S. Census of Population and Housing: 1960*.

56. For the role of nature in the creation of suburban place-based identities, see Sellers, *Crabgrass Crucible* and Geismer, "Don't Blame Us!"

57. Staggs Oral History; Long Oral History (1987), PHP.

58. Pomelo Estates advertisement, *AR*, Feb. 15, 1953, IV, 8.

59. Fairway Park advertisement, *AR*, Feb. 10, 1952, III, 2.

60. Hamilton, *Resources of Arizona*, 30–31.

61. Paradise Park advertisement, *AR*, Feb. 6, 1955, II, 6.

62. John F. Long Oral History (1987), PHP. Peter Siskind emphasizes the different nature of suburban construction occurring on farm fields versus wooded or hilly lots. Siskind, "Fractured Suburbias: Exploring Land Use Liberalism in the 1960s and 1970s," paper presented at The Diverse Suburb conference, Hofstra University, Oct. 23, 2009.

63. Staggs Oral History, PHP.

64. Title III authorized the FHA to charter private national mortgage associations that would repurchase mortgages from initial lenders. In the four years after passage of the NHA, few private lenders proved willing to form such associations. Fannie Mae was designed not only to purchase primary mortgages, but also

278 • Notes to Chapter 2

to make them more attractive investments by increasing their circulation and to encourage investors to treat the new standardized mortgages created by federal policy like other capital instruments that could be traded like stocks and bonds. Freund, *Colored Property*, 136–38, 190–93.

65. Haar quoted in Freund, *Colored Property*, 192.

66. Carl Bimson Oral History, VNB.

67. Ibid.

68. Valley National Bank, *President's Annual Report to Stockholders*, 1956.

69. Walter Besson Oral History, VNB.

70. In theory, this ownership structure, allowing corporate ownership of a wide geographical range of utilities, protected investors from catastrophe at the same time it encouraged utilities toward efficiency and interconnection. As S. Z. Mitchell, the innovator of the holding companies of the 1920s, wrote, "If men combined their investments in a large number of plants, widely diversified geographically, the floods will never come to all at once; a depression in business is unlikely to come to all at once, if the diversity is widely made." In practice, however, holding companies quickly became pyramid schemes. Financiers could control local utilities with little personal investment by purchasing controlling shares of parent companies. In 1930, Samuel Insull's investment of $27 million in the Insull Utilities Investment Company allowed him to control subsidiary companies in thirty-two states with assets of at least $500 million. Perched atop the pyramids, Insull and others financial barons could, as critics of the "Power Trust" charged, extract revenue by charging fees for financial, management, and engineering services. See Thomas Hughes, "The Electrification of America: The System Builders," *Technology and Culture* 20 (1979); and Rudolph and Ridley, *Power Struggle*, 57–68.

71. Rudolph and Ridley, *Power Struggle*, 57–68.

72. For the particulars of this plan, see CALAPCO, *Annual Report*, 1925–34. For a small utility like CALAPCO, these relationships did enable the attraction of capital, the main struggle the utility faced in the early 1920s, when two separate bond offerings went undersubscribed. All bond offerings after CALAPCO's consolidation into AP&L were fully purchased, and their advertisements contained the phrase "All common stock is owned by the American Light and Power Company . . . thus securing supervision by the Electric Bond and Share Company, one of the largest and most successful public utility operators in America." Quote from Pacific Co. Investment Securities, Ltd. Advertisement, *LAT*, June 24, 1930, 12; for other advertisement of 1930 bond offering, see Security-First National Company advertisement, *WSJ*, June 19, 1930, 13.

73. For details of the devolution of CALAPCO to local control, see Frank Snell Oral History, Arizona Bar Foundation, Oral History Project: Arizona Legal History, AHS-Tucson. See also "Arizona Seeking Public Ownership of Electric Utilities within State," *WSJ*, October 26, 1945, 6; "First Boston-Blyth Win Arizona Light Common; Are Reoffering Today," *WSJ*, November 8, 1945, 9. For board of directors, see CALAPCO, *Annual Report*, 1945–51 and APS, *Annual Report*, 1952–66.

74. Snell Oral History, Arizona Bar Foundation; APS, *Annual Report*, 1952.

75. For power line mileage, see U.S. Federal Power Commission, *Statistics of Electrical Utilities in the United States . . . Classes A and B, Privately Owned Companies* (Washington D.C.: Government Printing Office, 1947–70).

76. For a visual representation of this expansion, see the service maps in APS, *Annual Report*, 1955–62.

77. Federal Power Commission, *Statistics of Electrical Utilities in the United States . . . Privately Owned Companies, 1946*.

78. Bureau of Reclamation, "Advance Power Program, 1950–1959," 1949, RG 115, Records of the Bureau of Reclamation, Field Office Records, NARA-D, 3–2; for power shortages in Phoenix, see "Power Program, 1947–1952," 1946, RG 115, Records of the Bureau of Reclamation, Field Office Records, NARA-D, 98–100.

79. Federal Power Commission, *National Power Survey, 1947* (Washington, D.C.: Government Printing Office, 1947), 238.

80. For APS power plant construction, see *Annual Reports*, 1952–59. For electrical sales and purchases, see FPC, *Statistics of Electrical Utilities in the United States . . . Privately Owned Companies*, 1945–56.

81. APS, *Annual Report*, 1954, 1956, 1959.

82. Ibid., 1955; Shadegg, *Century One*, 40.

83. Arizona lacked the extensive interconnection between different load centers that characterized the electric utility industry in the Northeast, Midwest, and California. For those systems, see Hughes, *Networks of Power*, and James Williams, *Energy and the Making of Modern California* (Akron: University of Akron Press, 1997).

84. For details of the development of this strategy, see Richard Hirsch, *Technology and Transformation in the American Electric Utility Industry* (New York: Cambridge University Press, 1989), and *Power Loss* (New York: Cambridge University Press: 1999).

85. Quotes from prospectuses of stock and bond offerings come from untitled prospectus announcements in the *Wall Street Journal* on the days of the various offerings, respectively 3/26/1952, 10/30/1953, 10/7/1957, 3/27/1959, and 4/26/1960. On purchase of preferred shares, see FPC, *Statistics of Electrical Utilities in the United States . . . Privately Owned Companies*, 1962. Stock prices taken from, respectively, Frank Snell Oral History, Arizona Legal History, and *WSJ* stock listings for May 12, 1961.

86. Both article titles and quote taken from Hirsch, *Technology and Transformation in the American Electric Utility Industry*, 52–53.

87. Whitmore Villa advertisement and APS, "Electricity Is a Family Affair" ads, *AR*, 2/16/1953, 22.

88. Tobey, *Technology as Freedom*, 92–126. Tobey effectively shows that it was the New Deal's commitment to extending electrical modernity (involving both the FHA's underwriting guidelines and efforts to expand public power with the REA and Bureau of Reclamation), rather than the initial phase of electrification in the early twentieth-century that effectively democratized the residential use of electricity.

89. "Adequate Wiring Essential to Full Use of Housepower," *AR* 2/1/1959, V,

23; APS ad, "Adequately Wired for Modern, Electrical Living," *AR* 2/27/1955, V, 4.

90. SRP, "An Electric Dryer Beats the Sun," *AR* 2/6/1955, V, 2; Appliance Manufacturer's Association ad, "A Freezer Pays for Itself," *AR* 2/18/1952, 13.

91. For the key role gender inequalities embedded in postwar credit policies played in buttressing male authority over household purchases, see Cohen, *Consumer's Republic*, 147–50.

92. APS, "Electricity Is a Family Affair," *AR* 2/23/1953, 7; and 2/27/2953, 22.

93. APA, "Take the Work out of Washday," *AR* 2/16/1953, 18.

94. SRP, "Electric Valentine," *AR* 2/10/1957, V, 8; Hallcraft Homes, "Note to the Ladies," *AR* 2/16/1959, V, 12. For the gendering of spaces of domestic consumption, see Cowan, *More Work for Mother*, and Nye, *Consuming Power.*

95. For APS contest, see "Confidential to Members," 3/18/1955, 1955 Scrapbook, "Page 12–31" Folder 1, Box 2, Homebuilders Association of Central Arizona Records 1953–87, AHS.

96. For SRP's postwar residential consumption, see Federal Power Commission, *Statistics of Publicly Owned Electric Utilities* (Washington, D.C.: Government Printing Office, 1945–52).

For postwar construction program, see Shadegg, *Century One*, 30–34. For quote, see Houghton, "Problems of Public Power Administration in the Southwest," 123.

97. For annual details of SRP's residential consumption, see *Statistics of Publicly Owned Electric Utilities*, 1947–70. For the promotion of the all-electric home as a development strategy, see Rome, *Bulldozer in the Countryside*, ch. 2.

98. "Arizona: Air-Conditioned Desert."

99. In Ralph Staggs Oral History, he does indicate that some home builders returned to swamp coolers during the recession of the late 1960s. Ralph Staggs Oral History, PHP. For the technological history of air conditioning, see Cooper, *Air Conditioning America*; Ackerman, *Cool Comfort*; and Raymond Arsenault, "The End of the Long Hot Summer: Air Conditioning and Southern Culture," *Journal of Southern History* 50 (1984), 597–628.

100. Owen Ely, "Analyzing Utility Stocks," *Analysts Journal* 11 (February 1955), 19–22.

101. For Phoenix's annexation policies in the 1950s, see Carol Heim, "Border Wars: Tax Revenue, Annexation, and Urban Growth in Phoenix," University of Massachusetts Political Economy Research Institute, Working Paper Series, Number 112, July 2006, 8–9. Available at http://www.peri.umass.edu/fileadmin/pdf/working_papers/working_papers_101–150/WP112_revised.pdf; and John Wenum, *Annexation as a Technique for Metropolitan Growth: The Case of Phoenix, Arizona* (Tempe: Institute for Public Administration, Arizona State University, 1970).

102. See Amy E. Hillier, "Redlining and the Homeowners' Loan Corporation," *Journal of Urban History*, 29 (4) (2003), 394–420.

103. McMichael quoted in Clement Vose, *Caucasians Only: The Supreme Court, the NAACP, and the Restrictive Covenant Cases* (Berkeley: University of California Press, 1959), 219–20.

104. Lincoln Ragsdale, testimony, *Hearings before the United States Commission on Civil Rights*, Phoenix, Arizona, Feb. 3, 1962, 48.

105. Roy Yanez Oral History, PHP. Luckingham, *Phoenix*, 178.

106. For the geography of black Phoenix, see Matthew Whitaker, *Race Work: The Rise of Civil Rights in the Urban West* (Lincoln: University of Nebraska Press, 2007).

107. O'Neill, *Working the Navajo Way*, 95.

108. The 1960 census defined deteriorating housing as needing "more repair than would be provided in the course of regular maintenance. It has one or more defects of an intermediate nature that must be corrected if the unit is to continue to provide safe and adequate shelter," while dilapidated housing failed to "provide safe and adequate shelter. It has one or more critical defects, or has a combination of intermediate defects in sufficient number to require extensive repair or rebuilding, or is of inadequate original construction. Critical defects result from continued neglect or lack of repair or indicate serious damage to the structure." U.S. Census Bureau; U.S. Censuses of Population and Housing: 1960. Census Tracts. Final Report PHC(1)-11. U.S. Government Printing Office, Washington, D.C., 1962.

109. 1960 Census of Population and Housing; John Camargo Oral History, PHP; British magazine quote from Bolin et al, "The Geography of Despair: Environmental Racism and the Making of South Phoenix, Arizona, USA," *Human Ecology Review* 12 (2005), 164. Andrew Kopkind, "Modern Times in Phoenix: A City at the Mercy of Its Myths," *New Republic* (November 1965), 15.

110. 1960 U.S. Census of Population and Housing, Phoenix Census Tracts.

111. Camargo Oral History.

112. Ragsdale quotes and accounts of interracial efforts to integrate northern Phoenix in Mary Melcher, "Blacks and Whites Together: Interracial Leadership in the Phoenix Civil Rights Movement," *Journal of Arizona History* 32 (1992), 203.

113. Rev. Bernard Black Oral History; John Camargo Oral History.

114. Sam Mardian, testimony, *US Commission on Civil Rights*, Phoenix, 8.

115. Sugrue, *Origins of the Urban Crisis*, xvi.

116. Heim, "Border Wars."

117. Benjamin Brooks, testimony, *US Commission on Civil Rights*, Phoenix, 53.

118. Kopkind, "Modern Times in Phoenix," 15.

119. Walter Bimson, "The Businessman as Area Developer: Opportunities for Business Leadership in Area Development," Western Area Development Conference, San Francisco, November 17, 1954, Box 29, Folder 254, VNB.

120. Goldwater quoted in Phillips-Fine, *Invisible Hands*, 136.

121. Ralph Burbacher Oral History PHP.

122. Luckingham, *Phoenix*, 193–97.

123. Long Oral History (1987), PHP.

124. Edward Abbey, "The Blob Comes to Arizona," *NYT* 5/16/1976, 184.

125. Long Oral History (2000), PHP.

Chapter 3: Turquoise and Turboprops

1. For the planning and accounts of the Sperry Rand recruiting visit, see *Phoenix Action*, September and December 1955. For the Thunderbirds' origin, duties,

attire, and official titles, see "The Phoenix Thunderbirds," *Phoenix Magazine* (June 1966), 4–7. For the Thunderbirds' attire and recruitment style, see Martin, "The New Millionaires of Phoenix." For further details of the recruitment, see Lara Bickell, "Eugene Pulliam: Municipal Booster," in *The Human Tradition in the American West*, Benson Tong and Regan Lutz, eds. (Wilmington: Scholarly Resources, 2002), 148.

2. Carl Bimson Oral History, VNB; Ralph Staggs Oral History, PHP.

3. For details of the inducements offered to Sperry Rand to locate their aeronautics electronics division in Phoenix, see Michael Konig, "Toward Metropolitan Status: Charter Government and the Rise of Phoenix, Arizona, 1945–1960" (Ph.D. diss, Arizona State University, 1983), 200–202, 214–15; and Luckingham, *Phoenix*, 156–57.

4. Carl Bimson Oral History, VNB. Frank Snell Oral History, PHP; and Konig, "Toward Metropolitan Status," 200–202. For details on the development of Sperry Phoenix's operations, see Hogan Smith, "Awakening the Valley's Sleeping Giant," *Phoenix* (December 1966), 7. Halpert's quotation is from Arizona Public Service Company, *Industry Views: Phoenix and the Valley of the Sun* (Phoenix, 1962), 162.

5. Self, *American Babylon*, 25.

6. Quotes from Bolin et al., "The Geography of Despair," 159–62 For "workscape" as a description of industrial space, see Andrews, *Killing for Coal*, ch. 3. For the historical development of zoning as a tool of racial exclusion, see Freund, *Colored Property*, 45–98.

7. Luckingham, *Phoenix*, 102; Carl Bimson Oral History, VNB; Dean Smith, "Military Bases Everywhere," in *Arizona Goes to War: The Home Front and the Front Lines in World War II*, Dean Smith, ed. (Tucson: University of Arizona Press, 2003).

8. Frank Snell Oral History, VNB; Orme Lewis Oral History, PHP-AHS.

9. Matthew McCoy, "Desert Metropolis: Image Building and the Growth of Phoenix" (Ph.D. diss., Arizona State University, 2000), 41.

10. Fifty-Ninth Fighter Wing History Office, "Luke Field/AFB and 56th Fighter Wing Chronology, 1941–2008" (March 2009) http://www.luke.af.mil /shared/media/document/AFD-110209-028.pdf.

11. Smith, "Military Bases Everywhere."

12. Stephen Shadegg, "The Sun Is Our Fortune," *AH* (Aug. 1943), 7.

13. *Statistics of Electrical Utilities in the United States . . . Privately Owned Companies* and *Statistics of Publicly Owned Electric Utilities*, 1945–52.

14. Abbott, *The Metropolitan Frontier*, 10.

15. Monroe, "Bank Knight in Arizona," 25.

16. Luckingham, *Phoenix* 158–59; Shermer, *Sunbelt Capitalism*, 122–26.

17. "Goodyear Announces Plant," *AR*, 9/21/1940, 1; Horton, *A Survey of Phoenix*.

18. Shermer, *Sunbelt Capitalism*, 89–90.

19. Carl Bimson Oral History; Patrick Downey Oral History, PHP-AHS.

20. Walter Besson Oral History, VNB.

21. Cohen, *Consumer's Republic*, 98–114; Self, *American Babylon*, 61–95; Shermer, "Drafting a Movement: Barry Goldwater and the Rebirth of the Ari-

zona Republican Party," in *Barry Goldwater and the Remaking of the American Political Landscape*, Elizabeth Shermer, ed. (Tucson: University of Arizona Press, 2013).

22. For other works considering the actions of these groups, see Molotch, "The City as a Growth Machine"; Molotch and Logan, *Urban Fortunes*; Kruse, *White Flight*, ch.1; and Lassiter, *The Silent Majority*. For Dallas, see Michael Phillips, *White Metropolis: Race, Ethnicity, and Religion in Dallas, 1841–2001* (Austin: University of Texas Press, 2006). For a more extended consideration of the origins and significance of Charter Government, see Shermer, *Sunbelt Capitalism*.

23. For details of the coordinated efforts of businessmen and politicians to draw defense dollars in the immediate postwar years as a means of buttressing metropolitan economies in other cities in the West, see Lotchkin, *Fortress California*, and Richard Kirkendall, "The Boeing Company and the Military-Metropolitan-Industrial Complex, 1945–1953," *Pacific Northwest Quarterly* 85:4 (Oct. 1994).

24. Kotlanger, "Phoenix, Arizona, 1920–1940," 60–65.

25. McCoy, "Desert Metropolis." For the broader reorientation of the Chamber, see Shermer, "Drafting a Movement," 42.

26. McCoy, "Desert Metropolis," 49–51.

27. Shermer, "Drafting a Movement," 49–50.

28. Frank Snell Oral History, VNB.

29. McCoy, "Desert Metropolis," 100–101.

30. Shermer, *Sunbelt Capitalism*, 79.

31. Shermer, "Drafting a Movement," 50.

32. Joseph Stocker, "Phoenix, City Growing in the Sun," *AH* (April 1957), 36.

33. Patrick Downey Oral History, PHP.

34. Ibid.; "King-Sized Man Hours," *Fortune* (Jan. 1948), 211. For similar advertisements, see Valley of the Sun Club, "So that's your branch office in Arizona's Valley of the Sun," *Fortune* (Dec. 1947), 71; see also *Fortune* (Nov. 1948), 186. For Cronon's explanation of the natural advantages touted in the nineteenth century, see *Nature's Metropolis*, 31–41. For similar ideas of urban development in another city, see Ari Kelman, *A River and Its City: The Nature of Landscape in New Orleans* (Berkeley: University of California Press, 2003).

35. Fannin quoted in Shermer, "Drafting a Movement," 51.

36. Quote from Bickell, "Eugene Pulliam: Municipal Booster," 146. For Pulliam's influence on local politics, see Bickell, "Southwest Sunbelt Booster Eugene C. Pulliam and His Changing Vision of Phoenix, Arizona, 1946–1975" (Ph.D. diss., Pepperdine University, 1975); Rick Perlstein, *Before the Storm: Barry Goldwater and the Unmaking of the American Consensus* (New York: Hill and Wang, 2001), 23–30.

37. For Goldwater's early political actions and their relation to "right-to-work," see Phillips-Fine, *Invisible Hands*, 117–19; and Shermer, "Counter-Organizing the Sunbelt: Right to Work Campaigns and Anti-Union Conservatism, 1943–1958," *Pacific Historical Review* 78 (February 2009), 81–118.

38. For labor's attack on the power of the Chamber, see "Right-to-Work or Starve? *Times* Presents Both Sides," *Arizona Times*, July 18, 1948. M. A. DeFrance Oral History, PHP; Darwin Aycock Oral History, PHP. Thomas Sheridan, *Arizona: A History* (Tucson: University of Arizona Press, 1995), 277.

39. Luckingham, *Phoenix,* 150.

40. Leonard Goodall, "Phoenix: Reformers at Work," in *Urban Politics in the Southwest,* Leonard Goodall, ed. (Tempe, 1967), 114. Amy Bridges, *Morning Glories: Municipal Reform in the Southwest* (Princeton 1997), 32–51.

41. McCoy, "Desert Metropolis," 79–86.

42. Ray Busey Oral History, PHP.

43. Sheridan, *Arizona,* 301; Philip VanderMeer, *Desert Visions and the Making of Phoenix, 1860–2009* (Albuquerque: University of New Mexico Press, 2010), 210–35.

44. Dix Price Oral History; Rhes Cornelius Oral History, PHP.

45. Robert Goldberg, *Barry Goldwater* (New Haven: Yale University Press), 57.

46. Phillips-Fine, *Invisible Hands,* 119.

47. VanderMeer, *Desert Visions,* 235. "Our Rising Taxes," AR, 10/20/1949, 6; "What Our City Needs," AR, 10/21/1949, 6; "Worthy of Confidence," AR, 10/28/1949, 6; "Wasting the City's Cash," AR, 10/22/1949, 6.

48. "Arizona Nuisance Taxes Ripped at Chamber Meet," AR, 10/22/1949, 1.

49. "Move the Barrier," AR, 10/23/1949, 6.

50. For "apple throw," see the bottom of the front page of AR for 10/31, 11/1, 11/2, 11/3, 11/4, 11/5, 11/6, 11/7, all 1949.

51. "CHARTER TICKET SWEEPS CITY," AR, 11/9/1949, 1.

52. Konig, "Toward Metropolitan Status," 74.

53. Jack Kelso, "Phoenix Makes a New Start," *National Municipal Review* 39 (Sept. 1950), 383–94. Konig, "Toward Metropolitan Status," 172.

54. Bridges differentiates between low-income areas, with median family incomes between $4,500 and $5,100, and poor areas, with median incomes below $4,000. Of these communities, the low-income areas were 11.8 percent Latino and 5.1 percent black and had 10.1 percent voter turnout, while poor communities were 39.7 percent Latino and 20.3 percent black and had 10 percent voter turnout. In contrast, middle-income sections of the city were 2.7 percent Latino and 0.1 percent black and voted at a rate of 18.5 percent; affluent sections were 1.7 percent Latino and 0.1 percent black and voted at a rate of 20.7 percent. Bridges, *Morning Glories,* 131–32, 144, 146. Allegations of voter intimidation and excessive enforcement of literacy standards in Phoenix were directed at William Rehnquist in his confirmation hearings for the Supreme Court, see Peter Irons, *Brennan vs. Rhenquist: The Battle for the Constitution* (New York, 1994).

55. Bridges, *Morning Glories,* 150.

56. Monica Perales, *Smeltertown* (Chapel Hill: University of North Carolina Press, 2009), 232.

57. Patrick Downey Oral History, PHP-AHS; Bob Saback Oral History, Box 3, Folder 35, VNB. For the emergence of "business climate" as a description of political economy, see Shermer, *Sunbelt Capitalism,* 147–50.

58. Patrick Downey Oral History.

59. Carl Bimson Oral History. For details of the recruitment of General Electric, Unidynamics, Motorola, and Sperry Rand, see Shermer, *Sunbelt Capitalism,* 248–66.

60. APS, "Industry Views: Phoenix and the Valley of the Sun" (Phoenix: Arizona Public Service, 1962).

61. Luckingham, *Phoenix*, 154.

62. U.S. National Security Council, "NSC 68: United States Objectives and Programs for National Security," April 14, 1950, www.fas.org/irp/offdocs/nsc -hst/nsc-68.htm.

63. Markusen et al., *The Rise of the Gunbelt*, 31. For the strategic and military components of Eisenhower's "New Look," see Campbell Craig and Fredrik Logevall, *America's Cold War: The Politics of Insecurity* (Cambridge: Harvard University Press, 2009), chs. 4–5. For General Electric's defense of "the free enterprise system" in the 1950s, Phillips-Fine, *Invisible Hands*, chs. 5–7.

64. Markusen et al., *Rise of the Gunbelt*, 37.

65. Quotes taken from Peter Gallison, "The War Against the Center," *Grey Room* 4 (Summer 2001), 14–15.

66. "Industry Finds Its Place in the Sun," 3.

67. Valley of the Sun Club, "Arizona's Valley of the Sun is the perfect spot to combine business with pleasure," *Fortune* (Jan. 1948), 211; see also *Fortune* (Dec. 1948), 138. For other promotional ads, frequently placed by power companies, see ads for Georgia Power Company, "Plant the Future in Georgia," *Business Week* (Nov. 11, 1946), 106; Bank of America, "What Does California Hold For You?" *Business Week* (Nov. 3, 1945), 58; "This Summer a City Larger than Detroit Will Move to Colorado," *Fortune*, (Nov. 18, 1948), 5; San Diego Gas & Electric, "San Diego, Where Climate, Labor, and Management Form a Profitable Team," *Business Week* (Nov. 21, 1949), 32; and Iowa Development Commission, "Industry Is Turning to Iowa," *Fortune* (Dec. 4, 1947), 168.

68. Study results reported in "Valley Manufacturing: A Snowball in the Desert," *Phoenix* (February 1964), 4. David Harvey foregrounds urbanization as a process whereby capital is fixed in place to accumulate surplus. See particularly Harvey, "The Urbanization of Capital."

69. Sam Maridan Oral history, PHP.

70. Wesson Barrett Oral History, Box 2, Folder 24, VNB.

71. "National Advertising Committee Reports," Phoenix (Nov. 1965), 6.

72. For the rise of industrial relocation consulting, see Elizabeth Shermer, "'Take Government out of Business by Putting Business into Government': Local Boosters, National CEOs, Experts, and the Politics of Midcentury Capital Mobility," in *What's Good for Business: Business and American Politics since World War II*, Kimberly Philips-Fine and Julian Zelizer, eds. (New York: Oxford University Press, 2012).

73. Snell Oral History PHP.

74. Bickell, "Eugene Pulliam: Municipal Booster," 148; Shermer, *Sunbelt Capitalism*, 255–58.

75. Snell Oral History, PHP.

76. Bickell, "Eugene Pulliam," 149.

77. Shermer, *Sunbelt Capitalism*, 7–12.

78. For this incident in 1961, see Konig, "Toward Metropolitan Status," 263–75.

79. APS, *Annual Report*, 1953.

80. APS, *Industry Views*.

81. As Ronald Tobey demonstrates, private utilities had privileged industrial consumers since the earliest days of the electrical industry, at times discouraging residential consumption for fear it would limit utilities' ability to serve industrial consumers. Tobey, *Technology as Freedom*, 14–25 ; Richard Hirsch explains in detail the importance of industrial consumers in the postwar years. Hirsch, *Technology and Transformation*, 55–72.

82. Federal Power Commission, *Statistics of Electric Utilities . . . Private Utilities*, 1961–70.

83. Comparison compiled from Federal Power Commission, *Federal Power Commission Electric Rate Survey* (Washington D.C.: Government Printing Office, 1950–70).

84. Ibid.

85. FPC, *Statistics of Electric Utilities . . . Privately Owned*, 1947–70; *Statistics of Publicly Owned Electric Utilities*, 1947–70.

86. FPC, *Statistics of Publicly Owned Electric Utilities*, 1954–70.

87. Plant sizes taken from Phoenix Chamber of Commerce, "Annual Report of Manufacturing Increase, 1964" *Phoenix* (January 1965); and from APS, *Industry Views*.

88. Frank Snell Oral History, PHP.

89. FPC, *Statistics of Electric Utilities . . . Privately Owned*, 1947–70; *Statistics of Publicly Owned Electric Utilities*, 1947–70.

90. FPC, *Statistics of Electric Utilities . . . Privately Owned*, 1947–59.

91. APS, *Annual Report*, 1958; "Blackout in South Phoenix," *AR*, 5/14/1957, 3.

92. APS, *Annual Report*, 1960; "Much of City Faces Day-Long Electricity Loss," *AR* 8/19/1959, 1; "Fire at Power Plant Cause of Blackout," *AR* 8/20/1959, 3.

93. Richard Vietor, *Contrived Competition: Regulation and Deregulation in America* (Cambridge: Belknap Press, 1996), 104.

94. In their public statements about their rationales for beginning to utilize coal for generation, neither Arizona Public Service nor the Salt River Project mention limits on the supply of natural gas. Rather, they claim rapid increases in the *cost* of natural gas occurred in the late 1950s, leading the utilities to seek less expensive fuel to keep electricity prices low. In investigating this decision, however, I could find no indication of a rapid increase in gas prices during the 1950s. As Richard Vietor's study of the regulation of El Paso Natural Gas demonstrates, rate changes had to go through a gauntlet of regulatory and judicial review on both the state and federal level, making rapid changes in gas prices unlikely. Vietor portrays the 1950s and 1960s as an era of stable prices, with prices rising only when supply levels begin to drop precipitously in the late 1960s. Vietor, *Contrived Competition*, 105–15. Peter Wiley and Richard Gottlieb indicate that El Paso Natural Gas informed Arizona Public Service not that prices would rise but that it could not guarantee supply. Wiley and Gottlieb, *Empires in the Sun*, 41. For Arizona Public Service's claims about increasing gas prices, see *Annual Report 1961*. For the Salt River Project's claims, see Shadegg, *Century One*, 39.

95. Department of the Interior, Office of the Secretary, "Salt River Project,

Summary of Negotiations on Transmission Arrangements and Wheeling Proposals," February 20, 1958, Box 166, SLU.

96. Hirsch argues that constant increases in supply during the 1950s were regarded as necessary components of interconnections, *Technology and Transformation*, 56–59.

97. Stanford Research Institute, "Study of Future Electrical Generation in the Southwest: Prepared for Arizona Public Service Company," 9/19/1955, SRI Archives, Palo Alto, California. Richard Hirsch's analysis of the postwar electric utility industry has, in fact, demonstrated this very point. *Technology and Transformation*, 68.

98. Vietor, *Contrived Competition*, 74.

99. "Coal Power Utility Unit Planned," *LAT*, December 30, 1957.

100. John Herbert, *Phoenix: Economic Capital of the Great Southwest Sun Country! . . . "Phoenix Is the Driest, Sunniest Resort Area in the United States"* (Phoenix, 1958).

101. Tim Kelly, "The Changing Face of Phoenix," *Arizona Highways* (March 1964), 33.

102. Environmental Protection Agency, "Superfund Site Overview: Motorola, Inc. (52nd Street Site)" http://yosemite.epa.gov/r9/sfund/r9sfdocw.nsf/ViewBy EPAID/azd009004177?OpenDocument. As Aaron Sachs has shown for the case of Silicon Valley, the legacies of environmental pollution from "clean" industries are persistent in many locales. Sachs, "Virtual Ecology: A Brief Environmental History of Silicon Valley," *World Watch* (January/February 1999).

CHAPTER 4: MODERNIZING THE NAVAJO

1. Jones quoted in Marshall Tome, "Coal Mine Will Help Navajo Tribe," *NT* July 27, 1957, 1, 22. "Mining Lease—Tribal Indian Lands, Navajo Tribe of Indians and Utah Construction Company," July 26, 1957, Folder 5015, Box 128, Central Classified Files, 1940–157, Navajo, RG 75, Records of the Bureau of Indian Affairs (hereafter BIACF, Navajos), National Archives and Records Administration, Washington, D.C. On the various names for the landscape of Navajo Mine, see Powell and Long, "Landscapes of Power," in Smith and Frehner, *Indians and Energy*.

2. Quotation from Iverson, *Barry Goldwater, Native Arizonan*, 42–43.

3. Philip Vanderhoof, general manager of Navajo Tribal Utility Authority, quoted in Glaser, *Electrifying the Rural American West*, 168. Paul Jones, quoted in "Tribal Council Meets," *NT*, 8/12/1957, 2.

4. Bureau of Reclamation, *Study of Future Transmission in the West* (Washington, D.C.: Department of the Interior, 1952), RG 115, Records of the Bureau of Reclamation, Transmission Division Records, NARA-D.

5. Hiltzik, *Colossus*, 382–95.

6. Bureau of Reclamation, "Advance Power Plan, 1950–1959," 10/1947, BRTD, 3–3.

7. Ibid., 3–4.

8. Bureau of Reclamation, *A Study of Future Transmission*, xx.

9. Katharine Hamill, "Cheaper Power Through Higher Voltages," *Fortune* June 1959, 141–47.

10. Bureau of Reclamation, *A Study of Future Transmission*, xx.

11. Ibid. This was not the first time a centralized system of coal-fired electrical production had been envisioned. Gifford Pinchot's Giant Power concept, developed in the 1920s, would have remade Pennsylvania's electrical network in much the same way as the Bureau outlined. For Giant Power, see Phillips, *This Land, This Nation*, ch. 1.

12. *A Study of Future Transmission*, xx.

13. United States, Department of Interior, *The Navajo: A Longterm Plan for Navajo Rehabilitation*, (Washington D.C., 1949), vii.

14. Ibid., 23.

15. Press Release, War Assets Administration, Dec. 31, 1947, Box 313, Folder 7, AAIA.

16. James Preston, testimony before House Committee on Public Lands, Subcommittee on Indian Affairs, *Navajo and Hopi Rehabilitation*, Eighty-First Congress, 1st session, April 18, 19, 22, May 16–18, 1949, 73 [hereafter *Navajo-Hopi Rehabilitation Hearings*].

17. O'Neill, *Working the Navajo Way*, 86–87. For the broader experience of Navajos during World War II, see Iverson, *Diné*, 180–205.

18. Quoted in Rosier, *Serving Their Country*, 123.

19. William Warne, *Navajo-Hopi Rehabilitation Hearings*, 29.

20. Ibid., 9.

21. For McNickle's life and career as an activist, see Frederick Hoxie, *This Indian Country: American Indian Activists and the Place They Made* (New York: Penguin, 2012).

22. Kenneth Philp, *Termination Revisited: American Indians on the Trail to Self-Determination, 1933–1953* (Lincoln: University of Nebraska Press, 1999), 83–92.

23. Ruth Kirk to Krug, 11/14/47, Box 313, Folder 7, AAIA.

24. Collier, "Forces of Destruction," *Salt Lake Tribune*, 9/27/49, Box 313, Folder 7, AAIA.

25. Rosier, "'They Are Ancestral Homelands': Race, Place, and Politics in Cold War Native America, 1945–1961," *Journal of American History*, vol. 92, no. 4 (March 2006).

26. William Pemberton, "Truman and the Hoover Commission," *Whistle Stop: The Newsletter of the Harry S. Truman Library Institute* 19 (1991).

27. Will Rogers, Jr., "Starvation Without Representation," *Look*, 2/17/1948, 4–7.

28. Peter Iverson, *The Navajo Nation*, 54.

29. Rosier, *Serving Their Country*, 117.

30. For the politics and policies of the termination era, see Rosier, *Serving Their Country*, 109–60; Kenneth Philp, *Termination Revisited*; Roberta Ulrich, *American Indian Nations from Termination to Restoration* (Lincoln: University of Nebraska Press, 2012); and Donald Fixico, *Termination and Relocation: Fed-*

eral Indian Policy, 1945–1960 (Albuquerque: University of New Mexico Press, 1986).

31. Warne, *Navajo-Hopi Rehabilitation* hearings, 32, 33.

32. Alexander and Dorothea Leighton to Alexander Lesser, 11/14/1947, Box 313, Folder 7, AAIA.

33. For Stewart's plan, see O'Neill, *Working the Navajo Way*, 145.

34. Warne, *Navajo and Hopi Rehabilitation Hearings*, 20.

35. Ibid., 32.

36. O'Neill, *Working the Navajo Way*, 134.

37. A representative of the Arizona Associated Farmers suggested directly to the congressional committee overseeing Rehabilitation that Navajos could replace braceros, whose labor the Mexican government was withholding in a dispute over working conditions and legal safeguards, testifying that, "the Mexican Government has increased its safeguards by requiring a minimum of housing and other things for Mexican nationals, and it has been increasingly difficult for us to get Mexican nationals or to get white labor from further east. Therefore, there is a great deal of labor opportunity for Navajo Indians, or any other Indians, to do this work. I just throw this out, that the need is there." *Navajo and Hopi Rehabilitation Hearings*, 172.

38. O'Neill, *Working the Navajo Way*, xx.

39. Iverson, *Diné*, 205–207; Hoffman and Johnson, *Navajo Biographies*, 215–36. As Richard White argues, such balancing of wage work and pastoralism was a key way of managing risk in a harsh environment. White, *The Roots of Dependency*, ch. 11.

40. Warne to Albert Emerson, 12/8/47, Box 313, Folder 7, AAIA.

41. Alexander and Dorothea Leighton to Alexander Lesser, 11/14/1947, Box 313, Folder 7, AAIA.

42. Sam Ahkeah, Sheely Tso, and Navajo Tribal Council to Richard Welch, Styles Bridges, Hugh Butler, and John Taber, 3/18/1948, Box 313, Folder 7, AAIA.

43. Max Drefkoff, "An industrial program for the Navajo Indian Reservation: a report to the Commissioner of Indian Affairs," Jan. 1948, Box 18, Folder 28, Theodore Hetzel Papers, Fort Lewis College, Durango, Colorado. "Chicagoan Offers Plan to Aid Indian and Businessman," *WP*, 8/27/1947, B2.

44. Ed Ainsworth, "Attempt to 'Sovietize' Navajo Tribes Told," *LAT*, 8/28/1948, p.1; "In Navajoland, Where Indians Fight for Free Enterprise," *AR*, 4/26/1948, 1; Ainsworth, "Indians' Sheep Business Factor in 'Soviet' Plan," *LAT*, 5/1/1948, 2; "U.S. Aide Quits over Navajos," *LAT*, 4/16/1948. For Drefkoff's resignation, see Rosier, *Serving Their Country*, 130–31.

45. Sam Ahkeah, *Navajo and Hopi Rehabilitation Hearings*, 58.

46. Joe Duncan, *Navajo and Hopi Rehabilitation Hearings*, 58.

47. Ibid., 100.

48. Sam Ahkeah, *Navajo and Hopi Rehabilitation Hearings*, 59.

49. Iverson, *Diné*, 190.

50. The best accounts of the infrastructure improvements funded by the act are Iverson, *Diné*, 184–90; and Iverson, *The Navajo Nation*, 55–60. For a summary of the program, see *The Navajo*, 13–49.

51. Harry S. Truman, Veto of S. 1407, 10/17/1949, Box 314, Folder 2, AAIA.

52. "A Bridge Is Burned," *AR*, 10/19/1949, 6.

53. For quotation, see Goldberg, *Barry Goldwater*, 47.

54. Ibid., 74.

55. Ibid., 132.

56. Orme Lewis, "I Was the Great White Father," *SEP* (12/17/1955), 98.

57. John Frank, *Lewis and Roca: A Firm History, 1950–1984* (Phoenix: Lewis and Roca, 1984), 6–7.

58. The classic history of the politics of western public lands is Paul Wallace Gates, *Fifty Million Acres* (Ithaca: Cornell University Press, 1954). For a more recent examination of public land administration and the Taylor Grazing Act, a frequent component of Lewis's legal practice, see Karen Merrill, *Public Lands and Political Meaning: Ranchers, the Government, and the Property between Them* (Berkeley: University of California Press, 2002).

59. Orme Lewis testimony, "Hearing before the Committee on Interior and Insular Affairs, United States Senate, 83d Congress, February 5, 1953" (Washington, D.C.: Government Printing Office, 1953).

60. Lewis, "Use Is the Essence of Conservation," *Pacific Fisherman* 52, 1 (January 1, 1954): 1.

61. Laurence Lee, Speech to National Lumber Manufacturer's Association, 11/13/1952, Box 4, OLP; Lee, "Land Freedom," *American Forests* 59 (Feb 1953), 27.

62. Lewis, "I Was the Great White Father," 98, 100.

63. See, for example, Mark W. T. Harvey, *A Symbol of Wilderness: Echo Park and the American Conservation Movement* (Albuquerque: University of New Mexico Press, 1994).

64. The legacies of such beliefs reached back to the so-called peace policy of the 1870s and 1880s, which saw the eradication of tribal identity as a necessary step toward the incorporation of Indian peoples into modern society. See Frederick Hoxie, *A Final Promise: The Campaign to Assimilate the Indians, 1880–1920* (New York: Cambridge University Press, 1989), and Cathleen Cahill, *Federal Fathers and Mothers: A Social History of the United States Indian Service, 1869–1933* (Chapel Hill: University of North Carolina Press, 2011).

65. Watkins, quoted in Rosier, "'They Are Ancestral Homeland.," On Lewis's role in termination bills, see Fixico, *Termination and Relocation*, 130–35. On the American Indian Research Fund, see Larry Burt, "Factories on Reservations: The Industrial Development Program of Commissioner Glenn Emmons," *Arizona and the West* 19 (Winter, 1977).

66. "Why Are We So Far Behind," Memorandum from Tom Shiya to Bimson and Lewis, undated (1953?) in both Box 3, Folder 5, OLP; and Box 34, VNB.

67. Ibid.

68. Ibid.

69. William H. Kelly, "Suggestions for the Clarification and Solution of Some Indian Administration Problems in Arizona, A Confidential Memorandum Prepared for Richard A. Harvill, Walter Bimson, and Orme Lewis," August 14, 1953, Box 3, Folder 5, OLP.

70. Kelly, "Suggestions for the Clarification . . ."; Shiya, "Why Are We So Far Behind."

71. Bimson to Carl Hayden, 2/16/54, Box 34, Folder 305, VNB.

72. Bimson's report is printed in House Committee on Interior and Insular Affairs, *Survey Report of the Bureau of Indian Affairs*, Committee Print 14, 1/26/1954 (Washington, D.C.: Government Printing Office, 1954). Hereafter, Bimson *BIA Survey*.

73. Larry Burt, "Roots of the Native American Urban Experience: Relocation Policy in the 1950s," *American Indian Quarterly* 10 (Spring 1986), 90.

74. Bimson *BIA Survey*.

75. Orme Lewis to Walter Bimson, 9/17/1953; Walter Bimson to Orme Lewis, 10/14/1953, both Box 35, Folder 317, VNB.

76. Lewis to Bimson, 9/17/1953.

77. Lewis to Goldwater, 5/14/1954, Box 3, Folder 5, OLP.

78. Lewis, "I Was the Great White Father," 99.

79. Ibid.

80. Iverson, *Diné*, 133–36.

81. Iverson, *Diné*, 208.

82. "For Our Navajo People," 39. For Paul Jones's history before becoming chairman, see Iverson, *Diné*, 211–13; Hoffman and Johnson, *Navajo Biographies*, 256–74.

83. R. B. Clay to Commissioner, Bureau of Indian Affairs, 12/13/1956, Central Classified Files, 1940–57, Navajo, Box 143, Folder 3385–56 (part 1), RG 75, NARA.

84. Clinton Anderson, hearing transcript, Joint Committee on Navajo-Hopi Indian Administration, May 21, 1957, contained within letter, Anderson to Rep. Stewart Udall, May 24, 1957, Box 38, SLU.

85. Maurice McCabe, hearing transcript, Joint Committee on Navajo-Hopi Indian Administration, May 21, 1957.

86. For details of the IMLA and the process of negotiation between energy conglomerates and the BIA, see James Allison, "Sovereignty for Survival: American Energy Development and Indian Self-Determination" (Ph.D. diss., University of Virginia, 2013).

87. Pierre Bretey, "Coal: The Giant Revived," *Financial Analysts Journal* 27 (Jan–Feb 1971), 54.

88. For arguments about underpayment, see Lorraine Ruffing, "The Navajo Nation: A History of Dependence and Underdevelopment," *Review of Radical Political Economics* 11 (Summer 1979); as well as Ruffing, "The Navajo Nation;" and "Navajo Mineral Development," *Indian Historian* 11 (Spring 1978), 28–41; Lynn Robbins, "Energy Developments and the Navajo Nation," in *Native Americans and Energy Development*, Joseph Jorgenson, ed. (Cambridge, Mass., 1978), 35–48; and Joseph Jorgenson, "The Political Economy of Native American Energy Business," *Native Americans and Energy Development II*, Jorgenson and Sally Swenson, eds., (Cambridge, Mass., 1984), 10–51. For the counterargument that compares lease rates on Indian lands with those of off-reservation leases, see Brian Morton, "Coal Leasing in the Fourth World," Ph.D. diss., University of California, 1984.

89. Morton, "Coal Leasing in the Fourth World," 124–30.

90. The exact statutory language is as follows: "Mining leases may be made for a specified term not to exceed ten years from the date of approval by the Secretary of the Interior, or his authorized representative, and as much longer as the substances specified in the lease are produced in paying quantities" (IMLA, Part 171.10, Title 25, Code of Federal Regulations).

91. Glaser, *Electrifying the Rural American West*, 159.

92. Larry Burt, "Factories on Reservations," 322–25.

93. Shiya to Lewis and Bimson, "Why We Are So Far Behind."

94. David Kamper, *The Work of Sovereignty: Tribal Labor Relations and Self-Determination at the Navajo Nation* (Santa Fe: SAR Press, 2010), 131.

95. Burt, "Factories on Reservations," 325–26.

96. Glaser, *Electrifying the Rural American West*, 155–69.

97. Jones quoted in Glaser, *Electrifying the Rural American West*, 161–62.

98. Ibid.

99. Bernard DeVoto, "The West: A Plundered Province," *Harper's*, August 1934.

CHAPTER 5: INTEGRATING GEOGRAPHIES

1. Victor Heilweil and Geoffrey Freethey, "Hydrology of the Navajo Aquifer in Southwestern Utah and Northwestern Arizona," *Engineering and Environmental Geology of Southwestern Utah* (1992), 213–24. Daniel Higgins, "The Black Mesa Case Study: A Postaudit and Pathology of Coal-Energy Groundwater Exploitation in the Hopi and Diné Lands, 1968–2008" (Ph.D. diss., Arizona State University, 2011). "Fossil groundwater" is from Cindy Yurth, "Report: Mining Depleted N-Aquifer More than Predicted," *NT* (7/28/2011).

2. For the actions of John Boyden, who secretly represented both the Hopi Tribe and Peabody Coal, see Charles Wilkinson, *Fire on the Plateau: Conflict and Endurance in the American Southwest* (New York: Island Press, 2004).

3. Shirley Powell, *People of the Mesa: The Archaeology of Black Mesa, Arizona* (Tucson 1987); Robert Jerome Glennon, *Water Follies: Groundwater Pumping and the Fate of America's Fresh Waters* (Washington, D.C. 2002), ch. 11; Suzanne Gordon, *Black Mesa: The Angel of Death* (New York 1973). Groundwater pumping amounts from Yurth, "Report," *NT* (7/28/2011).

4. As the previous chapter explained, Arizona Public Service's Four Corners Power Plant was located across the border in New Mexico. Nevertheless, it primarily served APS's customers in Arizona.

5. The phrase "strong transmission system" appears repeatedly in Bureau of Reclamation planning documents in the late 1950s and early 1960s. For examples, see Bureau of Reclamation, "Transmission System Report, Colorado River Storage Project, April 1960," Box 282, Bureau of Reclamation Project Files, Bureau of Reclamation General Records, RG 115, NARA-D.

6. For the increasing importance of groundwater pumping in Western farming, see Donald Worster, *Rivers of Empire*, 148–54, 236–43. For the role of the Bureau of Reclamation in powering groundwater pumping, see Toni Linenberger,

Dams, Dynamos, and Development: The Bureau of Reclamation's Power Program and the Electrification of the West (Denver: Reclamation Bureau, 2002), 158–76.

7. For the formation of the Bureau of Reclamation, see Donald Pisani, *To Reclaim a Divided West* and *Water and American Government*; Norris Hundley, *The Great Thirst*; and Donald Worster, *Rivers of Empire*.

8. The Bureau of Reclamation had first faced the question of how to distribute electricity generated at its dams with the construction of Hoover Dam. As explained in chapter 1, the Bureau solved the problem in that case with a one-time solution of allowing public and private utilities to build transmission lines themselves to the Hoover Dam power plants. For information on the Bureau's preference customer policy and its repayment strategy, see Linenberger, *Dams, Dynamos, and Development*, 14–24, 54–65, 102–34.

9. This estimate of the Salt River Project's electrical load taken from Stephen Shadegg, *Century One*, 33. Hoover Dam was another exception to the Bureau's tendency to concentrate on agricultural consumers. As explained earlier, Hoover's electricity policies are anomalous, considering its early completion date.

10. See chapter 4.

11. For details of the Bureau of Reclamation's transmission system, see Linenberger, *Dams, Dynamos, and Development*, 56–89. I have drawn much of my understanding of how this system worked from R. A. Hore, *Advanced Studies in Electrical Power System Design* (London: Chapman & Hall, 1966).

12. See, for example, the Colorado River Storage Project, U.S. Statutes at Large, Public Law 485, 70 Stat 106, April 11, 1956.

13. Until CRSP, all major Bureau of Reclamation projects had occurred in the Lower Basin states of California, Arizona, and Nevada, with most of the resources of the project going to California. Passed in 1922, the Colorado River Compact divided the Colorado River into Upper and Lower Basins at Lee's Ferry, Arizona, apportioning 7.5 million acre-feet to each basin. See Hundley, *Water and the West*.

14. The literature on this battle between the Sierra Club and the Bureau of Reclamation is extensive. The best treatment is Harvey, *A Symbol of Wilderness*. See also Russell Martin, *A Story that Stands Like a Dam: Glen Canyon and the Struggle for the Soul of the West* (New York: Henry Holt, 1989); Fradkin, *A River No More*; and Reisner, *Cadillac Desert*.

15. Lee Olson, "Power Fight Shakes Reclamation: Electrical Utilities Battle to Forestall Federal Network in Colorado River Basin," *Denver Post*, August 6, 1961, located in Box 170, SLU.

16. For costs and construction plans for the various proposed all-federal systems, see Bureau of Reclamation, "Transmission System Report, Colorado River Storage Project, April 1960," RG 115, Bureau of Reclamation Project Files, Box 282, NARA-D. See also Olson, "Power Fight Shakes Reclamation" for an excellent explanation of the structure of the Bureau's system and the political support of Seaton and Udall for the all-federal system.

17. Olson, "Power Fight Shakes Reclamation."

18. American Electric Council, "Public Power's Red Roots," Box 154, SLU.

For concerns of Arizona Public Service about these power lines, see Walter Lucking, President, Arizona Public Service, to Stewart Udall, August 4, 1961, Box 74,
SLU, and Arizona Public Service, *Annual Report 1961*, 4–5.

19. Olson, "Power Fight Shakes Reclamation." Bureau of Reclamation to
Udall, September 8, 1961, Box 166, SLU. Details of this plan, along with Udall's
disagreement, can be seen in Steward Udall, circular letter to Congress, September 8, 1961, Box 166, SLU.

20. For Udall's earlier belief in public power, see "Constituent Letters," of
March 4, 1957, Box 34, September 8, 1957, Box 35, February 1, 1958, Box 35,
and March 16, 1958, Box 35, SLU.

21. Francis Irist, Tucson, Arizona, to Udall, June 23, 1961, Box 166, SLU.
Somewhat surprisingly for arguably the most influential secretary of the interior
in the postwar era, published biographical material on Stewart Udall is very limited. The best sources are Udall's own book, *The Quiet Crisis* (New York 1963),
and the limited biographical note at the Stewart Udall Manuscript Collection,
University of Arizona Library, Special Collections, Tucson, Arizona. The note is
also available at http://dizzy.library.arizona.edu/branches/spc/sludall/biography
.htm.

22. Bureau of Reclamation, "Transmission System Report, Colorado River
Storage Project, April 1960," RG 115, Bureau of Reclamation Project Files, Box
282, NARA-D.

23. Floyd Dominy, Commissioner of Reclamation, to Udall, September 8,
1961, Box 154, SLU. American Public Power Association, Press Release, September 10, 1961, Box 166, SLU.

24. Steward Udall, circular letter to Congress, September 8, 1961, Box 166,
SLU.

25. Ibid.

26. "Hosmer Denounces Federal Plan," *Arizona Republic*, September 13,
1961, found in Box 170, SLU.

27. Stewart Udall, circular letter to Congress, September 8, 1961, Box 166,
SLU.

28. This division was conceived as so absolute that preference customers were
forbidden from reselling CRSP power to private utilities. An Interior Department
staff memo clarified:

> The marketing criteria for CRSP, as approved by the secretary on 5/18/60,
> stated that project power is not to be sold to a preference customer for sale or
> exchange to a nonpreference customer for resale. This principle, that a prefer-
> ence customer will not be permitted to be a conduit through which private
> utilities obtain government power for resale if needed by preference customers
> for their own purposes, has been adhered to by both Democratic and Re-
> publican Administrations. The only way [a preference customer] might obtain
> CRSP power for resale to private utilities is through waiver by all preference
> customers of their rights.

Staff Memo, Neinberg to Udall "Re: Resale of CRSP Power to Private Utilities,"
January 11, 1962, Box 166, SLU.

29. Olson, "Power Fight Shakes Reclamation."

30. Federal Power Commission, *National Power Survey* (Washington, D.C. 1960), 230.

31. Ibid., 230–50.

32. U.S. Department of the Interior, Office of the Secretary, "Press Release: Interior Department Makes Decision on Colorado River Storage Project Transmission System," Box 166, SLU.

33. "Hosmer Calls Udall Plan Power Grab," *AR*, February 22, 1962.

34. American Public Power Association, Press Release, February 20, 1962, Box 166, Folder 3, SLU.

35. Department of the Interior, Office of the Secretary, "Public Service Company of New Mexico, Summary of Transmission and Interconnection Arrangements," February 20, 1962, Box 166, SLU.

36. Ibid., "Public Service Company of Colorado, Summary of Transmission Interconnection Arrangements," February 20, 1962, Box 166, SLU.

37. Example taken from "Basin Power Plan Looks Sound," *Denver Post*, February 22, 1962.

38. This understanding of the benefits of balancing generation between multiple sources comes from Hore, *Advanced Studies in Electrical Power Systems*, 18–28, and from "Basin Power Plan Looks Sound."

39. Department of the Interior, Office of the Secretary, "Arizona Public Service Company, Summary of Negotiations on Transmission Arrangements and Wheeling Proposals," February 20, 1962, Box 166, SLU.

40. Pascual Gonzales, Phoenix, Arizona, to Udall, June 23, 1962, Box 166, SLU. See also Arizona Public Service, *Annual Report 1962*. For more detail about the way the struggle between APS and SRP influenced the politics of taxation in Phoenix and Arizona at large, see Andrew Needham, "The End of Public Power: The Politics of Place and the Postwar Electric Utility Industry," in *What's Good for Business*, Phillips-Fine and Zelizer, eds.

41. Staff Memo, Neinberg to Udall, Re: Power Line Right-of-Way Approval, December 31, 1962, Box 166, SLU.

42. Walter Lucking, President, Arizona Public Service, to the Bureau of Land Management (copied to Carl Hayden, Barry Goldwater, John Rhodes, Morris Udall, and George Senner), January 23, 1963, Box 166, SLU.

43. Ibid.

44. Quote and photo taken from "Western Utilities Intend to Develop Facilities Jointly," *WSJ*, September 23, 1964, 2.

45. The initial members of WEST Associates were Arizona Public Service, El Paso Electric, Nevada Power, the Public Service Company of New Mexico, the Public Service Company of Colorado, San Diego Gas and Electric, Sierra Pacific Power, Southern California Edison, Tucson Gas and Electric, and Utah Power and Light. Later the same day, the Los Angeles Department of Water and Power joined WEST; later that year, the LADWP was joined by Burbank (Calif.) Public Service, Glendale (Calif.) Public Service, Pasadena Municipal Light and Power, and the Imperial Irrigation District. For accounts of the press conference announcing WEST, see Gene Smith, "10 Utilities in 9 Western States Map a $10.5

Billion Expansion," *NYT*, September 23, 1964, 67; "Western Utilities Intend to Develop Facilities Jointly," *WSJ*, September 23, 1964, 2; "Utilities Plan Massive Growth," *NT*, October 1, 1964, 1.

46. Smith, "10 Utilities in 9 Western States Map a $10.5 Billion Expansion."

47. While the Los Angeles Department of Power and Water served Los Angeles proper, Southern California Edison supplied the rest of the Los Angeles basin and Orange County. For details on the electrical systems of Southern California, see Williams, *Energy and the Making of Modern California*.

48. "Western Utilities Intend to Develop Facilities Jointly."

49. For the growth of generating capacity in the late 1960s, see Richard Hirsch, *Technology and Transformation*.

50. The utilities participating in the Four Corners expansion were Southern California Edison (48 percent), Arizona Public Service (15 percent), the Public Service Company of New Mexico (15 percent), Tucson Electric Power (10 percent), and El Paso Electric (10 percent). The Salt River Project would later purchase generating capacity from Tucson Electric Power, El Paso Electric, and PSC–New Mexico. See "Western Utilities Announce Power Plant Expansion," *WSJ*, November 11, 1964, 13.

51. Hirsch, *Technology and Transformation*, 89–104.

52. "Western Utilities Announce Power Plant Expansion."

53. Glennon, *Water Follies*, ch. 11; "So Cal Edison Announces New Power Plant," *Los Angeles Times*, December 12, 1964, 3.

54. "Four Corners Power Plant Begun," *Albuquerque Journal*, October 12, 1966, 1.

55. "Udall Sorry Utilities Kept WEST Secret from Interior," *Grand Junction Daily Sentinel* (Grand Junction, Colorado), October 11, 1964, Box 166, SLU.

56. Arizona Public Service, *Annual Report*, 1963.

57. I could find no direct evidence stating that WEST's power-pooling plan was designed to avoid the Department of the Interior's right-of-way rules. However, the plan did render the potential use of those lines moot.

58. "Udall Sorry Utilities Kept WEST Secret from Interior."

59. While residential use increased 1,000 kwh approximately every five years, agricultural use increased 1,960 kwh during that same time. Federal Power Commission, *National Power Survey 1964* (Washington, D.C. 1964).

60. Bureau of Reclamation, "Transmission System Report, Colorado River Storage Project, April 1960," Bureau of Reclamation Project Files, Box 282, NARA-D.

61. Harvey, *A Symbol of Wilderness*, 343.

62. "Udall Sorry Utilities Kept WEST Secret from Interior."

63. James Henderson, Assistant Secretary, Federal Power Commission to Bureau of Land Management, February 26, 1963, Box 166, SLU.

64. *National Power Survey 1964*, 45.

65. Ibid., 46–49.

66. Bureau of Reclamation, Office of the Secretary, "WEST Associates, Summary of Transmission Interconnection Arrangements," October 13, 1965, Box 162, SLU.

67. Salt River Project, "Press Release: Salt River Project to Join WEST Associates," October 13, 1965, Box 156, SLU.

68. "Udall Pledges Cooperation with Utilities: Prophecies Great Future," AR, June 24, 1965.

69. "Four Corners Power Plant Begun."

70. "Udall Pledges Cooperation with Utilities."

71. "Lighting the West," Popular Mechanics (November 5, 1967), 34. Box 200, SLU.

72. On the Pacific Northwest–Pacific Southwest Intertie, see Department of the Interior, Office of the Secretary, "Press Release: Pacific Northwest–Pacific Southwest Intertie Arrangement Complete," Box 182, SLU; "Udall Discloses Plan for Power Intertie in West," Wall Street Journal, June 26, 1964, 5; "Northwest, Southwest to Begin Unique Seasonal Power Swap," The Oregonian, September 20, 1967, 3.

73. Raymond Moley, "A New Electric Age," Newsweek (May 15, 1967), 96.

74. The story of the Mercury astronauts seeing the plume of Four Corners comes from Alvin M. Josephy, Jr., "Kaiparowits: The Ultimate Obscenity," Audubon 78 (March 1976): 64–90.

CHAPTER 6: THE LIVING RIVER

1. "The High Cost of Arizona," NYT, 5/18/1966, 18.

2. U.S. Bureau of Reclamation. Pacific Southwest Water Plan (Washington D.C.: Government Printing Office, 1963).

3. Richard White emphasizes that a bureaucratic mindset in which production itself and not social demand formed the rationale for projects drove Reclamation's postwar planning. See White, The Organic Machine, 34–50.

4. Hundley, The Great Thirst, 304–305; see also Rich Johnson, The Central Arizona Project, 1918–1968 (Tucson: University of Arizona Press, 1977), chs. 2–4.

5. Hundley argues that the decision was based on a fundamental misunderstanding of the Boulder Canyon Act, which had included a division of the lower basin's water that was merely suggestive, rather than binding. The Great Thirst, 306. On the litigation of Arizona v. California, see Hundley, "Clio Nods: Arizona v. California and the Boulder Canyon Act—A Reassessment," Western Historical Quarterly (January 1972).

6. U.S. Department of Interior, Bureau of Reclamation, "Pacific Southwest Water Plan," I-3-I-6, Box 174, SLU.

7. For the importance of this boundary, see Martin, A Story that Stands Like a Dam, 235–38.

8. Grand Canyon National Park Act of 1919 (40 Stat. 1175).

9. Wayne Akin, Chairman, Arizona Interstate Stream Commission, and C. A. Calhoun, Chairman, Arizona Power Authority, to Paul Fannin, Governor, Arizona, February 1, 1961, Box 166, SLU. The Federal Power Act of 1920 granted authority to the Federal Power Commission to regulate dam construction on interstate rivers.

10. Stewart Udall to Carl Hayden, June 12, 1963, Box 166, SLU.

11. "Introduction: The Pacific Southwest," *Pacific South West Water Plan*, I-1–I-6.

12. U.S. Bureau of Reclamation, "Introduction: The Pacific Southwest," *Pacific South West Water Plan*, I-1, I-4; "Chapter I: The Power Market," 7.

13. See, for example, "Central Arizona Project," *AR*, January 2, 1963, 4; and "Pass CAP Now," *AR*, January 15, 1963, 4.

14. "Pass CAP Now," *AR*, January 15, 1963, 4.

15. "Human Beings Are Valuable Too," *Arizona Daily Star*, June 17, 1966.

16. Francois Leydet, *Grand Canyon: Time and the River Flowing* (San Francisco: Sierra Club Books, 1964).

17. Brower, "Preface," *Time and the River Flowing*, vi.

18. For details of this campaign, see Robert Righter, *The Battle over Hetch Hetchy: America's Most Controversial Dam and the Birth of Modern Environmentalism* (New York: Oxford University Press, 2006).

19. On the Echo Park controversy, see Martin, *A Story that Stands Like a Dam*, 46–72; Harvey, *A Symbol of Wilderness*.

20. Wallace Stegner, *This Is Dinosaur: The Echo Park Country and Its Magic Rivers* (New York: Knopf, 1956), vii.

21. Lewis, "I Was the Great White Father," 98.

22. David Brower, *Glen Canyon: The Place No One Knew* (San Francisco: Sierra Club Books, 1963), 7.

23. Martin, *A Story that Stands Like a Dam*, 184.

24. Robert W. Jasperson, General Counsel, Conservation Law Society of America, "Grand Canyon and the Law, Prepared for the Sierra Club, David Brower, Executive Director," Aug., 25, 1963. Otis (Dock) Marston Papers, Box 209, "Sierra Club" Folder, Henry E. Huntington Library, San Marino, California.

25. U.S. Department of Interior, National Park Service, "Appendix to and Evaluation of Pacific Southwest Water Plan," Box 174, SLU.

26. Rich Johnson, "Dams are for People . . ." *Tucson Sun*, April 30, 1965, 2.

27. Leydet, *Time and the River Flowing*, 52.

28. Ibid., 84.

29. Ibid., 85.

30. I draw this analysis from Martha Sandweiss's writing about the intersection of photography and narrative. Sandweiss, *Print the Legend: Photography and the American West* (New Haven: Yale University Press, 2002), 6–9, 35–36.

31. Brower, *The Place No One Knew*, 15.

32. Leydet, *Time and the River Flowing*, 19.

33. Martin, *A Story that Stands Like a Dam*, 248.

34. "Grand Canyon Not for Sale!" *NYT*, 12/20/1964, 12.

35. Russel Werneken, letter to the editor, "Reader Says Sierra Club Wants a Private Canyon," *AR*, 4/1/1966, 4.

36. Floyd Richardson, letter to the editor, *AR*, 6/14/1965, 6.

37. Robert Ashley, letter to the editor, *AR*, 12/18, 1965, 5. As Jared Farmer has noted, Floyd Dominy, director of the Bureau of Reclamation, helped create such notions of the dam's recreational, as well as utilitarian benefits. Farmer, *Glen*

Canyon Dammed: Inventing Lake Powell and the Canyon Country (Tucson: University of Arizona Press, 2004).

38. Editorial, "Nailing a False Statement about the Grand Canyon," *Arizona Daily Star*, 6/20/1966, 6.

39. "Barry, Swinging Late, Hits Hardest at Canyon Forum," *AR*, 4/1/1966, 1.

40. Editorial, "Clearing the Air," *AR*, 6/26/1966, 5.

41. Johnson, "Dams are for People," *AR*, June 29, 1966, 5.

42. Editorial, "A Few People Make a Lot of Noise," *AR*, July 29, 1966, 6.

43. Editorial, "Human Beings Are Valuable Too," *Arizona Daily Star*, June 17, 1966.

44. "A Few People Make a Lot of Noise."

45. "Nailing a False Statement about the Grand Canyon."

46. Editorial, "Fanatics to Subdue," *AR*, 6/16/1966, 3.

47. Leydet, *Time and the River Flowing*, 132–33.

48. Ibid., 135.

49. *Outside Magazine*, for example, wrote in its February 2001 obituary profile of David Brower, "Full-page ads in The New York Times and The Washington Post are now standard weapons for enviro campaigns, but no one had thought of using advertising as a cannonade before Brower. (And what ads! When the feds suggested the proposed Grand Canyon dams would let tourists float closer to the cliffs, the Sierra Club asked, "SHOULD WE ALSO FLOOD THE SISTINE CHAPEL SO TOURISTS CAN GET NEARER THE CEILING?" Game over.)" Bruce Barcott, "Our Son of a Bitch," *Outside Magazine* (February 2001), 23–27.

50. For the advertisement, see display ad, *NYT*, 8/27/1966, 11; see also same day edition of *Washington Post*, 15; *San Francisco Chronicle* and *Los Angeles Times*, pages unknown. The advertisement was actually the third similar advertisement that the Sierra Club had run in those newspapers. The first suggested that the damming of the Grand Canyon would open up all other national parks to resource development; the second called on Secretary Udall to cancel the dams. The first advertisement also led Morris Udall to request that the Internal Revenue Service investigate the Sierra Club's tax exemption, which eventually resulted in the Sierra Club's loss of that exemption and a resulting rise in membership from people objecting to Udall's and the IRS's tactics. See Martin, *A Story that Stands Like a Dam*, 248–56; "I.R.S. Threatens Sierra Club," *NYT*, 6/12/1966; and "The Sierra Club Case," *NYT* 12/20/1966. For the historical association of America's natural wonders with European masterworks, see William Cronon, "The Trouble with Wilderness, or Getting Back to the Wrong Nature;" and Marguerite Shaffer, *See America First: Tourism and National Identity* (Washington, DC: Smithsonian, 2001).

51. Ethan Thorney (name partially illegible on original) to Ottis [*sic*] Peterson, Assistant Commissioner of Reclamation, 10/4/1966, Box 169, SLU; Ben Yellin, Bakersfield, California, to Stewart Udall, Secretary of the Interior, 8/12/1966, Box 169, SLU; George James, Rochester, New York, to Udall, 12/22/1966, Box 169, SLU. For more such letters, see Box 169, SLU.

52. For various versions of these forms, see Box 168, SLU.

53. Edith Selbo to Orren Beatty, Assistant to the Secretary of Interior, 8/9/1966, Box 169, SLU. All underlining present in original letter.

54. See, for example, Abbey, "The Second Rape of the West," in *The Journey Home*.

55. For this exchange, see Martin, *A Story that Stands Like a Dam*, 264.

56. U.S. House, Committee on Public Lands, Subcommittee on Irrigation and Reclamation, *Lower Colorado River Basin Project: Hearings before the Subcommittee on Irrigation and Reclamation*. 89th Congress, 2nd sess. 5/6/1966.

57. For Saylor's role in the Grand Canyon controversy, see Thomas G. Smith, *Green Republican: John Saylor and the Preservation of America's Wilderness* (Pittsburgh: University of Pittsburgh Press, 2006), 180–221.

58. Walter Heller, Chairman, President's Council on Economic Advisors, to Philip Hughes, Assistant Director for Legislative Reference, Bureau of the Budget, 4/3/1964, Box 167, SLU.

59. Ibid.

60. The Bureau of Reclamation had calculated the long-term repayment rates using "the weighted average of outstanding long-term Treasury bonds, which responds very sluggishly to changes in market conditions. This runs directly counter to the principle . . . that interest rate charges be directly related to market conditions." Ibid.

61. Ibid.

62. Pearson, 83–86. For "economy bloc," see Morris Udall, circular letter to Congress, 3/1/1968, Box 169, MKU.

63. For these objections, see Byron Pearson, *Still the Wild River Runs: Congress, the Sierra Club and the Fight to Save the Grand Canyon* (Tucson: University of Arizona Press, 2002), 88–95; and Martin, *A Story that Stands Like a Dam*, 224–64.

64. For the details of these legislative developments, see Pearson, *Still the Wild River Runs*, 124–80.

65. Morris Udall to John K. Rhodes, Legislative Memorandum, 4/22/1966, Box 169, MKU.

66. Pearson, *Still the Wild River Runs* 158–79; Martin, *A Story that Stands Like a Dam*, 260–68; for one such editorial, see "Spending in West Pays off For US," *Denver Post*, July 25, 1966, 15.

67. Brower revealed that Reclamation economists had failed to eliminate their estimate of evaporation from the reservoir at Echo Park in their evaluation of a CRSP built with only Glen Canyon Dam. Martin, *A Story*, 63. As Brian Balogh argues, scientists and technical experts played a major role in federal agencies throughout the Cold War. As a key part of what Balogh calls the "prominstrative state," experts set agendas and made policy, as well as providing vital support for legislation. Expert confusion, he argues, created a power vacuum. Brian Balogh, *Chain Reaction: Expert Debate and Public Participation in American Commercial Nuclear Power, 1945–1975* (New York, 1991).

68. Norman Brooks, Vito Vanoni, and Frederick Raichlen, California Institute of Technology, Pasadena, California, to House Subcommittee on Irrigation and Reclamation, 5/14/1966, Box 158, SLU. See also testimony by Brooks, Vanoni, and Raichlen in *Lower Colorado River Basin Project: Hearings before the Subcommittee on Irrigation and Reclamation* [hereafter *Lower Colorado River Basin Project Hearings*].

69. Alan Carlin, Rand Corporation, testimony, *Lower Colorado River Basin Project Hearings*

70. Brooks, Vanoni, and Raichlen, *Lower Colorado River Basin Project Hearings.*

71. Floyd Dominy, Commissioner of Reclamation, *Lower Colorado River Basin Project Hearings.*

72. Ibid.

73. Carlin, testimony, *Lower Colorado River Basin Project Hearings.* For the celebration of dams as unique accomplishments of American engineering, see Nye, *American Technological Sublime.*

74. For this request, see United States, Department of the Interior, Office of the Secretary, "Request for Study—Water and Power Division," 10/23/1966, Box 166, SLU.

75. The renamed dam represented part of a larger effort by dam supporters to garner support for the projects as providing economic opportunity for the Southwest's native peoples. In an agreement negotiated in 1965, the Hualapai Tribe would receive $93 million in rent payments by 2047, would be allowed to buy power at the lowest market rates, and would control the revenue generated by tourists using the south shore of the reservoir. Wayne Aspinall wrote that it would be a good strategic move to "have an Indian, preferably the Chief of the Hualapai Tribe . . . testify . . . in support of the bill." Such testimony, Aspinall believed, would "put those who opposed Bridge Canyon Dam in the position of being anti-Indian." See Byron Pearson, "'We Have Almost Forgotten How to Hope': The Hualapai, the Navajo, and the Fight for the Central Arizona Project, 1944–1968," *Western Historical Quarterly* 31 (Autumn 2000), 297–316.

76. U.S. Department of Interior, "Analysis of Alternative Plans, Colorado River Basin Project," December 1966? [date questioned on original], Box 169, SLU; U.S. Office of the Secretary of the Interior, Stewart Udall, "Draft Memorandum for the President, Subject, Colorado River Basin Project: The Best Alternatives," unknown date, Box 174, SLU. Since this latter memorandum summarizes the conclusions of the former report, I assume it was written in December 1966. James McMillan to Morris Udall, 6/15/1966, Box 134, MKU. For Wayne Aspinall's authority over Western water projects, see Stephen Sturgeon, *The Politics of Western Water: The Congressional Career of Wayne Aspinall* (Tucson: University of Arizona Press, 2002).

77. "Analysis of Alternative Plans, Colorado River Basin Project"; Udall, "Draft Memorandum for the President"; Walter Lucking to Stewart Udall, 11/22/1966, Box 169, SLU; Udall to Lucking, 12/11/1966, Box 169, SLU; Lucking to Udall, 1/12/1967, Box 169, SLU.

78. U.S. Department of the Interior, Office of the Secretary, "Press Release: Revised Lower Colorado River Plan Announced by Udall," 2/1/1967, Box 167, SLU; see also "U.S. Drops Plans to Build 2 Dams in Grand Canyon," *NYT*, 2/2/1967.

79. The other utilities drawing power from Navajo Generating Station were the Salt River Project (21.7 percent), the Los Angeles Department of Water and Power (21.2 percent), Arizona Public Service (14 percent), Nevada Power (11.3 percent), and Tucson Electric Power (7.5 percent). Lucking to Udall, March 23, 1967, Box 169, SLU.

80. See, for example, "Analysis of Alternative Plans, Colorado River Basin Project"; and U.S. Department of the Interior, Office of the Secretary, Assistant Secretary for Water and Power Development to Udall, "Memorandum: Colorado River Basin Project—Alternative Plans," 1/26/1967, Box 169, MKU.

81. For quote, see Martin, *A Story that Stands Like a Dam*, 268.

82. For reaction to the announcement, see "U.S. Drops Plans to Build 2 Dams in Grand Canyon," *NYT*, 2/2/1967, 1. Martin, *A Story that Stands Like a Dam*, 283.

83. For a good summary of the broad support for the bill, see Morris Udall, circular letter to Congress, 3/11/1968, Box 169, MKU. Udall listed the only opponents of the bill as John Saylor, who was opposed not to the CAP but to some additional projects that were tacked onto the bill; "the Northwest raiders," a set of Northwestern representatives still suspicious that the bill would open the door to the export of water from the Pacific Northwest; and the economy bloc.

84. Leydet, *Time and the River Flowing*, 8.

85. Both quotes ibid., 134.

86. Brower, testimony, *Lower Colorado River Basin Project Hearings*.

87. For more on this enduring environmental faith in technological solutions, see Andrew Kirk, *Counterculture Green: The Whole Earth Catalog and American Environmentalism* (Lawrence: University Press of Kansas, 2007).

88. "Grand Canyon Saved," *Washington Post*, 2/2/1967; 33.

89. "Victory for Grand Canyon," *NYT*, 2/2/1967, 34.

90. "Udall's Decision," *AR*, 2/2/1967, 17.

91. Hyde, quoted in Charles Hagen, "Land and Landscape," *Aperture* 120 (Late Summer 1990), 16.

92. John McPhee, *Encounters with the Archdruid* (New York: Noonday Press, 1971).

CHAPTER 7: A PIECE OF THE ACTION

1. I use "imagine" here deliberately, in order to evoke Benedict Anderson's argument that nations do not naturally come into being, but are actively created in the language historical actors use in discussing them. I will later contend that MacDonald used the political imagining of the potential power of a Navajo state to attempt to win support for his program from Navajos and concessions from power companies. Benedict Anderson, *Imagined Communities: Reflections on the Origins and Spread of Nationalism* (London: Verso, 1983).

2. Statistics on mining wages and employment from "Black Mesa Mine, Peabody Coal Co.," and "Navajo Mine, Utah Int'l Co.," Ephemera Collection, AHF. Four Corners' wages and employment drawn from "Nakai Delivers Inaugural," *NT*, 1/16/1967, 1. On the creation of Navajo Community College, see Wayne Stein, "Tribal Colleges and Universities: Supporting the Revitalization in Indian Country," *Tradition and Culture in the Millennium: Tribal Colleges and Universities*, Linda Sue Wagner and Gerald Gipp, eds., (Charlotte: Information Age

Publishing, 2009), 20. The *Navajo Times* reported circulation of fifteen thousand on its masthead for 1968.

3. Iverson, *Diné*, 226–30.

4. "Industrial Development of the Navajo Reservation," memorandum prepared for BIA Commissioner Roger Bennett, Box 6, Records of the Office of the Commissioner of Indian Affairs, Office Files of Commissioner Robert L. Bennett, 1966–69, RG 75, NARA (hereafter CIA-RLB).

5. Demands to locate operations on reservation land had killed negotiations earlier that year to build a BVD textile mill. For details of negotiations, see weekly "Navajo Reports" from BIA Commissioner Bennett to Interior Secretary Udall between 7/1/1966 and 9/23/1966, Box 6, CIA-RLB.

6. Text of Nakai inaugural contained in Bennett to Udall, 2/21/1967 Box 6, CIA-RLB.

7. For industrial recruitment, see reports in *NT* on 2/15/1968, 6/23/1968, and 3/18/1969. For mining operations, see "Mining Brings New Economic Activity," *NT*, 4/20/1969.

8. "We Will Not Surrender Black Mesa," *DBH*, Oct. 1970, 7.

9. "The Rape of Black Mesa," November 1971; "You Are Being Robbed!!," June 1970; "The Sacred Mountain Will Die," Feb, 1971; "Clean Up Your Act, Honkey," Nov. 1970, Death's Head cartoon, Nov. 1971, all *DBH*.

10. For analysis of internal colonialism by native scholars, see Vine Deloria, Jr., and Clifford Lytle, *The Nations Within: The Past and Future of American Indian Sovereignty* (New York: Pantheon, 1984); Jodi Byrd, *The Transit of Empire: Indigenous Critiques of Colonialism* (Minneapolis: University of Minnesota Press, 2011); and the essays in *The State of Native America: Genocide, Colonization and Resistance*, M. Annette Jaimes, ed. (Boston: South End Press, 1992).

11. Bradley Shreve, *Red Power Rising: The National Indian Youth Council and the Origins of Native Activism* (Albuquerque: University of New Mexico Press, 2011), 140–211.

12. Ibid., 140.

13. Herbert Blatchford Oral History, American Indian Oral History Collection, University of New Mexico Library Special Collections.

14. Shreve, *Red Power Rising*, 156–80.

15. "Dineh for Justice Responds," *NT*, October 3, 1968.

16. "Who Is *Diné Baa-Hani*," *DBH*, February 1969, 3; Shreve, *Red Power Rising*, 185.

17. "Dineh for Justice!" *NT*, 9/20/1968.

18. "Indians Against Exploitation," quoted from David Salmanson, "Facing Mount Taylor," unpublished manuscript in author's possession, 200–20.

19. Navajo John, "Supernavajo in Gradgeation or Quit-chation," *DBH*, May 1970.

20. Supernavajo in Gradgeation or Quit-chation!!" Such comparisons with African and Mexican Americans were rare in the *Navajo Times*, which more frequently portrayed African Americans as a counterpoint to Navajos. African Americans, especially urban African Americans, were portrayed in that paper mainly through reference to rioting and lawbreaking. During the early 1960s,

the *Navajo Times* characterized the civil rights movement as chaotic and illegal compared to the legal and legislative efforts of Native Americans to gain greater recognition. The paper went so far as to accuse African American civil rights workers of utilizing Native American grievances to gain their own political ends. *Diné Baa-Hané* avoided this rhetoric and adopted many of the terms utilized by black nationalists ("honkey," "the Man").

21. This critique is most evident in early Chicano historiography. See Rodolfo Acuna, *Occupied America: The Chicanos Struggle toward Liberation* (Albuquerque 1972).

22. John Redhouse, letter to the editor, *NT*, September 10, 1970.

23. Orville McKinney, "Giant Powerplants Post Threat to the Beauty of Navajoland," *DBH*, September 1970.

24. Esther Patrick, letter to the editor, *NT*, September 3, 1970.

25. Caleb Johnson, letter to the editor, *NT*, October 22, 1969. In this letter, Johnson indicates some of the anger of traditional leaders who refused to recognize the authority of the Hopi Tribal Council. As Charles Wilkinson has demonstrated, the Hopi Tribal Council was virtually created by John Boyden, the Hopi Tribe's lawyer. Wilkinson has discovered that at the same time Boyden worked for the Hopi Tribe, he also worked for Peabody Coal, a staggering conflict of interest that Wilkinson has argued led to a lease unduly favorable to Peabody. Part of the Peabody lease area lay on land claimed by both the Navajo and Hopi Tribes, a conflict that would lead to a long-running land dispute throughout the 1970s and 1980s. Wilkinson, *Fire on the Plateau*.

26. Such critiques can be seen in Esther Patrick's letter; the manifesto of Dineh for Justice!, and in many articles in *Diné Baa-Hani*.

27. Douglas Dunlap, letter to the editor, *NT*, November 5, 1970; William Beaver, letter to the editor, *NT*, June 4, 1970; and Michael Gruber, letter to the editor, *NT*, July 8, 1971.

28. "They're Just Saying That," *DBH*, September 1970.

29. "Profits vs. Preservation," *NT*, September 24, 1970.

30. Louis George, letter to the editor, *NT*, June 18, 1970.

31. Betty Boyd, letter to the editor, *NT*, September 10, 1970.

32. Louis Rogers, letter to the editor, *NT*, June 18, 1970.

33. Peter MacDonald, "Text of MacDonald's Inaugural Address," *NT*, January 7, 1971.

34. MacDonald was essentially an auxiliary member of the celebrated Code Talker regiment. He never actually served with the group but was still associated with it. Iverson, *Diné*, 246.

35. Iverson, *Diné*, 246–47; Peter MacDonald, with Ted Schwarz, *The Last Warrior: Peter MacDonald and the Navajo Nation* (New York: Crown, 1993).

36. "The Candidates for Chairman," *NT*, October 17, 1970. Ironically, MacDonald was borrowing much of this populist language from Nakai, whose 1963 campaign had established a new populist language for appealing to voters and who had begun insisting on the use of "Navajo Nation." Described by Peter Iverson as "the first modern Navajo politician" for his ability to use the media to forge a direct bond between himself and Navajo, Nakai had argued that the tribal

government in Window Rock had become remote from "the people" and that Navajo politicians relied too much on non-Navajo experts. Iverson, *Diné*, 228.

37. I base this conclusion on a comparison of two speeches reprinted in the *NT*: "MacDonald Speaks in Kayenta," *NT*, September 18, 1970; and "Pete Addresses Crowd," *NT*, October 8, 1970. The latter speech was given in Window Rock.

38. "Election Returns," *NT*, November 11, 1970.

39. "Opposes Leasehold Tax: Pete Talks in Phoenix," *NT*, March 4, 1971.

40. "MacDonald Warns Against Continued Exploitation of Indian Energy Resources," *NT* January 6, 1972.

41. "Indian Tribes Must Get Fair Return for Resources," *NT*, April 22, 1973.

42. See A. Wolff, "Showdown at Four Corners," *Saturday Review* (6/3/72), 29–41; R. J. Ashton, "Black Sky over the Southwest," *National Parks and Conservation Magazine* (October 1971), 25–28; "High Price of Supplying Power," *Business Week* (June 12, 1971), 63–64; "Bad Day at Black Mesa, Furor over Four Corners Plant," *Newsweek* (June 7, 1971), 39.

43. "Navajo Learns of Ecology from White Man's Smog," January 29, 1971; and "Navajos Learn White Man's Smoke Signal," January 30, 1971, both *Kansas City Times*.

44. Fern Morgan, Overland Park, KS to BMG, 2/5/71; Michael and Merly Domina, Chicago, to BMG, 12/11/70; Douglas Molitor, New York to BMG, udt.; Eric Karlstrom, Flagstaff, to BMG 2/18/71; all Box 194, Folder 2, BMG. Letters about energy development in Box 194, Folder 2; Box 195, Folder 24; Box 186, Folder 11; Box 339, Folder 15; Box 188, Folder 2; Box 336, Folder 15; and Box 290, Folder 10, BMG.

45. "Navajos Learn White Man's Smoke Signal," January 30, 1971, *Kansas City Times*.

46. "MacDonald Testifies in Washington," *NT*, March 24, 1972.

47. "In Washington Speech Chairman Outlines Resources Development Plan," *NT*, October 5, 1974.

48. "MacDonald Names Major Sources of Future Tribal Revenue," *NT*, July 18, 1974.

49. For accounts of the energy crisis of the early 1970s, see Vietor, *Energy Policy in America since 1945: A Study of Business-Government Relations* (New York: Cambridge University Press, 1987); Paul Sabin, "Crisis and Continuity in US Oil Politics, 1965–1980," and Tyler Priest, "The Dilemmas of Oil Empire," both *Journal of American History* 99 (June 2012). For political demands to speed domestic energy production, see Environmental Protection Agency, "EPA Position Paper on the Energy Crisis," January 1974, Box 128, SLU.

50. "The Navajos and the National Energy Crunch," *NT*, February 17, 1972.

51. For the development of OPEC in relation to state power, see Coronil, *The Magical State*, 52–56.

52. Jim Benally, "Navajos, Arab-Style, to Cash in on Resources," *NT*, March 13, 1974.

53. "MacDonald Announces CERT Terms," *NT*, December 12, 1975.

54. Ibid.

55. See Wilkinson, *American Indians, Time, and the Law: Native Societies in a Modern Constitutional Democracy* (New Haven: Yale University Press, 1988) for a full account of the development of modern legal sovereignty. For the evolution of federal policy from termination to self-determination, see George P. Castile, *To Show Heart: Native American Self-Determination and Federal Indian Policy, 1960–1975* (Tucson: University of Arizona Press, 1998).

56. "MacDonald Announces CERT Terms."

57. "MacDonald Named CERT President," *NT*, April 15, 1976.

58. "The Emerging Navajo Nation Theme of Second Inaugural," *NT*, January 12, 1975.

59. U.S. Commission on Civil Rights, *The Navajo Nation: An American Colony* (Washington, D.C.: Government Printing Office, 1975), 7, 10.

60. Nixon, "Clean Energy Message," June 4, 1971, in Vietor, *Energy Policy in America since 1945*, 236.

61. "Gasification: A Crucial Issue," *NT*, January 23, 1975.

62. Ibid.

63. "Big Potential Seen in Coal Gasification Plants," *NT*, February 15, 1973.

64. Ibid.

65. "Pete Testifies," *NT*, February 18, 1975.

66. "MacDonald Discusses Tribe's Fiscal Status; Urges Economic Development," *NT*, July 1, 1976.

67. "Gasification: A Crucial Issue"; "MacDonald Gets Commitments Prior to Energy Development," *NT*, both March 16, 1976.

68. Peter MacDonald, "Navajo Tradition," *NT*, February 17, 1974.

69. "Gasification: A Crucial Issue."

70. Committee for Navajo Development, "Stop Coal Gasification and Support Navajo Development," *NT*, October 23, 1975.

71. Harold Foster, letter to the editor, *NT*, December 30, 1976.

72. "Coal Gasification in Navajoland."

73. "Coal Gasification—Part III."

74. Harris Arthur, quoted in "Coal Gasification, Part III;" Martin Begay, letter to the editor, *NT*, September 16, 1975.

75. For estimates of population increase, see Dine Coalition, "Coal Gasification—Part III," *NT*, August 23, 1973; for "unmanageable boom towns," see Harold Foster, letter to the editor, *NT*, December 30, 1976.

76. Statement of the Coalition for Navajo Liberation, "Coalition Opposes Gasification," *NT*, February 19, 1976.

77. "Coal Gasification in Navajoland."

78. "Burnham Votes on Gasification," *NT*, May 14, 1973; "Burnham Rejects Gasification," *NT*, May 28, 1973; "Benally Urges Burnham to Vote for Gasification," *NT*, October 19, 1975; "Burnham Rejects Gasification Again" *NT*, November 2, 1975.

79. In a meeting between Peabody and tribal officials nearly a week into the occupation, Peabody agreed to put $100 into escrow for each acre of land that had been strip-mined since 1964 to compensate families whose land had already been mined. Furthermore, Peabody agreed to participate in the Black Mesa Re-

view Board. The tribe had established the Board two years earlier to give Black Mesa residents a forum to register complaints against the company. Until the occupation, Peabody had avoided appointing a member to the board or even participating, but in the wake of the occupation, they appointed a member and began sending representatives to its meetings. For AIM's occupation, see "Aim Protest Halts Peabody Mine," October 17, 1974; "Black Mesa Cooling After Recent Protest," and "MacDonald Says AIM Action at Peabody Coal Inevitable," both October 24, 1974. For AIM's demands, see "Black Mesa Complaints Listed," October 31, 1974. For negotiations between AIM, MacDonald, and Peabody, see "Black Mesa Cooling After Recent Protest." All references from the *NT.*

80. "AIM Seizes Fairchild, Issues Demands," *NT*, March 15, 1975.

81. "Pete Settles Fairchild Dispute," *NT*, March 29, 1975; "Fairchild Shuts Doors, Blames AIM," *NT*, July 18, 1975.

82. The Navajo-Hopi land dispute took place on land nearby, where Peabody Coal's mine intersected the border of the two reservations. See David Brugge, *The Navajo-Hopi Land Dispute: An American Tragedy* (Albuquerque: University of New Mexico Press, 1994); Jerry Kammer, *The Second Long Walk: The Navajo-Hopi Land Dispute* (Albuquerque: University of New Mexico Press, 1980); and Emily Benedek, *The Wind Won't Know Me: A History of the Navajo-Hopi Land Dispute* (New York: Knopf, 1992).

83. WESCO, Draft Environmental Impact Statement, Burnham Coal Gasification Plant, 1975, Special Collections, Cline Library, Northern Arizona University. For the impact of NEPA on development, see Hal Rothman, *The Greening of a Nation? Environmentalism in the U.S. since 1945* (New York: Harcourt Brace, 1995), 120–27; Samuel P. Hays, *Beauty, Health, and Permanence*, 143, 279–81, 446–47.

CONCLUSION: "GOOD BYE, BIG SKY"

1. J. Neary, "Hello, Energy; Goodbye, Big Sky," 61.

2. Ibid., 62, 63.

3. Bretey, "Coal: The Giant Revived," 54–55.

4. U.S. Energy Information Administration, "Table 8.2b: Electricity Net Generation: Electric Power Sector, 1949–2011," *Annual Energy Review* (September 2012) available at http://www.eia.gov/totalenergy/data/annual/pdf/aer.pdf.

5. U.S. Cong., Senate, Committee on Interior and Insular Affairs, *Problems of Electrical Power Production in the Southwest*, report, pursuant to S. Res. 45, 92nd Congress, 2nd sess. (Washington, D.C., 1972).

6. Pollution figures taken from U.S. Environmental Protection Agency, "Facility Detail Report—Hazardous Air Pollutants Four Corners Power Plant, 2002," http://iaspub.epa.gov/airsdata/adnti.site_detail?siteid=350450002&emis=A&year=2002&geoinfo=st~NM~New%20Mexico.

7. Four Corners' carbon emissions estimated using U.S. EPA, "Greenhouse Gas Equivalencies Calculator" http://www.epa.gov/cleanenergy/energy-resources/calculator.html.

8. Lewis Mumford, *Technics and Civilization* (New York: Harcourt, Brace, 1934), 233–56. For "democratic pyramids," see Mumford, "Architecture of Power," *New Yorker* (June 7, 1941), 58.

9. Phillips, *This Land, This Nation*; Tobey, *Technology as Freedom*; Nye, *American Technological Sublime*.

10. The centrality of coal to the development of postwar American modernity portrayed in this work stands in contrast to Timothy Mitchell's argument that a transition from coal to oil as a primary source of global energy occurred in the immediate postwar years, both producing global political differences and constraining labor's political power. The case of the modern Southwest suggests that this transition was neither as comprehensive nor as dependent on oil as an energy source as Mitchell suggests. Instead it seems that coal as well as oil could be used politically to fulfill the promises of infinite growth. It is the embedding of an implied promise of energy without limit within American politics and the spatial distancing of production from consumption, rather than the particular source of energy itself, that helped produce modern America's imperial approach toward energy supplies, not only overseas but at home. Timothy Mitchell, *Carbon Democracy: Political Power in the Age of Oil* (New York: Verso, 2011).

11. Michael Harrington, *The Other America: Poverty in the United States* (New York: Touchstone: 1962), 4.

12. For the belief that Indian peoples had "missed out on modernity," and analysis of the key place of Indian people in the construction of modernity early in the twentieth century, see Philip Deloria, *Indians in Unexpected Places* (Lawrence: University Press of Kansas, 2004).

13. "Roads to Navajoland," *AH* (June 1963), 4.

14. Quotes from Laura Paskus, "The Life and Death of Desert Rock," *HCN* (8/16/2010). For jobs and revenue estimates, see Tony Barbosa, "Pollution for Jobs: A Fair Trade?" *HCN* (9/5/2005).

15. Barbosa, "Pollution for Jobs."

16. Quoted in Powell and Long, "Landscapes of Power," 240.

17. Ibid., 239.

18. Quotes from Mireya Navarro, "Navajos Hope to Shift from Coal to Wind and Sun," *NYT* (10/25/2010), I-4.

19. Powell and Long, "Landscapes of Power," 235; Miguel Bustillo, "Edison to Shut Down Polluting Coal Plant," *LAT* (12/30/2005), I-7; "Edison to Decommission Mohave Power Plant in Nevada," *LAT* (6/11/2009), I-13; Cyndy Cole, "Tribe Reap Benefits of Closed Coal Plant," *ADS* (2/14/2013), 1.

20. Chuck Slothower, "Power Plants Awaits Coal Contract," *Farmington Daily Times* (12/6/2012), 1.

21. Press Release, "Navajo President Ben Shelly Testifies Before Appropriations Panel," Navajo Nation, Washington Office, (3/29/2012) http://nnwo.org /content/navajo-president-ben-shelly-testifies-appropriations-panel.

22. Anne Minard, "Navajo Council Forms Liability Company to Buy Navajo Mine," *Indian Country Today*, May 6, 2013; http://indiancountrytodaymedia network.com/2013/05/06/navajo-council-forms-liability-company-buy-navajo -mine-149216.

23. Anne Minard, "Navajo Nation Is Coal Country as Mine Sale Finalized," *Indian Country Today*, Jan. 6, 2014; http://indiancountrytodaymedianetwork.com/2014/01/06/navajo-nation-coal-country-mine-sale-finalized-152981#.UvEY339A9Cw.email.

24. Gunderson and Curley quotes from Andrew Curley, "2013: Navajo Nation Doubles Down on Coal," *NT*, Jan. 16, 2014; protests detailed in KPFA radio interview with Lori Goodman, DINE-Care, Nov. 24, 2013; http://www.anngarrison.com/audio/2013/11/25/475/bhp-billiton-and-the-navajo-nation.

Index

Page numbers in italic type indicate a figure or table on that page. Entries for U.S. presidents or other government leaders may refer to the individual, the administration, or both.

Thomas, David, 107
Time and the River Flowing (Sierra
    Club), 191, 194–96, 201, 210
Tobey, Ronald, 279n88, 286n81
Tovrea, Philip, *59,* 94–95
Treanor, Thomas, 23
Truman, Harry, 132; NHRA and, 138
Tucson Daily Star, 191
Tugwell, Rexford, 5
Turner, Frederick Jackson, 3; literature
    on, 262n8

Udall, Morris, 204–5, 209
Udall, Stewart, 163, 166–67, 174,
    208, 209; biographical sources and,
    294n21; on Bureau of Reclamation,
    163–64; at Four Corners in 1966,
    178–79; Glen Canyon dam and,
    187, 188; on hydroelectricity, 177;
    on regional economic development
    and, 178; second plan of, 207–8; on
    WEST Associates, 175, 176
uranium, mining and processing of,
    13, 264n24
US News, 65
Utah International Construction Com-
    pany, 123; APS and, 152, 245; coal
    and, 148–50, 233; mineral explora-
    tion permit and, 247; Navajo Mine
    closing and, 247; WESCO and, 241.
    See also BHP Billiton

Valley of the Sun, 61–65; idealization
    of, 55–56; Navajos and, 64–65; as
    political project, 56
Vanderhoof, Philip, 152
Vasey's Paradise (Hyde), 194–95
Vietor, Richard, 286n94
Villiard, Oswald, 133
Vogue, 62

Walker, Brett, 13
Wall Street Journal, 77

Warne, William, 131–32, 133–34, 135
Warrior, Clyde, 220
Washington Post, 131, 140, 196, 211
Watkins, Arthur, 133, 141
Wayland, W. R., 74
Weisiger, Marsha, 43, 44, 48; on Col-
    lier, 274n105; *Dreaming of Sheep,*
    273nn73–76
Welch, H. W., 107
Werneken, Russel, 197
WESCO, 237, 238–39, 241
WEST Associates, 171; APS and, 175;
    Bureau of Reclamation and, 202;
    joint financing and, 172–73; mem-
    bership of, 295n45; Navajo Nation
    and, 174; power-pooling plan and,
    296n57
Western Energy Supply and Trans-
    mission Associates. *See* WEST
    Associates
Western Systems Coordinating Coun-
    cil (WSCC), 179
White, Richard, 9, 51, 274n105, 297n3
White, Sarah, 253, 257
Whyte, William, 199
Wiebe, Robert, 26
Wilbur, Raymond, 33, 271n41
Wiley, Peter, 286n94
Wilkinson, Charles, 304n25
Williams, Herbert, 99–100
Williams, Jack, 15, 104
Wilson, Ray, 104
Wooten, E. O., 45
Worster, Donald, 38
Wright, Frank Lloyd, 110

Yazzie, Burton, 45
Yazzie, Curtis, 254, 257
Yazzie, Duane, 256

Zahnziner, Howard, 191
Zeh, William, 135
Zipp, Samuel, 264n24

Printed in the USA
CPSIA information can be obtained
at www.ICGtesting.com
JSHW081816040624
64296JS00003B/26